SHADOW PLAY

Information Politics in Urban Indonesia

Focusing on government-organized relocations of street vendors in Indonesia, *Shadow Play* carefully exposes the reasons why conflicts over urban planning are fought through information politics.

Anthropologist Sheri Lynn Gibbings shows that information politics are the principal avenues through which the municipal government of Yogyakarta city seeks to implement its urban projects. Information politics are also the primary means through which street vendors, activists, and NGOs can challenge these plans. Through extensive interviews and lengthy participant observation in Yogyakarta, Gibbings shows that both state and non-state actors engage in transparency, rumours, conspiracies, and surveillance practices.

Gibbings reveals that these entangled information practices create suspicion and fear, form new solidarities, and dissolve relationships. *Shadow Play* is a compelling study explaining how we cannot understand urban projects in post-Suharto Indonesia and the resistance to them without first understanding the complexities embedded in the information practices.

(Anthropological Horizons)

SHERI LYNN GIBBINGS is an adjunct professor in the Department of Global Studies at Wilfrid Laurier University and a research affiliate at the University of Manitoba.

ANTHROPOLOGICAL HORIZONS

Editor: Michael Lambek, University of Toronto

This series, begun in 1991, focuses on theoretically informed ethnographic works addressing issues of mind and body, knowledge and power, equality and inequality, the individual and the collective. Interdisciplinary in its perspective, the series makes a unique contribution in several other academic disciplines: women's studies, history, philosophy, psychology, political science, and sociology.

For a list of the books published in this series see page 305.

Shadow Play

Information Politics in Urban Indonesia

SHERI LYNN GIBBINGS

UNIVERSITY OF TORONTO PRESS
Toronto Buffalo London

© University of Toronto Press 2021
Toronto Buffalo London
utorontopress.com

ISBN 978-1-4875-0819-7 (cloth)   ISBN 978-1-4875-3773-9 (EPUB)
ISBN 978-1-4875-2572-9 (paper)   ISBN 978-1-4875-3772-2 (PDF)

Anthropological Horizons

Library and Archives Canada Cataloguing in Publication

Title: Shadow play : information politics in urban Indonesia / Sheri Lynn
   Gibbings.
Names: Gibbings, Sheri Lynn, author.
Series: Anthropological horizons.
Description: Series statement: Anthropological horizons | Includes
   bibliographical references and index.
Identifiers: Canadiana (print) 20210159596 | Canadiana (ebook)
   20210159723 | ISBN 9781487508197 (cloth) | ISBN 9781487525729
   (paper) | ISBN 9781487537722 (PDF) | ISBN 9781487537739 (EPUB)
Subjects: LCSH: Street vendors – Government policy – Indonesia –
   Yogyakarta. | LCSH: Business relocation – Indonesia – Yogyakarta. |
   LCSH: Business and politics – Indonesia – Yogyakarta. | LCSH: City
   planning – Political aspects – Indonesia – Yogyakarta. | LCSH:
   Yogyakarta (Indonesia) – Politics and government.
Classification: LCC HF5459.P5 G53 2021 | DDC 381/.180959827 – dc23

This book has been published with the help of a grant from the Federation
for the Humanities and Social Sciences, through the Awards to Scholarly
Publications Program, using funds provided by the Social Sciences and
Humanities Research Council of Canada.

University of Toronto Press acknowledges the financial assistance to its
publishing program of the Canada Council for the Arts and the Ontario
Arts Council, an agency of the Government of Ontario.

Canada Council   Conseil des Arts
for the Arts   du Canada

ONTARIO ARTS COUNCIL
CONSEIL DES ARTS DE L'ONTARIO
an Ontario government agency
un organisme du gouvernement de l'Ontario

Funded by the   Financé par le
Government   gouvernement
of Canada   du Canada

Canadä

Contents

Figures

Acknowledgments

This book has been over a decade in the making. It is the result of many relationships and intellectual debts, as it spans my time at graduate school at the University of Toronto, a brief postdoc at the University of British Colombia, my job at Wilfrid Laurier University, and beyond.

My greatest thanks go to the people in Yogyakarta who shared their time, knowledge, and insights with me. It was through the support of so many generous and kind individuals that I was able to complete my fieldwork. I want to thank so many members of the community in *kampung Pajekson* for making me feel welcome and allowing me to be part of their everyday lives while I lived in their neighborhood.

I initially spent time with street vendors on Malioboro Street, where I slowly widened my network to include a good number of organizational leaders, shop owners, and people involved in parking on the street. I am so grateful to the many people on Malioboro Street who allowed me to spend time with them and to learn about "street life" in Yogyakarta. Although many of these individuals do not appear in this book, my interactions with them were essential in providing me with insight into the processes, politics, and relationships involved in street vending.

It was my connections from Malioboro that helped me to enter into and later understand the street vendor relocation project that is discussed in this book. This project involved four groups of street traders: the Pethikbumi, Independent, Asem Gede, and Southern Square traders. I deeply appreciate the relationships that I developed with these people. Although I would love to name everyone with whom I spent time, I must preserve their anonymity in order to protect their identities. In particular, I want to thank the leaders of the four street vendor organizations and their members for their time and for allowing me to follow their processes. I also want to thank the non-profit organizations, municipal officials, and other people involved in the relocation who generously shared their insights with me. So many went out of their way to patiently answer my questions. Outside the immediate circle of my research, I also want to thank a group of girlfriends, Rani Fajri, Risti Madyayanti, Pupu Purwaningsih Wahyud, and Novriyanti, whom I met when I initially arrived in Indonesia. They tolerated my initial faux pas and we remained friends throughout.

The University of Toronto, where this project began, provided an important intellectual and collegial environment. This project started when I began my PhD under the mentorship of Joshua Barker, who encouraged me to consider fieldwork in Indonesia. Joshua's own work on imagined communities and the state has had a profound effect on my own thinking about Indonesia. I am deeply indebted to Joshua for creating the intellectual space for this project to develop over time, for the many conversations across the years that have enriched my ideas, and for his support for this project from start to finish. I was also lucky to have Tania Li join my PhD committee. Tania always goes above and beyond for her students, and my experience was no different. She was supportive during my fieldwork, and her counsel was essential when it came time for me to write up my research. Her thoughtful and often tough comments played an important part in shaping the outcomes of this project. Tania also helped to devise the idea of shadow play as a key concept of my work. Janice Newberry carefully read and provided thoughtful comments on my dissertation, and her ideas about how I might transform it into a book have been immensely helpful. My fellow graduate students Mieke deGelder, Lauren Classen, Kori Allen, Jim Stinson, Sharon Kelly, Zoe Wool, Emily Hertzman, Lukas Ley, and Jessica Taylor have offered friendship, intellectual engagement, and support. I thank Katherine MacIvor, too, for her editing help.

After finishing my PhD, I received a SSHRC Postdoctoral Fellowship, allowing me to work with someone I admire deeply, Abidin Kusno, who was based at the University of British Columbia. Over the course of that year, I started to revise my dissertation into a book, and he provided me with thoughtful comments and support. During this postdoc, I also had the opportunity to spend time in Leiden at KITLV (Koninklijk Instituut voor Taal-, Land- en Volkenkunde/Royal Netherlands Institute of Southeast Asian and Caribbean Studies), where I was able to share some of my work and receive feedback from a number of scholars. I want to thank Henk Schulte Nordholt and Gerry van Klinken, in particular, for their support.

I arrived at Wilfrid Laurier University in 2012, where I was warmly welcomed by colleagues in Global Studies, Anthropology, and beyond.

I would like to express my thanks to Alex Latta, Alicia Sliwinski, Ashley Lebner, and Tanya Richardson for their many conversations about my work. Tanya was an important mentor in this process, providing me with guidance and encouragement. I owe much to Jessica Taylor, as she agreed to read and provide extensive feedback on the chapters as I significantly rewrote them; so many of the ideas that appear in this book were fostered in these conversations with Jessica. Once the draft of the manuscript was done, Tanya again generously made time in her busy schedule to read the chapters and provide insightful feedback. I also want to thank Lukas Lay for providing comments on a chapter, and Paul Jenkins from the Institute for the Humanities at the University of Manitoba for providing me with an opportunity to present a chapter to a group of colleagues. Additionally, my thanks to Derek Johnson and Fabiana Li from the University of Manitoba for their support.

After I had a revised draft of my book manuscript, there was the difficult work of editing, streamlining, and polishing. It was then that I started to work with Tom Cho, who has a keen reader's eye, perfectionist tendencies, and great communication skills. His editorial support made this long process manageable. I also extend my gratitude to the manuscript readers. Their theoretical insights, regional and subject knowledge, and writing experience helped me to pinpoint how I could streamline and improve the manuscript. I want to thank Douglas Hildebrand, my original contact and source of advice at University of Toronto Press, and Jodi Lewchuk, who then guided me through UTP's publishing process. Thanks also to Ryan Perks for his careful copyediting at the final stages, and to Siusan Moffat for putting together the book's index. I am grateful that Pak Asnar Zacky from the Indonesian Art Institute of Yogyakarta (Institut Seni Indonesia Yogyakarta) provided the drawing for the front cover.

The research and writing of this book were supported by multiple institutions and granters. My thanks to the Wenner Gren Foundation for Anthropological Research and the Social Sciences and Humanities Council of Canada, both of which funded my fieldwork in Indonesia. The Dr. David Chu Scholarship in Asia-Pacific Studies helped to fund language study and an initial visit. I am grateful for sponsorship from the Asia Pacific Centre (Pusat Asia Pasifik) and Dr. Paschalis Maria Laksono at Gadjah Mada University in Yogyakarta, which made this research possible. Thank you, as well, to Dr. Pujo Semadi for sponsoring my follow-up research in Yogyakarta and for helping me to find a research assistant. I also had a SSHRC Postdoctoral Fellowship that provided me with time to work through my material. Aspects of my arguments and ethnography appeared as a chapter in *Citizenship and*

Democratization in Southeast Asia, edited by Ward Berenschot, Henk Schulte Nordholt, and Laurens Bakker, and as an article in *City & Society*.

This funding also supported a number of research assistants. Agus Nur Prabowo helped me to make initial contacts during my fieldwork and assisted in other ways during the early days while I learned the ropes. Hidayah Utama Lubis and Nanda Wirabaskara did the hard work of transcribing the interviews. Novi from Gadjah Mada University helped near the end of my research in 2008. Elan Ardi Lazuardi, a skilled researcher, served as a research assistant when I conducted follow-up research in 2014. Khidir Marsanto and Elan were also central in helping me to "fact-check" and complete any follow-up questions I had when I was doing revisions to the manuscript in 2016 and beyond. The major revisions I did to the manuscript would not have been possible without their intellectual insights and unwavering support.

Many of my friends outside of academia have been an important source of support and encouragement during this long process. This includes Emily Alexander, Genevieve Chui, Amy Patterson, Manzur Malik, Janna Cumming, Sonia Chandarana, Kirstin Rondeau, Jennifer Plewis, Charleen Jordaan, and Ashley Wagner. I would not have been able to write this book without the support and friendship of those who provided care for my son and daughter, giving me the opportunity to write, especially Angela Falk, Accalia Robertson, Andrea Earl, and Nancy Bilibli.

I am endlessly indebted to my parents, Edith and Neil Gibbings, who taught me early on about kindness and empathy towards others. For as long as I can remember, they have prioritized education and fostered a deep curiosity in learning and travelling. Without their unwavering support, I would never have started, let alone finished, this project. I am also grateful to my siblings, Anita, Derrick, and Julie, whose friendship and advice I have sought along the way. Julie, thank you for all the conversations and for serving as a role model and sounding board for so many of my ideas. Finally, I am profoundly grateful to my husband, Rob Winter, who has given me endless encouragement and support.

I dedicate this book to my son, Charles, and daughter, Lily Anne, who have given me the energy and willpower to keep writing and to see this project to its end. I wanted to show them my love for anthropology, not only as a profession or field of study, but as a world view and a way of being. Thanks, Charles and Lily, for making my life so fun and meaningful.

SHADOW PLAY

Information Politics in Urban Indonesia

Chapter One

Introduction

It was a warm September evening in 2007 on Mangkubumi Street in Yogyakarta.[1] The dimly lit sidewalk was crowded, with hundreds of young people winding up and down the street. As far as the eye could see, street traders arranged their new and used merchandise in front of the colourful retail and travel shops whose doors were closed for the night. Although most of the streetgoers were enjoying an evening out with friends, the vendors from Pethikbumi – a street vendor organization refusing a municipal government–organized relocation to a newly renovated marketplace – were on alert. The Pethikbumi leaders had recently told their members not to trust anyone on the street except for the group's known representatives, and not to answer any questions regarding the relocation, even if they appeared to be from an innocent visitor.

Early in the evening, a small group of university students came to the street to ask the Pethikbumi leaders for permission to conduct a study on the street traders for a class. After a brief discussion, the leaders rejected the request, suspecting that the municipal government, having failed to collect sufficient data, was merely using these students to gather information on the traders. As I observed this exchange, the Pethikbumi leaders' response did not surprise me. A month earlier, they had asked my research assistant to stop videotaping the street because they were worried that the footage would be used against their members if it fell into the wrong hands.

A couple weeks after the university students had sought permission for their study, Mas[2] Eko and Pak Pramana,[3] two Pethikbumi leaders, phoned me and asked if we could meet up. They said over the phone that we should meet on nearby Malioboro Street because Mangkubumi Street was no longer a safe place to talk. They feared that an undercover police agent might overhear our conversation, and that *preman* (thugs)[4] who had lately been hanging around the street might ask for money in exchange for support against the relocation. When we met up, they said that a parking agent (a person who watches parked vehicles in exchange for a fee) had reported to the Pethikbumi leaders that some other students had also tried to collect data the night before, and Mas Eko and Pak Pramana wanted to know if I knew about this group of students from my connections to the local university, Universitas Gadjah Mada (UGM). Surprised by this update, I explained that I was not aware of these students or their research project, and I assured Mas Eko and Pak Pramana that all the information I was collecting was not being shared with UGM, or with anyone for that matter. Satisfied with my response, Mas Eko and Pak Pramana ended our conversation by recommending that I develop a plan in case the government or police decided to pressure or intimidate me into sharing my information about the anti-relocation traders.

Mas Eko and Pak Pramana's apprehensiveness reflected persistent concerns among the Pethikbumi traders during much of my ethnographic research on the municipal government's street vendor relocation project. During this research, I heard the traders express concern that the government was trying to obtain information about them in an underhanded manner; that it had not responded to their requests for information; that it had illegally drafted a new regulation because the drafting was done without consultation (i.e., in secret); that civil servants had falsified one of the trader's signatures; and that officials had claimed that traders had agreed to the relocation when they had simply signed the minutes to a meeting. As a result, the traders and their NGO supporters developed different tactics to try variously to withhold information, obtain information, and determine if the information they received could be trusted. Stories also circulated about the government bribing the traders and using *preman* to intimidate them. Some anti-relocation traders told me that there was a person working behind the screen to create a conflict between those refusing the relocation and those accepting it. Some of the anti-relocation traders were convinced that Pak Herry Zudianto,[5] the mayor of Yogyakarta, was secretly creating the conflict (for a list of the key figures involved in the relocation project and their roles, see List of Protagonists). Meanwhile, others raised the possibility that the person might be internal to the anti-relocation group, an *oknum* (an individual who uses his or her official position for secret or underhanded goals; see Ryter 2001, 126n9).[6]

This book is about the *information politics* of an urban infrastructure project – that is, the repertoire of information practices that street vendors, NGOs, and government officials engaged in during a street vendor relocation project. In what follows, I make two main arguments. The first is straightforward, perhaps even obvious: I argue that when these information practices – such as transparency, rumours, conspiracies, and surveillance – are viewed together, they provide a more complete picture of urban politics in a post-authoritarian city. I call this totality of practices an *ecology of information practices*. The government's use of rumours cannot be separated from its attempt to inform the traders about the relocation project through face-to-face consultations. The government's ability to implement this project was tied to its capacity to create confusion and distrust among the anti-relocation traders while simultaneously engaging in an open dialogue with them. By the end of the book, I hope that readers will agree that it is impossible to understand this urban project without understanding how these different information practices occur alongside each other.

The second argument is that focusing on information politics is a way to understand and study state-society relationships. Anthropological literature on the state suggests that the boundary between the state and society is often blurred and is continually produced and reproduced (Mitchell 1988) through such practices as the laying of roads (Harvey and Knox 2015) and the writing of letters and texts (Mathur 2016). A focus on information politics allows the researcher to map how different types of information are used and circulate differently, and how they bring together or divide different entities such as citizens, municipal officials, the police, political parties, and NGOs. In Indonesia, the state has never exerted total control, but during the Suharto era – that is, the New Order period (1965–98) characterized by the authoritarian rule of then president Raden Suharto – it operated through militias or criminalized figures (Barker and Van Klinken 2009, 22). While a certain understanding of information politics has always been required in order to function in Indonesian society during times of "contentious politics" (Tilly and Tarrow 2015, 14–15), it is increasingly necessary as information politics is more centrally used as a mode of governance in an era in which transparency, communication, and non-violent actions are increasingly expected and demanded by both citizens and the larger international community. In this ethnography, I argue that a focus on the information politics used by state and societal actors helps us see in practice how state-society relationships come into existence, and that information is the mediator that brings people together at certain moments and divides them at others (cf. Hull 2012b, 21).

In addition to information politics in general, this book uses the term *information ideologies* to examine how people's beliefs about information shape both collective and government action. I have developed this term from language ideologies (M. Silverstein 1979; Bourdieu 1991; Woolard and Schieffelin 1994) and media ideologies (Gershon 2010). One common definition of *language ideology* is "sets of beliefs about language articulated by users as a rationalization or justification of perceived language structure and use" (M. Silverstein 1979, 193). Drawing on this field,[7] Ilana Gershon (2010) has argued that we can view a parallel set of media ideologies that "are sets of beliefs about communicative technologies with which users and designers explain perceived media structure and meaning" (3). The term *information ideologies*, then, refers to sets of beliefs that underpin how people talk about information, the mediums through which information is circulated, and discussions about where, when, and by whom information should be produced, circulated, and interpreted.

Although my focus is on Indonesia and a group of street traders, the ecology-of-information-practices framework has broader relevance for understanding urban, national, and global politics in the present. We live in a time of uncertainty about "official" versions of the truth; one need only think about online networks like WikiLeaks that are dedicated to open information and whistle-blowing. With the rise of Donald Trump, we have witnessed the president of the world's most powerful country turn against traditional media sources by accusing journalists of producing false stories or "fake news." And yet it is not just the United States that is facing this crisis. In September 2018, Indonesia's communications ministry announced plans to hold weekly briefings on fake news stories in an attempt to inform the public about the spread of disinformation in the country.[8] In Brazil, fake news circulated on WhatsApp ahead of the 2018 presidential election: one study of 100,000 images shared to millions on that app indicated that more than half contained misleading or false information.[9] In South Africa, Facebook has launched a new anti-fake-news tool that enables users to flag articles for fact-checking by third-party services.[10] The emergence of the global COVID-19 pandemic in 2020 has also generated a plethora of conspiracy theories and incorrect scientific information circulating on social media in countries around the globe.[11]

This book, then, is a call to rethink and study the central role and place of information and trust in twenty-first-century politics. It encourages us to explore how people's beliefs about the structures of information shape the kind of information they produce and how they interpret the information they both produce and receive. This requires, however, looking at how people's ideas about information are influenced by a myriad of factors, such as new structures of power, ideas about the past, and the different mediums through which information travels.

The production, circulation, and withholding of information is central to how governments assert and maintain power and how members of society relate, resist, and engage with the state. A study of information politics is therefore an important way to understand state-society relationships, and how these relationships shift and transform over time.

Information Politics and State-Society Relationships in Indonesia

Information politics are central to shaping social, political, and economic relationships in Indonesia. Patricia Spyer (2006) has described, for instance, how journalists inspired by the democratic ideal of transparency have invented new ways of writing about violence within the Moluccan conflict that she calls "stripped-bare reporting" (153). In the lead-up to the 2019 Indonesian presidential election, rumours circulated that someone was storing millions of marked ballots at a Jakarta port.[12] In Indonesia, information and its sources, validity, and forms are topics of concern that are widely debated in the public sphere (e.g., Bubandt 2009; Strassler 2004).

Two central concepts associated with these discussions of information in Indonesia are trust and belief, and these concepts can be translated into Bahasa Indonesia as a variety of related terms, such as *percaya*, *kepercayaan*, *yakin*, or *keyakinan*.[13] During the Suharto era, the Indonesian government sought to control information, and all information that circulated in the country was subject to review and modification by the Ministry of Information (Kitley 1994; Lim 2003, 280). While most citizens took information from the government at face value, others – especially middle-class activists, intellectuals, and artists – were more critical and sceptical of official information, a stance that goes back to the early days of the New Order (Aspinall 1996, 215). Those who were critical of information produced under Suharto generally used irony, humour, art, and even acronyms to express their scepticism (e.g., M. Clark 2006).[14] For instance, the headlines in *Tempo,* a weekly news magazine, would often take the form of a question whose answer suggested a critique of the government's version of the truth.[15] The emergence of the Internet in Indonesia in the early 1990s also played a significant role, allowing people to access controversial information on such topics as Suharto's corruption and details related to the Indonesian Communist Party (Partai Komunis Indonesia, or PKI) (Lim 2003, 280).[16] The builders of the Internet in Indonesia, who worked independently from the state, in fact constructed "a sociotechnical imaginary that linked the technology to a politics of freedom" (Barker 2015, 200). Writers and activists such as George Aditjondro were also important; Aditjondro revealed information about the Suharto family though his "list of Suharto's wealth" (*Daftar Kekayaan Suharto*), which circulated through email (Lim 2003, 280–1).[17] These new nodes of online information-sharing interacted with traditional forms of networking and information-sharing in the 1990s, thereby allowing a growing number of citizens to have greater access to information that was not controlled by the government (282).

The transition to democracy in Indonesia did not establish a radically new epistemological relationship between truth, trust, and information. As Doreen Lee (2016) writes, "Post-Suharto regimes have failed to secure a system of accountability and transparency in Indonesia, further reinforcing the epistemological distance between *korban* [victims] and perpetrators, civil society and the state" (145). Scholars have noted that gossip in post-Suharto Indonesia can gain authority in the eyes of Indonesian citizens if it is converted into written material (see Bubandt 2008; Herriman 2010, 726), highlighting how certain mediums are viewed as more trustworthy than others. Unlike the Suharto period, there is now increasingly widespread public debate and discussion about whether information or facts from the government or social media sources can be trusted.[18] In the post-Suharto era, technological transformations – and especially those related to social media – have spawned widespread debate over whether certain sources of information can be trusted or whether they are "hoaxes."[19]

Given these increasingly widespread reflections on information and its validity in Indonesia, it is not surprising that I quickly learned during my fieldwork in Yogyakarta that information was of central concern to the Pethikbumi traders. I witnessed these anti-relocation vendors trying to learn how to channel, request, manipulate, and correctly interpret information in order to challenge the government's project. It also became apparent to me that the strategic use of information was a central government tactic for implementing this controversial urban project. In particular, since Indonesia has transitioned to a democracy, the ideal of "sharing" information is now embedded within deeply contested beliefs about how information should be distributed, circulated, and interpreted. To fully understand this politics of information, I argue that it is necessary to go beyond a narrow focus on particular information practices, such as revealing information in newspapers or generating and circulating rumours, and that we must instead consider these practices as part of a larger repertoire that combines both "democratic" and "non-democratic" practices in the aid of conducting urban politics. As Aradhana Sharma (2013) has argued, "bureaucratic and sovereign modes of state power (W. Brown 1995) are at odds with the ideal of transparent governance and subvert it from within" (320).

For the anti-relocation street vendors I studied, *informasi* (information) was sometimes obtainable through such avenues as official documents, face-to-face consultations with government officials, and surveillance. At other moments, these face-to-face meetings seemed to provide the vendors with "no information." What is noteworthy, however, is that the vendors' efforts to protest the government's relocation project involved a whole *range* of information practices, and the government's attempts to control and inhibit the vendors' organizing also involved a series of information practices that went beyond creating and circulating documents, and that were not always framed in relation to democracy or transparency. *Informasi* in Indonesia is generally used in a similar manner as in the North American context, where it is associated with obtaining the facts or being given a message or details. *Informasi* is associated with statements (*keterangan*) that are mostly verbal in practice, and with different forms of evidence (*bukti*) such as official documents. Increasingly in Indonesia, *informasi* is also being used in the context of the idea of fake news; there is so much information, and people are struggling to sift through the information they are receiving. With the growing concern over fake news, the central Indonesian government now works to mitigate it. For example, following the 2018 earthquake and tsunami in Sulawesi, the Indonesian government rebutted hoaxes surrounding the disaster that were circulating on Twitter and Facebook.[20]

In this book, I move back and forth between describing the experiences of the anti-relocation traders and their supporters during the relocation, and the municipal government's efforts to curb their resistance and convince them to join the relocation. I seek to tell the story of urban politics in post-Suharto Indonesia by starting with the idea that information is a central means of shaping political action in urban environments writ large. In the most immediate and descriptive sense, I show that information politics in Indonesia is currently being shaped by the processes of democratization that have emerged since 1998, when the political system began to allow people to demand access to information and to participate more freely in politics. As state agents, traders, and non-governmental actors engage in these political practices, information politics are co-produced. It is important to note, however, that it is not just the present post-authoritarian period in Indonesia that generates information politics; Indonesia has always had different kinds of information politics. Rather, the present generates new kinds of information politics and practices that draw on the past to react to the present as well as an imagined future. Therefore, one cannot understand people's ideologies and practices of information without understanding the social and political context of Suharto's New Order.

In many ways, the history of the Indonesian state during the Suharto era has been told through studies of its different information practices and their mediation through technology. Most of these works drew on Benedict Anderson's *Imagined Communities* (1991), which discussed how different information technologies such as print-capitalism, maps, and censuses made certain territorially based communities like "Indonesia" imaginable. Joshua Barker (2005) argues that a generation of Indonesian engineers, entrepreneurs, and government officials acted as "human mediators" of the new satellite technology of the time by altering older discourses (or information) about the role of communication technologies in nation building and development (703). The study of Indonesia's newspaper and television media during the Suharto era also pointed to the role the media played in reproducing Indonesia's state ideology – an ideology that promoted cultural unity while silencing its critics (Sen and Hill 2007; Kitley 2000). Overall, the "imagined community" approach was able to show how national communities were formed through technology-mediated information.

While the state tried to control information about itself, there was a political economy comprised of the counterfeit things and information circulating in Indonesia during the Suharto era. James T. Siegel's (1998) work on criminality during the period noted that the Indonesian press – both lower- and middle-class newspapers – often published stories about counterfeiting (*palsu*) (52). Indeed, the list of items reported to be counterfeit was extensive: from an entire fictive university to fake revenue stamps or false divorce certificates (52). Siegel argues that "what is remarkable, but common in stories of falsification, is that the source is no guarantee of authenticity" (54). Counterfeiting was so common that a neologism, *aspal*, was created. *Aspal* combines the word for "original" (*asli*) with the word for "fake" (*palsu*) to make a word that can be translated as "original-but-fake" or "authentic-fake." It refers to a kind of counterfeit produced by "insiders" who specialize in genuine-but-false document or goods (54). Siegel concludes that "falsity simply pervades the Indonesian world. One knows that one cannot rely on signs; they are as likely to mislead as not" (55).

Studying the cultural logics of information politics has remained important for understanding relationships between citizens and the state in post-authoritarian Indonesia. With the transition to democracy, scholars are continuing to explore the role that fake documents and rumours play as agents in the mediation of conflicts across Indonesia.[21] Studying the role of fake documents in the North Maluku conflict,[22] for instance, Nils Bubandt (2008) describes the context in which these documents made sense to the parties involved, arguing that "the social efficacy and, indeed, the agency of these pamphlets [had] to do with their capacity to be 'in the true' in a variety of evocative plots" (792). In further work on this, Bubandt (2009) notes that although individuals from both sides of the conflict knew the documents were false, the documents nevertheless remain very powerful because people still see them as having authority (556). With regard to post-conflict and post-disaster Aceh, Annemarie Samuels (2015) likewise examines what makes rumours so "affectively powerful" and what kind of emotional effects they produce in people (230). Karen Strassler (2004) has also examined the debates about proof (*bukti*) mobilized by activists with regard to the rapes of mostly Indonesian Chinese women that occurred in 1998. She points to the fact that debates over proof have to be situated in discussions of transparency within the country, the important role played by photographs in these deliberations, and the popular images of "heroic male-on-male violence" that shaped what was recognizable as state violence and the political action around these incidents (690). All of this research points to the powerful influence that information politics continues to have over the shaping of societal relationships in post-Suharto Indonesia, and the fact that we cannot begin to understand Indonesian politics and culture without investigating the practices, contexts, and meanings from which these information politics emerge.

Scholars of the Suharto and post-Suharto eras have noted that information politics – whether we are talking about rumours, fake documents, or technologically mediated information – are central to any understanding of relationships in Indonesia (e.g., Bubandt 2008; Spyer 2006; Strassler 2004, 2000). My book builds on this scholarship by examining information politics in the post-Suharto era during a low-level conflict. It shows that information politics continues to remain central to how citizens and the state relate to each other in the post-authoritarian era. In the following chapters, I consider how information politics brings together different information practices, each with their own relationship to the past and an imagined democratic future. In the post-Suharto era, it is not only state officials who use information politics to govern in new ways in a democratic environment: citizens also engage in information politics to challenge the government and assert power. I argue that when the channels, forms, and practices of information-sharing change, new forms of suspicion arise since people need new ways to determine reliability and truthfulness. As Jodi Dean (1998) says, "when the truth is out there but we can trust no one, more information heightens suspicion" (23).

Towards an Anthropology of Information

In the eighteenth century, the word *information* emerged from the "medieval Latin term *informationem* and old French *enformacion*, meaning 'formation of the mind, or teaching'" (Weller 2011, 5). During the late eighteenth and nineteenth centuries, there was a growth in print culture, as well as a variety of infrastructures like the telephone and postal systems, that helped information to move (4). As new information became more widely available, people started to view information as separate from "information content, persuasion, and rhetoric" (5). As a result, the nineteenth century saw a shift from the understanding of information as an "implicit part of education" to the idea that it is a concept in its own right (5).

Although early anthropologists did not take "information" as their central analytic concept of concern, information has been of interest to anthropologists for a long time. Approaches that looked at culture or social relationships explored the role that information practices such as gossiping (Radcliffe-Brown 1933; Gluckman 1963a; Benedict 1934, 60), spreading rumours (Firth 1955), and joking (Radcliffe-Brown 1940, 1949) played in human behaviour.[23] In particular, in the 1960s and '70s, anthropological interest in rumour, gossip, and scandal sparked lively debates over the function and role of these information practices. Max Gluckman (1963b, 1968), for instance, saw gossip as enforcing conformity and maintaining boundaries, while Robert Paine (1967) viewed gossip less as a mechanism of social control and more as a means to advance one's own political goals against rivals and to control the flow of information.

F.G. Bailey's edited volume *Gifts and Poison* (1971a) explored the "small politics" of European villages by focusing on their information practices in order to understand how reputations were made and challenged. Insights into everyday practices of information-sharing are scattered throughout the book. For example, Heppenstall describes how in an Austrian village "the information channels (by word of mouth) are far more important than direct observation," and that "there are right and wrong ways of handling information" (1971, 154). This volume points to the power of informal information practices, such as gossiping, to alter individual reputations and rework social relations.

Into the 1980s, although information had still not appeared as a central analytic term, anthropologists continued to flesh out the complexities of particular information practices like gossiping.[24] For example, in studying the flow of information in an American neighbourhood, Sally Engle Merry (1984) argued that people are removed from the consequences or effects of gossip because of their wealth, control over resources, or marginal social status (48). James C. Scott (1985) also observed that, "For the poor … gossip achieves the expression of opinion, of contempt, of disapproval while minimizing the risks of identification and reprisal" (282). In these works, information was seen as playing an important role in shaping power relationships among people of different social and economic classes.

Later in the twentieth century, information became a highly valued principle for Western governments, especially in the 1990s after the end of the Cold War (Sharma 2013, 310). "The collapse of the USSR reinforced the ideological equations between secrecy and authoritarianism, on the one hand, and freedom and Western liberal democracy, on the other" (310). Transparency, closely associated with the concept of information, also became a key criterion by which the World Bank and the Asian Development Bank ranked governments in terms of their good governance and efficiency (310). At the same time, the growth of information technology helped to foster a desire for citizens to have information easily available at all times (311).

In the 1990s and 2000s, scholars – mostly information specialists – started to explore the idea of information in different historical contexts (Weller 2011, 5), and largely from a quantitative perspective (Day 2008, 5). While questions of epistemology (concerns with forms or ways of knowing) and ontology (forms of being or existing) have recently become areas of concern and debate in anthropology (e.g., Holbraad, Pedersen, and Viveiros de Castro 2014; Kohn 2015; see also Lebner's contribution in Lebner et al. 2017), we have still seen less anthropological engagement with the idea or concept of "information," at least as a central analytic term (see Hetherington 2012; Riles 2001). Annelise Riles (2001) suggests that while academics view capital as a mode of analysis, information, by contrast, "is understood to be a thing in the world" (113). It is hardly surprising, then, that anthropologists have not engaged substantially with the term when "information" feels all-encompassing and is hard to define.

Yet one way that anthropologists can study information is by investigating the different information ideologies and information practices of our informants, and how these practices and ideologies occur in relation to or alongside each other. When we see these information practices and ideologies together, we can understand them as part of a larger repertoire of strategies and practices that bring relationships – such as those between state and society – into existence through concrete, performative engagements with information.

Although there is not really an anthropology of information per se, as there is an anthropology of infrastructures, anthropologists have long been interested in studying information ideologies, along with information practices such as transparency and surveillance, in a variety of contexts. Rather than defining what *information* is, most anthropologists and other social scientists have examined what *different practices of information* mean to their informants in a particular context, and how these practices often have unexpected political and social outcomes. In my research, the sharing and withholding of *informasi* was the basis of relationships between government officials, traders, and other actors involved in the relocation project. To be interested in information, then, is to be concerned with understanding relationships. Because anthropology has long been interested in the study of relationships of various kinds, the discipline can offer an ethnographic study of information: what information means to our informants, the range of practices they develop around it, and how it impacts their social, political, and economic relationships. While "information" has not been the point of departure for many anthropological studies, anthropologists have focused on a range of information practices like transparency, documentation, and surveillance – practices that were important to my informants and that influenced how the street vendor relocation unfolded.

Anthropologists studying transparency have examined how the state, people, and activists are developing new practices and ideas of the self (Ballestero 2012, 160; Schumann 2007, 840; Morris 2004; Strathern 2000b), as well as new relationships based on these ideals (Webb 2012). For example, Kregg Hetherington's (2011) work examines how the ideals of transparency were important in shaping how peasant farmers (*campesinos*) in Paraguay interacted with the government. Despite being characterized as "threats" to transparency because of their allegedly backward ways, the *campesinos* decided to participate in transparency practices, thereby becoming what Hetherington calls "guerilla auditors" (8). He argues that when guerilla auditors engage with documents, they see them as sites of possibility and a means to achieve political goals. For the Pethikbumi traders I studied, documents were viewed as a tool to hold the government accountable, and much of their activism focused on obtaining documents about the relocation in the hope that they could later use these documents to pressure the government to uphold its promises.

In India, Sharma (2013) examines how the technical procedures demanded by transnational transparency discourses and practices ended up shaping how activists sought to imagine change on the part of the state. Ironically, these changes ended up supporting the state's elusiveness, as government officials started changing how they communicated and what they recorded in order to obstruct accountability

(318–19). In a similar way, the municipal officials in Yogyakarta who were involved in the relocation project were under pressure from the public to be more transparent, and as a result, these officials claimed in the public sphere to be dialoguing with the traders. However, rather than bringing about greater transparency on the part of the state, the state's "transparent" practices occurred alongside other less transparent practices like falsifying documents, causing the Pethikbumi traders to grow increasingly suspicious of the state's motives and behaviour.

While transparency as an ideal is supposed to create more equality between different actors, anthropologists have shown that in reality the situation is far more complex. For example, in India, efforts to develop new transparency measures generated new relationships of brokerage between activists and those who sought their assistance as mediators vis-à-vis the state (Webb 2012). Transparency is based on the idea of bringing information to the people and empowering the individual, but "more often than not, the agents of reform find themselves dangling as before in inscrutable relations and dependency" (Hetherington 2012, 243). In this book, I describe how the Pethikbumi traders looked to a group of lawyers and NGOs to help them navigate the information politics of the state's relocation project. While the lawyers and NGOs helped the Pethikbumi traders to navigate this terrain, the relationship between the Pethikbumi traders and their supporters became entangled in its own information politics when the state portrayed the lawyers and NGOs as having "unnamed interests." The state also played an important role in mediating the relationship between the Pethikbumi traders and their supporters because the state circulated conspiracies about the latter that generated mistrust between both groups.

The material forms of documentation and communication (which can be the result of transparency initiatives or not) also mediate relations between people, things, places, and goals. For example, in Islamabad, Matthew S. Hull (2012b) notes that different documents have diverse ways of moving, and they "often function less as instruments of documentation than as tools for building coalitions or oppositions" (22). In India, Nayanika Mathur (2012) found that the "transparent-making documents" required for a new development scheme shaped the participation of contractors, political leaders, and officials in this project (179). She writes, "To get all the papers in order that would allow for the funds to be spent required a radical overhaul of extant systems of governance and the crafting of … new ones premised on an intricate dance of perfectly synchronised transparent-making documents" (179). When the municipal government of Yogyakarta failed to circulate documentation about the relocation, this brought the Pethikbumi leaders and their membership closer as they mobilized together to demand access to documentation about the relocation. However, when the government circulated documents in unusual ways, and ultimately falsified one document, the Pethikbumi leaders became even more distrusting of the state. Documents are important mediators of relationships; they can create new networks, shift existing ones, and/or cause people to maintain old ones.

While transparency and auditing[25] might seem like the opposite of surveillance and its secrets, practices of surveillance also create new relationships, often of suspicion, among people. Ilana Feldman (2015) notes that in "low-tech human surveillance," relationships among people are central to how surveillance functions. In Gaza, surveillance relationships involved direct relations (connections between police and informants), but also "in a more conceptual relational field, which shaped people's understandings of the character of their connections" (52). These relationships were affective, producing suspicion, uncertainty, and isolation in some instances, but also camaraderie and friendship in others (52).[26] In the case of the Pethikbumi leaders and their supporters, they looked to close friends and members of their network to help in surveilling the actors associated with the state as well as the traders' own members. While engaging in surveillance was empowering for some of the traders and their supporters, for the members who were the targets of it, it was disempowering, creating more fear and distrust.

Although state surveillance appears all-encompassing, Allen Feldman (2000) has illustrated how republican paramilitaries in Northern Ireland evoked rumours as a way to challenge state surveillance in their private lives. He describes these rumours as a "reaction to the actual, diffuse, capillary threading of the state surveillance and power through the warp of everyday life" (48). Paul A. Silverstein (2000) argues that in a context of strong surveillance and the punishment of activists, Algerian diasporic media circulated conspiracy theories in the 1990s. Silverstein sees these conspiracy theories as a kind of local knowledge that gives power to both the accuser and those doing the accusations (10). Individuals and groups escaped or challenged surveillance through other information practices such as spreading rumours, engaging in fake conformity, and creating conspiracy theories. For the Pethikbumi traders, the practices of state surveillance occurred alongside another practice, that of managing impressions – or *conspicuous visibility*, a term I borrow and modify from Erik Harms (2013a) – whereby the Pethikbumi leaders told others about their meetings and relationships with government officials in an attempt to curb suspicion that they were secretly working with the government. One information practice was often entangled with another. This enmeshment of information practices is key to this book: as previously noted, my aim here is to explore a multiplicity of information practices alongside each other, rather than focus on one or two practices in isolation, as a way to understand state-society relationships. Information practices rarely, if ever, occur in isolation.

More broadly, this book takes up Kregg Hetherington's (2012) call for anthropologists to return to the concept of information, which he says "never fails to make an appearance in the ethnography of transparency but is rarely defined" (245). Moreover, my book demonstrates the centrality of information politics – the daily questioning, production, manipulation, and evaluation of information – to social and political relationships. I argue that information politics are not just instruments of state power; they constitute both the state and its subjects (cf. Hull 2012a, 253), as well as the relationships between these entities.

In this book, I home in on a wide range of information practices because my informants did. In particular, although my anti-relocation trader-informants cared about transparency and democracy, their aim was also to oppose the government and its information tactics in order to maintain their livelihoods. This took other skills and tactics that did not always fit easily within the framework of transparency and democracy. From the perspective of the anti-relocation traders, the transition to democracy not only produced new demands for transparency; it produced different kinds of information politics that required attention and skill to navigate. For these traders, then, information was not just restricted to the revelation of "facts," but also involved the spreading of rumours and the concealment of certain actions. Of course, these types of information practices existed prior to the transition to democracy. But in this new era of democracy, traders and members of civil society felt that they could draw on a wider range of practices in bolder ways, while the government officials needed to use information to work towards their goal of ensuring that the vendor relocation proceeded according to plan and without violence or excessive upheaval.

While some scholars have approached the question of democratic transition narrowly by examining the formal practices of democracy (such as voting, protesting, and engaging with political parties), this book, by contrast, considers both the formal and informal practices of information politics that contribute to the formation of political identities, and it argues that the emerging information politics work both for and against democracy. These newly allocated rights to information are producing new relationships and practices that lead people to take up their rights to the city, in ways that are not limited to the formal practices of democracy.

How information in a democracy should be produced, circulated, and interpreted is not apparent. There are no hard and fast rules governing this process, especially during and shortly after a transition to democracy in which citizens are demanding more and new access. Moreover, when a new regime takes power, it can also quickly shift information practices, as we have seen with the Trump administration in the United States, for which "fake news" has become a new information ideology resulting in a series of new information practices. Anthropologists, scrambling to make sense of these changes, are exploring topics such as the role of lying in politics (McGranahan 2017), the use of Twitter in the 2016 US presidential campaign (Stolee and Caton 2018), and the role of "big data" analysis (González 2017). A focus on information politics, then, is a call to treat these different information practices in relation to each other and to study them ethnographically. Because Indonesia underwent a significant transition to democracy in 1998 after thirty years of authoritarian rule, it is a useful place to investigate information politics in an effort to understand how state-society relationships are transforming.

Shadow Play

The anti-relocation street vendors I studied often talked about and understood the government's information politics through the metaphor of the *wayang kulit* (shadow play), a reference to the popular Indonesian form of puppet theatre. According to this interpretive framework, in life there is the play that can be observed unfolding before your eyes, but behind the screen there is always a puppet master (*dalang*) controlling the show. While some traders used the terms *wayang kulit* or *dalang* to describe the actions of the government, others used terms like *provokator* (provocateur) or *oknum* (in this context, referring to a figure imagined to operate secretly in order to benefit personally). All of these figures were understood to operate in the off-stage realm, concealing the work of others behind the screen.

The anti-relocation traders and their supporters used this framework to understand what appeared to them to be an invisible realm of politics. In this framework, what happens "behind the screen" is often viewed as more real than what happens in front, which is mere illusion. The New Order government was invested in creating an appearance of order (through, as John Pemberton [1994] argues, the staging of traditional rituals and Javanese culture), but behind that there was chaos. This idea continues to pervade everyday life in Indonesia, where people are suspicious of appearances and believe that behind every appearance lies an alternative reality (Bubandt 2014, 32; Spyer 2002). Drawing on Strassler (2004, 692), Nils Bubandt (2014) states, "dreams of democracy and discourses of transparency (I. *transparansi*) and openness (I. *terbuka*) are, accordingly, in constant tension with the 'orchestrated' (I. *direkayasa*), the 'dark' (I. *gelap*) and things 'hidden' (I. *tertutip*) in politics)" (32).

In the course of my research, I found that certain actors – namely, government actors, NGOs, and street vendors – took advantage of this interpretive framework in order to create confusion among their opposition. I describe some of these practices using the vernacular concept of "shadow play" to refer to the confusion and secrecy created through the (mis)use of information; it is a mode of control. Confusion, secrecy, and falsification are often viewed as mere effects rather than actual strategies of governance. The concept of shadow play helps to make sense of the elite (often state) practice of generating confusion, uncertainty, and distrust when trying to implement controversial urban infrastructure projects. This generally top-down practice not only reproduces visions of state/elite power but also creates a feeling of powerlessness and frustration among those who are exposed to it. The practice helps the state/ elites to accumulate and maintain power, especially during the implementation of controversial projects affecting the livelihoods of the poor and marginalized. However, as shown in my research, state practices of shadow play also generated agency among the anti-relocation street vendors and their supporters as they responded by engaging in their own counter shadow play, developing practices that would help them identify the *dalang* (see Chapter 4: Democratizing Surveillance), reveal the government's shadow play to the wider public (see Chapter 5: Press Releases and Silent Critiques), and generate confusion about their own agency (see Chapter 6: The Talk of Violence). Although shadow play can be a mode of governance, it can also be used as a method to challenge it.

I describe shadow play as a way to get at the paradoxical nature of urban governing practices in Indonesia, where the Yogyakarta municipal government shifted between an open dialogue with the anti-relocation street vendors and the strategic manipulation, hiding, and publicizing of information in order to generate confusion. These practices created uncertainty about the "true" interests of government officials, and caused the traders and their supporters to develop their own practices of shadow play to engage in this conflict over information. This oscillation between dialogue and democratic practices on the one hand, and secrecy and manipulation on the other, was possible because one can be upheld and promoted in the public sphere while the other can be mostly hidden from the residents of Yogyakarta. Following Michel Foucault (1995), I argue that while the practice of shadow play can be read as repressive, it is in fact still productive, giving rise to new forms of behaviour like paranoia and distrust, rather than only inhibiting forms of behaviour. Although some of the traders did accept the world view that shadow play creates, most were not simply dupes of ideological pressures, but questioned, reflected on, and conspired about what was happening. Some tried to resist the government's shadow play while others sought to benefit from or take advantage of the situation for their own financial or political gain. Power, then, is not something that is held by those in government, but something that is performed – a strategy. Shadow play was one of the strategies in the toolkits of all of the actors involved in the relocation project – elites, government officials, NGOs, and street vendors. It was used to accumulate and exert power, and it was deployed largely through the strategic utilization of information.

Street Vendors through an Information-Politics Lens

Street traders are a particularly fruitful group in which to study shadow play and its related information practices because of their fraught relationship with the public and the state. Since street vending is often very contentious, gaining access to information, sharing information, and controlling its circulation is important for traders' success and survival. Early work by Clifford Geertz (1978) recognized that street vendors in a marketplace in Morocco operated through "the search for information – laborious, uncertain, complex, and irregular" (30). Geertz went on to describe how searching for information is a highly developed skill or "art" that is developed and maintained through certain structures in the marketplace. And yet, despite Geertz's important work on the importance of information practices for traders, the idea of information did not develop as a main line of study in the work on street vendors.

Street vendors have nonetheless been held hostage by a kind of information politics produced by scholars and bureaucrats that has impacted street-vending policies globally. Once the concept of an "informal economy" was developed by scholars in the late 1970s to characterize street traders (and other self-employed urban labourers), it was taken up problematically by the International Labour Office as being "synonymous with poverty" (Portes and Haller 2005, 404), and by other policymakers as being associated with "low levels of productivity" and a "low capacity for accumulation" (404). Some scholarly approaches saw the informal sector as upsetting society's proper trajectory, "either by draining resources or by facilitating powerful elites' exploitation of the disenfranchised poor" (Lewinson 1998, 209). Traders had to face an information politics not of their choosing as governments and bureaucrats decided on the labels of *informal sector* and *informal economy*, setting up systems to collect information about this sector without people involved in it having much say. The traders themselves were also considered informal because information about their practices existed out of state control.

Despite some actors' negative usage of these terms, other scholars have used the concept of the informal sector in a more positive way. Keith Hart (1973), who coined the term, characterized the informal sector as an example of the fact that urban dwellers are not simply passive actors, but people who can generate income based on their own initiatives. Others have recognized that formal and informal activities are connected and interdependent rather than in opposition to each other (e.g., Lewinson 1998; Lindell 2010), and that even though some traders might be outside of the formal state system, in practice, they are often regulated and controlled by their own rules and organizations (e.g., Gibbings 2013; Lazar 2007). Rather than being seen as economic relics of the past, traders have also been presented as the products of recent socio-economic and political changes, and as embedded in the cultural practices and norms specific to their places of operation (e.g., K.T. Hansen, Little, and Milgram 2013, 3).

Despite the more progressive concepts of the informal sector and informal economy that academics are increasingly putting forth, the traders I studied in Yogyakarta faced a public and government that largely imagined street vendors as violating modern visions of the city as a place of formal employment, cleanliness, and centralized planning. The traders countered these discourses by presenting themselves as actually contributing to the city: they were not, after all, unemployed, nor were they asking the government for help. They also tried to portray themselves as clean and orderly, two important values from the Suharto era that gave them credibility. I found that many of these traders asserted their relative status by suggesting that their work was *halal* (permissible in the eyes of Allah) and that they were "aspiring entrepreneurs" or "bosses" of their own businesses. Even before the relocation was underway, the street traders were embedded in an information politics about street vending and modernity.

A focus on information politics allows us to see how what is called "information" comes to bear little resemblance to some ideal of neutral or objective facts, but instead becomes a space of negotiation among street traders and the state (cf. Anjaria 2016) and central to the formation of relationships in practice. The scholarship on street vending has understood that street vendors have a complex and contradictory relationship with the state (e.g., A. Brown 2006; Cross 1998; G. Clark 2013, 29). John Cross (1998) found that traders' leaders in Mexico City were able to create alliances with important officials within the state structure without becoming dependent on the administrative apparatus of the state. Walter E. Little (2014) uses the term *urban spatial permissiveness* to describe how regulations are not tightly enforced in Antigua, Guatemala, but are negotiated and flexible because the vendors' interests are in alignment with others such as the national government and the international tourist industry. Daniel Goldstein (2016) describes how government officials at Cancha marketplace, in the Bolivian city of Cochabamba, applied certain preferred forms of regulation while ignoring others (7). He describes this as the "absent presence" of the state, a situation where state actors enforce certain rules but not others (6). This literature on street vending has shown just how fragmented the state can be, and how government officials, in their dealings with street vendors, often operate in contradiction to the ideal image of the state acting democratically. However, this line of research has focused less on the fact that information practices can be central to the ways that these state-vendor relationships form in the first place, are strengthened, and break apart.

In my own research, the conflicts, friendships, trust, and disbelief that I witnessed among the traders themselves, and between the anti-relocation traders and the state, were mediated by different information practices such as surveillance, *sosialisasi* (the practice of communicating a plan to citizens), and conspiracy. A focus on the information practices of the government, traders, and advocates demonstrates that all parties engaged in information practices, some of which could be considered informal and "off the books." The government's ability to carry out this relocation project depended on the use of informal information practices like the falsifying of documents. The street vendors likewise relied on practices that challenged the government's project, such as indirectly revealing information in newspapers about the government's relocation plan.

The information practices of the anti-relocation traders were often shaped by other groups and individuals, such as NGOs and lawyers, who could help these traders tackle the information politics. Although many of these street vendors were university educated and could be considered lower-middle class because of their incomes, they had less experience interacting with the government and opposing a government project, and therefore looked to activists and lawyers for support.

The NGOs, lawyers, and student organizations involved in opposing the relocation took up important roles in helping to organize the anti-relocation street vendors by providing them with regular guidance. While these middle-class activists helped the street vendors articulate their grievances, they were less equipped to deal with the suspicions and distrust that emerged between themselves and the vendors. These new activist leaders understood how to easily engage in some practices of information politics, but they were less capable of navigating other, concurrent streams of information politics involving potential government interference and the impact of rumours and conspiracies among the traders they were supporting. The Suharto-era propaganda continued to linger as the government depicted these middle-class activists as outsiders and troublemakers who were taking the street vendors down a wrong path of dissent against the state. Yet the street vendors also picked up on new information practices they learned alongside the NGOs and incorporated these practices into their repertoires of action against the state.

In a contemporary global moment that fetishizes secrecy and revelation, truth and fake news, street vendors are one group in which to study information politics in order to understand how relationships are negotiated, made, and remade in practice. Street vending has often been studied through the lenses of formality and informality, legality and illegality, as a means to understand how the state-trader relationship works. The study of information politics offers another way to understand how traders negotiate their relationship with both the state and others in ways that have little to do with official laws or policies. A focus on information politics allows us to see how what is called "information" is not comprised of independent facts but instead constitutes its own category that is granted the ability to enable some forms of political action while foreclosing others. Because street vending is deeply embedded in information politics, it becomes a revealing site through which to think about the state of democracy, national politics, and even global politics.[27] At the same time, while street vendors are the site of the present study of information politics and the play of power, they have been struggling with the state for a much longer time. Their current information politics must be understood in relation to this history.

The Struggle over Street Traders in Indonesia

Although the information politics I describe in this book are part of a new logic of urban governance associated with the transition to democracy, it is important to recognize that street vendors have long been faced with an information politics that characterizes them as "unmodern." As a result, successive governments across Indonesia have sought to remove them or relocate them to marketplaces as a solution. The struggle over street traders in Indonesia is a long one, beginning in the colonial period and continuing to the present. Towards the end of the nineteenth century, Indonesian cities were organized with the logic of preventing urban radicalism. In 1891, a national by-law on public order permitted street traders to operate only if there was insufficient space in official, government-sanctioned marketplaces (Colombijn 1994, 317).[28] Wary of any subversive movements, the colonial rulers created a spatial and visual order that sought to prevent urban movements from arising (Kusno 2005, 494). Part of this spatial organization was the placement of street sellers in marketplaces to ensure a clear view of the street. The organization of street traders into marketplaces was not only concerned with repression and control, but also "modernity" and "hygiene" (Kusno 2005).

During the Japanese occupation (1942–5) and the subsequent revolution that led to Indonesia's independence, many urban residents took up trading since imported goods were difficult to obtain (Jellinek 1991, 72). In the 1950s and early 1960s, the traders evoked government intervention. There was little concern over the traders as a security threat; instead, they were viewed as inhibiting Indonesia from ushering in the modernity that independence had promised.[29] The national government had not yet developed a system to identify, record, or count the traders. They were instead grouped and relocated to marketplaces where possible, especially if they occupied major streets. In the newspapers, they remained voiceless bodies.

In the 1960s, the economic situation in Indonesia was dire, and in 1966, Suharto forcefully took power after the army and anti-communist citizens massacred hundreds of thousands of so-called communists and left-leaning individuals. Many were sent to prison or detention camps. It was in this context of massive displacement, political upheaval, and poverty that the modern-day incarnation of the street vendor, which came to be known as the *pedagang kaki lima*, emerged. With thousands of people unemployed due to their alleged communist ties, street vending grew in popularity because it provided freedom and anonymity. In particular, street vendors were considered part of the "floating mass," a category that emerged after the popular anti-left radicalism of the 1960s. That is, the traders were considered to be potential communists in hiding or part of the underclass that had migrated from rural to urban areas, and the government was hopeful that these individuals could be transformed into productive subjects. This population was not documented statistically, but nevertheless their presence could be felt in the city because of their visibility.

By the start of the 1970s, petty trading in *kampungs* (lower-class residential neighbourhoods or slums in an urban setting) was the most important means of earning a livelihood, with approximately 50 per cent of the workforce engaged in the sector (Jellinek 1991, 72). Some food sellers pushed mobile carts through neighbourhoods and on main streets, while others parked their carts in one place for a longer time. Many individuals sold food door to door; others had small food stalls in their neighbourhoods of residence. By the mid-1970s, many petty traders were finding it difficult to survive because the costs of raw materials had increased but their customers were generally poor (73). A new range of affordable packaged goods was available from supermarkets, cafés, and shops. Despite these challenges, many individuals chose to sell on the street because of unemployment and increasing rental costs in marketplaces. Yet while many of the traders selling in the same areas knew each other, shared information, and helped each other out, there existed no formal vendor organization.

By the 1980s, the term *pedagang kaki lima* (five-legged seller; *pedagang* translates to "seller" and *kaki lima* translates to "five feet") had solidified as the most popular name for street traders, and a local variant for the internationally recognized terms *street vendor* and *hawker*.[30] In the face of increasing global attention to the subject, *pedagang kaki lima* became a way to refer to the local Indonesian experience of the street vendor in cities across the archipelago. Through numerous studies in the 1980s (see, for example, Fakultas Hukum, Universitas Katolik Parahyangan 1980), the idea of the street vendor as pedagang kaki lima was firmly established, and the term has since become ubiquitous. Central to these studies was the effort to define this new category. Indeed, throughout the 1980s, all such studies on the pedagang kaki lima seemed to have the same goal: to "know" the street vendor according to a series of criteria.[31] This allowed the pedagang kaki lima to be viewed as a discrete population, a group with certain characteristics that could be known, monitored, and most importantly, compared across cities, across Asia, and indeed across the globe.

During this period, the "floating mass" of street vendors also became a cause for government concern at multiple levels in Indonesia and for citizens who feared that this group might be mobilized by political organizations and engage in populist politics ("Masalah Pedagang Kaki Lima" 1980). Due to these concerns about vendors mobilizing for radical ends, municipal governments supported street vendors in forming cooperatives, seeing these organizations as a means to control vendors and organize them around upcoming national elections.[32] This trend began on Yogyakarta's main street, Malioboro. In June 1981, some street vendors in Yogyakarta formed PPJ-Y (Persatuan Pedagang Pinggir Jalan Yogyakarta, or Roadside Traders Union Yogyakarta), an organization that in 1982 expanded to become a cooperative under the name Tri Dharma.[33] The state also contained the possible radicalism of street vendors by encouraging the formation of other cooperatives that supported and promoted state ideologies. It was also around this time that municipal governments started to create regulations that specified which traders could be given permits and the conditions for granting these permits.

With traders organized in cooperatives, governments continued to relocate or remove traders throughout the 1980s and the early 1990s. There was minimal overt resistance from traders, even though street vendor relocations or removals generally resulted in little financial success for the traders. During this period, harsh and even excessive measures were used to ensure stability; but this was merely the appearance of order (and an eerie one at that), and any uprisings were quickly suppressed. Most resistance to these relocations or removals thus took subtle forms that James C. Scott (1985) has described as "foot-dragging": after being relocated for a few weeks, street vendors would often simply return to their original selling locations or find new ones, thus avoiding direct confrontation with the state.

The 1997 Asian economic crisis unleashed thousands of unemployed workers, many of whom circulated through cities across Indonesia looking for work. In May 1998, after months of economic instability, dictator Suharto was unseated from power after nationwide student-led demonstrations and violence in Jakarta (May 13–14) shook the New Order regime. The movement that toppled Suharto on 21 May 1998 was called *Reformasi* (Reform). These rapid economic and political transformations caused many people to look to street vending to make a living, because there were few alternatives and it was relatively easy to become a street trader (requiring only a small amount of capital and a location). In Yogyakarta, new trading locations popped up around the city, in places where no or few traders had previously operated.

Most municipal governments initially turned a blind eye to the growth of urban street vending around the city during the economic crisis of 1997. But after the crisis subsided and democracy took hold, street vendor relocations became a common practice again. Municipal governments have been keen to relocate traders in the wake of the decentralization that has followed the end of the Suharto regime. With greatly expanded functions, municipal governments have needed to increase their revenues to finance their greater level of responsibility.[34] As a result, these governments have been more aggressively pursuing local revenue through collecting taxes from street vendors by relocating them to a marketplace or licensing them (Peters 2009). Government officials have also been collecting a small daily selling fee from traders who are officially recognized. Other traders who have not obtained official permits sometimes pay officials in the form of bribes.

Prior to Reformasi, municipal governments typically used force to remove street traders. This was also the case in Yogyakarta during the authoritarian period. From 2006 to 2007, Pak Achmad was involved in the planning and redevelopment of Kuncen Marketplace (which was previously a livestock market), where the Mangkubumi Street vendors were to be relocated. As Pak Achmad explained, "[during the New Order] the approach of the municipal government of Yogyakarta had always been 'force' (pemaksaan), since the initial idea was always from the government and rarely involved the public in policy formation during the [tenure of] Mayor Widagdo (1994–1998)" (Hardiyanti 2008, 99).[35]

In the post-Suharto era, some city governments continue to remove street vendors by force without providing an alternative location, while some of the more "progressive" governments provide alternative places, such as marketplaces. Governments in Yogyakarta and Surakarta, for example, have renovated marketplaces for unwanted street vendors and provided incentives for them to relocate, such as subsidies for the first few months of selling, access to credit and skill-building resources, and tax deferrals. In Surakarta in 2008, the government proudly claimed to have met with local street vendors fifty-four times before the vendors agreed to relocate to a marketplace. The government officials involved in these relocations have used terms such as demokrasi (democracy) and pengembangan (development), claiming to provide a voice for these small sellers and an opportunity for them to progress.[36] When Pak Herry Zudianto became mayor of Yogyakarta in 2001, the municipal government shifted its approach away from the use of force to that of dialogue. Under the leadership of Pak Herry Zudianto, there were approximately seven different street vendor relocations between 2005 and 2010 (Retno 2012, 12). Relocating traders without violence, chaos, or conflict is increasingly desirable for mayors because, among other things, it has allowed them to demonstrate to other leaders and citizens across the nation that they are "good" and "democratic" leaders. Mayors such as Pak Herry Zudianto have hoped that this will become part of their legacy.

The democratic transition has created conditions in which street vendors can now openly come together, with the help of NGOs and other members of civil society, to defend their urban territory against the state. To date, however, most of these efforts have been ad hoc, as street vendors only mobilize when their ability to sell is under direct threat. The alliances rarely involve street vendors from across Yogyakarta, but only those in a particular area who are in immediate danger. Many of the street vendors I spoke with, who traded at various locations across the city, were sceptical of the government relocation programs that were supposedly meant to help them. Their scepticism stemmed from their direct or second-hand experiences with anti–pedagang kaki lima policies, numerous failed relocations (leading to loss of income or bankruptcy), and the difficulty of obtaining government-issued operating permits. Although many of the movements against vendor relocations or evictions have been unsuccessful, these efforts are nonetheless pushing the boundaries of citizenship by playing information politics. However, information politics is not easy to engage in in a complex landscape marked by differences and divisions among the street vendors.

Street Vendors: Divisions and Belonging in Yogyakarta City

From the outside, all street vendors might appear the same. They are all found on the streets and are engaged in what can be considered precarious work. Yet, as Gracia Clark (1988a) has argued, traders are far from monolithic and their "responses [to the state] also reveal critical subdivisions within their ranks" (58).

Selling Conditions, Ethnicity, Age, and Religion

In my own research, I found that government officials, citizens, and even the vendors themselves drew distinctions between the traders by where they sell (an expensive and secure location versus an insecure location in a less desirable part of the city) and what they sell. Many of the street vendors selling new items (shoes, batik, belts, jeans, or T-shirts) saw themselves as different from those who sell second-hand goods. The second-hand sellers regarded the vendors who sell new items as lacking in talent, reasoning that because vendors of new items can buy their goods from a distributor and sell them at a fixed price to make a profit, their work requires less effort. The second-hand vendors, by contrast, viewed their own buying and selling as requiring "real" skill and knowledge, because they needed to be able to determine the value of used goods such as watches, glasses, or antiques. The way they saw it, they are good sellers if they can buy a watch for a tenth of its value from an inexperienced seller.

Among the street vendors I studied, distinctions were also drawn according to ethnicity – first and foremost, between the Javanese and those from other islands, such as Madura (off the north-eastern coast of Java), and then between "local" people from Yogyakarta and those from elsewhere in Java. People from Yogyakarta city, or at least from the Special Region of Yogyakarta, were viewed as having a greater right to sell on the street than outsiders. One of the unverified rumours circulating during my fieldwork was that the majority of street vendors on Malioboro Street were in fact outsiders – people from Madura or Sumatra with more capital who had bought out the Yogyakartans and the Javanese. Among people who considered themselves as Yogyakartans, the fear over the loss of a traditional "Javanese culture" unique to Yogyakarta – including Javanese trading traditions – intersected with their concern about losing control of their economy with the arrival of so-called outsiders. The latter often entered into street vending through kampung ties or through relatives. For example, Pak Akbar, the leader of the Pethikbumi street vendor organization on Mangkubumi Street, had numerous relatives and at least one individual from his kampung who had relocated from Sumatra to Yogyakarta. Upon coming to the city, they had initially stayed at his house and helped him with his trading for several months before setting up their own selling locations.

While traders in Yogyakarta are often a wide array of ages, many of the Pethikbumi members selling used cell phones and new clothing and accessories were under forty. Those members selling second-hand goods (besides cell phones) tended to be forty and older. As will be discussed later in this chapter (see An Ethnography of Information Politics), there were also three pro-relocation trader groups, one of which traded on Mangkubumi Street. Among these pro-relocation groups, although there were a number of traders in their twenties and thirties, the majority were forty and older. Taken as a whole, there was therefore a wide span of ages across all four groups; on Mangkubumi Street itself, one of the oldest traders was eighty-four years old, while the youngest was twenty.

Generally, most of the street vendors I interviewed followed Islam,[37] but loosely. Thus, although the ideas and practices of Islam varied among the street vendors, this was not a point of tension. The majority had not studied Islamic traditions in *pesantren* (traditional Islamic educational institutions) and did not follow the regular practices, such as praying five times a day. Most maintained the basic principle that if you are good and nice to other people, others and Allah will treat you well. This philosophy also influenced how people reflected on their sales. If they received little takings that day, it was considered Allah's will, and they had to accept this outcome as a part of a divine plan. If they did not receive enough money that day to eat, then hopefully tomorrow they would. This generally relaxed approach to Islam fits with the laid-back attitude and freedom generally associated with the life of the street vendor. This freedom is what makes street vending appealing to many people. The social and cultural expectations are less stringent than in other places, like the office or the kampung.

Gender and Pemuda Masculinities

In Southeast Asia, women typically dominate petty trade, a position that evokes mixed reactions of both respect and condemnation (e.g., Atkinson and Errington 1990; Brenner 1998; Leshkowich 2011). On the island of Java in particular, women have traditionally dominated marketplaces and neighbourhood trading because money and the marketplace are considered to lie outside the sphere of prestige (see J.T. Siegel 1986, 164; Brenner 1998). In *The Domestication of Desire*, Suzanne Brenner (1998) argues, however, that women in Solo, Java, served as the main agents of "domestication," converting the money they received from trading batik into status for themselves and their families (16).

In my own research in Yogyakarta, I found that whether it is considered appropriate for women to work as street vendors depends on their location and the items they sell. For instance, on the well-established Malioboro Street, I observed more women selling than on other streets in Yogyakarta. The vendors on this street mostly hold vending permits from the government, and they are viewed as a tourist attraction; thus, the women who sell on this street are subject to fewer (although still many) negative connotations than those at other locations. The women who do sell on the street often sell food or clothing, which are also symbolically linked to women. On Mangkubumi Street, where my study is focused, the majority of sellers were men: in the Pethikbumi membership book, there were just 10 women listed out of a total of 377 members.[38] There were two reasons for this. Firstly, the goods sold there included second-hand electronics, cell phones, or other merchandise associated more closely with men because these objects were considered "dirty" (*kotor*) and were sometimes viewed as stolen. Those traders selling new items sold goods that tended to appeal to male customers, such as men's clothing. Both these new and second-hand items were indeed more often bought by men. Secondly, the majority of sellers were men because the selling only took place in the evenings, until around 10:00 p.m., with meetings and general socializing sometimes occurring afterwards (see figure 1). Most of these male street vendors

Figure 1. Mangkubumi Street traders, 10 November 2007. Photographer unknown.

were unaccompanied by their partners or children, not only because they worked for three to four hours each evening, but because the street was associated with stolen goods and considered unsafe. Girlfriends, children, or wives rarely visited, preferring to stay at home. Moreover, in terms of the Pethikbumi group specifically, the organization's leadership was exclusively male; the few women in the general membership often sold alongside their partners rather than on their own.

I argue in this book that the Pethikbumi leaders drew on various concepts of manliness, particularly those tied to the idea of *pemuda*, a term used to refer to "youth," and more generally to "political activists, especially those working outside the structure of government and social institutions" (Steedly 2013, 333). The word typically refers to men; even though there is a feminine variant, *pemudi*, it is rarely used (Lee 2011, 946).

Pemuda were important figures during the revolutionary period in Indonesia (1945–9) because youth were frustrated by the Japanese occupation and waged an armed struggle against the remaining Japanese troops, followed by the British and Dutch troops who were trying to gain control of the region (B. Anderson 1972). The role of this younger generation in the development of the Indonesian National Revolution has been widely narrated as a central aspect of Indonesian history. As Benedict Anderson (1972) states, "On the Indonesian side, a whole literature of glorification attests to an exultant consciousness of the sudden emergence of youth as a revolutionary force in those critical times" (1).

At various points since, when youth have challenged the government, the idea of the pemuda has resurfaced, and although their role has changed over time, pemuda remain important historical figures as heroes and nationalists. For instance, in 1965–6, pemuda, operating in cooperation with the army, played an important role in the removal of President Sukarno (1945–67) (Ryter 1998). Reformasi brought about the idea of the pemuda movement again when young activists called for a wide range of changes, such as democratic elections and press freedom (Steedly 2013, 321). Lee (2016) describes how the youth of the Reformasi era, many of them students, engaged in "pemuda fever," with activists identifying themselves with different periods of pemuda activism throughout history and seeing themselves as the pemuda generation of 1998.[39]

This activism of the 1980s and '90s has since become more widespread and is now being taken up by groups outside of traditional youth and student activist circles. Lee (2016) describes this development of the pemuda figure as "the slow-motion spread of student activism from its campus-based, moral-force roots in the 1980s and 1990s to its social-movement climax in the years of Reformasi and finally to its diffuse form more than a decade later as a 'repertoire' of masculinist poses, images, and mass political techniques that others have appropriated to serve the diverse needs of the public domain (Taylor 2003)" (210). While woman were present in the Reformasi movement, they were not equal in number or significance (Lee 2011, 946). Moreover, women activists were evaluated according to the same measure as their male counterparts, and were expected to be "as militant, as radical, as potentially violent, and as wild as men" (946). In this book, I argue that the activism of the Pethikbumi leaders – who, as has been noted, were all men – and their supporters in the PPIP (Pergerakan Pemuda Indonesia untuk Perubahan, or Indonesia Youth Movement for Change) – who were also mostly men[40] – can be viewed in light of the collective memory and practices of pemuda. Many of the information practices of Pethikbumi and its PPIP supporters evoked some of the "repertoire" of masculinist poses, ideas, and methods used by the Reformasi pemuda (see Lee 2016).

Networks and Ties

Although many of the street vendors who sell beside each other enjoy friendly ties, solidarity among street vendors across Yogyakarta city was nonetheless fragile. Of the many attempts to create citywide and even region-wide vendor organizations, most failed to mobilize the street vendors for any single cause over a sustained period of time. When I asked various street vendors about why they did not support other vendor groups that were targeted by the government, many said they were too busy (*terlalu sibuk*): they were just trying to survive and did not have the time or money to invest. Others did not want to put their own positions in jeopardy by helping other vendors who were not in the government's favour.

The residents in the neighbourhood where I lived most often met and interacted with the street vendors at the mosque. On Fridays, streams of vendors could be observed coming to the mosque for prayer, and many neighbourhood residents ate lunch in the local *warung* (casual food stall, shop, or café), where food was cheaper. In my neighbourhood, one of the street vendor organizations rented a house for their office, so the appearance of street vendors in the area was a regular occurrence. During street vendor relocations, support from the surrounding neighbourhoods was important. In the case of the project to relocate the Mangkubumi Street vendors, for instance, Pethikbumi sought the support of the nearby kampungs, hoping that the residents could pressure the government to change its mind. The sheer numbers of kampung dwellers could help the cause. The preman in the kampungs were also an important component as they could be mobilized on either side to intimidate or generate trouble. Both the government and the Pethikbumi traders watched and lobbied for neighbourhood support during the relocation.

As well as vendor groups and preman, a wide range of other actors have an interest in street vendors and their relocation: political parties, landowners, corporations, NGOs, mass organizations (organisasi massa; ormas), customers of vendors, and the municipal government. Initially, before the Mangkubumi Street vendor relocation project, the vendors (both those for and against the relocation) were not closely tied to larger sociopolitical networks in the city. However, as the relocation rapidly approached, the vendors were drawn into these networks through their informal leaders, such as human rights advocates. The emergence of these alliances suggests that political groups in the city are fragmented, flexible, and formulated during and through urban projects.

During the relocation project, a wide range of non-state actors appeared on the scene, some of whom challenged state power, while others worked to consolidate and maintain it (see Wilson 2012b). These non-state groups provided street vendors, who were members of the informal economy, with a network of solidarity and opportunities. The groups helped the vendors voice their needs in a context in which they have few rights, since the majority of these vendors were illegal according to municipal by-laws (Pemerintah Kota Yogyakarta 2002).

The network of individuals who supported the pro-relocation traders was backed by Pak Herry Zudianto, who was a member of the National Mandate Party (Partai Amanat Nasional, or PAN) and a local businessman. He developed the vision for Kuncen Marketplace and implemented the relocation plan with the help of his relocation team, a group of municipal civil servants. The main informal leader supporting the mayor was Pak Didik. As well as being an advocate for the pro-relocation traders, Pak Didik was a human rights activist and director of an NGO, Indonesian Law Monitoring Alliance (ILMA). His vision was to promote democracy and human rights in Indonesia. He was informally connected to PPP (Partai Persatuan Pembangunan, or the United Development Party), an Islamic political party, and he helped rally other informal leaders in the city behind the relocation plans. However, the Pethikbumi traders and their supporters questioned the ethics and validity of his work, knowing that he was close to and worked with preman.

The anti-relocation traders' network of supporters included the following organizations: the NGO Forum, a coalition of NGOs in the city concerned with human rights and democracy; PPIP, a radical youth organization comprised mostly of Marxist-leaning university students;[41] and BPHK (Badan Pelindung Hak Kemanusiaan, or Human Rights Protection Agency), a non-profit comprised mostly of lawyers. All of these groups considered themselves part of the movement to promote democracy and human rights in Indonesia. Mbah Ahmad, the leader of ethnic organization KMY (Ikatan Keluarga Madura, or Madura Family Alliance), also expressed his disapproval of the relocation. Other street trader organizations in the city disagreed with the relocation but did not offer any substantial support to the anti-relocation traders. Finally, besides having limited resources and time, many individual traders not involved in this specific relocation, despite generally being opposed to it, expressed concern that joining forces and opposing the relocation would put their own right to sell at risk. It was in the context of these different alliances and allegiances that the information politics of the relocation took place.

An Ethnography of Information Politics

This book is based on a long-term engagement with street vendors during the implementation of this urban infrastructure project in Yogyakarta city, including my two consecutive years of ethnographic research from 2006 to 2008 and my follow-up research conducted in 2013 and 2014 over several months. I became interested in studying this particular street vendor relocation after reading about it in a newspaper in April 2007. I had been spending my time with street vendors on nearby Malioboro Street, where the majority of the vendors, having managed to negotiate temporary permits with the government, were relatively secure. They had profitable locations on the most famous tourist street in Yogyakarta, and they were also very well organized. I was interested in comparing what I had been observing on Malioboro Street to Mangkubumi Street, where a group of traders, Pethikbumi, existed in a more precarious situation in which they were threatened by the relocation project. In August 2005, Pethikbumi had 377 members,[42] although this number was closer to 500 by March 2007; by October 2007, it was estimated that 800 Pethikbumi traders were selling on Mangkubumi Street.[43] Pak Denny, who worked with the community policing organization on Malioboro Street, said that he knew many of the traders on Mangkubumi Street because he also acted as security there. He introduced me to one of the Pethikbumi leaders, Mas Arief, who was the group's secretary. Luckily, I arrived at just the right time: Mas Arief and the other Pethikbumi leaders were open to having a foreign researcher witness and observe their organizing against the relocation.

After meeting with the Pethikbumi leaders, I quickly learned that there were three groups of pro-relocation street traders – the Independent, Asem Gede, and Southern Square traders – working with the government to achieve the relocation. The Independent group sold on Mangkubumi Street. Formed in November 2006 after Pethikbumi decided to refuse the government's relocation, it had, by my estimation, approximately 100 members throughout the period of the relocation project. The Asem Gede group, which had 120 members,[44] sold at Asem Gede, a neighbourhood near Mangkubumi Street. The Southern Square group, which had 80 members,[45] sold at the Southern Square (Alun-Alun Selatan), a city square located south of the Sultan's palace and a few kilometres south of Mangkubumi Street and Asem Gede.[46] I approached these leaders to request approval for my research and thereafter started spending time with the various pro-relocation traders and leaders. I chatted with them at their selling locations and attended some meetings organized by their NGO advocate, Pak Didik. Although the pro-relocation traders had no problem with me, Pak Didik was more hesitant about me attending their official meetings, especially at the start of my research. However, I developed a positive relationship with him fairly quickly when he realized that we knew a number of the same people in Yogyakarta who were willing to confirm that I was a researcher who could be trusted. After that, I was invited to spend time at his office, where I would regularly drop in to hear his perspective on the relocation.

Although I spent significant time with the pro-relocation traders while they traded on the street, I decided to spend more time with the anti-relocation traders as well, partly because they invited me to observe all of their meetings and demonstrations. (Although I was invited to – and attended – some of the pro-relocation meetings, the pro-relocation groups did not hold as many of these gatherings as the anti-relocation group.) The Pethikbumi traders and their lawyers were welcoming to me because, besides wanting to be transparent in their dealings, the anti-relocation traders liked the idea that a foreign researcher was observing and could record how unfair, from their perspective, the government was being towards them. While I was sympathetic to Pethikbumi, I was also sympathetic to, and wanted to understand, the pro-relocation traders. In order to move between the two sides, I described myself as a researcher, not an advocate, who was trying to understand the perspective of the different parties and who promised to uphold the confidentiality of everyone involved. In addition to spending time with the street vendors from both sides and their supporters, I also regularly spent time at the city government offices. I rotated through a number of different departments to learn about their activities, collect documents, and understand more generally how the municipal government functioned. I also observed and interacted with government officials during the meetings they held with the traders about the relocation.

John Borneman and Joseph Masco (2015) argue that "there are many parallels between anthropological fieldwork and espionage. Both involve looking, listening, eavesdropping, taking notes, recording conversations, snapping photos, and establishing trusted confidants" (781). Conducting anthropological fieldwork on a politically charged topic like a street vending relocation was challenging in Indonesia precisely because of these parallels. Throughout my fieldwork, people I met, interviewed, and spent time with joked with me about my being an intelligence agent, and they informed me, in a joking manner, that I, too, was under surveillance. Although these jokes often generated laughter from myself and my interlocutors, I do believe that certain individuals seriously considered or suspected that I was working as an intelligence agent for the Canadian government. Because I was regularly placed in the subject position of an intelligence agent, I was often disturbed by a research process that required me to carry out tasks not that different from those of an intelligent agent, such as closely observing and recording the political minutiae of what was unfolding (although I was obviously not hiding my identity).

Therefore, as the relocation proceeded and tensions and suspicions grew among all the groups involved, conducting research became even more difficult. There was a general sense among all of the groups that no one could be trusted, and that behind outward appearances there might be another reality. Although at times the research was not easy because of these suspicions, I believe I managed to convince most people that my work as a researcher could have some value for understanding the challenges involved in the relocation project from different perspectives.

Finally, as a researcher, I brought along my own information ideologies. During the early days of my research, when I was perhaps more naive, I assumed that the truth was obtainable if I spent endless hours observing and verifying information through multiple people. After months of research, my information ideologies started to shift. I started to see the world more like my informants did. I saw that perhaps we would never really know who was behind the screen generating the conflict between the pro- and anti-relocation traders. I also grew more paranoid about whether I could trust what people were saying and doing.

After I left the field, I felt like a failed researcher because I had not joined all the pieces of the puzzle. It took me a long time to accept the fact that I would never know what really happened, that in fact no one involved really knew the entire story. Although I collected extensive data on both the anti- and pro-relocation traders, I also had to begin selecting what I would focus on because research and writing always involves a process of selection. I decided to write about the anti-relocation movement because I found their strategies fascinating. As I worked through the materials, I started to reflect more on how we relate to information, and how our ideas about information depend largely on our context. Over years of working through my field notes and interviews, I have come to see that information is less a discrete concept than an analytical starting point for understanding relationships and power. Individuals and groups engage in information practices and in so doing enter into and transform their relations with each other. By situating information practices in relation to power, I also began to recognize that power asserted through information politics can be limited and subject to change and challenge.

Information Politics and the Structure of This Book

In his study of peasant movements, Scott (1985) notes that far too much attention has been paid to open revolts, despite their rarity, so instead he turns his attention to everyday forms of resistance. He argues that, because of state power, peasants were usually not overtly rebellious, but they did resist the state through foot-dragging, dissimulation, and joke telling. For the street vendors involved in the relocation that I studied, information constituted the politically contentious site through which they fought for their rights not only to their livelihoods but to participate in the urban planning process more generally. As I will demonstrate in this book, disputes over the control of land have brought questions of governance and information to the forefront of urban planning, illustrating that conflicts over urban space are also disputes over how information should be used and circulated in the democratic era.

Access to information is a central tenet of democracy; as such, it is often a new desire and possibility for citizens after a country transitions from an authoritarian regime to a democracy. By tracking interactions between state agents, NGOs, activists, and street vendor networks in Yogyakarta city in the context of the vendor relocation project, I analyze how each of these actors leveraged, manipulated, and played with information in order to secure their claims and position themselves in relation to the relocation. As I demonstrate in each of the following chapters, the anti-relocation street vendors and their supporters, like the municipal government, developed a variety of strategies and practices to utilize information as power. In some ways, this emerging "rights consciousness" around information inspired new forms of agency and collective action. However, these new claims and rights practices were also embedded in a context in which the street vendors remained illegal and did not own the land on which they sold their merchandise. By seeing information as intertwined with politics, this book illustrates how the urban poor, those living on the margins of the city, come to inhabit political roles that transform and are transformed by emerging information practices in this new democracy. The different array of information practices, in turn, shapes the forms and practices of urban politics.

In Chapter 2: The Politics of Containment, I describe how the government began to consider relocating the street vendors to a marketplace. While the NGOs had promoted the idea of participatory planning, government reports on the potential relocation focused on a different information ideology – *sosialisasi*, which in these reports referred to the practice of communicating a plan to citizens via face-to-face meetings.

After tracing the history and meaning of this term during the Suharto era, I argue that, in government reports, *sosialisasi* was shaped by the fear of resistance and therefore was embroiled in what I call the *politics of containment*. The politics of containment involved trying to reduce the possibility of resistance among the street vendors by studying their perceptions of the relocation before starting the process of sosialisasi, and by sharing information strategically in order to curb any possible opposition.

Following on from the government's planned approaches to engaging in sosialisasi, Chapter 3: Dialogue, Documents, and Distrust describes how the government's use of sosialisasi in fact involved practices of shadow play. I discuss the different ways in which government officials and Pethikbumi members imagined and viewed the processes of sosialisasi. Rather than viewing it as having the same meaning for governments, NGOs, and citizens in Indonesia, I argue that, in the case of the relocation project, sosialisasi was often associated with competing ideologies and practices. While government officials viewed it as sharing information orally and getting close to all the traders affected by the relocation, the Pethikbumi traders wanted more meaningful discussions and access to documentation. I show that, although the government engaged in sosialisasi, it also used sosialisasi to engage in shadow play by circulating documents in unusual ways and with altered content. While the municipal government's sosialisasi practices created an idea among the public that the government was openly communicating with the street traders, the circulation of these government documents generated suspicion and uncertainty among the vendors.

Chapter 4: Democratizing Surveillance explores surveillance as a particular practice of shadow play. The chapter starts with a brief discussion of Indonesia's history of surveillance and how, during the Suharto era, the state, though fragmented, imposed a vision of itself as a powerful and coherent body capable of closely watching its citizens. During the relocation process, the government engaged in shadow play by using intelligence agents to watch the anti-relocation traders and then revealing these surveillance practices to them. This chapter describes, however, how the anti-relocation traders and their supporters also used surveillance tactics to collect information about their opponents and, in the case of Pethikbumi, their own members. Outlining these activities, I argue that surveillance is now imagined not only as a tool of the state but also as a useful practice available to citizens who seek to verify the actions and loyalties of others. I demonstrate that surveillance is a privileged technique among citizens who wish to counter suspicion in a political environment in which ideas of state conspiracy and distrust of appearances remain strong.

Chapter 5: Press Releases and Silent Critiques describes another type of shadow play used by the government, and how the anti-relocation street vendors and their supporters sought to challenge this practice through public engagement. The government supported preman who protected the pro-relocation street traders as they collected data at Mangkubumi Street, creating fear and uncertainty among the anti-relocation traders. After debating different strategies for releasing information about this practice to local newspapers, the anti-relocation traders and their supporters decided to indirectly accuse the government of being involved. While scholars have recognized that journalists in Indonesia often engage in self-censorship, I argue that the NGOs and anti-relocation street vendors also reported information to journalists in an indirect fashion, assuming that their units of discourse would move from their vendor meetings to the pages of the newspaper. Exploring these assumptions about how information should be circulated to the wider public, I argue that the practice of making indirect accusations anticipates particular reading practices on the part of newspaper consumers.[47]

In Chapter 6: The Talk of Violence, I describe how the government's uses of shadow play created fear among the anti-relocation traders that the government might use repression against them. These traders tried to clarify whether the government would use violence through discussions in meetings and in the newspapers. However, I demonstrate that the anti-relocation traders also engaged in their own practices of shadow play. They purposely created confusion about whether their opposition might eventually lead to an eruption of violence. These fears were subject to a different regime of circulation, however, surfacing in face-to-face discussions and on T-shirts that some Pethikbumi members wore, and they only appeared in the newspapers in an indirect fashion. I argue in this chapter that the "talk of violence" among the street vendors simultaneously engendered an environment of fear and addressed a particular set of fears as the Pethikbumi leaders created rumours of impending violence in an attempt to prevent such violence. The chapter also shows how newspapers became both a site of shadow play and a vehicle for the pursuit of truth.

In Chapter 7: Conspiratorial Knowledge, Allah, and State Power, I explore the effects that shadow play had on the anti-relocation traders and their supporters. The alliance between these traders and their allies broke down after a secret meeting involving an unusual grouping of people. The traders, NGOs, and lawyers thought that someone within their group was an *oknum* (in this case, someone secretly working for the government), and some individuals felt the need to account for themselves while also casting suspicion on others. These individuals started naming the oknum because they sensed that an actor from the state's off-stage play had infiltrated their group. There was a sense of relief when the traders could claim defeat at the hands of these unseen powers. However, there was also a sense of shame that their group might not be as pure or democratic as they had claimed, and naming the oknum thus remained a private business.

In Chapter 8: Agents and Brothers, I discuss contrasting versions of the shadow play that happened during the relocation from the perspectives of two informants, which I collected when I returned to the field in 2014. The first informant, a police officer who had been working behind the scenes to oversee the relocation, described how his approach relied on managing informal circuits of information and money in the interests of both the municipal government and himself. In contrast, a leader among the street vendors described how he had used information to protect himself from preman, as well as to demonstrate that he was under threat because of his role as the leader of an anti-relocation group. I argue that both of these stories, told six years after the events in question, relied on underlying sets of ideas about when it is appropriate for information to circulate in post-authoritarian Indonesia.

Chapter 9: Marketplace Relations briefly describes life in Kuncen Marketplace after the relocation, and how the pro- and anti-relocation traders have fared and how they relate to each other today.

Finally, I close with Chapter 10: Conclusion, which summarizes the main arguments of the book before discussing in broad terms the idea of information politics and how the study of information politics and ecologies of information in Indonesia can make a useful contribution to the anthropology of information. It also argues that information politics provides another way to understand how street vendors and the state negotiate their relationships. As I show in the chapter, urban politics in Indonesia is shaped by practices of shadow play.

In Indonesia, governments since the colonial period have sought to move street vendors to marketplaces in an attempt to clean up the streets and make them look attractive to foreign and national tourists, visiting dignitaries, and the local middle and upper classes. From the perspective of residents, marketplaces can be a fair solution since the traders are given a new location without being violently evicted. From the perspective of the state, marketplaces can also become a means to govern these traders more easily, extract taxes from them, and achieve the state's goal of appearing modern and clean. As relocations continue to be a common solution to the "urban problem" of street vendors globally, it is as important as ever that we understand what these relocations promise to the traders, why traders accept or disagree with them, how the process of relocation unfolds, and, ultimately, its long-term effects. As this book argues, in Indonesia, information politics becomes the battleground for new kinds of urban politics centred on the manipulation, control, and use of information.

Chapter Two

The Politics of Containment

In Indonesia, if a government department wishes to implement any new project, the process of communicating about it with local communities is usually referred to as sosialisasi. Sosialisasi is a kind of information practice that involves informing and consulting with community members in face-to-face meetings before and during a project's implementation. In this chapter, I argue that information politics in the context of the vendor relocation project involved sosialisasi in a politics of containment, with government officials explicitly identifying the potential resistance to the project by studying the stakeholders involved and producing reports. This information was then used in an attempt to contain the stakeholders' potential resistance by using sosialisasi strategically, as part of a largely top-down technical solution. The government officials associated with the relocation project operated according to an information ideology that suggested that experts should produce information about how the project should be implemented, and that they should control the circulation of this information to outside parties in such a way as to reduce oppositional politics.

I have developed the term *politics of containment* in relation to James Ferguson's (1994) work on anti-politics and Tania Li's (2007) work on "rendering technical." In his study of development in Lesotho, South Africa, Ferguson argues that the identification and creation of a "problem" is closely linked to the formation of potential solutions. In a similar way, I describe how the Yogyakarta municipal government, working within a politics of containment, looked to and anticipated resistance that was closely related to the formation of the solution – sosialisasi. The politics of containment also involved a process of "rendering technical"[1] (Li 2007, 7), with the government claiming for itself the ability and right to determine the plans and approach while citizens were subjected to direction through the process of sosialisasi. Finally, the politics of containment involved focusing on the causes of resistance and politics with the sole aim of curbing them. There was no attempt to address or remedy the underlying causes; rather, sosialisasi was the only solution that fell within the government's repertoire. The fact that sosialisasi was used so frequently during the New Order as part of Suharto's "Festival of Democracy"[2] (Pemberton 1994, 19) raises questions about the extent to which the meanings and practices of sosialisasi are changing in the current era. I argue that government officials have to think more strategically about sosialisasi in the post-Suharto era because there is more potential for open and organized resistance to state projects and greater expectations among citizens and stakeholders that the government must be transparent in the way it advances these projects. In the case of the vendor relocation project, government-commissioned consultants discussed in their reports how the sosialisasi (or the participation) of citizens should unfold. Rather than worrying about participation, however, these government consultants worried about containment and ensuring that their process of consultation would inhibit any potential resistance.

This politics of containment can be contrasted with another project (discussed in the following section). In the early 2000s, a group of NGOs tried to make the traders into stakeholders by involving them in the planning of the street; by this logic, the traders would be kept on the street but organized in a better, more "rational" way. However, as will be seen over the course of this and subsequent chapters, once the government's plan to relocate the traders got underway, the traders were nonetheless converted into objects of the relocation project.

Citizens as Stakeholders: Moving towards the Relocation

Historically, Mangkubumi Street was part of Yogyakarta's most famous tourist thoroughfare, Malioboro Street, which today is a location for the sale of souvenirs (*oleh-oleh*) to both domestic and foreign tourists. During the period of Dutch rule, a train station and tracks were built, dividing the two streets from each other. People have described this division as a challenge to the Javanese since the Dutch blocked a powerful axis that ran past these streets from the Yogyakarta Palace (Kraton Yogyakarta) to Mount Merapi.[3] When I visited in 2006, Mangkubumi Street, unlike Malioboro Street, was not a popular tourist destination; it housed a variety of shops and businesses, such as hotels, banks, motorbike shops, a newspaper office, travel agencies, and furniture stores (see figure 2). The majority of people visiting the street during the day either lived nearby or needed to purchase a specific item from a store in the area.

Figure 2. Mangkubumi Street, 2007. Photo by author.

Since 1998, Mangkubumi Street has seen a rise in the number of informal street vendors occupying the sidewalks. In 1998, the selling locations
were still mostly available to anyone who could pay a small fee to the
local street vendor organization. From 1999 to 2001 (the early years after
Reformasi), instead of selling items to tourists, many of these traders,
who were mostly men, sold second-hand items from their own homes
or from those of their neighbours. In 1998, there were only around ten
street vendors; by 2001, there were almost two hundred – again, still
mostly men – selling more new items than before, along with an influx
of used cell phones. The Mangkubumi Street vendors generally had
less capital than more established traders elsewhere, such as those on
Malioboro Street, some of whom were legally licensed by the municipal
government. Some of the Mangkubumi Street vendors sold during the
day, but the majority did their business in the evenings, when most of
the shops on the street were closed. New parking lots had also been created to accommodate customers who wanted to park their motorbikes.

In 2001, a group of non-profit organizations including Urban Forum,
Oxfam, and LINGKUP Indonesia (Yayasan Lingkar Lingkungan Hidup

Indonesia, or Indonesian Environmental Circle Foundation) started a program for Mangkubumi Street called *Kota untuk Semua* (City for Everyone).[4] These NGOs saw Mangkubumi Street as an opportunity to implement participatory planning in response to how "crowded" (the English term was used) the street had become, a goal developed with a comparative eye on the nearby, and quite congested, Malioboro Street. The NGOs involved in the project played important roles as mediators and educators, and this would impact how the street vendors viewed themselves years later.

The NGOs were interested in changing the information ideologies of the citizens with whom they were working. During the New Order period, the state controlled what information was available to citizens and how it circulated. The massive wealth of Suharto's family, his role in the government takeover in 1965, the nationwide killings of communists and others in 1965–7, and communism itself were all topics that could not be discussed, circulated, or read about without putting oneself at risk. All Chinese publications and the use of the Chinese language were also banned after 1966 (Hoon 2011). At the same time, the government institutionalized restrictions and legislation to control the press (Hill 2006, 11). After the fall of Suharto in 1998, the media was able to publish information more freely and there was an increasing demand on the part of the public for access to information. While these changes were taking place, there was a growing perception that members of the informal economy, including street traders, should have access to the plans and regulations that influence their livelihoods, and that they should be consulted during the development of these plans.

Thus, rather than assuming that the government should determine and then inform citizens about urban plans in a top-down fashion, the NGOs encouraged the street vendors, parking agents, and shop owners to see themselves as stakeholders who should have a say in how and by whom urban plans should be made. To this end, the NGOs facilitated discussions among these citizen-stakeholders on a regular basis, and they shared information and documents with them. If the New Order state had sought to withhold documents and information, these NGOs were concerned with ensuring that all the information from their meetings was written down and circulated. They wrote up their studies, meeting minutes, invitations, and newsletters, all in an attempt to record and make information accessible to themselves, the stakeholders, and the government.[5]

Although the NGOs helped to circulate information and tried in meetings to convince the citizens of their role as stakeholders, as a group, these parties had trouble agreeing on a way forward, and they often deferred the decision-making process to a later date. For example, during meetings in May 2002, there remained disagreements about whether to move the motorbikes from the west to the east side of the street. Pak Adi from Urban Forum suggested that the group of stakeholders needed to develop rules for how they would manage the area, and he repeated an idea that often surfaced in these meetings: "They [the City for Everyone project] couldn't just involve one group." These commonly repeated statements about representation served to delay the implementation of any project by postponing decisions to some future moment when representation would finally be achieved. This discourse also helped to diffuse the situation when things became tense (see Nuijten, Koster, and de Vries 2012, 163).

In 2002 – the year in which the NGOs' City for Everyone program ended – the municipal government began to discuss the idea of relocating the traders after receiving a letter of complaint from some shop owners (Hardiyanti 2008, 64). Most of these owners had to squeeze out of their front doors, if they were not blocked entirely, because of the number of traders and customers on either side. The shop owners were also displeased by the garbage that the traders left behind, the smell of late-night bathroom breaks, and the crowdedness of the street in the evenings, with young men smoking and chatting into the late hours. Yet most of these shop owners did not vocalize their disapproval to the street traders. Many people, including the vendors, considered the shop owners – a significant portion of whom were of Chinese descent – outsiders. In Indonesia, ethnic Chinese have faced a long and complicated history of discrimination and scapegoating (see Purdey 2006; S. Turner 2003; Wibowo 2001).

After receiving complaints from shop owners, and fearing that Mangkubumi Street would soon be overrun with traders, the government decided to move forward with a relocation project involving traders from three areas in the city: Mangkubumi Street, Asem Gede, and the Southern Square. In contrast to the vision laid out by the NGOs in their City For Everyone program, according to which the stakeholders would be involved in both the development and implementation of the plans, the government's vision involved two main stages: data gathering by professionals that would lead to a government-conceived plan, followed by sosialisasi to inform the community about the plan and obtain its (minimal) input. Pak Susanto, an employee from the municipal government's Department of Marketplaces, explained how before any of the formal sosialisasi meetings took place, departmental staff searched for information about the street vendors' perceptions of the relocation in order to learn what the traders might demand. He said,

"Then they [the government] would hold a formal meeting internally to anticipate the situation prior to meeting with the community" (Hardiyanti 2008, 109).

Sosialisasi as Information Politics

Sosialisasi is a key information practice that governments, NGOs, and corporations in Indonesia use when they want to inform the public about a new project and/or gain input from citizens. The practice of sosialisasi is often entangled in politics because, while the actors doing the sosialisasi can claim that they are consulting and informing the public in an open manner, in reality sosialisasi might be done strategically to achieve these individuals' own interests of implementing a project they have already planned. In the reports that were produced around the relocation, sosialisasi was indeed entangled in information politics, with the reports recommending that the government include sosialisasi in its repertoire of information practices to control and contain any potential unrest that might emerge around the idea of the relocation project.

Under Suharto's New Order, instructions or orders from the government were conveyed primarily through community meetings, with minimal record-keeping. As explained above, this process was called sosialisasi. After the fall of the New Order, that term has continued to be used to suggest the sharing of information, often through face-to-face communication.[6] One standard textbook used in middle schools describes sosialisasi as "a process of transferring values and norms through agents, actions, and patterns" (Maryati and Suryawati 2006, 105). This textbook identifies the agents of sosialisasi in the middle-school context as the students' parents, peer group, and school, as well as the media.

One of the most common definitions of sosialisasi describes the training or shaping of people's behaviour.[7] Dozens of reports were produced in the 1980s and '90s that looked at the sosialisasi of poor neighbourhoods in South Sulawesi (Hamid, Suprapti, and Bale 1987), Yogyakarta (Salamun 1993), and Padang (Sumarsono 1987). Sosialisasi was carried out on a national scale during the New Order government through courses that sought to instil the principles of the Indonesian state, known as P4 or Pancasila (P4 stands for Pedoman Penghayatan dan Pengamalan Pancasila [Guidelines of the Learning and Implementation of Pancasila]). During the New Order era, the government's use of sosialisasi thus focused on changing the behaviours of marginal groups and the poor, who were perceived to be ignorant or uneducated. For street traders, this could include providing information and knowledge about such topics as how to cook food hygienically or how to throw away garbage.

Despite its paternalistic connotation, sosialisasi is considered part of the democratic process in the post-Suharto era. Consultants and civil servants have different experiences and definitions of sosialisasi, although most continue to experience it as a vertical rather than a horizontal process. Ibu Fatima, who works at a study centre at UGM, described how sosialisasi events at the university – staged when the centre is invited to help with government studies – often take place only at the academic level or only among those invited to these events. She noted, "It is rare that we engage in the sosialisasi of a project [at] the level of most small communities."[8] Pak Yohanes, a civil servant since 2005, described sosialisasi as important but found that its intended purpose and beneficiaries were often missed in practice.[9] By contrast, Pak Johar, a civil servant since 2010, said that even though the input from sosialisasi might not influence the material being socialized, the fact that this input is allowed at all is significant, since this was not always possible during Suharto's authoritarian rule.[10]

The term also appears in newspapers to describe how the legislative branch or other institutions communicate with communities about new programs or issues such as health care, the effects of drugs, or electoral processes.[11] However, the meaning of sosialisasi is changing in post-Suharto Indonesia. People are now commonly using it to complain that the government or governmental institutions have *not* communicated sufficiently about a new project or topic. For example, a member of a legislative committee (*komisi*) in Jakarta praised the government's plan to develop an electronic road-pricing system, but criticized it for not engaging in sosialisasi with the community (*kurang disosialisasikan*).[12] Evident in many of the discussions about sosialisasi in the public sphere is the sense that sosialisasi, while it is still often used to transform people's behaviours, is now also concerned with transparent communication, with the implicit assumption that sosialisasi as a form of one-way communication is a good in and of itself. In practice, sosialisasi often still means strategically sharing some pieces of information while withholding others to elicit a form of consent. Moreover, sosialisasi can be a practice of shadow play (see Chapter 3: Dialogue, Documents, and Distrust), because when information is not given openly or in expected ways, it generates confusion and uncertainty.

Information as Social Unrest

Sosialisasi is typically carried out after government studies into the feasibility and effects of a project have been completed. According to my communications with a number of civil servants in Yogyakarta, although many civil servants are supportive of sosialisasi, some, especially those trained in the social sciences, are more critical of the studies that the municipal government typically completes before it conducts sosialisasi. Through my discussions with local civil servants and consultants involved in producing government reports, I learned they generally assumed that the reports were not widely read and were written to support already existing plans rather than to question or challenge them.

For instance, Ibu Novri works at the Centre for the Study of Culture at UGM and has been involved in a number of feasibility studies that the centre has conducted for the municipal government. She found that the government does not always implement the recommendations contained in these studies, but instead sometimes draws from them in a piecemeal fashion or sometimes not at all. She said, "These studies are usually only used to legitimize the program that already exists in the minds of the administrators."[13] Ibu Fifi, a civil servant for the provincial government, reported similar experiences. In her opinion, local governments have the responsibility to carry out studies before implementing projects. Yet when she conducted a food security assessment for the provincial government, she felt they were focused on finishing the task simply to fulfil the political expectation that the assessment be completed. Indeed, the office staff only used the report internally. Furthermore, even though most of the studies that her staff generated were registered with the DPRD (Dewan Perwakilan Rakyat Daerah, or Regional People's Legislative Assembly), Ibu Fifi believed that they were never even read.[14] Based on these observations, we might assume that the municipal government's reports providing technical expertise on the street vendor relocation would bear little resemblance to the way the project would eventually be executed.

Between 2004 and 2005, several reports[15] were written for the government to aid in the planning and execution of the relocation. These documents were used to communicate relevant information about the project to government officials, but also to show that the project was sound; the government is required to carry out such studies before a project is implemented. As I will go on to show, although conversations about the relocation did take place between some of the street vendors and relevant government officials during this phase, these conversations were done with the purpose of determining the vendors' stances on the project in order to successfully implement it rather than to alter it in any significant way. The government studies were meant to provide officials with more information and to aid in the development of a strategy for sosialisasi, and the reports remained in the hands of government officials and the parliament. Although it was not clear to me whether these documents were strictly for internal use, to my knowledge none of the street traders had received any of these reports. I was only given a copy after the relocation had taken place, and by a government official who was not directly involved in the project.

In October 2004, Yogyakarta's Environmental Impact City Office, along with a consultant, C.V. Bangun Cipta Persada, produced an environmental impact study of the relocation project.[16] The study's purpose was to ensure that the plan to relocate the street vendors to Kuncen Marketplace met the government's environmental standards. The government also wanted to identify the potential impact of the development of Kuncen Marketplace on the street vendors, the surrounding neighbourhood, and the livestock traders being moved out of the marketplace. Despite the expected benefits of this plan, such as the reduction of livestock smells in the city, it was noted that the proposal would require sosialisasi with the community around the marketplace, the animal traders, and the second-hand[17] street traders. The report described this process in the following terms: "Generally, the sosialisasi material should be the development concept and plan that will be done. The emphasis of the material for each segment of the group will be different and depend on the interests of that group" (Kantor Pengendalian Dampak Lingkungan Pemkot Yogyakarta and C.V. Bangun Cipta Persada 2004, II-3[18]).

As indicated by this description, the report suggested developing different approaches to sosialisasi based on each group's particular "interests" (*kepentingan*) or fears. For example, in the case of the livestock traders, the report suggested stressing how easy trade would be in the new location, because what these traders feared most was that the new location would be worse for business (II-4). The information given to the livestock traders was not necessarily true or based on studies (which, for instance, could determine the ease or challenges of the new location), but was driven simply by the need to appease the traders' by asserting that their fears would not be realized. The study also explained that the second-hand street vendors already felt content in their selling locations, and therefore, the report predicted, "sosialisasi towards these groups will not likely be easy." Because of these different fears, the report suggested that "the material shared, and the approach of sosialisasi (*pendekatan sosialisasi*) towards each of the groups does not have to be the same. In general, the traders need to be told about how comfortable (*nyaman*) the new place will be from an economic standpoint" (II-5). Again, there was no study or information provided in the reports that actually backed the claim that the new marketplace would be better from an economic standpoint; instead, the report suggested that government officials simply claim the second-hand vendors would be better off economically because this would counter the vendors' concerns.

The report argued that the sosialisasi process would also have to be tailored to the different reactions of each group. The report explained that "the data given suggests that the traders before sosialisasi had started to agree, become resigned to, be ambiguous about, or refuse the relocation" (IV-2).[19] It warned that if the sosialisasi process was not "smooth," unrest might emerge (IV-6). Although the NGOs involved in the City for Everyone project in the early 2000s had wanted to generate dialogue among the stakeholders on the street in order to reduce potential unrest, the government feared that if the sosialisasi for the relocation project was not done correctly it could actually *cause* unrest. Sosialisasi as information politics, while it was a technique of the politics of containment, could also, if not done correctly, produce the very thing it sought to prevent.

The report warned that unrest might emerge because the traders were concerned that their incomes would be smaller in the new location (IV-14). Unlike some development agencies, which sideline questions about the politics of resource allocation (Ferguson 1994; Li 2007), these reports identified these issues (in this case, concerns over access to the best locations) as central to potential vendor resistance. In this report, sosialisasi was therefore something that was done *after* the government had understood the fears of the different groups involved. It assumed that all the information did not need to be shared with everyone, and that only specific pieces of information should be targeted towards the stakeholders' specific fears. It also suggested that a *kedekatan* (closeness) could be developed by sharing this information, especially with the groups that were more resistant.

In addition to an environmental impact study, a feasibility study was completed in July 2005 by another consultant, C.V. AKA.[20] One of the goals of the resulting report was to bring together information about the Kuncen Marketplace plans in order to ascertain the opinions of the traders and members of the nearby community (Pemerintah Kota Yogyakarta, Badan Perencanaan Pembangunana Daerah [Municipal Government of Yogyakarta, Regional Development Planning Agency] and C.V. AKA 2005, I-3). The findings in the report were based on surveys with traders and the citizens living near Kuncen Marketplace (III-10). Like the earlier report, this one argued that the relocation should only happen after the municipal government had undergone the sosialisasi process with the traders and community members near Kuncen

Marketplace (V-13). Both reports were progressive insofar as they suggested that the government communicate with the traders – something that might not have happened during the Suharto period. Although the 2005 feasability study did not focus on the specific groups of street vendors and the differences among them, as had the 2004 environmental study, it did conclude that the municipal government must consider the input of the leaders of street vendor organizations and the various community leaders near Kuncen Marketplace as part of the relocation process.

In order to reduce problems during sosialisasi, the second report suggested that the traders form an organization that would then collect data on their activities well in advance of the relocation process. Although this was never explicitly stated in the report, having a trader organization would give the government leaders a specific group of individuals to work with, individuals who could control and engage in their own sosialisasi with their members. The data – which would include traders' names, addresses, and the types of goods they sold – needed to be collected before the relocation was officially announced because it was assumed that once the announcement was made, new traders might flock to the newly renovated Kuncen Marketplace with the hope of securing a selling location there. This idea of the state working *through* the community was not unusual, but was in fact a common approach during the Suharto era (see Barker 1998; Newberry 2006). In this way, the state was able to use the community to do its work – in this case, to collect the information that it needed about the traders without being directly present.

The approach to sosialisasi evidenced in this second report was much like the first. As there was a fear of potential resistance among the traders, it was assumed that information should be withheld until sosialisasi could be done properly. In this report, too, it was recommended that sosialisasi should be done strategically – after the fears and interests of the groups were understood. However, unlike the first report, the second highlighted the need to prepare organizations, data, and laws before sosialisasi was started. The information provided through sosialisasi was thought to be of a sensitive nature, something to be carefully guarded until all the structures were in place to carry out the project.

In September 2005, a more detailed design for the former Kuncen Marketplace was completed. Authored by consultants P.T. Cipta Nindita Buana, who were hired by the municipal government's Regional Planning Board, this report[21] presumably built on the two earlier documents. It noted that the municipal government needed to engage in sosialisasi during the pre-construction phase. It described this process as follows:

> It involves an initiator (for this project, this person would be the municipal government) giving information through meetings and generating a schedule of activities for the local community. The initiator should give the necessary background information around the need to develop the second-hand and antique marketplace in Kuncen Marketplace, and estimate the problems that might arise and the restrictions of the location, and provide the necessary information on the development plans and the technical implementation to be undertaken. The community can be given hope that it will participate in the development of the marketplace by giving suggestions and opinions that will be considered by the initiator in order to minimalize the impacts that might emerge. (Pemerintah Kota Yogyakarta, Badan Perencanaan Pembangunana Daerah [Municipal Government of Yogyakarta, Regional Development Planning Agency] and P.T. Cipta Nindita Buana 2005, VI-2–VI-3)

In this report, sosialisasi was imagined as giving citizens "hope" that they could participate in the development of the marketplace, despite the recognition that the plans, both general and technical, were already being developed by experts.[22] In reality, then, citizens' contributions would be considered only insofar as they curtailed any negative consequences. Sosialisasi was therefore a strategy for obtaining input while sidelining any larger political questions, such as whether Kuncen Marketplace was the right place for these traders, or whether relocation was indeed the best solution.

Like the earlier reports, this one suggested that sosialisasi should also seek to anticipate potential unrest. It noted the need to anticipate in advance who would control the parking areas and the security around Kuncen Marketplace in order to avoid future conflicts (VI-6). The report also expressed concern that security could be disrupted if a negative perception of the Kuncen Marketplace plan was allowed to develop. In order to mitigate this problem, the report recommended that the government recruit people from across the city to rebuild the marketplace, so it did not appear that the workers were coming from only one area (VI-14). In this report, like the two before it, information was also portrayed as the potential cause of social unrest, and here, too, the recommendation for reducing this unrest was ensuring that individuals from various communities, especially unemployed youth, were given roles in the relocation process and made to feel involved.

The authors of this latest report also recommended that if negative talk about the relocation emerged among the traders and their allies, the municipal government needed to work more closely, intensively, and openly with those in the community so that they would understand the project. The circulation of competing or erroneous information was also viewed as a potential cause of social unrest, and sosialisasi events were seen as forums where the information the government wanted to circulate could be shared. The report reads, "We are scared that this [resistance] will happen in the community because they [local citizens] don't know [about the project] or the information they have received is wrong" (VI-11). In anticipation of potential misunderstandings, the report suggested several solutions, including providing complete information in a transparent way to the community and inviting the community to give suggestions and ideas for the development of the marketplace. Unlike the first report, which suggested that the traders be given different information according to their different fears, this report championed a more universal approach to sosialisasi. And while the other report suggested carefully managing the information that was to be shared, this one suggested that complete information be given more "openly." But although each of these reports contained different ideologies of information, their goal was the same: to manage information (whether by circulating it strategically or more openly) in order to contain any politics that might emerge.

Many of the government officials I spoke with perceived resistance to the relocation as a normal part of the relocation process; while it was something to be contained, it was nonetheless expected. On 21 November 2007, I spoke with Pak Joko, an architect by training and an official with the Yogyakarta city government's Management of Regional Goods Office (*Pengelolaan Barang Daerah*), a department formed in 2006. Pak Joko had been involved with some of the early reports (discussed above) that the municipal government created on Kuncen Marketplace. In Pak Joko's opinion, the relocation was a non-profit investment for the benefit of the public because the government was giving the kiosks to the traders for free and, through the process of relocating the vendors, improving their status from illegal to legal traders. He believed that the relocation project provided a generous arrangement for the street vendors, but considered the vendors' resistance to the relocation as "normal" (*wajar*). He explained the resistance by comparing it to the idea of people moving houses:

> If there is resistance, I think it is normal enough, because in Javanese culture if you move houses it feels different. Psychological adjustment is not

necessarily easy. So if there's turmoil it is a psychological reaction of those who are used to operating in places that are free (*bebas*) [of rules], and they enter into a place that now has rules. Hence it is normal to have resistance.[23]

Thus, for Pak Joko, the vendors' opposition was based on defiance to discipline and the desire to be free of regulation. He viewed the street as having fewer rules than a marketplace, whereas in the marketplace, traders would have to pay formal taxes. However, from my conversations with the street traders who were refusing the relocation, they were less concerned about having to pay taxes in the new marketplace than about losing their customer base.

Pak Joko helped design Kuncen Marketplace so that it was open but protected from the sun and rain. He was certain that those traders who relocated to the marketplace would be happy because their legal status would be clear. However, he admitted that the government's relocation team was fearful that the street vendors might abandon the marketplace if it was not successful in attracting enough shoppers.[24]

Conclusion

As I described earlier in this chapter, in the early 2000s, a number of NGOs in Yogyakarta saw the transition to democracy as an opportune moment for changing people's relationship to urban planning, to shift their information ideologies, and to connect the macro processes of democracy to citizens' lived experiences. Unlike in the past, when the government provided citizens with little information about urban planning (Widianingsih and Morrell 2007, 2), a group of NGOs, through their 2001 project City for Everyone, hoped that citizens involved with Mangkubumi Street could now have a say in how their street was managed.

A few years later, the municipal government was interested in consulting with the traders on Mangkubumi Street about the vendor relocation project, but not in treating them as citizen-stakeholders who had a say in developing the project from its inception. Instead, the government developed the project with the help of experts, and it sought to use sosialisasi as a technical strategy to communicate with the traders only after the general idea of the project had been developed and the government knew what it was up against in terms of potential resistance. The municipal government was particularly concerned about community resistance to the project and ultimately its potential failure, and this shaped government perceptions of the appropriate strategy for sharing information about the relocation project, as well as who should have the agency to participate in shaping it. The government imagined that sosialisasi would take place through face-to-face communication with the traders in formal meetings.

Ferguson (1994) has argued that the development apparatus has a depoliticizing effect. He calls it an "anti-politics machine" since it masks political realities while increasing the power of the state bureaucracy. Ferguson found that because development agencies have fixed budgets and are positioned as mostly apolitical and technical, they cannot respond if problems are framed as political or structural. In Yogyakarta, the municipal government was engaged in a slightly different kind of anti-political information politics. Here, the main concern was how to contain and control politics through information so that a project presumed to benefit the citizens would be successful. I have used the idea of the politics of containment to understand how the municipal government sought to study, predict, and strategize around its desire to prevent resistance when implementing a controversial project – in this case, the street vendor relocation. The studies leading up to the project were "anti-political" because they sought to contain or reduce the potential resistance to the relocation without taking seriously why there might be resistance in the first place. The resistance was characterized as emerging from fears that could be overcome with the right information, or from fears caused by receiving the wrong information. These characterizations rendered "technical" (Li 2007) the process of informing the traders about the relocation project because the government was positioned as the one with the ability and right to determine the plans and approach, while the citizens needed to be subjected to direction through the information practices of sosialisasi. Controlling information through the process of sosialisasi was therefore viewed as central to the project's potential success.

According to these reports, proper sosialisasi included understanding the positions of the street vendors and other citizens affected by the relocation prior to sharing detailed information with them. It involved knowing who they were and understanding their fears around the project. In addition, proper sosialisasi included setting up certain structures before the relocation took place. Street vendor organizations, relevant data, and the appropriate laws all needed to be put in place. Only then could the government engage in deeper conversations about the project with the community leaders and vendors. One of the reports suggested tailoring the information to the traders' specific fears, while another suggested sharing information in a more open manner in the hope that traders would "feel involved." All of the reports suggested that traders should have input into the project, but the main goal – engaging in a relocation – was non-negotiable. The politics of containment therefore involved seeking input within the boundaries of the assumed project. Unlike other participatory projects described by such as scholars Monique Nuijten (2013) and Roberto Barrios (2011), the government in this case was more explicit or conscious – at least among the reports' limited audience of government officials – about also trying to limit resistance through the participatory mechanism of sosialisasi. Although the reports described the context in which the relocation was being carried out, my conversations with civil servants suggest that these documents were to serve a largely symbolic role. The reports were not often read, and if ideas within them did not match the mayor's vision, they were simply ignored. Yet despite the fact that they were rarely read, these reports suggest that the government and other actors involved in the relocation operated with the idea that information was a central means through which resistance could be contained and curbed.

Postscript: Growing Unrest and Resistance

After the more detailed design of Kuncen Marketplace was completed in September 2005, a meeting was held on 16 January 2006 with the leaders of the different vendor groups involved in the relocation – the first of many such face-to-face meetings with the traders. In this meeting, the group leaders were told that they would be moved to Kuncen Marketplace after it was renovated. They were also told that the relocated traders would have legal status in the new marketplace, and that the government hoped to make this marketplace a tourist location (*ikon wisata*).[25]

Pak Wahyu, the general chair of Pethikbumi, was supportive of the relocation, but many of his members were sceptical and wanted more information. This created unrest within Pethikbumi itself. As concern over the relocation grew among the Pethikbumi membership, some eventually engaged a neighbourhood organization to survey all of the street vendors on Mangkubumi Street from 11 to 13 November 2006. The results confirmed the Pethikbumi members' suspicions: the majority (93 per cent) of the vendors surveyed disagreed with the relocation, with 6 per cent in favour of the relocation and 1 per cent abstaining from answering the questionnaire (Paguyuban Kawasan Mangkubumi Yogyakarta [Yogyakarta Mangkubumi Regional Organization] 2006).

On 17 November 2006, Pak Wahyu was removed from Pethikbumi, ultimately because the other Pethikbumi leaders determined that he was
telling the government that the organization's membership was supportive of the relocation despite clear resistance.[26] The other Pethikbumi
leaders had also recently found out that Pak Wahyu was a civil servant
for the provincial government – a piece of information that made the
traders further suspicious of his actions. The fact that Pak Wahyu was
employed by the government made the Pethikbumi leaders suspect
that he might be a puppet of the municipal government. His removal
from Pethikbumi was the start of the group's efforts at transparency
and accountability – two ideals that would shape many of their actions
in the days and months to come.

After Pak Wahyu was removed, the general chair role was split
among three people. Pak Akbar became the first general chair, Pak
Pramana became the second general chair, and Mas Basri became the
third general chair (these numerical designations reflected a hierarchical ranking from most senior to least senior). This new leadership
was more sceptical of and resistant to the relocation. A few days later,
on November 23, Pethikbumi sent a letter to the government informing it of the leadership change.[27] As Pethikbumi's resistance to the
relocation grew, the group held a public demonstration at City Hall
on 2 February 2007, where they requested to speak directly with the
mayor. The Pethikbumi leadership was told that the mayor was not
available to meet; instead, they were invited to speak with the vice
mayor, Pak Haryadi Suyuti. Along with some local journalists, I followed the Pethikbumi leaders and a number of their key supporters
into City Hall, where we were led to a meeting room. We were joined
there by the vice mayor and some other government officials, and
the Pethikbumi leaders again insisted that the group's traders did not
want to be relocated.[28] As the new leader of Pethikbumi, Pak Akbar
declared, "We ask that the city government of Yogyakarta not relocate
the *klithikan*[29] traders. Because the klithikan market [on Mangkubumi
Street] is already established and there are many visitors. If we are
relocated to Kuncen Marketplace, who will be responsible for the fate
of the traders? Because [Kuncen Marketplace] is located on the edge
of the city and is quiet."[30] Pak Akbar's comment again reflected the
Pethikbumi leaders' concern that it would take a significant amount
of time to attract a new customer base at the marketplace. Another
trader and adviser to the Pethikbumi leaders added that, whatever the
outcome of the sosialisasi, Pethikbumi would refuse the relocation.
He said, "We will fight to be able to continue selling on Mangkubumi
Street."[31]

As shown in this section, despite the consultants' recommendations that the government use sosialisasi to contain the politics of the relocation, the early days of sosialisasi created precisely what the consultants had hoped to avoid: a climate of growing unrest and resistance to the relocation. As I show in the next chapter, this climate of resistance would continue as the government's process of sosialisasi proceeded.

Chapter Three

Dialogue, Documents, and Distrust

At the demonstration the other day, we brought a fake human coffin as a symbol of the death of the clear conscience between the government and the little people (*rakyat kecil*).

– Mas Arief, secretary of Pethikbumi, April 2007

In August 2007, the government's relocation team began visiting Mangkubumi Street to meet with the anti-relocation traders in a series of occasional visits that continued into September. This relocation team, which usually included senior officials Pak Ari and Pak Galang, would come to the street at ten thirty in the evening. They would sit on straw mats on the sidewalk and chat with the traders for hours. An important goal of these meetings was making the traders feel like they had access to the officials, and that at some point in the future they might be able to contact them for assistance. These meetings also helped the government show that they were going out of their way to dialogue with the traders. However, the meetings did not usually go very far. The traders would often explain why they disagreed with the relocation (e.g., it would take years for them to develop their businesses again since the marketplace was not located in a strategic area), and why they disagreed with how the process had been carried out thus far (e.g., the government had not given them the appropriate documents they needed). They also suggested that an alternative project be developed for those who did not want to move. The administrators, for their part, were unwilling to entertain this type of discussion in their sosialisasi practices. Instead, they focused on how good things would be in Kuncen Marketplace since the traders would be able to operate legally there.

As discussed in the previous chapter (see Information as Social Unrest, Chapter 2), in 2004 and 2005, the government conducted a series of confidential surveys to analyze the relocation project's impact on the traders, the surrounding community, and the land. These studies helped to justify the relocation plan while also recognizing that there might be citizen resistance. The solution to this problem of potential resistance was "socialization" (sosialisasi). And yet, since the government's sosialisasi process had begun in January of the previous year, it had become increasingly clear that the municipal officials and the Pethikbumi leaders each had a different view of what this should look like. The municipal government publicly claimed that it was "dialoguing" (i.e., consulting) with the Pethikbumi traders; however, the details of the project and plan had already been under discussion for years, mostly without any input from the traders.[1]

This chapter discusses how information regarding the relocation was shared with the Pethikbumi street vendors after the organization came under the new leadership of Pak Akbar and adopted an anti-relocation stance. I describe how the government's sosialisasi practices involved shadow play as documents were withheld and falsified. I also explore the government's and the Pethikbumi traders' different ideologies of sosialisasi, or their competing beliefs about how the government should share information with the community. However, people's ideologies of sosialisasi were not only defined in relation to the New Order practice of sosialisasi; they also revolved around citizens' ideas about how the government should act in the post-Suharto era, as well as the role that documentation should play in government-citizen communication. I argue that while the government engaged in sosialisasi, it simultaneously engaged in shadow play by circulating documents in unusual ways and with altered content. The Pethikbumi traders viewed the government's use of sosialisasi as shadow play because while the government appeared to share information face-to-face with them during the process of sosialisasi, the traders were suspicious that other information was being hidden "behind the screen." While the government appeared to dialogue with them in front of the screen, the traders sometimes came to learn of the government's less-than-transparent activities. The traders' experiences of seeking information that had been withheld, while occasionally learning of previously unknown information that attested to the government's lack of transparency, generated suspicion and uncertainty among both the traders and their NGO supporters. Mathur (2016) notes that documents in India, while they might be a product of the ideology of transparency, do not make the state more transparent but instead "build up another order of state-created reality that can materially attest to the transparency of the government" (172). In the case of the vendor relocation project, while the government documents materially attested to practices of transparency expected by the public, their questionable alterations were uncanny reiterations of the authoritarian past.

In this chapter, I start by describing how civil servants, including the mayor, perceived sosialisasi as a process through which vendors would be persuaded that the relocation was in their best interests. Alongside the New Order term *sosialisasi*, however, the mayor often referred to his process as involving *dialog* (he used the Indonesian term) in order to distinguish his approach from New Order practices. Government officials below the mayor carried out his vision of dialoguing by meeting with the anti-relocation traders numerous times in an effort to get close to them. While the NGOs involved in the City for Everyone project deferred the decision-making process because of the difficulty of finding agreement among the Mangkubumi stakeholders (see Citizens as Stakeholders: Moving towards the Relocation, Chapter 2), the government used postponement during sosialisasi to its advantage as it hoped to eventually appease the traders' opposition. While government officials met regularly with the Pethikbumi street vendors, they always postponed decisions and the "real" discussion until a later date. This strategy – a "politics of postponement" (J. Gibbings 2020) – used time as an instrument of power (Harms 2013b; Verdery 1996).[2] It made it appear as if the government was engaging with the traders while substantial engagement with their concerns was always deferred to a later date. This politics of postponement was a subtle form of shadow play as it created frustration and confusion among the traders.[3]

When Pethikbumi claimed that the government did not sufficiently *socialize* the vendors about the relocation, they were not using the term in the same way as the government. Some of the Pethikbumi traders wanted the process of sosialisasi to be more meaningful, to allow for the possibility that the plan might change to meet their concerns and needs. They also felt that the government's use of sosialisasi, with its face-to-face conversations, was too informal and not trustworthy; they sought official written documents instead, which could be used to hold the government accountable.

During Suharto's thirty-two years of authoritarian rule, citizens viewed official documents with suspicion, since many were withheld from circulation in the public sphere and those that were circulated were often fake (J.T. Siegel 1998). Since the transition to democracy in 1998, citizens have taken up the discourse of "transparency" (*transparansi*), and they expect that authentic documents related to urban projects will be widely and openly circulated. Yet during this period of sosialisasi with Pethikbumi, the documents that did appear were part of the government's shadow play; they generated confusion and uncertainty rather than transparency or clarity due to the way they were circulated or the information they contained. The circulation of these documents also suggested to Pethikbumi's leaders that the government had two different faces: when facing the public, it claimed to want to "dialogue" with and "get close" to the traders, while its private face suggested that through the strategic circulation of documents, it was engaged in shadow play "behind the screen" of sosialisasi.

Getting Close and Speaking Their Language

During my fieldwork, government officials often described the strategy of sosialisasi as a process of "getting close" to the various stakeholders. This meant spending time with traders and community members who would be affected by the relocation. In one of two interviews with me, Pak Herry Zudianto described his sosialisasi strategy with the traders as involving a process of "speaking in their language," as opposed to speaking in the language of bureaucracy. He met the traders in places where they felt comfortable, such as a food stall rather than a stuffy office. He proudly told the story of how he had invited the traders to his private home in order to make them feel welcome, following the Javanese philosophy of *witing tresno jalaran soko kulino* – the idea that love/respect grows through familiar or frequent communication.[4]

Pak Herry Zudianto was born in March 1955 and was elected mayor of Yogyakarta for two terms (2001–6 and 2006–11). He was born and raised in a family of entrepreneurs who were part of the well-known families of Batik Margaria Group and Batik Terang Bulan Putera Group, two large parent companies in the batik fashion industry. After graduating from university, Pak Herry Zudianto worked briefly for a batik company before starting his own. Although his main business interests lay in batik, he also expanded into other areas. In diversifying his family's business interests, he grew his company from five employees to one that today employs about a thousand. In 2001, the political party PAN, where he had previously served as treasurer, nominated him as their mayoral candidate. Pak Herry Zudianto was inspired to join PAN because of Amien Rais, a PAN politician who played an important role in leading and inspiring the Reformasi movement in 1998. Pak Herry Zudianto had not planned on a career in politics, but he hoped to provide a new perspective and approach to the Mayor's Office, which previously had been dominated by military leaders.[5]

One of Pak Herry Zudianto's strategies when running for mayor was to publish his ideas in newspapers with the goal that if he lost the mayoral race, it would not be because he did not have a vision but because of politics. During his tenure as mayor, Pak Herry Zudianto described himself as open-minded and interested in creating space for discussion. Unlike many of the civil servants working beneath him, Pak Herry Zudianto preferred the word *dialog* (dialogue) over *sosialisasi* because he felt the latter had "too much history," whereas *dialog* suggested more reciprocal communication.[6] In engaging with the general public, he facilitated communication by encouraging citizens to send him text messages and by hosting the radio program *Mengapa Walikota?* (*Why, Mayor?*), where he would respond directly to their concerns. He sought to influence others with his ideas but not to impose or force these ideas through fear. He wanted people to adopt his ideas out of respect for them.[7]

In 2004, Pak Herry Zudianto decided to remove approximately one thousand street vendors from the premises of a shopping centre called Sri Wedani Market. The area was later turned into a children's museum and playground called Taman Pintar. Pak Herry Zudianto said that his staff were sceptical about his decision to relocate the traders because the previous mayor had twice tried to do so without success. He explained, however, that he had learned from his staff why many of the city's previous attempts at relocating street vendors had failed. Based on this knowledge, he decided to initiate a dialogue with the street vendors at Sri Wedani Market so they would "understand" (*mengerti*) his program.

During a conversation we had at Pak Herry Zudianto's house, he explained that he learned from the resulting relocation that dialogue was the key to success. It was important to not assume that traders will agree with a relocation. He said, "Who knows why they disapprove of it – perhaps it is because they don't fully understand."[8] Pak Herry Zudianto explained that the traders' dreams for themselves were rarely significantly different from the government's vision for the city. Therefore, the job of the government was to find a way to translate its visions into the language of its citizens.

When conducting a street vendor relocation such as the one to Kuncen Marketplace, Pak Herry Zudianto usually selected a team of ten people to work on the project. Following his philosophy of "speaking their language," he chose individuals who could communicate well with citizens on the ground. Pak Herry Zudianto appointed these people to dialogue with the traders because he chose to not be personally involved in the discussions until the end. He described this strategy as follows: "Usually I'm the ending; I'm the key. If [most of the vendors have] agreed [with the relocation but] there are one or two who still don't agree, then we will end with me."[9] There is some irony in this:

although Pak Herry Zudianto promoted the idea of dialogue, he did not make himself available to dialogue about the relocation to Kuncen Marketplace until the very last minute, which frustrated many of the Pethikbumi leaders. The traders had been able to meet with him earlier in the sosialisasi process, during an informal meeting at his house on 9 February 2007. However, this meeting had proved to be more of a top-down information-sharing exercise focusing on details such as the capacity of the new marketplace,[10] and Pethikbumi had found it difficult to obtain a meeting with him after that. Pethikbumi requested meetings with the mayor on a number of occasions during the relocation because they hoped that by meeting with him face-to-face he might be willing to reconsider the project. Largely inaccessible for eight months of this project, the mayor only met with the traders once they felt they had little choice but to accept the relocation. For the traders, the mayor's refusal to meet with them was part of the government's shadow play: they felt that without meeting with the mayor directly, lower-level[11] government officials had no power to alter the relocation plans substantially. The mayor, from their perspective, was working somewhere in the background, out of their view.

Pak Herry Zudianto explained that there were staff who carried out sosialisasi throughout the relocation plan, and that it was important that they use everyday language (*bahasa asam*).[12] The civil servant Pak Galang could speak the "street language" (*bahasa gali*) particularly well.[13] "It is not easy," Pak Herry Zudianto said. "It has to be in their frequency. For instance, [he went on to describe a potential conversation] 'Well, what will happen later if we don't make money?' 'OK, if you don't make money, then for six months you won't have to pay taxes so you won't be out of money.' Later there are more complaints – [to which one of the staff carrying out sosialisasi might respond] 'OK, I have a program for marketing like this.'"[14]

Pak Herry Zudianto also had a specific strategy for dealing with the lower classes, and especially what he called the "psychology of the little people" (*psikologi orang kecil*) or "the psychology of lower society" (*psikologi masyarakat bawah*), when he was carrying out sosialisasi. He explained that it was important to give poor people status so that they felt respected. "I respect them and it turns out they respect me even more," he said.[15] Pak Herry Zudianto claimed that marginalized people often felt sidelined. "As soon as they are recognized, feel cared for, and we reach their hearts, they directly surrender."[16] Pak Herry Zudianto elaborated:

> If we are talking about serving the community, we must know the social psychology of [the community]. We must apply it. Like the example I gave

earlier, [in which] street vendors came late at night to my place because I invited them. What is the first thing I say to them? "Eh, we are equals (*sederajat*) tonight. We are both leaders. You have responsibilities and I have responsibilities." This is an example of how I will lift them up. I position them at the same level as myself. After they are positioned at the same level with me, [their anti-relocation movement] dies (*mati*). At that time, they have clear thinking and they will not feel right [refusing his government's needs]. Finally, [they say] "Yes, I believe Herry." It is like that.[17]

Pak Herry Zudianto's vision of getting close to citizens through dialogue (*pendekatan yang dialogis*) was therefore about making the traders (or other citizens he was negotiating with) feel like equals – not because they were equals, but rather as a psychological strategy to get them to support his position. Since this tradition did not exist during the New Order, he believed that citizens were still learning the culture of dialogue. Pak Herry Zudianto also thought that many citizens were not ready to dialogue in a "rational way." As a result, sometimes getting to the level of dialogue required patience. "When I was dialoguing with them [the Pethikbumi leaders], sometimes I was angry (*hati saya sudah panas itu*). This person was really not easy [to dialogue with],"[18] he admitted. He described how he usually continued to smile even though he was tired and wondered why "this person" did not understand what he was trying to convey. What was important to Pak Herry Zudianto was that his goal could be achieved. "Well, for me it's like a challenge. It is interesting. The challenge is how to subdue them (*menundukkan mereka*)."[19] In Yogyakarta, while the public sphere was characterized by a repressive mode of interaction during the New Order, under Pak Herry Zudianto it shifted to a hegemonic one according to which elites ruled by trying to convince others of their ideologies. Even though this method was less overtly repressive, it was still problematic for the Pethikbumi traders because they remained concerned that there were other activities taking place behind the screen.

Pak Supriyanto, who was the head of the Department of Industry, Trade, and Cooperatives from 2003 to 2006, described how the municipal government's approach to relocating the Mangkubumi Street traders used "humanity" (*kemanusiaan*). In an interview with a UGM student, he said, "The approach of humanity here is defined as the art of leadership that looks at the conditions on the ground, gathering, and becoming close through jokes. The process involves touching the hearts of the policy objects first. It was applied in the process of dialoguing with the klithikan traders. This is a Javanese cultural concept that teaches us to humanize people. As Javanese say, if we sit people in our laps then that person will die (or obey our will)" (Hardiyanti 2008, 76).

Pak Supriyanto shared Pak Herry Zudianto's philosophy that being "close" was key to curbing any potential resistance. Pak Herry Zudianto's strategy of not meeting directly with the street vendors himself early on in the relocation discussions did not sit well, however, with the Pethikbumi traders; this was part of their frustration with the government's process of sosialisasi. Pethikbumi argued over and over in meetings with lower-level government officials and in the newspapers that it was difficult to contact the mayor. During the relocation project, Pethikbumi held various demonstrations at which they requested a direct meeting with him (see, for example, Postscript: Growing Unrest and Resistance, Chapter 2). Lower-level government officials were largely responsible for sosialisasi, but these officials were perceived as having little power to actually change the project. A government official I interviewed described how important sosialisasi was to the Kuncen relocation because there was often resistance to such relocations among the vendors. He said:

> Actually, by the year 2006 the project could have been implemented, but [it was delayed] because there were lots of interests at play from political leaders and people, and because the sellers did not agree [to move]. Ultimately, we needed to convince them that if they sold [in Kuncen Marketplace] they would sell more than in the old place. So we had to get close to them, so that the result is one unified language that is good and that they can understand. And that is a long process.[20]

This process of "getting close" to the traders involved lower-level government officials setting up regular meetings with them. Pak Ari and Pak Galang were the main municipal officials in communication with the Pethikbumi leaders on a regular basis. Before becoming the head of the Department of Industry, Trade, and Cooperatives (Dinas Perindustrian, Perdagangan dan Koperasi, or Disperindagkop),[21] Pak Ari had previously worked at the Regional Development Planning Board of Yogyakarta (Badan Perencanaan Pembangunan Daerah Kota Yogyakarta, or BAPPEDA). He was known for his ability to speak calmly and reason with people. In all the meetings that I attended at which he was present, he never raised his voice or showed any sign that he was bothered by any conversation, no matter how heated the Pethikbumi members became. Pak Galang, who was in his early fifties, was the head of the Department of Marketplaces in the city, and was described by the traders as "well connected" since he ran his own *pesantren* outside of the city. Pak Ari and Pak Galang had both been involved in previous vendor relocations, and these had been successful even in the face of resistance.

On 6 July 2007, to the discomfort of the officials in the government relocation team, the Pethikbumi traders and their supporters requested the involvement of a third party in the remainder of the sosialisasi process. This request was made around two months into the sosialisasi process. Pethikbumi's lawyers, BPHK, had recommended that they write to the Special Region of Yogyakarta Ombudsman Institution (Lembaga Ombudsman Daerah Istimewa Yogyakarta, or LOD DIY) about their case and request that LOD DIY both investigate and act as a mediator. On 11 September 2007, LOD DIY brought Pethikbumi and the government relocation team together to facilitate the remainder of the sosialisasi process. In this mediated setting, Pethikbumi criticized the government for various acts, including not giving them written copies of the relocation plan in a timely fashion and not listening to their proposal to reorder Mangkubumi Street instead of relocating the vendors.

During one of the first meetings, the new mediator asked the government to justify and explain its approach to sosialisasi. Pak Ari and Pak Galang both argued that they were currently in the process of sosialisasi and that they were planning on having deeper conversations with Pethikbumi. That they were engaging the traders in this process was, they argued, more important than what was actually said. In many of the meetings that I had attended thus far, the municipal government had promised the traders that there would be more meetings and opportunities for sosialisasi, thereby deferring the process of agreement or understanding to some unknown future date. In this early meeting with LOD DIY, Pak Galang also promised future sosialisasi: "We are undertaking sosialisasi, whether informal or formal. We will focus more on the formal sosialisasi in the upcoming months as we approach October."[22]

Besides being a way of "getting close" to the traders, sosialisasi was also seen as an opportunity to show the traders how sincere the government was. In the September 11 meeting mediated by LOD DIY, Pak Ari said, "We really truly believe in economically empowering the people. If we are talking about Cokroaminoto Street [where Kuncen Marketplace was located], I think in two or three years' time it will be an area of rapid growth and development. It will become a premium area."[23] Pak Galang, following Pak Ari, also explained that the government wanted to empower the traders, which was why the traders would not have to pay *retribusi* (retribution – that is, taxes to the municipal government) for the first six months in the new marketplace, and after that they would only have to pay a small amount. "The government is giving a big subsidy to the community for the economic empower-ment of the people. That is what the government is really like," Pak Galang explained.[24] This was in keeping with the statements I heard in the many sosialisasi meetings I had already attended, where it was common for the government officials to try to persuade the traders that the government was in fact looking out for their welfare and interests.

For Pak Galang and Pak Ari, sosialisasi was not only about showing that the government was sincere in its desire to improve the welfare of its citizens; it was also an attempt to sell certain ideas. In the September 11 meeting with LOD DIY, Pak Galang described what he thought the process of sosialisasi involved:

> It is like I'm a salesperson and I am going to tell you about a product that is good. If you drink this, you will be strong. If a prospective buyer wants it or not is another issue. If we used a method that was not acceptable, then that would be a problem. Otherwise, let the process continue. We are consulting [with the traders], whether it is informally or formally, and will do this more aggressively in the months ahead before we approach the end of October … We need to continue, because lots [of traders] still do not understand [the benefits of the relocation].[25]

The mayor, too, later described to me how sosialisasi was like sell-ing a product. He narrated what he had said to the traders: " 'Please go ahead and compare the promise I have made you with the promise made by the NGOs. Which one is more logical? If [the promise] is not realized, is it easier to prosecute the NGOs or me?' So I influenced them by asking, 'Which is more rational?' It was like selling a product."[26] Government officials most often blamed the resistance to the relocation on a lack of understanding. They believed that with more sosialisasi the traders would eventually change their minds, which is why the govern-ment's job was to sell this project to them in the traders' own language.

Pak Herry Zudianto deployed his methods of "social psychology" to convince the traders and to win them over. However, in practice he did not respect their wishes or take their concerns seriously. He assumed that they spoke a different language from bureaucrats and that they did not understand the relocation project, thereby providing a ratio-nale for his paternalistic approach. In turn, suggesting that the trad-ers did not understand the project served as a mechanism to dismiss their concerns. As a tactic of avoidance, it allowed the government to defer the negotiation process to a later date. The traders' resistance was merely a "challenge" to be overcome by deploying various strategies. The lower-level officials also carried out Pak Herry Zudianto's strategy of trying to "get close" to and speaking the language of the traders. Like Pak Herry Zudianto, they thought the Pethikbumi membership did not understand the project, which allowed them to deflect and deny the underlying reasons for why Pethikbumi opposed the relocation in the first place. However, the Pethikbumi leaders were not dupes. Although they did not know all the details of the relocation, they knew from their own experience and from the experiences of other vendors that relocations did not always mean economic success for street traders. They understood the project and did not agree with it. Over time, they grew increasingly frustrated with the politics of postponement, the endless sosialisasi meetings at which the government tried to convince them that the project was good for them without addressing their real concerns. For the municipal government officials, what mattered was that they were spending time with the traders. They could say in the newspapers and to agencies like LOD DIY that they had met with the Pethikbumi traders regularly and that they were being "transparent." The manipulation of time in these meetings also acted as a form of social control because the government officials imposed on the traders a form of "waiting for the real discussion" (Crapanzano 1985; Harms 2013b, 352). Yet waiting did not cause the Pethikbumi leaders to yield to the state's desired temporality; instead it furthered Pethikbumi's interest in critiquing the state (see Mathur 2016, 143) and in trying to make the officials respond to their questions and concerns in an immediate way.

Details and Documents

If sosialisasi was a face-to-face sales pitch for the government officials, the Pethikbumi traders viewed it as a process that should involve detailed information about the project communicated not only orally but also through documentation. When one of my research assistants asked Mas Arief what sosialisasi should ideally look like, he responded, "Sosialisasi should be interactive, effective, and, if nothing else, comprehensive. We should at least be given an explanation of the project in a detailed way. But at the start of the relocation project, the government did not make the purpose of the relocation clear to the traders."[27] Mas Arief explained that the street vendors had been told in these sosialisasi meetings that they would be relocated to Kuncen Marketplace, and they were given the kiosks in the marketplace for free without having to pay any taxes and electricity for the first six months; beyond that, no more detail was provided.

Indeed, most of the information given during these sosialisasi meetings was general and vague. Mas Arief remembered that some of the basic questions he asked could not be answered. For instance, the government could not specify how many hours the traders would be expected or allowed to sell in the marketplace. It was only after being asked this question over and over that the government eventually produced a document that was distributed to the Pethikbumi leaders listing selling hours from ten in the morning until eleven in the evening.

The first steps of sosialisasi had involved the government inviting the leaders of all the vendor groups to meet with them to talk about the program. This had occurred on 16 January 2006 (see Postscript: Growing Unrest and Resistance, Chapter 2). The government had also invited these leaders on a comparative study trip to Bandung, West Java. Mas Arief went on this trip but remembers that its purpose was not clear to him at the time. He saw the markets in Bandung, but observing them did not make him want to join any relocation effort. This use of sosialisasi – in this case, going on the trip – was futile for him. Although Mas Arief did not see the trip as a form of bribery, other traders did. They thought the purpose of this "free" trip was to convince them to agree to the relocation since the government had taken them on an all-expenses-paid tour.

Despite the government's efforts to communicate the project to the traders, the Pethikbumi leaders refused to agree to the relocation because they said they were not being given enough detail about the relocation process. Mas Arief explained that they not only wanted verbal clarification about the project but also supporting documentation. He said, "If nothing else, we wanted the government to write down their promises on paper so that one day, if we need to make demands, the evidence would be right there." Laughing, Mas Arief said, "Promises without written evidence are certainly broken."[28] He remembered how the municipal government made a promise in the sosialisasi meetings that the kiosks would be free of charge in Kuncen Marketplace. Pethikbumi requested, however, that this promise be written down in an official document. Pethikbumi communicated its concerns over this lack of detail and documentation in the newspapers. As *Kedaulatan Rakyat* reported, "The leader of Pethikbumi, Pak Akbar, said the concept developed by the municipal government regarding the relocation was not transparent (*tidak transparan*), especially with money ... 'I also have asked for a detailed relocation concept (*konsep relokasi*), but I haven't been given it,' said Pak Akbar."[29]

According to the Pethikbumi leaders' shared information ideology, documents held the most weight and therefore could be trusted to hold the government accountable. Mas Arief explained, "We had a principle. We thought that if the government wants to promise us this, it must be written down ... It must be written in black and white."[30] In a later interview, he expanded on this view:

> In the context of such a relocation, the city government should ideally prepare documents or evidence of the things that we were promised. Written, complete, legal, and all leaders should know. In the document, the name and the signature of the mayor must also be included so we know who is responsible. Those being relocated can use documents such as this as proof (*bukti*) in case there is anything that is promised that does not materialize, or at least they can recognize things that remain unrealized.[31]

When the Pethikbumi traders did receive documents, however, they did not generate further trust or clarity, but rather greater fear and distrust. In this sense, documents comprised just another part of the government's toolkit. In the next section, following a more general discussion of the role of documentation in contemporary Indonesian society, I will discuss how the Pethikbumi leaders perceived the documents they did or did not receive during the sosialisasi process.

Shadow Play with Sosialisasi

In Indonesia, the increasing use and circulation of documents related to urban planning projects must be seen alongside calls for democratization since the fall of Suharto in 1998. During the country's authoritarian period from 1967 to 1998, activists were suppressed, the media was carefully controlled, and fabricated elections were held. During this period, the state rarely shared documents related to urban planning with its citizens.[32] When documents did circulate, they were often counterfeit. Siegel (1998) explains how government insiders often produced what he calls "genuine-but-false verification[s]" (54). These documents, while they were fake and illegally produced, looked real because they carried official stamps and signatures. Falsity was thus part of everyday life, and as a result, Siegel argues, it was difficult for Indonesians to trust documents (55).

Bubandt (2008) argues that because in post-Suharto Indonesia people are still "wary of the truth," "fake letters are therefore written and read with a fundamental distrust of official forms of veracity and a deep sense that the state forms of authority that provide a measure of authenticity to the fake letters may themselves be counterfeit" (561). Bubandt argues that a particular kind of transparency has emerged in the post-Suharto era where a person purposely creates a false letter in order to reveal what they consider to be the truth (566). In Indonesia, then, while documents are never entirely trusted, they still remain a respected medium of communication since even copies or forgeries might have an important story or "truth" to tell, depending on who produced them.

The desire for documentation therefore exists in a context in which document forgery is common. Indeed, I was surprised to learn the extent of the forgery practised by government officials and consultants in Yogyakarta. This was described to me by a friend named Pak Ettes, who had worked for two years (2011–13) for a consulting firm that cooperated closely with the national, regional, and municipal governments. The firm conducted policy research, mostly around tourism and culture, to inform the creation of new legislation. It also worked closely with the municipal government to support the development of new tourist destinations. Formed in the 1990s by three academics from a local university, the firm was able to get many government contracts because one of its founders was close to a government minister in power from 2009 to 2014.

Pak Ettes explained, "From the ten projects ... that were done by the firm every year, at least during my time there, [the implementation of] almost all of them was manipulated or falsified."[33] For instance, he described how the firm often did not complete all the components they were required to carry out for their studies, such as surveys or focus-group discussions. If they were supposed to conduct a focus group with a hundred participants, they would only do it with fifty and then "mark up" the missing attendees. The employees of the firm were often asked to create signatures. On one occasion, Pak Ettes was asked to invent five different names and a signature for each. Pak Ettes described how staff at the firm also frequently asked for his signature, which was used to record his attendance at a particular event even though he was not involved. Even photos were forged for reports – old photographs were digitally edited to produce a record of an event that never really took place. In a measure of just how institutionalized falsification practices had become, the firm even had a special division for handling these activities. Moreover, falsification was also done when drawing up budgets. The finance division always made two versions of a project budget: one for the process of tendering, and another to be used if the bid was successful.

Pak Ettes said, "All of this falsification is closely related to bribery and corruption."[34] Ministry elites, for instance, usually received money from any project undertaken by the consultants. Pak Ettes said that the minister who was close to one of the firm's founders almost always got gifts or cash from projects done by the firm. He explained that the minister would participate in events organized by the firm, in the middle of which a staff member would deliver a parcel with hundreds of millions of rupiah in cash to the minister's hotel room. Pak Ettes suggested that such practices were "normal" and that, judging from his experience, this firm had likely been embedded in this tradition since the Suharto era, and continued it after Reformasi. This evokes Sylvia Tidey's (2013) study of the Department of Public Works in Kupang, in which she argues that official documents in Indonesia increasingly display the kind of transparency required by international anticorruption programs without actually being transparent (190). In the case of the Department of Public Works, she asserts that these documents allow for the existence of "informal gift-giving practices" and "new forms of corruption" through which departmental officials appear to adhere to new rules and regulations (190). In this way, governments have found new methods of falsifying documents while meeting transparency requirements.

Despite these practices, the street vendors still wanted access to documents – not because they could trust the information in them or because that information described an eventual reality, but because they might be able to mobilize around them. Unlike words spoken at a meeting, documents were something that the traders assumed could be used to hold the government to account. As Hetherington (2011) noted in the case of the *campesinos* in Paraguay, "information … is the quality of a document that always belongs to the document's future as a form of possibility" (151). The power of documents for the Pethikbumi leaders lay in the opportunity they gave them to challenge the government's claims and to pressure it to carry through with any promises in the future.

The first request for a relocation document occurred during the initial sosialisasi meeting on 16 January 2006 (see Postscript: Growing Unrest and Resistance, Chapter 2). Mas Arief later explained to me why this initial meeting had generated distrust. At the meeting, the municipal government had asked the traders to sign a blank document – apparently an attendance sheet – without providing them with a written outline of the relocation. Shortly after the meeting, Pethikbumi requested a copy of the minutes to share widely with its membership. Almost six months later, the minutes had still not been released. Mas Arief recounted that it was only after the traders held a demonstration, with the help of the student activist organization PPIP, that the minutes were finally released.

Enclosed with the released minutes were the signatures of those who had attended the meeting. "The municipal government started saying that with our signatures, we had agreed to the relocation," Mas

Arief explained.[35] According to Mas Nasir, an advocate from PPIP, this method of asking that the traders sign an attendance sheet, only to later claim that these signatures indicated their agreement with the relocation, was a common practice. Thus, although the traders were shocked and angered by this misuse of their signatures, Mas Nasir was not surprised. He had witnessed this practice in two other cases involving street vendors in Yogyakarta city (at Selokan Mataram and UGM). He described the process in the following terms: "With the attendance form they usually use a blank sheet. They have the name, address, phone number, and signature. It is like that. At the time of the meeting, there was no writing on the form, but just a signature. After, when they [the municipal government] meet with the legislature, they claim that the street vendors already agreed with the relocation ... These are the methods they often use."[36]

Another worrying fact for Mas Arief was that a forged signature appeared on the document: "There was a leader from Pethikbumi who was new, Pak Sarwan, and he became the treasurer in July 2006, but in the minutes from the meeting on January 16 his signature appears. He had not become a leader yet, and did not know anything about the relocation."[37] During the Suharto era, it was not uncommon for vendors, under the threat of violence by police, to sign up for relocations or promise not to sell on the street (Hadiwinata 2003, 208). These practices perhaps heightened Mas Arief's sensitivity to the power and danger of giving the state his signature, because the signature lends itself to forgery, unauthorized circulation, and certain performative effects that might be beyond his intention (see Das 2004, 245). The relative instability of the vendors' signatures, then, left an immense amount of room for politics (see Hetherington 2011, 8), and the forged signature in particular became a major turning point for many of the Pethikbumi traders. It was a sign that the government would go to great lengths to show the traders' support for the relocation, and that the government's use of sosialisasi was entangled in practices of manipulation and forgery. The fake signature was, moreover, effective in generating suspicion because it was identified with the power of the state (see Bubandt 2009). The state's manipulation of the meaning of the signatures and its use of falsification also confirmed the Pethikbumi leaders' belief that the state was engaging in shadow play.

In addition to the manipulation and forgery of signatures, the Pethikbumi leaders also held the lower-level civil servants responsible for another act: purposely circulating different relocation concepts. Pethikbumi had been seeking an outline of the relocation plan – that is, a relocation concept – in writing. In February 2007, after making numerous informal requests to the government, they made a formal written request for the relocation plan. They finally received a copy in March. In June, however, Pethikbumi received a different plan, one that focused on how the street was going to be greened. "There are two types of concepts that have been offered by the municipal government," Pethikbumi's BPHK lawyers wrote in a press release.[38] Outlining them both, the press release argued that Pethikbumi was refusing the relocation because the two concepts were not consistent, which raised serious concerns about whether additional concepts were circulating and about whether the information provided could be trusted. The way that documents circulated therefore mattered. Despite the government's attempts to build "closeness" through formal discussions, the documents, which the traders hoped would bring greater clarity and trust to the process of sosialisasi, did the opposite: they only generated further distrust because they were open to duplicity and misrepresentation.

The government's withholding of documents also continued to generate frustration and suspicion from Pethikbumi. In June 2007, the organization's leadership had taken steps to obtain the necessary forms from the local sub-district office to apply for official trading permits, which, according to a 2002 mayoral regulation, would make the Pethikbumi members legal traders, giving them more legitimacy to refuse the relocation.[39] Mas Arief recounted that the group's leaders had asked the sub-district office for the paperwork to obtain the permits on four separate occasions. The first time, when they went directly to the sub-district office to ask for a form (blanko), the head of the office said there were none left. Three days later, Mas Arief sent a text message to the office head, who said they still did not have any forms. Based on the advice of their lawyers, after two more informal requests, the traders decided to send an official request to the sub-district office. Mas Arief remembered that at first the Pethikbumi leaders were confused: "How could the form be out for more than a month?" Then they realized that this was a strategy the government was probably using to prevent them from applying for legal status, because if they were successful that would challenge the government's argument that the relocation would benefit them by converting them from illegal to legal traders.[40] The traders never did receive the forms from the sub-district office.

Pethikbumi were also critical of a regulation affecting the relocation that had appeared in writing without their prior knowledge or input. In July 2007, Pethikbumi learned that a new regulation (Pemerintah Kota Yogyakarta 2007), which would officially make street vending on Mangkubumi Street illegal, had been drafted without their knowledge. An informal community leader (not a member of the government) gave

Pethikbumi a draft of this new regulation, which would make the traders illegal – permit or no permit – within two months. News of this secret regulation quickly circulated among the traders, and they publicly criticized the government for not consulting them first. This new regulation would give the government the legal authority it needed to relocate the traders in the upcoming months. Pethikbumi and its supporters argued that it was illegal for the government to produce this document without prior sosialisasi, since developing new legislation required the government to consult with the groups who would be impacted. In a newspaper article, Mas Arief was quoted as saying, "We ask for the support of members of parliament to repeal the [Mayoral] Regulation No. 45, 2007. Because we do not feel included in the development of this regulation that appeared suddenly."[41] The unearthed document eventually became the basis of a lawsuit launched against the government by five members of Pethikbumi. With the help of BPHK, a ten-page document was produced outlining how this new regulation was illegal.[42] Regarding the regulation, Mas Nasir explained, "In reality, the regulation is the result of the 'play' of the bureaucracy. They released it, no? At that time there was no sosialisasi beforehand."[43] Mas Nasir referred to the production and the release of the new regulation as a kind of shadow play because it was constructed "behind the screen" and out of the traders' view.

After the traders held a protest against the regulation outside the municipal courts on 7 November 2007 (see figure 3), a newspaper article described the situation in the following terms: "The traders feel that the regulation breaks the law because it was done without a process of rationalization and sosialisasi. The reason for the [relocation] project is to make the area [Mangkubumi Street] green (taman), but from their perspective it is only to evict traders."[44]

Similar to sosialisasi, which made the Pethikbumi leaders wait for a "real" discussion, the delayed release of documents also used time as an instrument of power (Verdery 1996; Harms 2013b). Acting as a subtle mechanism of control, these practices created an oppressive structure of "waiting" (see Harms 2013b). The Pethikbumi leaders were not indifferent to this waiting because they also felt the urgency of the relocation project as it was moving forward, and the passage of time meant that they might have even less ability to contest it. While the municipal government used the delayed release of certain documents as a "temporal tactic," the municipal government also moved quickly to draft legislation that would make street vending on Mangkubumi Street illegal, perhaps once they realized that the Pethikbumi leaders were trying to apply for permits to become legal traders. This "playing with time"

Figure 3. Pethikbumi protest outside the municipal courts, 7 November 2007.
Photo by author.

(Hoskins 1997), whether slowing down or speeding up the production of documents, was a practice of government shadow play. In the case of the relocation project, it created confusion and uncertainty as the Pethikbumi leaders and their supporters wondered not only about the content of these documents, but the extent to which the government officials were purposely playing with time.

Reflecting on these incidents involving state documents, Ibu Marini, director of BPHK, was convinced that if the government had given the traders the documents directly, without delay, the conflict around the relocation would not have become so intense and the Pethikbumi would not have had to file a lawsuit against the municipal government. Ibu Marini considered that it was perhaps government oknum who were responsible for how these documents circulated, but she was less certain about the extent to which the mayor might have known about these activities. Ibu Marini said, "Who inside the government was playing the role (*memainkan peran*) of withholding these documents? There had to have been a person 'playing' (*bermain*), an oknum, who did not release the documents even though they might have been reporting something different to the mayor. It is possible that the mayor did not know at the time that there was this play, below him, at the level of his subordinates."[45] By using the term *bermain*, Ibu Marini was referring to the idea of shadow play and how lower-level officials seemed to be operating behind the screen. What Ibu Marini was less certain about, however, was the extent to which the mayor was involved in or aware of the shadow play taking place.

Mas Nasir was likewise suspicious of the lower-level officials; he said that they were involved in withholding these documents, but, like Ibu Marini, he was uncertain about whether or not the mayor knew of these actions. He said, "There is [an Indonesian] tradition of 'as long as the boss is happy' (*asal bapak senang*). As long as the leader is happy, they [lower-level civil servants] can do whatever they want. 'As long as I receive recognition from the mayor, I'm going to use whatever method I can.'"[46] Mas Nasir perceived both the withholding and the strategically timed release of documents as methods that lower-level civil servants would deploy in an attempt to generate fear and uncertainty among the traders. These methods were used because they could leave traders feeling powerless and thus more likely to accept the relocation. Meanwhile, higher-level individuals like the mayor might have little idea of the drama unfolding below them. Mas Nasir assumed that the lower-level civil servants were willing to engage in these questionable tactics because they would likely be promoted if the project was successful.

As discussed throughout much of this chapter, Pethikbumi's leaders were trying to push the boundaries of the government's sosialisasi by requiring the government to be more open and transparent with information, in particular by providing them with documentation. Yet it is worth noting that the Pethikbumi leaders had their own problems when it came to sosialisasi with their membership. For example, they were expected to inform and consult with members about their activities through both face-to-face communication and documents. To this end, the Pethikbumi leaders regularly circulated information sheets to their membership containing updates on the status of the relocation and explaining why the group continued to refuse or challenge the government's relocation. At times, however, the Pethikbumi leaders told their members only convenient versions of the truth. This practice was in fact encouraged by one of the group's NGO partners, who said in a meeting, "I hope that our friends that are here will really promise to engage in sosialisasi and give members information about what we have spoken about this evening, but you don't need to share some things that will scare them."[47]

During internal Pethikbumi meetings, the leaders also increasingly placed pressure on their members. Often in these meetings, a distinction between "traitors" (*pengkhianat*) and "enemies" (*musuh*) was invoked to describe those who had decided to switch sides and support the relocation. In one late-night meeting, a leader said, "I am here asking for you to stay strong and not to become a traitor, and to defend Mangkubumi Street with everything (*mati-matian*)."[48] The Pethikbumi leaders also threatened their members, warning that if they joined the relocation they would not be given a selling location on Mangkubumi Street. As Edward Aspinall and Meredith L. Weiss (2012) suggest, civil society can be as much a place for the "reproduction of social inequality as it is a site from which that inequality is challenged" (214).

Conclusion

An attention to different information practices and ideologies shows that urban projects such as vendor relocations are far more than just a conflict over land and livelihoods. In the case of the vendor relocation to Kuncen Marketplace, different perceptions of sosialisasi were shaped by how street vendors, their NGO supporters, municipal government officials, and the mayor perceived and believed information should circulate during this urban project, and their different goals in relation to the relocation. Focusing on these ideologies and practices of sosialisasi allowed me to approach the study of participatory planning without assuming the existence of shared beliefs between my interlocutors and myself or among my different interlocutors. The government's post-Suharto ideologies of sosialisasi were shaped in relation to newer demands for democracy and dialogue and by fears of potential resistance to their project. Meanwhile, the traders' competing idea of sosialisasi was influenced by their fears of manipulation and falsification and in relation to newer demands for transparency through documentation.

Civil servants involved in the relocation, including the mayor, viewed all of the trader groups as one larger body that needed to feel close to the government in order to "understand" the relocation. The lower-level officials justified their actions through their concept of sosialisasi. They claimed in the newspapers and in meetings that they were doing their job by informing the traders about the project through face-to-face meetings. Yet their firm conviction that they were being democratic and inclusive meant that their ideas about participation were different from those of the traders. For Pak Ari and Pak Galang, government documents and regulations were viewed as extraneous to the process of sosialisasi, and sharing them with the traders was not a priority.

The discourse of sosialisasi can, on one level, be read as a legitimizing strategy used by the government to justify how it carried out the relocation. The discourse of sosialisasi can be further viewed as creating the image of "participation" that has been documented and critiqued in so many development projects around the world (e.g., Mosse 2005; Sivaramakrishnan 2000). The government's discourse of sosialisasi could also be seen as a continuation of the New Order practice in which the government and various interested parties carried forward projects in "consultation" with stakeholders, when in reality they simply used sosialisasi to persuade those stakeholders to agree with their own viewpoint. Yet the government's discourse of sosialisasi vis-à-vis Pethikbumi was also a departure from this practice in the sense that the government officials in the post-Suharto era were under greater pressure from the public, NGOs, and the Pethikbumi traders themselves to meet with Pethikbumi and engage in sosialisasi. The government also took the "softer" approach of trying to "get close" and "speak the language" of the traders, an approach likely supported by many development agencies.

Based on my observations of these sosialisasi meetings, the government was often less concerned with dealing with the traders' concerns in a substantial way, and more concerned with holding the meetings so that it could tell the public and other interested parties that it had met with the traders. This involved what I have called, following Julie Gibbings (2020), the "politics of postponement," because while meetings were indeed held with the street vendors, the "real" discussion was always deferred to the next meeting. By playing with time in this way, the municipal government was able to exert a subtle form of control that allowed it to move forward with the project while appearing as if it was fulfilling its obligations to engage in sosialisasi. However, these delay tactics were not met with indifference and disinterest (cf. Harms 2013b) among the traders. Recognizing these delay tactics, the traders tried to push for information from the government through formal requests and by inviting LOD DIY to mediate the sosialisasi.

In contrast to the government, the Pethikbumi leaders expected different things from the sosialisasi process. Although they did not mind "getting close" to the government, they expected to be given information in an open manner and for the government to engage in a more meaningful consultation process when it came to plans that impacted their livelihoods. While the government tried to "speak their language," it failed in the sense that the language of the traders was also one of written documentation. The government perhaps underestimated the expectations, education, and demands of this group of traders when it came to sosialisasi. These different information ideologies and practices also precipitated the formation of shifting networks (cf. Hull 2012b, 22), with Pethikbumi looking to lawyers, activists, and LOD DIY for support while questioning the practices of the lower-level officials. Yet despite their demands that government officials engage in sosialisasi in more meaningful ways, the Pethikbumi leaders and their NGO supporters did not always engage in transparent sosialisasi practices with the Pethikbumi members. At times, they decided not to share some information that might deter these members from continuing to refuse the relocation.

While the civil servants attempted to make the traders trust them by speaking in their language and meeting with them on the street, the way the government circulated documents, and the contents of these documents, had the opposite effect – namely, they generated more fear and distrust. How and under what circumstances the traders accessed these documents had a profound influence on how they experienced and perceived them. Their engagement with the documents was haunted by a New Order legacy in which documents are seen as a site of both authority and suspicion. Even though the traders and their supporters were suspicious of lower-level government officials, there was confusion and uncertainty about whether the mayor was informed about these officials' practices.[49] The Pethikbumi traders and their supporters thus distinguished between various kinds of state officials rather than seeing the state as a unified or coherent entity. Through this understanding of the state, the Pethikbumi traders and their supporters drew from their social interactions with lower-level officials the idea that certain components of the state were potentially dangerous and should not be trusted. The traders viewed the sosialisasi practised by these lower-level officials as a kind of shadow play wherein the information given to them in front of the screen was different to what was taking place behind it.

Chapter Four

Democratizing Surveillance

As the government pushed forward with the relocation despite Pethik-bumi's opposition, suspicions ran high among everyone involved, especially once it was apparent that government documents were being falsified, withheld, and leaked through different channels. The Pethikbumi leaders were increasingly suspicious that anyone they met or anyone who was involved in their organizing – including other traders, along with their NGO, legal, and activist supporters – might be secretly working for the state because information was somehow being leaked to the government after Pethikbumi's own internal meetings. During a break in an internal meeting held by the Pethikbumi street vendors and their NGO supporters, one trader, Pak Mujib, asked a couple other traders to join him at the back of the room. There, he told them that he suspected me of being a government informant, and he threatened to break my recording device if it was true. The two traders, whom I knew better, said they doubted that I was a government informant because I had promised them confidentiality. They decided not to invite me to the next Pethikbumi meeting (without me knowing) to see if any information discussed there was still leaked to the government. When information was indeed relayed to the government after that gathering, the traders concluded that someone else must be the internal informant. After they determined that I was innocent, Mas Eko revealed to me their tactic of not inviting me to the meeting.[1] Through this and similar incidents, I quickly realized that it was very important for the Pethikbumi traders and their supporters to be able to control and manipulate the production, circulation, and interpretation of information. It was an effective way to both challenge the government's relocation project and its associated policies, and to confirm and maintain the loyalty of their members.

During Suharto's rule, traders opposing an eviction or relocation would operate under the assumption that intelligence agents were watching them, inhibiting their ability to organize against the state. The Indonesian state during the Suharto era was fragmented, but it had the power to impose its own vision of itself on the social world, which meant it was able to project a certain power and coherence (Van Klinken and Barker 2009). Today, although street traders continue to believe that the state and its associated actors are omnipresent, they are confused and suspicious about who is working for, with, or against the state. With the growing number of political actors on the scene, one never knows if one's friend, co-worker, or NGO supporter is secretly working on the side of the state. In this context, the traders I worked with tried to use surveillance to map the state's activities, to understand the activities of the pro-relocation vendor groups, and to verify that their own colleagues were loyal. The anti-relocation traders, then, were not rendered docile despite the surveillance (and the revelation of this surveillance) they faced by the police and other actors.

Recent work on the state suggests that we should understand it not as a natural or given apparatus but as a historical and contingent entity (see T.B. Hansen and Stepputat 2006). In particular, scholars emphasize that the state is shaped through cultural imagination and the practices of everyday people (e.g., Aretxaga 2003; Das and Poole 2004; Gupta 2005). In this chapter, I approach the state not as a coherent system of institutions but as part of a "social imaginary"[2] and an everyday practice (see Mueggler 2001, 4). Even though the state is a loosely coordinated system, I argue that the Pethikbumi traders and their activist supporters imagined the state as a powerful body engaged in shadow play through surveillance and capable of working through non-state actors. This caused the traders and their activist supporters to become suspicious of each other, and to develop their own practices of surveillance targeting individuals they suspected of working with the government, including their own members and friends. The traders and their supporters therefore shared the state's information ideology with regard to surveillance: they assumed that surveillance was a means to obtain the truth. Another information ideology shared among the Pethikbumi street vendors and their supporters (both pro- and anti-relocation) was the belief that divulging information gained from spying to the person being watched was a form of power: it suggested that one was in possession of information that was otherwise meant to be kept secret. The anti-relocation traders and their supporters seemed to understand these techniques of shadow play, and they were willing to use them.

In this chapter, I describe how the Pethikbumi street vendors and activists adopted and adapted the state practice of both using surveillance and revealing this surveillance to others. In addition, the

Pethikbumi traders and their supporters developed their own techniques of "managing impressions" to ensure that other anti-relocation leaders did not become suspicious of them. I argue that with the advent of the democratic era, these traders and activists now felt they had a right to engage in information politics in new ways, and to take up practices that were in the past confined mostly to the state and its associated actors. These practices of controlling, manipulating, and producing information were an important part of the traders' collective political action. I also argue that these surveillance and impression-management practices were performative and affective – they generated pleasure, enjoyment, and also fear. They played on desires for and fantasies of transparency under democracy. Yet they also simultaneously utilized "undemocratic" practices such as intimidation and secrecy to achieve these ends. Moreover, I argue that the traders and the activists who engaged in these practices of surveilling and revealing felt empowered and were able to occupy new political positions. By contrast, those who were the target of these practices felt disempowered and helpless in the face of intimidation. This does not mean, however, that Indonesian democracy is a failed democracy or a deviation from "true" democracy. Instead, it suggests the possibility that in Indonesia, democracy is sometimes achieved through opaque and undemocratic political practices (see Bubandt 2014).

Much of the anthropological literature on urban planning has focused on the use of surveillance cameras that privatize public spaces in the growing number of gated communities (Low 2001; 2006) and fortified enclaves (Caldeira 2000). However, face-to-face policing and surveillance of civilian politics, especially among oppositional groups, remains important for governments and corporations (Heyman 2014, 286). Josiah Heyman (2014) describes how transnational meetings among the elites are often met with opposition from transnational activists, and he argues that political policing plays an important role in shaping the political action, such as free speech, of these activists (286). I will argue that surveillance is an important component of the urban planning apparatus because it can be used to intimidate citizens, especially those organizing to oppose an urban project. The state surveillance system in Indonesia plays a central role in urban planning projects because it generates suspicion and uncertainty among citizens, thereby helping to break down trust among those opposing these projects. Yet like the other parts of the urban planning apparatus, citizens are also staking a claim by appropriating these surveillance practices and making them their own.

Deanna Barenboim (2016) describes how the "spectre of state surveillance" and the threat of law enforcement produces new forms of (im)mobility among Mayan migrants from Yucatan living in Marin County, California. By "spectre of state surveillance," Barenboim (2016) refers to "the power of the state as imagined, envisioned, anticipated, and, ultimately, embodied by migrants" (80). In the case of Mayan migrants, the "politics of (im)mobility takes form through spatial *tactics of invisibility and visibility*" (80; emphasis in the original). In a similar way, in this chapter, I describe how the anti-relocation street vendors and their supporters engaged in a variety of tactics of invisibility and visibility in order to inhibit state surveillance, manage rumours about themselves, and produce their own secret knowledge about others through surveillance. I argue that these practices took place in the context of Indonesians' newfound desire for, and pleasure in, the revelation of secrets in the public sphere.

In this chapter, I also describe how the Yogyakarta city government and its pro-relocation supporters (a lawyer and a police officer, in particular) conducted surveillance in an attempt to engage in shadow play, and ultimately to create confusion and uncertainty among the anti-relocation traders and their supporters about what information was known or unknown by the government. This surveillance also constituted a form of intimidation, especially when it was revealed to the Pethikbumi traders. I then discuss how the Pethikbumi leaders and the student activists engaged in the surveillance of Pak Didik, who, as noted earlier, was seen as an associate of the state who supported the pro-relocation traders. I describe the other surveillance practices of the student activist group PPIP, and how the Pethikbumi leaders also used surveillance techniques against their own members. I argue that the Pethikbumi leaders, in addition to these practices of surveillance, had to manage information about – and by extension, other people's impressions of – themselves.

Finally, it is worth noting that these surveillance and impression-management practices were not conducted in a symbolic vacuum; they were closely associated with the actions and ideas of the masculinized figure of the pemuda, which serves as a powerful "imagined community" in Indonesia (Lee 2016, 7). As Lee (2016) states, "Youth activism is a mode of citation and documentation that strengthens and shapes the role of collective memory in nationalism and political resistance" (6). While the pemuda figure is associated largely with masculinity (Lee 2011, 2016), it is a fluid set of practices and ideas upon which both men and women can draw to assert their identity.[3] Indeed, as Lee (2011) argues, "the trope of masculinity acts as an inclusive and hegemonic ideal, informing activist definitions of political success and behavior" (943), despite the fact that the idea of pemuda does not reflect all those involved in street politics (947).[4] Like the pemuda of the Reformasi period, the Pethikbumi leaders and their supporters used state practices for their own purposes (Lee 2016). In this respect, through their mirroring of the state practice of surveillance, the Pethikbumi leaders, and in particular their PPIP supporters, at times embodied the masculinist identity of the pemuda figure.[5]

Indonesia: Surveillance and Its Democratization

Suharto's regime inherited the Dutch East Indies' colonial regime of surveillance and built what Merlyna Lim (2002) calls a " 'panopticon' of constant surveillance over national territorial space" (386). Suharto's regime was known for its parades and visible presence in public spaces, as well as its strong surveillance of the populace in these spaces. Panopticism was relatively successful in Indonesia because there was a well-developed cultural apparatus aimed at reminding citizens that they were being watched. As Lim (2002) writes, "wherever people went, whatever they thought, they felt that they were under the eye of the state" (386).

Most Indonesian citizens who were alive during the New Order have memories of the government's surveillance system. One of my research assistants, born in Yogyakarta, remembered how when he was in grade 2 in 1992, he asked his mother about President Suharto and his political party, Golkar. His mother quickly responded, "Shhh ... do not talk nonsense about it or we will be arrested!"[6] For him, this stern warning was a clear indication that talking about President Suharto and his politics was taboo. Pak Freddy, who was in high school in the 1970s, remembers that his mother, a civil servant, slapped him because he claimed to support another political party over Golkar.[7] It was a public secret (*rahasia umum*) that talking politics was dangerous and that engaging in political discussions put one at risk of government detention.

Students involved in on-campus political activism during the New Order also remember the strong government oversight that met their activities. Moreover, for the pemuda or political activists of the Reformasi period, "*Intel* [intelligence agents] accusations and discoveries fueled the political intrigue within and between student groups, as the accusations unmasked intimates who turned out to be in the employ of the army or other state intelligence units" (Lee 2016, 135–6). Pak Haris was born in 1975 and grew up in Jakarta in a middle-class Chinese Catholic family.[8] The university campus was the place where he felt the weight of state surveillance the most. He explained that in the 1990s, it was an open secret among students that intel were listening in during discussions on campus. This made everyone suspicious (*curiga*) of each other and also on alert (*waspada*). Pak Haris remembers that every time he and his fellow students held a discussion, they would ask, "Ada Joni-joni, nggak?" (Is there *Joni-joni* or not?), *Joni-joni* being a Bahasa Indonesia term for intelligence agents. Alternatively, they would say, "Kayaknya banyak laler [lalat] nih" (It looks like there was a lot of flies here).

Pak Haris remembers that while travelling on the street, whether riding on a motorbike or in a car, he always checked behind to make sure no one was following him. Activists like him were particularly worried about being followed after a demonstration. Pak Haris described his approach: "I was usually silent and would stop at a corner alley and smoke one or two cigarettes while making sure the road was secure."[9] He also tried to avoid any association with intel, who often tried to contact students, whether by phone, coming to their home, meeting them on the street or on campus, or sitting next to them while they were eating at a *warung*. In these situations, the unknown person would reveal that they were intel. In particular, Pak Haris always tried to avoid meeting with intel one-on-one because he feared that his friends would become suspicious of him since intel also employed the practice of finding key informants through bribery.[10] As Lee (2016) has written in relation to youth activists during the Reformasi period, "it appeared that intel accusations were leveled at individuals whose backgrounds were unexceptional. Intel arose from the ranks of students and rakyat [the people] whom students were trying to recruit for their struggle" (137).

Despite its vast intelligence networks across the archipelago during the Suharto era, the surveillance regime was never solely under the control of the state because the state also worked with criminal elements. During the New Order, the government often worked with gangs or other criminals to maintain its power and conduct surveillance (Barker 1998; Ryter 2001). The New Order state attempted to appropriate local power by using both surveillance and discipline on individuals who controlled particular territories (Barker 1999, 8). Joshua Barker (1998) found that the state subjected gangs, security guards, and criminals to surveillance while also asking them to watch others and report their findings back to the state. Surveillance was thus used to control gangs and criminals, but also to help these same groups suppress others, particularly activists and so-called communists.

Scholars have characterized the post–New Order period as a time when state power is being appropriated or contested by various groups. For instance, Karen Strassler (2009) has described instances during the Reformasi period where citizens appropriated and played with symbols of state power. For instance, she describes "a street photographer capitalizing on the euphoric popular mood [who] enlarged to life size the Suharto postage stamp and charged people to have their photos taken in Suharto's place" (69). Strassler (2010) says, "the idea that 'you' could put yourself in the place traditionally occupied by state leaders and other important personages fit well with the general sense that the icons of state power are available, in new ways, for popular engagement" (162).

In a context that allows for new forms of engagement with state power, we see the democratization of surveillance put to diverse uses. Sarah Newman in *Inside Indonesia*, for instance, describes how in Aceh, vigilante groups are increasingly policing the sexuality of heterosexual unmarried couples through surveillance; members of these groups are portrayed as heroes in the newspapers for enforcing Aceh's prohibition against *khalwat* (a term used to describe an encounter between a man and an unmarried and unrelated woman).[11] She writes, "Neighbours will spy on a suspected couple until the early hours of the morning, just to confirm their suspicions, as a way of justifying their subsequent vigilante actions."[12]

Various government offices, bodies, and institutions are also using surveillance to uncover internal corruption. For instance, in a famous case that began in 2008, the Corruption Eradication Commission (Komisi Pemberantasan Korupsi, or KPK) bugged the Indonesian National Police's chief commissioner general and found him soliciting a bribe from a tycoon's lawyer. When the National Police countered with accusations that members of the KPK were themselves corrupt, a drama unfolded with the KPK and the National Police producing wiretaps of each other and their informants.[13] Within the government, then, surveillance has in some sense been democratized because it is no longer solely in the hands of the police, and various internal groups are "free" to make accusations against each other.

There are also cases of marginalized citizens developing their own surveillance techniques in order to protect themselves against vigilante groups or the state. For instance, a group of traders I observed near a university hired an individual to go undercover and watch for the Public Order Agency truck that was carrying the officers who would fine them and confiscate their merchandise for trading illegally. When the truck was spotted several kilometres away, text messages were circulated and the traders quickly hid and secured their merchandise (see also Gibbings 2016). The International Lesbian, Gay, Bisexual, Trans and Intersex Association (ILGA) and GAYa NUSANTARA (GN), the first LGBT advocacy organization in Indonesia, established surveillance and evacuation teams in the lead-up to a meeting they planned to host. The organizations recruited Muslims who were sympathetic to their cause to watch over the mosques and warn them if any groups (such as the Islamic Defenders Front [Front Pembela Islam, or FPI]) planned to protest. These organizations developed their surveillance tactics because the police were unwilling to provide protection for them.[14] It is therefore becoming more common for individuals, street vendors, and NGOs to engage in practices of surveillance for their own purposes, whether to locate a criminal and help the police or to protect themselves against the state or other groups. Steve Mann, Jason Nolan, and Barry Wellman (2003) developed the term *sousveillance* to describe the efforts or devices used to counter organizational surveillance. They argue that sousveillance involves a form of "reflectionism" because it mirrors and confronts bureaucratic organizations (333). As I will discuss later in this chapter (see Street Vendors Practising Surveillance), in the case of the vendor relocation project, the Pethikbumi traders and their supporters mirrored the actions of intelligence agents by using surveillance techniques against them and then revealing these practices back to them.

People's desire to engage in surveillance against the state and their fellow citizens is deeply connected to the wish for transparency in Indonesia. Jodi Dean in *Publicity's Secret* (2002) has argued that the public sphere is marked on the one hand by a desire for transparency, and on the other by paranoid beliefs in the power of secrets. The remedy is a political culture of transparency. She writes that "secrecy generates the very sense of a public it presupposes. The secret designates that which is desired to be known, that which hasn't yet been disclosed. In so doing, it presupposes a subject that desires, discovers, and knows, a subject from whom nothing should be withheld" (Dean 2002, 10).

In Indonesia, where there were many secrets hidden away from the public sphere during the authoritarian period (including cases of corruption), we can now see all kinds of revelations taking place (Kramer 2013). The media is playing a central role in revealing "secrets" and promising to expose the truth. Political corruption and sex scandals continue to make daily headlines. Transparency is publicly performed in the media, both because there is a public that is generally sceptical and because there is a pleasure derived from this process of revealing. As Elisabeth Kramer (2013) argues, "the public appear intrigued with the corruption scandals that emerge, demanding more news on corruption while the media fuels this interest with provocative stories highlighting the scandalous nature of corruption cases" (61).

But the media is not the only venue where practices of revealing and concealing have, in the new democratic era, taken place (and continue to take place). In this chapter, I describe how street vendors and activists who opposed the relocation both revealed and concealed information from each other in order to assert their power over the relocation process. These practices were driven by a new belief that truthful information was accessible through surveillance, and that street vendors – not just the state – could access this information and reveal it.

Being Shadowed

Prior to the municipal government's announcement of the relocation plan, traders on Mangkubumi Street already saw themselves as victims of the police. Often, police would come to the street and accuse the traders of selling stolen cell phones, demanding that they come to the police station and pay a fine without providing them with the proper documentation required to make such an accusation. Most traders paid an "off the books" fee rather than undergo the additional hassle of trying to obtain a lawyer and prove their innocence. Some would ask one of the leaders of Pethikbumi, who had closer relations with the police, to help them negotiate a smaller fee. By the spring of 2007, a number of the Pethikbumi street vendors had raised concerns about the municipal government's increased surveillance. They believed that intelligence agents were monitoring their meetings, conversations, and plans to protest the relocation, and one trader whom I knew well, Mas Eko, often asked to borrow my camera to photograph potential spies. The traders suspected both strangers and friends of being government spies; this included fellow traders, journalists, university students doing research on Mangkubumi Street, and even my research assistant after he asked to film a video. As shown in the preceding section, however, these types of suspicions were in some ways not new to Indonesia. This was particularly the case among student activists, who in the 1990s "were wary around trusting outsiders and newcomers, even if those outsiders were from other student groups" (Lee 2016, 136).

The suspected surveillance impacted vendors on the ground, and as a result the Pethikbumi street vendors engaged in the politics of escaping, screening, and tracking the surveillance. They also engaged in their own practices of surveillance to learn about the government's and their own members' possibly secret actions. On a daily basis, the traders tried to escape surveillance by meeting and discussing the relocation in private locations such as an empty café, a home, or an office. Several times, the leaders of Pethikbumi asked to meet me in unexpected places away from the street, where we would be less visible and less likely to be overheard by potential intelligence agents. Formal meetings and protests were announced through text messages at the last minute so that the government would be less likely to intercept the information. One street vendor leader changed his phone number regularly to avoid government monitoring. He and his colleagues thus operated under the assumption that their activities were under constant government watch. This belief shaped their notions of trust and their relationships (see Ali 2016).

The bureaucrats and their collaborators, meanwhile, did not deny their roles in watching over our conversations and actions; rather, they went out of their way to tell the traders that they were watching them. One day, while waiting for a meeting with a particular civil servant, I conversed with some members of the Satpol PP (Satuan Polisi Pamong Praja, or Civil Service Police Unit). I knew many of these officers, having spent time at their offices and observed their operations against traders, street children, and *becak* (pedicab/rickshaw) drivers across the city. They also had a team of undercover agents who kept track of activities on the street. One of the men jokingly said, "I saw you last night touching the hand of Pak Akbar."[15] He laughed about the romantic connotation, and then proceeded to describe how he saw me on the street meeting with this person or that person. When I asked how he knew this, he described how he sent people there to watch the activities on the street every night: "Sometimes they come as rickshaw drivers and other times they act as sellers or go as customers."[16]

An undercover police officer, Pak Ferry, also regularly reported my own activities to me. I knew that he was involved in "watching" the relocation, although he rarely went to the street himself. He openly shared with me that he had several people planted as street vendors who regularly reported to him.[17] Moreover, when I visited Pak Didik – the NGO advocate for the pro-relocation traders and director of ILMA – at his office, he made no attempt to hide his efforts to organize thugs to support the relocation. He proudly introduced me to his friend, a known preman who controlled activities in a region of the city near the palace. On several occasions, he described, in a joking fashion, who I had spoken to hours earlier and where I had done so.[18] He did not reveal his informant to me, but made it known that he was able to watch me from afar. Once, I even had an official from Satpol PP call me after a meeting to report what I had said there. As I found out, the purpose of the phone call was to warn me to remain neutral, since it was the one time during a meeting where I had made a recommendation to the group; but the phone call also indicated that someone in this internal meeting was working undercover.[19] While people often shared their ability to watch me from afar in a light-hearted manner, this was also a claim to power over my activities. It also made me concerned about whether I could truly provide my informants with confidentiality and/ or anonymity, despite my best attempts. Compared to my experiences in Canada, where I rarely thought about the government watching me, my expectations had shifted radically: I now assumed that everything I did was possibly being watched.

The leaders of Pethikbumi were also told of the fact that they were under surveillance, as well as the potential consequences of this surveillance. During a Pethikbumi meeting in October 2007, Pak Akbar recounted a conversation he had had with a government official. The official had warned him that if he refused the relocation, he would be labelled a provokator[20] and eventually arrested. Pak Akbar was also told that he would be "blacklisted"[21] by the municipal government, making all his future activities more difficult.[22] Pak Akbar regularly recounted the threats he received from lower-level government officials, and in doing so he circulated an image and sense of the state as having an all-powerful gaze.

Similar to activists during the New Order, the traders assumed that government intelligence was watching them, and they developed tactics to try to avoid this surveillance (see Lee 2016). But the traders and activists not only assumed or imagined that they were under surveillance – they were in fact told that they were. The government's shadow play involved a dual process of hiding at certain moments and then revealing, at a later time, the information that had been gathered. In this way, they simultaneously unmasked their secret without fully revealing it (for instance, by never disclosing the identities of specific informants). The suspected surveillance increased the traders' paranoia and suspicions, and the revealing of it by the government only furthered these feelings.

Street Vendors Practising Surveillance

One technique the anti-relocation traders used for obtaining information about actors associated with the government was going undercover. For example, the traders used their own intelligence-like methods to investigate Pak Didik. Since 2002, Pak Didik had acted to negotiate terms with the government for traders from the neighbourhoods of Beringharjo, Sriwedani, and Giwangan in Yogyakarta. He usually counselled groups of street vendors to accept government-organized relocations, but he also ensured that the mayor heard the vendors' concerns directly. In the case of the groups supporting the relocation to Kuncen Marketplace, he worked with lower-level government officials but would often – to the discomfort of these lower-level officials – go above them directly to the mayor. Many Pethikbumi traders viewed Pak Didik as working for the government, but also as working to coordinate thugs – especially individuals from the PPP – and other street-level actors. They believed that the municipal government was paying Pak Didik to persuade the traders to accept the relocation. Pak Didik held meetings in his office and strategized regularly with the pro-relocation vendors. He was said to work through other individuals, specifically a handful of traders to whom he had promised money and premier locations in the new marketplace. In my regular interactions with Pak Didik, he presented himself as a neutral NGO advocate trying to help poor street vendors, and he often highlighted his neutrality by stating that he could have been rich (*kaya*) if he had chosen another line of work or engaged in corruption.[23]

The Pethikbumi traders were concerned about preman and intelligence agents, but also about figuring out who was working with or behind these actors. Between 1983 and 1985, during a government campaign that has since come to be known as the Mysterious Killings (*Pembunuhan Misterius*), many preman were killed and their corpses left in the street for the public to see. Siegel (1998) argues that these killings were made public in order to shift the focus of interest from preman back to the state (120–4). In a similar sense, the appearance of certain individuals on the street, such as thugs, piqued people's fascination with the powerful actors operating behind them. Pak Didik was one such actor.

The Pethikbumi traders imagined the state as engaged in a conspiracy to make the street unconducive to selling by working through different types of actors (such as thugs, lawyers, or other traders). As a result, the group's leaders saw it as their job to identify others who were said to be involved in this conspiracy: the intelligence agents, the traders who had secretly switched sides, and the actors behind the thugs who appeared on the street. One trader, Pak Pramana, went undercover to find evidence of his suspicion that Pak Didik was working with the mayor. Like the other members of Pethikbumi, Pak Pramana was certain that the relocation project involved government surveillance and conspiracy. Pak Pramana was particularly upset that Pak Didik, whom he considered a thug, was presenting himself as the leader of an NGO. When Pak Pramana met Pak Didik at a neighbourhood ritual, he hid his own identity in order to find out the "truth" about Pak Didik. The street vendor leaders jointly wrote a detailed letter (which was typed up on a computer) describing the incident for the police, entitled "Kronologis intimidasi terhadap pengurus Pethikbumi" (Chronology of the intimidation faced by the Pethikbumi leaders).[24]

The letter noted the exact time and location of the encounter: Saturday, 14 April 2007, 9:30 p.m., at the residence of Pak Pramana's friend. It began by setting out the context and describing how Pak Pramana was invited by one of his friends to attend a neighbourhood Islamic ritual giving thanks for the birth of a new child.[25] It then described how Pak Didik arrived at the event, and how Pak Pramana and Pak Didik spoke to each other even though they had never met before in person. In the second paragraph, the letter recalled the specific conversation that took place between Pak Didik and Pak Pramana. The trader asked Pak Didik whether he controlled Mangkubumi Street, to which he responded that he controlled the pro-relocation second-hand traders. When the NGO advocate then asked Pak Pramana about his status on the street, Pak Pramana lied, saying that he only searched for merchandise on the street (in other words, he did not reveal that he was a Pethikbumi leader). Pak Didik then offered Pak Pramana a kiosk in the new marketplace, but Pak Pramana rejected the offer. Next, Pak Didik informed Pak Pramana that the leaders of Pethikbumi would be kidnapped because they were refusing the relocation. When the trader asked who would be kidnapped, Pak Didik listed the specific names. Pak Didik offered Pak Pramana another opportunity to register at the new marketplace, and again Pak Pramana politely refused. The letter concluded with the trader asking Pak Didik why some people came to Mangkubumi Street and brought weapons with them. Pak Didik responded, "Those were my men."

In this letter to the police, the traders provided an account of Pak Pramana's undercover attempts to discover Pak Didik's activities, thereby mirroring the state's own intelligence practices. The story reveals not only what they discovered but also their method of detection. Pak Pramana acted the part of an intelligence agent and discovered a case of possible terrorism in the form of a kidnapping plot. But while the bureaucrats used surveillance to *generate* fear, the traders used it to *illuminate* the state and its associated actors as a body that should be feared. This story suggests that the traders also drew upon the performative power of both surveillance and unmasking to reveal the government's secret activities (Taussig 1999).[26] The revelation to the police was in some sense not effective because the police never investigated the potential kidnapping. It was effective, however, insofar as it allowed the traders to show their capacity to access the the state's activities. This was a story that the Pethikbumi leaders proudly told their members. It showed how they were brave for putting themselves at risk of kidnapping and adept at tricking Pak Didik into giving them information. Shortly after Pak Pramana's conversation with Pak Didik, the members of Pethikbumi made an appointment with Pak Didik at his office, where they confronted him about the threat he had revealed. Pak Didik denied the accusation, declaring that it had been a joke. Information was used as a form of power here since the information they revealed to Pak Didik demonstrated that the traders were watching him and had been able to obtain information without him knowing.

Student Activists Practising Surveillance

Unlike the traders, members of the student activist group PPIP considered themselves to be close with government intelligence; they often used these connections to help map the urban conflicts in which they were involved, including the vendor relocation. Mas Totok was born in 1984 in Yogyakarta and had studied international relations at school. Over time, he became less interested in school and more involved in activism. Mas Totok joined PPIP in 2004, and for three years he was involved with a group of street vendors being evicted from Selokan Mataram, an area located in the Sleman region, just outside Yogyakarta city. In 2006, he started to work with street vendors on Mangkubumi Street. Mas Totok disapproved of the fact that the government often allowed traders to sell, and then only relocated them once they had a strong customer base and incomes, "even though in order to make the street busy [the vendors] had to work hard." Referring to the relocation project, he was blunt: "Of course there would be resistance under these circumstances."[27]

When PPIP became involved in advocacy work related to an urban conflict, they typically conducted an investigation, generating a map of actors involved (such as preman, political parties, NGOs, and whoever else). To produce this map, they sought the advice of people within PPIP as well as a network of friends with extensive knowledge of city politics. In addition, PPIP relied on the provincial police service (the Polisi Kota Besar, or Poltabes). Mas Totok said, "From the Poltabes' intelligence we could map who was involved. For example, those who are involved with violent groups, because the police would know more [about these people]."[28] Once PPIP knew who was entangled in the conflict, they tried to figure out who to contact in order to "balance" the situation.[29] For instance, if the traders faced intimidation from thugs, PPIP could determine who was behind it and try to counter it by approaching the thugs' leader or organizing other thugs in opposition to them.

Therefore, while the Pethikbumi street vendors were less friendly with intelligence agents, PPIP members saw these agents as potential allies. They were able to develop a police network (*jaringan*) because

PPIP took part in numerous demonstrations. For example, if the Indonesian president was coming to Yogyakarta city, government intelligence would often communicate with PPIP and ask them if they planned to demonstrate. "So we often shared information," Mas Totok explained.[30] Intelligence personnel would usually want information about the protest in order to write their reports. According to Mas Totok, this made the relationship between the two bodies "mutually symbiotic" because they both needed information from each other.[31] Despite this close relationship with government intelligence agents, PPIP nevertheless cross-checked the information they received from the government intelligence agents with other sources. They often had to wait until a later date to observe events unfolding in order to confirm the information's veracity.

Besides relying on government intelligence agents, members of PPIP had developed their own skills in intelligence and counter-intelligence. Mas Totok explained that PPIP had "borrowed" an educational book on intelligence and counter-intelligence from a police officer several years earlier, when a couple members of PPIP were arrested. He said,

> Usually with intelligence there are a number of stages. The first phase is the investigation. Then there is a phase of counter-intelligence. There is a phase of espionage and a phase of sabotage. These are the stages within an intelligence operation. So if we wanted to search for information about Sheri, what is associated with Sheri when she is in Indonesia? There is a passport or a report about where she lives. From here we can know, and in the investigative phase we can deepen our information.[32]

Within the investigation phase, PPIP also had specific techniques they would employ. Mas Totok explained how they used some of these methods on Pak Didik and a number of his staff. "In order to know more information about a person, we explored who this person had relationships with, and cross-checked that information with journalists, intelligence agents, and other people who were friends of PPIP," he explained.[33] In Pak Didik's case, they did not ask him any questions directly, but went through a friend of PPIP who became close to Pak Didik's staff because the friend went to the same university. "We placed someone to get close to them," Mas Totok said. Once PPIP had made the connection, they instructed their informant to not ask questions directly. Mas Totok role-played an example of how the friend seeking information was trained to speak:

> [The PPIP informant might say,] "What are you busy with now?"
> "Oh, with Mangkubumi Street."

"Oh, Mangkubumi Street, how is that?"

If you have a close relationship with the friend he will be more open, and that person will talk as a friend only. So if we are talking as friends [the member of Pak Didik's staff might ask], "Oh, you are doing research on Mangkubumi?"

I [in the role of the PPIP informant would] act stupid and ask, "How is the case?"

You [in the role of the member of Pak Didik's staff] won't be suspicious, because we are friends.[34]

Successful spying required approaching someone through a friendship – and in that sense, spying was not that different from ethnographic research. But unlike research, such approaches were done without revealing one's true intentions and when people were least suspecting. PPIP did not always share their information and strategies with the Pethikbumi traders, but used the information and strategies as a means to counter the pro-relocation group and the government's strategies. At different times, PPIP also used these tactics on third parties who were involved, including me, and even on the traders they were supporting, as Mas Totok later told me.[35] These "intelligence" tactics were thus not only used on outsiders but also to confirm the loyalties and "real identities" of the Pethikbumi members or the other actors involved with them.

Shadowing Their Members: The Pethikbumi Leaders

The Pethikbumi leaders shared in the performance of a certain masculine trope that acted as a hegemonic ideal and informed their definitions of political success and proper behaviour. This trope was often performed during meetings. In a late-night meeting at the end of August with the general membership of Pethikbumi, Pak Akbar said to the group, "Those who are playing (bermain) may be planning on accepting [the relocation] but look as if they are doing something else [i.e., refusing it]."[36] He said they could know this by the way these "players" acted and that actions were just as important as words. Actions could confirm information the leaders had about a person, and observing the actions of others through surveillance was therefore important.

The Pethikbumi leaders ascertained whether their members were changing sides by placing informants inside the marketplace in the days leading up to the relocation, when the government asked the traders to come to the marketplace to sign up for the lottery for kiosks in the new marketplace. In an early November meeting with BPHK, the

NGO Forum, and members of PPIP, Pak Akbar described how, the night before, he had gone up and down Mangkubumi Street searching for information to see who was lying to him. He knew who had signed up for the lottery for spots because he had informants, but he wanted to see what his members would say to him. He explained:

> When I got to group two[37] [on Mangkubumi Street], I asked Pak Benny how he was; I was fishing (*memancingnya*) for information. He said he would keep fighting [the relocation]. But I knew that he had already registered [for the marketplace]. But he said he would keep fighting. Then I went fishing again, and it turns out lots of people want to play (*bermain*) like that. They want to fight but [they] also registered.[38]

In this case, Pak Akbar had observed the traders' actions (by using an informant to spy on them) and then gone to see what information these traders would reveal to him. He had learned that the information that they had shared with him was false, which allowed him to demonstrate to the rest of the leaders and his members his ability to know the truth through the use of shadow play. Pak Akbar probably did not need to ask these traders to tell him their position, but he likely did this in order to demonstrate to others that words alone could not be trusted. This also served as a form of intimidation vis-à-vis his members since Pak Akbar's actions suggested that these traders were not free to act without consulting their leader first. It also suggested to the traders that they should fear the wrath of Pak Akbar if they did switch sides.

Conspicuous Visibility: Managing Impressions

Alongside the surveillance tactics that the Pethikbumi traders and their supporters used, the group's leaders also had to control and manage information about themselves. To overcome the suspicion that they might be engaged in some kind of shadow play with the government, the Pethikbumi leaders had to manage impressions through *conspicuous visibility*. I draw here from Harms's (2013a) use of the concept of "conspicuous invisibility," by which he describes the ways in which the figure of the Vietnamese boss manages the appearance of his wealth. In the case of the relocation, I use the term *conspicuous visibility* to refer to the practice of purposely making one's position and activities known to others. In the case of the traders, this entailed controlling the gossip and suspicion around their relationships with government officials by providing detailed accounts of their interactions, and by positioning those who did not reveal their true selves as traitors and enemies.

In meetings, Pak Akbar would often declare not only that he knew who had switched sides but also that he had been offered many bribes but had refused them. For example, he said in a meeting with the other Pethikbumi leaders and their NGO supporters that

> within recent days I have been promised many things. I met with the director of the Public Order Police (Dinas Ketertiban), [and] after that I was promised that I would meet with Pak Herry through him. After that I was promised that I would become a government official. I also met with Pak Mulyono [a municipal official] two days ago at Suhada [a mosque] at twelve thirty, and I was promised that if I wanted to move [to Kuncen Marketplace], Pak Galang and I would run the area behind the market-place. I would coordinate the rice and drink sellers if I wanted. So I see that that game is already ugly. It is not a pure game any more. If I wanted to betray my friends, maybe I would have already become a traitor. But I do not want that. I have a responsibility to all my subordinates.[39]

Even when Pak Akbar was not offered something, he told stories about these interactions and the things he could have done but did not because he was a moral person. As Sian Lazar (2008) writes in relation to Bolivia, "Telling a story about corruption generally serves more to highlight the moral integrity of the teller than anything else: corruption is always somewhere else, perpetrated by someone else" (110). Lazar argues that "corruption was the most important trope through which rumor and gossip were used to make and resist claims for power or leadership positions, as well as being a way to evaluate community leaders and articulate values about the use of power" (76). In a similar way, Pak Akbar used this talk of corruption to articulate his allegiances to the traders and to establish their moral high ground against the state. In this same meeting, he told of the following incident:

> Once I faced both Pak Ari and Pak Mulyono, and I could have asked for a transfer of money, and [I could have] said I wouldn't make a deal if the amount wasn't transferred to me by tomorrow at nine. That could have been done. But I did not do that because since I was small I was taught not to. And I will teach my children as well so they uphold their responsibility.[40]

These narratives occurred against the backdrop of the city, where people could expect to be seen essentially anywhere they went. Whether at a coffee shop, mosque, or office, individuals had to operate under the premise that others might see them and know of their meetings. With the decentralization of power from Jakarta to the local level, there has also been an increased need in Yogyakarta city to account for oneself in relation to state power, because political power in the city is shifting with the formation of new relationships among the growing number of political parties, NGOs, and other groups. Unlike other cities such as Jakarta, where there are upscale cafés, restaurants, or hidden massage saunas in which to remain relatively invisible, Yogyakarta city has fewer undetectable locations. Thus, as a relatively small city of half a million people, the spatial environment of Yogyakarta also shapes these practices of conspicuous visibility.

The need to manage impressions and control what could and could not be seen drove Pak Akbar's efforts. His stories of potential corruption described the bribes he had been offered from various government officials or the bribes he could have requested. By naming the specific government officials who had offered him money, jobs, or control of marketplace territory, he made visible to his membership not only the government's involvement in such activities but also his own innocence. This was especially important because Pak Akbar was vulnerable to accusations of corruption as a result of his close involvement with government officials. Instead of leaving these encounters open to interpretation, he provided detailed (and dynamically told) accounts of his interactions in order to signal his commitment to Pethikbumi and its anti-relocation cause, and to make it clear that he was not a traitor and did not need to be watched. Pak Akbar's approach to sharing information with his members and fellow leaders was based on the belief that distrust might be reduced if one openly disclosed one's meetings with government officials through stories that directly addressed people's concerns (corruption, two-faced actions). While surveillance helped people to find out the "truth" about *others*, the practice of conspicuous visibility helped to control information about oneself. The traders did this to ensure that others were not suspicious of them because they were already revealing their activities. The dual use of surveillance and conspicuous visibility were thus attempts to achieve transparency, to bring secrets into the public sphere.

Through these practices of conspicuous visibility, Pak Akbar not only positioned Pethikbumi in moral opposition to the government's corruption; he also drew an equivalence between himself and the image of the Reformasi pemuda, which, as was discussed earlier (see Gender and Pemuda Masculinities, Chapter 1), is a widely known and celebrated figure in Indonesia. As Karen Strassler (2005) explains, "an image of youth as idealistic, 'pure' actors had long been fostered in New Order narratives identifying 'youth struggle' (*perjuangan pemuda*) as the motivating force behind Indonesian history" (279). By detailing his refusal of government bribes, Pak Akbar was able to confirm his role as a hero and maker of history. These stories became "tokens of their own histories," of agency and engagement that could be retold to others (cf. Strassler 2005, 284).[41]

It was not only Pak Akbar who had to engage in the management of impressions but also the Pethikbumi supporters. Pak Toni, chair of the NGO Forum, and Ibu Marini, director of BPHK, claimed that their desire to help the street vendors for free was rooted in their desire to protect the interests of the poor and marginalized in the city. Yet, ironically, their ability to mobilize the traders, and even their lack of stated personal interest, made them susceptible to the claims of citizens, government officials, and street traders that these NGO actors had "unnamed interests" – that is, secret connections to other political interests. As a result, Pak Toni and Ibu Marini each had to regularly reaffirm that they were not receiving money, land, or other pay-offs. Ibu Marini also engaged in corruption talk. On one occasion, during an interview with me, she engaged in practices of conspicuous visibility, even though our interview, conducted one-on-one and in private, was relatively "inconspicuous." Describing how a government official had offered her money in order to handle an earlier relocation, she recounted her response: "I said that I was a lawyer and that I had no other interests, so why should I ask for land." She concluded that the official was trying to do two things: he wanted to test her and he wanted to make her a "silent partner."[42] By telling such stories, both Pak Toni and Ibu Marini tried to make their interests transparent to the traders, to me, and to other supporting organizations such as PPIP.

The Pethikbumi leaders also had to help clarify confusion about where their supporters' interests lay. In a Pethikbumi meeting in November 2007, one of the traders, speaking in front of a large group, said, "Here is Ibu Marini and we must give thanks to her because she fights for our livelihoods and does not receive anything."[43] I often heard the traders make note of this fact in meetings. When I met Mas Arief for the first time, he said to me, "Our movement is pure; there are not any other interests, only the interests of our stomachs. We search for incomes to help our families."[44]

Mas Totok from PPIP also went out of his way in one-on-one conversations with me and the other traders to illustrate his lack of political play in the relocation. During an interview with me he said, "Pak Galang tried to offer me two kiosks but I did not want them because I am not playing there. I am more interested in helping to mentor, that is it. [I'm] not [here] because I'm interested in politics or conspiracy."[45] He declared that PPIP received no money from outside funders, and that it merely wanted to support the people. Yet after the relocation, when his name was included on a list of those who had received a kiosk in the new market, people saw this as evidence that he might have been involved in some backstage play. Like Pak Toni and Ibu Marini, Mas Totok's declaration that he had "no interests" (*tidak ada kepentingan*) made him all the more subject to suspicion.

Conclusion

While in many cities around the world, cameras and other forms of media technology are transforming urban space through surveillance, in places like Indonesia, person-to-person surveillance remains an important feature of the urban landscape, and it is particularly important in shaping urban planning. In fact, we could consider the surveillance practices of both state and citizens as part of the urban planning apparatus. Although it is never talked about openly as part of any urban plan in Indonesia, surveillance plays an important role in shaping how these projects unfold because it reconfigures social relationships and, in some cases, acts as a form of intimidation. While governments, NGOs, and citizens discuss participatory urban planning, surveillance remains a public secret – a tactic of shadow play that is used in Yogyakarta to generate fear and distrust. The targets of this surveillance imagined those doing the surveillance as operating from a hidden place "behind the screen." The fact that the surveillance was partly revealed was oftentimes also a key element of the shadow play; to be effective was to control when and how information moved.

The Pethikbumi traders imagined the state as engaging in surveillance much like it had during the New Order regime, although, with the growing number of political actors on the scene, there was more confusion in the post-Suharto context over who might be working for or against the state. The state was not held at a distance; its agents were imagined as being recruited from neighbours, friends, and even street vendors (cf. Mueggler 2001, 6; Lee 2016). The local government was lodged within the community, and this made people, both unknown and known, equally subject to suspicion. To imagine the state this way was to see it as something both alien and familiar – something to be feared but also something that could be known. The model of New Order governance was thus a resource through which the traders understood the municipal government's power and actions in the post-Suharto era.

The activism of the Pethikbumi leaders and their PPIP supporters can also be viewed alongside the collective memory and practices of the pemuda, especially the youth activists of the late 1990s, when Suharto was forced to step down. These students developed a "repertoire" of masculinist subject positions and techniques to challenge the state (Lee 2016, 210), using state practices for their own ends while operating in a climate in which members of student groups could be unmasked as intel or their informants. The Pethikbumi practices of surveillance and managing impressions should therefore be viewed in light of this "repertoire" and the climate of accusation and suspicion in which it was performed. The imagined community of pemuda or youth activists likely helped the Pethikbumi leaders and their PPIP supporters feel that they were masculine political subjects whose movement was part of a larger history (see Lee 2016, 6; Strassler 2005).

In Indonesia in the democratic era, sensationalized stories about corruption are a common feature in the news (Kramer 2013). These stories are, among other things, a form of public transparency and revelation. Alongside such media, we see new forms of information-gathering and verification taking place on the street among ordinary citizens. I have described how the anti-relocation leaders and their activist supporters shared information ideologies that centred surveillance as an effective way of obtaining information. The act of collecting and revealing information to others operated as a form of power. The traders and their NGO supporters were interested in using surveillance tactics to map state power and to understand how and through whom it worked. They used surveillance to map the actors associated with the state, and even, in the case of Pethikbumi, their own members. In this sense, the Pethikbumi traders and their advocates were using surveillance, an authoritarian tactic, as part of the democratization process.

Although the World Bank and nation states around the world claim that democracy is about transparency and the sharing of information, these organizations have done relatively little to understand how these practices work either for or against democracy. In this chapter, the surveillance practices taken up by the traders and activists worked both for and against democracy. While they used surveillance as a means for transparency, these practices also had a dark side. They included intimidation and secrecy. For some of the traders, this was empowering because they were able to take up these state practices and engage in the culture of revealing. Yet for traders who were the objects of the surveillance, it was less empowering; indeed, it tended to generate fear. The use of state surveillance techniques by the "underclass" and related social movements is a reminder that the state is not a fully separate entity, and that its practices circulate.

The information that the government and the anti-relocation traders collected through surveillance was not shared with the wider public through the media. Instead, it was used in a performative way to assert each group's ability to watch from afar. As a result, the fruits of this watching were shared both with one's own friends and with the other side. In the next chapter, I describe how the Pethikbumi leaders and their supporters participated in shadow play when they used the newspaper as a medium to indirectly reveal some of the "dirty" tactics employed by the government.

Chapter Five

Press Releases and Silent Critiques

On 25 October 2007, the leaders of Pethikbumi gathered at the office of BPHK. They were there to discuss with representatives from BPHK, the NGO Forum, and PPIP the disconcerting events that had taken place two nights earlier. Less than two weeks away from the relocation deadline of October 31,[1] a group of pro-relocation traders had travelled to Mangkubumi Street in the company of preman to collect information about all of the street vendors who were operating there. This was a cause for concern not only because Pethikbumi leaders had not been consulted, but also because of the intimidating presence of the preman, who had been armed with sharp weapons. Most of the Pethikbumi leaders suspected that the municipal government had provided the funds to hire the preman.[2]

With the relocation approaching, the government had asked Pethikbumi's leaders for their members' names and addresses, along with information on the types of merchandise they were selling. Although such data had been collected years earlier, many new traders had since appeared. Indeed, there was uncertainty about whether there would be sufficient space in Kuncen Marketplace to house all the vendors who were to be moved there from three different locations in the city. As a dimension of their resistance to the relocation plan, Pethikbumi leaders had refused to provide the government with this information until the mayor agreed to discuss the possibility of reordering Mangkubumi Street instead of relocating the traders. On one occasion, uniformed government officials went directly to the street to collect data, but the data collection was stopped. Pak Pramana had grabbed the data from an official from the Department of Industry, Trade, and Cooperatives; he then ripped up the papers and threatened the official with violence if he continued. In response, the government officers left the street. Since this data collection had been unsuccessful, the government had pursued another course of action, with the leaders of the pro-relocation vendors (now known as Team 12[3] since they were twelve in number) conducting their night-time census in the company of preman and without the help of government officials.

In the aftermath of this incident, the anti-relocation traders and their supporters were interested in using the press to indirectly share this information about the night-time census with the wider public. Legal-aid supporters and activists had already played a particularly important role in assisting the traders. These middle-class supporters were therefore important mediators from within the local political field who could help the traders to further learn the mechanisms for transparency in the public sphere (see Webb 2012).

Michael Warner (2002), in his book *Publics and Counterpublics*, writes that "publics are essentially intertextual, frameworks for understanding texts against an organized background of circulation of other texts, all interwoven" (16). When a public opposes a dominant ideology and is defined by others as being in opposition to it, Warner argues, this public can be referred to as a *counterpublic* (56). In this chapter, I argue that the anti-relocation traders and their supporters aspired to reach a public whose members were sceptical of the government and who therefore might interpret the traders' indirect accusations against the government favourably. As I will show, by using self-censorship in the process of trying to reach this public, the anti-relocation traders and their supporters also anticipated particular reading practices (Hull 2003). The indirect accusations they shared in the newspapers were comprehensible to the different publics because of a shared assumption that there is a secret side to politics – in other words, shadow play. The work of the Pethikbumi leaders drew attention to the government's stagecraft; it also became a contagious subjectivity.[4] Readers of newspapers were called upon to read between the lines and decipher who was backstage pulling the strings.[5] The Pethikbumi leaders engaged in this practice because they were concerned that a direct accusation could have legal repercussions (such as defamation charges), while an indirect accusation allowed them to communicate their message with less risk. While the traders and their supporters were interested in creating and speaking to a public, the government tried to discredit the vendors' version of events by addressing the indirect accusation directly and demanding proof.

In the mainstream media, transparency is characterized as an important democratic practice. However, transparency is shaped by concealment as much as revelation (Strathern 2000b; Hetherington 2011; Mazzarella 2006; MacLean 2014; Morris 2004). Transparency-seeking practices are also often aesthetic and performative (see Barrera 2013). Marilyn Strathern (1991) has described aesthetics as "the persuasiveness of form, the elicitation of a sense of appropriateness" (10). While the production of information for the newspapers focused on political convictions and content, the form this information took also mattered deeply (see Riles 2001). The revealing and concealing of information in the newspaper by the anti-relocation traders and their supporters, as well as by the government, was performed according to the perceived interests of the audience, with particular attention paid to form. By focusing on how the traders and their supporters released information to journalists, I suggest that an examination of the relationship between form and content can demonstrate how practices of transparency gain authority and legitimacy. Although the "revealing" of this data-collection incident involving preman in the newspaper was an attempt at transparency, it was also an effort to paint a picture for the public of the municipal government's questionable tactics, and therefore to get the public to question the logic of this urban project in general.

Nancy Florida (1995) describes how writers in the Surakarta Palace in the nineteenth century, rather than seeking transparency, sought to produce truth through what she calls the "shimmer of *semu*" (298). *Semu* is about revealing glimpses of an event while maintaining a veil of secrecy. Florida's work on Javanese historical writings and Javanese etiquette point to the fact that, historically, the role of the "unseen" and the veils placed over "truth" were valued political aesthetics. In this chapter, I explore how new desires for democracy and transparency intersect with this shadow play practice of partial revelation. Rather than seeking to reveal the "really real," there is a continuing desire to operate under the shimmer of *semu* – to reveal while also continually concealing, since this is the safest way to operate.

The anthropology of news has increasingly come to focus on the politics of mass mediation from the perspective of journalists (e.g., Boyer and Hannerz 2006; Boyer 2005; Hannerz 2004; Pedelty 1995). While Mark Peterson (2001) describes how journalists interact with political actors in order to get a writeable story, the literature on the politics of mass mediation has focused less on how key actors in urban movements try to interact with and tell their stories to the media. While scholars have recognized that Indonesian journalists engage in self-censorship, I argue that other groups, such as those producing press releases, also engage in occasional self-censorship. I describe how the information ideologies of the street traders and their supporters prompted them to engage in self-censorship before releasing information to journalists, and to only indirectly accuse the government of being involved in the late-night data collection involving preman. They believed that if they gave information to journalists in an indirect fashion, it would be shared in the newspapers in a similar way. In other words, they assumed that the units of discourse would move from their meeting and into the pages of the newspaper (Bauman and Briggs 1990; M. Silverstein and Urban 1996). By sharing information with the public in this way, Pethikbumi and its supporters attempted to reveal the government's shadow play and non-transparent practices.

Newspapers in Indonesia

The role of the Indonesian press has changed significantly throughout the country's history, from a nationalist device during the colonial period (Adam 1995; B. Anderson 1991, 427–49), to a revolutionary instrument during the period of rule by Sukarno (Paget 1967), to a form of control and security under Suharto's authoritian rule (Hill 2006; Sen and Hill 2007; Romano 2003). During this latter phase, the media played an important role in legitimatizing the New Order government (Hill 2006), and as a result it was heavily censored. Journalists faced indirect and direct censorship through the threat of job loss, fines, or physical violence (see Romano 2003). The government largely controlled the information that was printed, and the Ministry of Information banned any newspapers that published articles with sensitive information in them (Tapsell 2012, 230). The Suharto government also continued to support earlier bans on the Chinese-language press, justifying its actions as an attempt to create national unity (Hill 2006, 132).[6]

Despite such censorship, newspaper journalists learned to write "in between the lines" to avoid being banned or fined. For example, Mary Steedly (1993) has described how, when the government killed many so-called thugs in the early 1980s in an effort to re-appropriate their power, the newspapers wrote about the "mysterious marksmen" by using "the wink-and-nudge transparency of newspaper accounts" (226). Another approach that journalists used to critique the New Order government was telling the stories of the victims of its policies (Steele 2011, 86). During this period, it was not uncommon for self-disciplined journalists to use suggestive language and "hidden messages" to communicate with their readerships (Romano 2003, 148).

In the 1990s, the *Kedaulatan Rakyat* newspaper published an article about self-censorship in Indonesia suggesting that any critique of the government should remain outside of the public sphere and be conducted "silently." In this article, entitled "Kritik secar diam-diam, cocok demokrasi 'semi-terbuka'" (Silent critique fits with a "semi-open democracy"), Doctorandus (Drs.) Khairuddin from the Indonesian National Youth Council (Komite Nasional Pemuda Indonesia, or KNPI) explained that many officials were still not open to receiving input or criticism from the community. He went on to state, "therefore, the community is scared (*dikhawatirkan*) that if they openly criticize (*secara terbuka*) [an official], then the official will become defensive (*defensif*) and stand their ground (*bertahan*), and this can bring '*extra-power-nya*' [this term was used in the original text] that will have bad effects (*akan berdampak tidak baik*)." As a result, Drs. Khairuddin recommended that it was better to become what he dubbed a "silent critic" (the English word was used) – that is, someone who delivered input discreetly, away from public channels so that such information could be consumed privately and used to make whatever changes were necessary.[7] Describing a similar phenomenon, Joseph C. Manzella (2000) writes about journalists in Jakarta who in 1997 provided criticism covertly via Indonesian newspapers:

> Journalists did take risks, however. Criticism was covert, and government officials seemed to understand a game was being skillfully played. That game involved elaborate "bridge action" strategies to subvert the system. Those strategies constituted an ongoing negotiation with the Information Ministry that was expressed in a form of an "I dare you to read between the lines" writing style. This style balanced the need to keep government censors at bay with the demands of a newspaper's readership. (316)

During this same period, the government itself also critiqued certain groups in an indirect fashion through the newspapers. The government's concern with communists or political organizing, for example, was often transmitted through newspapers in a similar way, with the reader positioned or cast into the role of a detective. One such article was entitled "Waspada, kelompok tertentu yang ingin mencapai ambisi politik" (Be aware, there is a certain group that wants to achieve its political ambitions).[8] It explained that while the Special Region of Yogyakarta was generally stable, there was nonetheless a risk that a certain "group" was trying to push its political ambitions forward in the region. The group was not named in the article, allowing citizens to imagine who could be involved. These indirect accusations were a powerful means through which the New Order government made civil-society groups aware that they were being watched, thus generating fear and terror and turning public opinion against them. The indirect accusations from both civil society and the government suggested that there was another world, simultaneously dangerous and secretive, outside the public sphere.

The post-1998 democratic reforms in Indonesia meant that people were free to organize against and critique the government in more overt and direct ways (see Manzella 2000, 322).[9] A large number of media watchdog groups emerged during this period to ensure that journalists would take up the democratic ideal of transparency (Spyer 2006, 152). However, there are still examples today of journalists facing threats and physical violence (Steele 2011). Although media censorship has declined since 1998, the role of the media in the post-authoritarian context is far from straightforward (Sen 2011, 2). Krishna Sen (2011), for instance, argues that there are "new modes of speaking and silencing in Indonesia. Sources of restriction are now more amorphous and criticism harder to target" (10). Kirrilee Hughes also argues that local newspaper journalists' low wages and long hours make it tempting for them to accept bribes (known as *kebudayaan amplop*, which literally translates to "envelope culture" – a reference to cash bribes given in envelopes).[10] Journalists in the post-Suharto era engage in self-censorship not necessarily because of government pressure but also because of pressure from the political and business elite (Tapsell 2012, 229). Nine business groups in Indonesia control half the print media and two-thirds of the television stations (Haryanto 2011, 104). Ross Tapsell (2012) argues that journalists "fear reprimands if they write about taboo topics or antagonize the powerful hierarchy" (236). While scholars have recognized that journalists and editors engage in self-censorship, in this chapter, I will show how these information ideologies were also shared among activists and street traders.

The Data Collection and a Direct Accusation

I first heard about the plan to collect data at Mangkubumi Street while attending a meeting on 21 October 2007 between the leaders of the pro-relocation vendors and the government relocation team. Organized by the Department of Marketplaces, the meeting was held in the morning at an office in Beringharjo, the largest marketplace in Yogyakarta. Pak Didik and two of his employees, along with the leaders of the pro-relocation vendor groups and the government relocation team, sat around a long table in a boardroom. There they devised the strategy for data collection. The pro-relocation leaders would go to the street on October 23 and collect the data directly, accompanied by private security (*keamanan*, the more formal and respectable term for preman, was used).

As I sat and listened to the meeting, I was surprised that no one raised any concerns about the plan to use private, non-state security to support the data collection; indeed, this was presented as an entirely legitimate and logical approach. One vendor later explained the reason for this decision: the data collectors might be threatened on the street by Pethik-bumi, and thus needed their own security for protection.[11] Hearing this scenario described in the meeting was nonetheless a difficult moment for me ethically, since I disagreed with this approach to data collection but had to remain silent as I was working hard to stay "neutral" in order to maintain my access to the various parties involved in the relocation. Revealing what I knew would jeopardize my research position, but not saying anything meant that people might get hurt.

That evening, I went over to the office of the Independent group, which was in the house of Pak Sarjadi, the group's treasurer. His house had been converted for this purpose because most of the group's leaders felt that the street was not suitable for meetings or for enlisting people to join the relocation. For months now, most of these leaders had not been selling on Mangkubumi Street. They were busy trying to organize the relocation and felt that Mangkubumi Street was no longer a favourable site for them.[12] Sitting in a sofa chair, I drank tea and discussed with the Independent traders how the relocation was unfolding from their perspective. After discussing more general topics, I took the opportunity to ask them about the data-collection process they were planning to carry out. "Aren't you worried about it starting a conflict?" I asked. One member responded,

> No, we are using security there to guard against the things that we do not wish for. We are not including the institution [the government], only our own members. We have good intentions – to invite them to join in the relocation.[13]

I changed the subject, as I did not want to force what felt like an increasingly awkward conversation. In the minds of the Independent leaders, however, their data-collection process made sense. They would not incite violence but would be protected against it. However, not all of the pro-relocation leaders agreed with this approach. The leaders from the Southern Square decided not to participate because they felt it was not their job to collect data on the Mangkubumi Street traders, and they also saw that this effort was bound to create further tensions, if not physical conflict, between Pethikbumi and the pro-relocation leaders.

On October 23, the night of the data collection, I sat on a bench on Mangkubumi Street chatting with one of the Pethikbumi leaders. I found myself getting anxious, however. I did not know how things would unfold and I was worried that the data collection might spark a violent encounter between the pro- and anti-relocation traders; tensions were already high, and preman would certainly be involved. At around 8:00 p.m., the data collection began. After twenty minutes, approximately eight to ten data collectors reached a Pethikbumi leader, Pak Mujib, who knew that the Pethikbumi leadership had no knowledge of this data collection and had not approved it.[14] Once the Pethikbumi members realized what was happening, they quickly sent text messages and made phone calls to mobilize other Pethikbumi leaders to come to the scene and help stop the data collection. As Pethikbumi members started to gather, I decided to remain across the street, away from the scene.

From what the Pethikbumi leaders told me after the event,[15] the leaders from the pro-relocation vendor groups were moving from vendor to vendor while twenty preman gathered along the southern and northern part of Mangkubumi Street, presumably signalling their control over the area. The exchange between the Pethikbumi leaders and the leaders of the pro-relocation vendors was heated, but it did not escalate any further because these pro-relocation leaders decided not to continue with the data collection after Pak Akbar asked them to provide an official government permit: without it, he argued, they did not have a right to collect data. The leaders from the pro-relocation vendor groups then requested that Pak Akbar provide a personally signed statement demanding that they stop, which he did. Both sides, fearing an escalation, went their separate ways shortly thereafter, with the Independent traders and preman leaving the street.

Once the data collection had stopped, the Pethikbumi leaders gathered together on the opposite side of the street to discuss what had happened. Mas Arief and Pak Akbar described what they had just witnessed, saying they could not believe that the municipal government would send a team to Mangkubumi Street to collect data about the vendors without Pethikbumi's permission. This was clearly another instance where the municipal government had breached any trust they had developed through sosialisasi. Within an hour of the data collection being stopped, there was a strong police presence on the street. This not only suggested that the police were concerned about a potential conflict; it also suggested to all involved that the state had control over Mangkubumi Street.[16]

On 25 October 2007, two days after the data collection, I attended the meeting between the NGO Forum, BPHK, and the leaders of Pethikbumi described at the start of this chapter. The discussion focused on how they could prepare in the case of a similar event. Pethikbumi's BPHK lawyers urged the group to stay united on the street, meaning that all leaders should be present on the street in case a group of preman arrived. Pak Akbar explained that most of the members of Pethikbumi had not yet arrived when the data collection started, and that a series of phone calls had been made to mobilize the leaders. The group, he said, needed to be more prepared and more observant of what was happening on the street.

The meeting then turned to the topic of who was behind the data collection. Pak Akbar immediately blamed one person: Pak Didik, who had close ties to the government and who had joined forces with the pro-relocation leaders in support of the relocation. Pak Akbar claimed to have proof of Pak Didik's involvement because one of the preman who was meant to join the data collection[17] had backed out at the last minute, and he later told Pak Akbar about Pak Didik's role in the collection.[18] Based on this information, Pak Akbar had sent Pak Didik a text message, to which he copied a few members of Pethikbumi. Pak Akbar opened the text message and read it aloud to us at the meeting:

> Before [the data-collection incident] you had a meeting [with the pre-man who accompanied the data collectors]. After that, you gave [the preman] [alcoholic] drinks, and [then] you gave [them] drugs (*pil koplo*)[19] and ... sharp weapons (*senjata tajam*)[20] – that is what I know. Mas Didik, I previously asked you not to create the conditions [for instigating a conflict] like you did [with the data collection] (*jangan dikondisikan seperti tadi*). I know that you are behind this. What was your intention (*maksudya*) in searching for data? [There was] *premanisme* (thuggery) to support the team [Team 12, the pro-relocation vendor leaders],[21] and before starting the data collection, [the preman] were gathered in front of the PLN [an electricity company building] to drink alcohol and be given *pil koplo* and sharp weapons ... For what intention? I have proof (*bukti*) for all of this.[22]

Pak Didik never responded to this accusation and no third party confirmed whether the allegations were true or false.

After the data-collection incident, the Pethikbumi leadership tried to tighten their control over the street by requesting that the coordinator of each group of street traders on Mangkubumi Street[23] phone or text the Pethikbumi leadership if the pro-relocation leaders appeared to be doing anything suspicious on the street. The Pethikbumi leaders decided that if any similar incident transpired, they would try to confront the pro-relocation leaders as a group. It was difficult to stop these leaders entirely, however, because they would often try to chat with the Pethikbumi traders, with the aim of eventually guiding the conversation in the direction of the relocation. As a result, the Pethikbumi leaders clarified that their members should not discuss the relocation on the street because there was already a place to talk about it: with the government, in the municipal offices.

The Press Conference: Constructing a Hidden Message

During this October 25 meeting, the Pethikbumi leadership and their NGO supporters also discussed another topic: their strategy for a press conference they had called for the next day. In this press conference, they planned to discuss two topics: their lawsuit against the government for developing – without consulting the street vendors – a regulation (Pemerintah Kota Yogyakarta 2007) that would make street vending on Mangkubumi Street illegal, and the data-collection incident itself. The choice of whether to accuse Pak Didik (and by extension, the pro-relocation leaders, since Pak Didik was their NGO adviser and organizer) or any government officials of engaging in premanisme was a difficult one. Making such an accusation would pit Pethikbumi's word against that of the accused, especially the government, and the Pethikbumi leaders and their supporters were worried about being charged with defamation.

In the post-Suharto era, various cases have highlighted the potentially serious consequences of "revealing too much" in Indonesia's newspapers. To take one example, in March 2003, Pak Bambang Harymurti, the editor in chief of the weekly news magazine *Tempo*, published an article suggesting that Pak Tomy Winata, a tycoon, was connected to a fire at Tanah Abang Market because he would be able to get a contract to rebuild the marketplace (Steele 2011, 85). Pak Bambang was originally sentenced to one year in jail for libel, although he eventually appealed the case successfully.[24] Many NGOs and journalists complained that this incident should have been processed under the 1999 Press Law rather than as a criminal case, which would have allowed Pak Tomy the right to reply or the court system to impose a fine rather than a jail sentence.[25]

Cases like this led Ibu Marini to advise the Pethikbumi leaders against using specific names because they did not have what she considered sufficient proof that the pro-relocation vendor leaders had engaged in premanisme. In the meeting she said, "If we talk about premanisme, we do not know who is behind it, because if we name one [perpetrator], later we will have to prove [the allegation]. Even though there was a witness … [this] does not equate to providing proof."[26] Pethikbumi had a harder time accepting this fact. Pak Pramana responded by saying, "There was more than one witness, Mbak."[27] He said that they could ask these witnesses – other traders who had observed how events unfolded when the preman were given drugs and weapons – to provide statements. However, Ibu Marini still insisted they not use names.

As she explained, "I am scared that later it will come back to us. If we say that the government did it and we do not have proof, it will be a problem. It is better that we just say that it was premanisme and that we do not know why this emerged."[28] In this context, statements from witnesses were insufficient because they pitted the word of ordinary citizens against that of the state. BPHK had prior experience working with the media, and therefore rather than leaving the self-censorship to journalists, Ibu Marini recommended that she and her allies do it themselves in order to avoid any repercussions.

In the meeting, Pethikbumi's lawyers and NGO supporters recommended that they frame the event as follows: the leaders of the pro-relocation vendors, who were working closely with the government, were collecting data for the relocation from the Mangkubumi Street vendors under the protection of preman. An accusation would not be made directly but the dots could be connected, since the data was being collected for the government's relocation project, and the government surely had to know about it in advance. Pethikbumi's lawyers concluded the meeting by advising everyone who would be speaking at the press conference – including the NGO Forum and Pethikbumi – not to name Pak Didik, any of the pro-relocation leaders, or any government officials; instead, they would say that premanisme had taken place while remaining vague as to who was responsible.[29] In other words, Pethikbumi and its lawyers decided to render their message implicit, allowing the audience to make the connection that someone behind the scenes had organized the thuggery – that someone (a subject position deliberately left blank), with his or her absence, had in fact produced a presence. They imagined that their vagueness would lead readers to interpret the facts themselves and to come to the conclusion that oknum government officials were involved.

Pak Toni from the NGO Forum also suggested that instead of naming people, especially government officials and Pak Didik, the Pethikbumi leaders and their representatives should ask questions. Pak Toni suggested that they ask why civilians joined in the data-collection effort when it was the responsibility of the government, not the community. Ibu Marini agreed and said that they should use language that avoided any charges of criminality. They would suggest that premanisme had occurred because those involved were unconnected citizens who were not affiliated with the matter of street vending, and thus did not have the right to involve themselves in it.[30] Pak Toni said,

> So they were outside the context of the government and outside the context of street vendors. They joined in and they did not have the right, and this is the indicator that it is premanisme. And there is an indicator of

intimidation because [the preman] brought sharp weapons (*senjata tajam*) and came to the location drunk.[31] These are the indicators that there was intimidation. Later [at the press conference] we frame it like this, yeah.[32]

Pethikbumi, BPHK, and the NGO Forum held the press conference on October 26. Several TV and newspaper journalists[33] in Yogyakarta city arrived at BPHK's office and sat cross-legged around the room. Ibu Marini then opened with a discussion of how Pethikbumi had tried to initiate a dialogue with the government concerning the possible renovation of Mangkubumi Street, but the government was only willing to discuss the relocation. She informed the journalists that no agreement had been reached in this more public forum of discussion. She then turned to the important point of the day, the recent data collection:

> Yesterday a concern emerged when there was a collection of data by Team 12 that was supported by around twenty people, and [the traders] from Pethikbumi said that [these people] were preman because [the traders] saw dark jackets (*jaket gelap*)[34] and these people had big builds (*badannya besar-besar*). [The preman] came with Team 12, who did [the data collection] in the name of the city government (*Pemkot*), who wanted to collect this data. This was done without coordinating with our friends [Pethikbumi]. When [Pethikbumi] saw it – others can later report on this – when [Team 12] started to collect data, there was almost turmoil.[35]

Ibu Marini paused briefly and then continued:

> The question then becomes, why did [Team 12] ask for the signature of the leader of Pethikbumi before they were prepared to stop the data collection? Indeed, in order to stop the conflict, Mas Akbar wrote a document that demanded that they stop the data collection and then signed it. We only know that Team 12 brought the document. When we asked [the government] why there was the data collection by Team 12, they said that they did not order them to do the data collection. And when my friends [Pethikbumi] the next day met with Pak Galang and Pak Sugianto [two government officials] from the relocation team ... they said that they never instructed [Team 12] to collect the data. Even if there was [to be a] data collection, it should be done by a government agency, and they must be in official uniforms. And this was not the first [such incident].[36]

By mentioning that the pro-relocation leaders had asked for a signature before stopping the data collection, Ibu Marini wanted to suggest that the data collection was in fact a formal initiative and that the pro-relocation leaders required the signature to report back to the government. When Ibu Marini concluded her speech by saying that this was not the first time that the government had done something like this, she was once again using insinuation, leaving her comment open to interpretation rather than providing details. She was, however, referring back to the previous Ramadan, when a group of men wearing dark clothes (*berpakaian gelap*) had appeared on Mangkubumi Street saying that they were searching for one of the Pethikbumi leaders. These men had generated fear among the Pethikbumi leaders that violent thugs were potentially seeking them out.

The press conference was then turned over to Pak Akbar, who reported further on the case:

> Peace be upon you (*Assalamualaikum wa rahmatullahi wa barakatuh*). It is true what Ibu Marini said earlier, that Mangkubumi has become a place where lots of different sides are at play. We do not know everyone who is behind them, [but] what is clear is that behind them are preman. We do not know who the preman are, but what is clear is that they are outsiders (*orang asing*).[37]

When Pak Akbar said, "We do not know everyone who is behind them," he was taking up Ibu Marini's advice that they avoid naming the people involved.[38] The preman were thus positioned as stand-ins for those unnamed individuals who were operating from beyond the street. Pak Akbar then highlighted that the street was the site of "play" for a multitude of different actors, many of whom were unknown to Pethikbumi and its supporters.

Thus, rather than asking the journalists to construct the hidden message, the NGOs, lawyers, and street vendors did it for them. They shared an information ideology often practised by Indonesian journalists and their readers – namely, that overly sensitive material that is hard to prove should be transmitted through hidden messages; people will understand these messages, and the senders of those messages (whether journalists or others) will be protected.

Charles L. Briggs and Daniel C. Hallin (2016) describe *mediatization* as the "transformations occurring as media become increasingly central to social life" (9). They examine some of the ways in which scholars of political communication have described how "older logics of political actions centering on institutions like parties and trade unions were displaced and transformed by new, mediatized forms of politics" (9). For instance, political candidates are "increasingly 'marketed' to publics, [who are] conceived of as aggregations of individual consumers" (9). In this new era, professionals trained in media skills are an important component of politics (9). In fact, media logics are now part of the culture and practice of politics (Strömbäck 2008). From the observations described above, we can see that the Pethikbumi street vendors, their lawyers, and their PPIP and NGO Forum allies relied on and interacted with the media in order to advance their advocacy, and they incorporated this logic into their political strategies.

Despite Pethikbumi's willingness to use the media to challenge the government, not all citizens are in a position to communicate their concerns to the government and public in this way. For example, the Chinese Indonesian shop owners – whose letter of complaint had originally prompted government discussions about relocating the vendors (see Citizens as Stakeholders: Moving towards the Relocation, Chapter 2) – did not engage with the media. When I asked Pak Nurdin, one shop owner along Mangkubumi Street, why he and his colleagues did not use the newspapers to air their criticisms of the street vendors, he said, "Because there are a lot of [shop owners] of Chinese descent. Instead of causing a conflict" – he paused and looked down – "well, we still are not free to speak."[39] Pak Nurdin was referring to the history of discrimination experienced by ethnic Chinese in Indonesia. So, rather than sharing their concerns through hidden messages in the media, the shop owners instead worked through less visible channels – in this case, by organizing meetings with government officials.

The Released Story and Its Repercussions

On October 26 and 27, several newspapers based in Yogyakarta city published articles on the topic of the relocation.[40] Not all of these articles mentioned the intimidation that the Pethikbumi traders faced in the data-collection incident, although many did.

On the twenty-sixth, *Kedaulatan Rakyat* published an article on the relocation that described Pak Herry Zudianto's belief that in five years' time Kuncen Marketplace would be an important economic centre in Yogyakarta. The article notes the various efforts that Pak Herry planned to undertake to promote the new marketplace, such as organizing door prizes to attract new customers. In the last half of the article, Pak Akbar is reported to have said that the government had proposed the concept (*konsep*) of the relocation to Pethikbumi, but that the Pethikbumi traders were still refusing to accept the relocation in any form. The article then mentions the data-collection incident:

> Pak Akbar admitted that there are a small number of traders who agree
> [with the relocation] but that is because there was intimidation from a

team that appears to be created by the Yogyakarta City government (*dari sebuah tim yang diindikasikan dibentuk oleh Pemkot Yogya*). The intimidation was done by approaching traders using ways that are the nature of pre-manisme (*Ujud intimidasi tersebut dilakukan dengan mendekati pedangan dengan cara-cara yang sifatnya premanisme*).[41]

In contrast, when the data-collection incident was reported in *Merapi* newspaper the following day, October 27, it appeared under the headline "Gubernur beri apresiasi: Klithikan Mangkubumi diintimidasi" (The governor gives his appreciation: Second-hand traders on Mangkubumi are intimidated).[42] Described in the second half of the article, the incident was reported with passive sentence constructions and thus evaded any direct accusation of the government. The article stated:

> Pethikbumi confessed that they were subjected to intimidation from a group under the name of Team 12, [who were] supported by the municipal government of Yogyakarta. They [Pethikbumi] were pressured two times in their opinion as twenty preman accompanied them [Team 12]. Pethikbumi thinks the intimidation is taking place because they are refusing to move to Kuncen Marketplace.[43]

The blame was openly placed on the leaders of the pro-relocation vendors, although a connection was nonetheless drawn to the government because of its support of the group.

An article published in *Radar Jogja* on October 27 described how BPHK, as the legal support for Pethikbumi, was asking the municipal government not to proceed with the relocation until there had been a decision on Pethikbumi's lawsuit against the municipal government. In addition, the article reported that BPHK had asked that the government not use repression or violence towards the traders:

> "There have been traders who have already been intimidated," said Ibu Marini to journalists the other day. On the 23rd of October at around 8:00 p.m., the traders were intimidated by a number of people who were operating on behalf of the city government (*mengatasnamakan pemkot*). They call themselves Team 12. The team of about 20 people collected data from the traders. Twenty guards suspected of being preman by the traders brought sharp weapons (*senjata tajam*). There was the smell of alcohol coming from their mouths.[44]

In the same article, a government official, Pak Winoto, responded to the accusation that the municipal government had engaged in intimidation. In his role as assistant secretary of development, he was quoted as saying, "This is a lie (*Ini fitnah*)! This is a lie (*kebohongan*) that is felt by the community (*meresahkan masyarakat*)." The article goes on to describe Pak Winoto's thoughts on the subject: "In his opinion, the municipal government has been following the procedures all along. Pak Winoto asks Pak Akbar to withdraw his statement." Pak Winoto was then quoted as saying, "If not, we will file a summons and take legal action to resolve this false statement."[45]

The government's response to the accusation of intimidation was also reported by *Merapi* on October 28. In an article entitled "Pethik-bumi galang tanda tangan: Pemkot bantah intimidasi" (Pethikbumi gathers signatures: The government denies the intimidation),[46] Pak Winoto once again opposed the claim and requested that Pak Akbar retract his statement: "Ini kebohongan yang dapat meresahkan masyarakat, fitnah besar" (This is a lie felt by the community; it is a significant slander). He told the newspaper that the government had taken all necessary procedural steps and communicated with the sellers. He also said that Pak Akbar should retract his statement unless he can prove that the municipal government really had intimidated them: "Silakan buktikan, jika tidak bisa membuktikan Pemkot dengan sangat terpaksa juga akan melakukan upaya hukum yang lain" (Please try to prove it, if you cannot prove it the municipal government will be forced to use other legal processes). Insofar as it failed to explain, for example, why the preman had appeared that night, the government's response was rather indirect. And yet it also made a direct counter-accusation when it demanded proof, recognizing how the public likely interpreted the traders' and supporters' original indirect accusation.[47]

The government's counter-accusation also claimed that Pak Akbar specifically – rather than all of Pethikbumi, or any or all of its supporters – was lying. In doing this, the government shifted the focus of its accusation by effectively redefining the subject of the disagreement. Pak Akbar was asked to account for his claim. Where was the proof? The government situated the story as a lie, not only to municipal officials but to the entire community, thus painting Pak Akbar in a negative light and publicly eroding his credibility. The government did not explain why the preman appeared that night or why the data collection was done or whether the government knew about it. It merely asked for proof. Yet both versions of the event (the government was responsible for intimidating the traders, or this was just a lie) left room for some suspicion. There was no moment of "truth" because there was no outside source used to verify the different competing claims.

I found it curious that no one, not even the journalists, tried to find out what really transpired that evening by interviewing different street vendors or individuals from the neighbourhood. The journalists, for their part, merely reported what both parties were saying. This was in keeping with Lukman Solihin's (2008) observation that *Merapi*'s criminal coverage is not presented as an investigation, but rather as a simple narrative. It is also written in a way that makes it appear politically neutral, since readers are only offered information about crime as it relates narrowly to the law (68). Janet Steele (2011) also argues that "a 'New Order mindset' still pervades the professional practice of journalists [in Indonesia], and is reflected in a style of reporting that includes a lack of context, too much privileging of official sources and an inclination towards reporting on events rather than underlying causes" (86). Many of the newspapers that reported on the data-collection incident nevertheless served as a medium through which Pethikbumi's story could enter the public sphere, thereby encouraging others to interpret this information. It was these two opposing stories, and journalists' seeming lack of interest in analyzing the differences between them, that created the contagious subjectivity that enabled strangers to place themselves in the role of understanding who might be responsible for the incident between the traders and the data collectors.

The Pethikbumi leaders and their supporters understood that newspapers are not only a place where transparency can be practiced; they are also a medium for shadow play and a place where politics gets done. Both the anti-relocation traders and their supporters, as well as the municipal government, tried to speak to the reading public through newspapers. The public to which they were speaking was a sceptical one; it assumed that government officials were corrupt, dishonest, and engaged in questionable practices. The choice of the street vendors and their supporters to communicate through the newspapers could be viewed as reproducing certain information practices from the New Order era – namely, releasing information in the newspapers and highlighting the limits of "openness." While the Pethikbumi leaders and their supporters sought to draw upon the public's ability to interpret their indirect accusations, the municipal government sought to win over the same public by calling out this practice and threatening legal action. Newspapers constituted the principal ground on which the conflict between the street vendors and the government was waged. (It is worth noting here that social media platforms like YouTube or Twitter were not widely used by Indonesian street traders at the time as a means to communicate information about themselves.) While the government could not deny the anti-relocation traders media space, it did seek to deny their version of events and to have the last word.

Conclusion

The Pethikbumi press conference involved the enactment of a familiar narrative that left some information missing: a performance that people, both the media makers (journalists, NGOs, traders) and consumers, were familiar with. Like most press conferences, it depended on an imagined audience of potential readers who could be reached through the journalists who attended the press conference. The NGOs, lawyers, and street vendors constructed their "hidden message" even before the journalists wrote their stories. This indicates that the hidden-message approach is a shared information ideology not only among journalists but also among a wider spectrum of individuals who engage with the media regularly. While journalists might still practise self-censorship because of pressure from media owners, the political and business elite, and editors, it is clear that some actors do so because they fear legal reprisal. In the case described in this chapter, the traders and their supporters sought to privilege a type of speech that could then be translated directly into a written or spoken form for larger circulation. Underlying the press conference was the use of concealment as a way to achieve transparency. Indirect revelation, however, turned the newspapers into one of the sites where each side (the anti-relocation traders and their supporters on the one hand, the government on the other) tried to win over public opinion and trust. In this scheme, the desire to reveal information was also deeply entangled with the pursuit of legitimacy and a good reputation. For the traders and their supporters, indirect transparency was a conduit for challenging the legitimacy of the state and its urban project while depicting their own movement as a victim of state intimidation.

It is only within the past ten years that ordinary citizens in Indonesia have begun to have more access to the newspapers, a medium that allows different groups to reach a larger public. In this case involving the Pethikbumi traders, we have witnessed how the desire for transparency was manifested as a form of indirect communication in the newspapers that was nonetheless recognizable to the parties involved; in fact, the government responded as if this was a form of direct communication. The use of hidden messages to reveal information existed during the New Order period, when the government raised concerns about political organizations in the newspapers without naming them directly. However, in the wake of the conflict between Pethikbumi and the municipal government, the traces of information that appeared in the newspapers provided readers with "clues" about how to comprehend the hidden story of this incident. It thus positioned readers as like-minded individuals who were encouraged to engage in the same process of using the proffered "clues" to "solve" this story.

Although I did not collect specific reactions to these articles, I have since confirmed with my informants that everyone familiar with the culture of writing and reading newspaper articles in Yogyakarta city would have known how to interpret these messages. The practice of reading between the lines is rarely talked about explicitly among ordinary citizens, but the existence of such a practice amounts to a sort of common knowledge among the reading public in Indonesia. It was ultimately that public, then, that was left to decide who was telling the "truth" and who was involved in the construction of a fake plot. The journalists only relayed the information and did not seek out an investigative role. Even though these indirect accusations seemed to indicate a lack of openness in Indonesian society, they also played a central part in reconstituting a public in which strangers can act collectively to challenge corruption, graft, and political play. The potential "truthfulness" of the claims depended on whether they were revealed and concealed in the right way; the right way meant not revealing – at least not directly – who the accusation was against. These claims then helped to generate a shared sense of contemporaneity based on a common past of silence and repression under the New Order.

The data collection performed by the pro-relocation leaders and their preman backers can be viewed as a form of shadow play on the part of the government and Pak Didik. It was seen as such because the municipal government organized the data collection and involved the preman while trying to hide its own role. In turn, this created uncertainty and fear because the government denied its involvement while preman appeared with weapons on the street. Rather than accepting this practice of shadow play, however, the Pethikbumi leaders tried to get to the bottom of how the data collection came about. Even though they ultimately decided that they had insufficient evidence to try to bring criminal charges against the municipal government, or even to accuse the government publicly, the Pethikbumi leaders and their allies tried to connect the dots back to the state. As a result, they decided to reveal this practice of shadow play to the public in a press conference that involved its own forms of shadow play. However, these revelations did not so much challenge the state's shadow play as reinforce the idea that it had the power to operate in hidden ways. The revelations did, however, show the government and the public that the Pethikbumi leaders and their supporters could engage in their own kind of shadow play by concealing and revealing information in the newspapers.

Finally, in this chapter I explored what happened when new desires for democracy and transparency intersected with ongoing fears about potential legal retaliation in the case of an accusation against the government. In the context of the vendor relocation to Kuncen Marketplace, I found that the NGOs, lawyers, and Pethikbumi leaders attempted to reveal information about the municipal government in an indirect fashion, and that these efforts were met with some success. Their message was received by the reading public, and it was also challenged directly by the municipal government with legal threats (with the government then taking no further action). In the next chapter, I explore how the anti-relocation traders and the state engaged in the "talk of violence" in a way that also involved the strategic revealing and concealing of information in both public and private settings. The ability to decide when and how information is revealed, and to control its circulation through different channels, was and remains an important way of doing politics in Yogyakarta city.

Chapter Six

The Talk of Violence

When I started studying the vendor relocation to Kuncen Marketplace, it had not entered my mind that it might lead to physical conflicts between the state and the street traders. Yet as tensions increased, I was so convinced by circulating rumours of forthcoming violence that I actually called the Canadian Embassy, explaining to them that I was studying a street vendor relocation. I wanted to let them know about the rising tensions so that they could support me if I was arrested or faced any serious threats in the coming weeks. Most of the street vendors hoped that the conflict with the government would not reach the point of violence, and some with more experience pointed out that this talk of potential violence was a regular aspect of these relocations. When the anti-relocation street vendors talked about violence, they were referring to the possibility that the Satpol PP or the police would use force to physically remove them and that the traders themselves might resist these efforts or use violence in response. It was not uncommon in Indonesia for physical altercations to erupt between traders[1] and Satpol PP officers during removals or evictions (e.g., Gibbings 2016). The Pethikbumi leaders had regularly watched violent clashes between Satpol PP and vendors play out across the archipelago on the evening news. Most traders in Yogyakarta had heard stories from friends who had moved from other cities such as Jakarta, where Satpol PP was known to be particularly repressive. Traders were also aware through the news that street vendors faced violent evictions around the world. Pethikbumi thus tried to prepare for this possibility; if a physical altercation took place, it was likely that some of the traders might end up in jail, and as a result, discussions took place about how they should respond in such a scenario.

The closer the relocation date loomed, the more unrealistic it seemed to hope for a solution through dialogue and democratic means. Neither the government nor the Pethikbumi leaders saw any progress from their attempts at dialogue through sosialisasi. As mentioned earlier (see Getting Close and Speaking Their Language, Chapter 3), on 6 July 2007, Pethikbumi asked LOD DIY to mediate the conflict. For the government, relocation was the only possibility; for Pethikbumi, renovation of the existing street – not relocation – was the answer. With no resolution in sight, the possibility of violence entered into the discussion. This talk of violence accompanied a mounting panic and a breakdown of communication between the government and the Pethikbumi traders. Eventually, on October 25, the original October 31 government deadline for the relocation was pushed back to November 10 because of the continuing disagreement between the municipal government and the anti-relocation traders, and because LOD DIY had recommended that the government not move forward with the relocation until a solution was found (Santoso, Budi, with Lembaga Ombudsman Daerah Istimewa Yogyakarta 2007).

Pemberton (1994) briefly describes how, during the 1982 election in the city of Surakarta (often referred to as Solo), rumours buzzed through the local food stalls about a possible moment of upheaval, known as a *saat* (5–6). This election campaign occurred at a time in the New Order period when elections were largely presented as "free," regardless of the fact that they were always contrived and controlled. They were shaped, however, by a momentary feeling that something revolutionary and radical might happen, only for that feeling to quickly pass. Talking about the possible saat was an important part of generating such a moment and making it move across the city.[2] From my perspective on the streets, the mounting crisis of the relocation was reminiscent of Pemberton's description of a saat – there was a growing feeling that something would happen.

During the Suharto era, social unrest was relatively uncommon, and when it did take place it was quickly eliminated. Pemberton describes how politics, including the holding of elections, were positioned within the realm of culture and ritual. For instance, the government called the 1982 election a "Festival of Democracy" (*Pesta Demokrasi*), framing it as a national ritual rather than a political event. As Pemberton argues, "the 'successing' of New Order national events such as the Festival of Democracy depends, to a significant extent, on the everyday sense of customary orderliness and stability that has accompanied the post-1965 emergence of a cultural discourse routinely anchored in constructs like 'tradition,' 'origins,' and 'ritual'" (10). The maintenance of this order required violence or the threat of violence.

In the post-Suharto era, while the concern for peace and order is still pertinent in Indonesia in general, it is particularly strong in Yogyakarta

because the provincial government, the Sultan, the municipal government, and Yogyakartans in general view the city (and region) as an
important site of "culture" and "tradition" in Java. Many, including the
Kraton of Yogyakarta (Royal Palace), declare Yogyakarta to be the "center of Javanese tradition" because of the Sultan's continuing importance
and because of the city's religious significance (Woodward 2010, 5). Slogans posted on billboards across the city, such as "Yogyakarta Berhati
Nyaman" (Yogyakarta is the Heart of Comfort),[3] remind residents to
keep Yogyakarta orderly, clean, and friendly.

People I met in Yogyakarta were proud of their city; they said it
was safe because it was a place where nothing happens. Many people
described to me how Yogyakarta was different because during the fall
of Suharto, Yogyakarta, unlike Jakarta and elsewhere, remained peaceful. The city was said to have experienced few moments of violence in
comparison to places like Poso in Central Sulawesi, which had experienced a "religious conflict"[4] after the fall of Suharto. This ideal picture
circulated – and continues to travel – through newspapers, television,
billboards, and tourist websites, both in Yogyakarta and beyond.

In this chapter, I describe how the relocation to Kuncen Marketplace
generated buzz around the possibility of a saat, and how these rumours,
which had circulated informally among the traders, eventually entered
the daily press. Discussions in the newspapers about the possibility of
violence included the voices of government officials, NGOs, the public
(here meaning ordinary citizens), and traders. In keeping with the post-
Suharto ideal of transparency, the anti-relocation traders tried to use
both newspapers and in-person meetings to ask for clarification from
the government regarding its potential use of violence. These traders
wanted to shift the discussion from one of mere rumour to one based
in fact, in this case by extracting a promise from the government that it
would not use repressive force.

Underlying this talk of violence was the fear that any violence associated with the relocation might fuel pre-existing religious and ethnic tensions in the city. This fear had a different regime of circulation, however,
surfacing in face-to-face rumours and discussions, on T-shirts that some
Pethikbumi members wore, and only appearing in the newspapers in
an indirect fashion. These fears were fuelled by the involvement of ethnic and religious networks (*jaringan*) from across the city and possibly
beyond. I show in this chapter how newspapers became both a site of
shadow play and a vehicle for the pursuit of truth.

Violence is connected to its representations, and narratives of violence can be an important part of generating violent acts. Charles L.
Briggs (2007) argues that "violence is inseparable from how we imagine

knowledge of it to be produced and circulated and how we are interpellated in this perceived process" (338). Different narratives of past violence can also have an important impact on shaping accountability and curbing violence in the present (Drexler 2006, 323). The talk of potential violence can help to create violent encounters, but it can also be used to reduce such instances. Using newspapers to talk about the potential of state violence allowed the anti-relocation traders to pressure the government to avoid using violent force against them. Moreover, as will be discussed in this chapter, when positioning themselves in less public forums as potential *agents* of violence, these traders drew on the fears shared by the government officials and the wider public – again, in order to pressure the government to avoid the use of force against them.

The "talk of violence" among the street vendors therefore both created and addressed certain fears. It was peculiarly performative in that the rumour of impending violence was spread in an effort to prevent that violence.[5] For the anti-relocation traders, fear came from the consumption of newspaper and television stories about violent street vendor evictions in Indonesia, and from their past experiences with the state (such as its use of thugs to intimidate them or the unusual circulation of documents). Although there were many ways in which the traders dealt with this fear, they addressed it first and foremost through talk (Barker 2009; Caldeira 2000).

In Teresa Caldeira's *City of Walls* (2000), she argues that the everyday "talk of crime" in São Paulo facilitated "a language for expressing the feelings related to changes in the neighborhood, the city, and Brazilian society more generally" (19). By talking in the newspapers about violence, the traders and other political actors communicated to the public their fear of violence in an environment where "peace" and "order" were under threat.[6] But in another narrative that circulated at this time, especially among the traders, their supporters, and the government, the traders positioned themselves as a force that the state and society should fear. This different "talk of violence" indexed other kinds of fears – namely, the political and religious transformations taking place across Indonesia and the reshaping of power relations in cities. In moments when Pethikbumi was associated with the possibility of violence, the traders assumed a threatening masculinity and potential criminality, not unlike how poor urban youth of lower-class origins are often viewed (see Lee 2016, 96).

In this chapter, I explore how engaging in urban politics and protesting the government requires an ability to strategically produce information and control the channels through which it circulates. I argue that the anti-relocation traders engaged in the "talk of violence" in the two different ways noted above in order to influence the state's implementation of the relocation project. The first positioned the traders as potential victims (*korban*) of state violence. As noted, the traders engaged in this talk to pressure the government not to use violence against them. This also had an ironic effect because, as the Pethikbumi leaders communicated their fears more widely, they made their members more afraid of what might happen. In the second talk of violence, the traders positioned themselves as potential perpetrators (*pelaku*) of violence. This was used to make the government less certain about the relocation project's potential impact on "peace" and "order" in the city. The Pethikbumi leaders were able to move between the subject positions of victim and perpetrator so fluidly because both positions represented moral claims against the state (see Lee 2016, ch. 4).

Moving between these two subject positions, the anti-relocation traders "played" with information and information ideologies in order to generate different results. While one could consider their discussion of violence in the newspapers as a transparency-seeking practice, in meetings with government officials this language revealed their interest in manipulating information in less transparent ways, as was seen in the discussion of surveillance in Chapter 4: Democratizing Surveillance. In order to effectively oppose the government, the anti-relocation traders had to engage in what could be considered "non-transparent" practices. If playing with information was an important part of opposing the government, then being "transparent" took a back seat. The ability to decide when and how information would be revealed and circulated was perhaps the most important tactic of effective resistance.

Newspapers: The Talk of Violence

In the lead-up to the relocation, the possibility of violence was discussed in the newspapers among members of parliament and the traders' supporters, with both groups raising concerns about whether the government would be repressive towards the traders once the relocation deadline arrived. In *Merapi*, the NGO Forum asked the mayor not to use violence when the deadline for selling on the street was reached. The article quoted Pak Cahaya from the NGO Forum as saying that "the mayor always campaigns not as ruler, but as the leader of the community of Yogyakarta. So to act repressively towards the street traders breaks Regulation 65, 2006, about human rights."[7] The government, traders, NGOs, and general public assumed that violence was a possibility. It therefore needed to be talked about so it could be prevented.

In *Kedaulatan Rakyat*, an unnamed individual was quoted as saying, "If there is protest, there will be a reaction. We are scared that Yogyakarta, up until now filled with friendliness, will be ruined if the regional government takes repressive action like that. The government should prioritize dialogue and not use repressive actions in moving the traders."[8] This individual was described as being on a "side that was scared if the municipal government went ahead with the relocation according to schedule." According to the article, on November 1 the parliament's Second Commission asked the executive of the municipal government to solve the problem of the Pethikbumi group refusing the relocation. Pak Zuhrif Hudaya, a member of the DPRD, told the newspaper, "Everything has to be discussed as well as possible. No side should feel that they have won or lost. Please solve the problem [of opposition to the relocation] first, and let's not get to the point where there is a person (*ada rakyat*) who is injured (*terluka*)." As was also noted in the article, members of parliament expressed their fear that if the relocation continued according to schedule, "new problems would emerge."[9]

Political parties also weighed in. In *Kompas*, Pak Syukri Fadholi from the PPP, who supported the relocation and was vice mayor during the early discussions over the project, said that the municipal government had already increased its communication with the traders: "With this, the possibility of things that are not wished for, such as violence (*seperti tindak kekerasan*) during the process of moving [the traders], can be reduced (*bisa diredam*)."[10] On 5 November 2007, *Kedaulatan Rakyat* also published an article whose title tried to instruct the government: "Jalan panjang menuju relokasi PKL: Menata klithikan tanpa kekerasan" (Long road to street trader relocation: Organize the klithikan without violence). The article continued: "As the date approaches, the voices of the traders who are refusing can still be heard. Yet the city government has remained adamant in its decision to relocate the traders to Kuncen Marketplace. Social upheaval must be stifled (*Gejolak sosial harus diredam*)."

In these newspaper articles, state officials, party leaders, and the supporters of the traders echoed the possibility of violence, often in vague and indirect ways. There was a fear that one incident of violence might lead to widespread conflict across the city. The more the possibility of violence was discussed in the newspapers, the more people hoped that violence would be avoided, and the more they mobilized to prevent it. In some sense, this discourse rejecting violence reaffirmed the image of Yogyakarta as a peaceful city. Each of these newspaper articles covered what might happen in the near future, and they included quotes from important officials and political figures in the city reaffirming the need for calm and speaking out against the possibility of violence. However, the stories avoided describing who beyond the traders might be involved in an outbreak of violence, thus concealing part of the story.

This discourse also operated on more than one level at once. The talk of violence was also representative of other kinds of fears that were not always talked about openly – namely, fears of religious and political violence in the city (see Caldeira 2000). These fears were related to transformations taking place in Yogyakarta, and across Indonesia more generally, during the democratic transition. As religious and ethnic tensions surfaced across the country, middle-class Yogyakartans felt new anxiety about the stability of their city. And as the relocation deadline approached, the fear of social unrest was projected onto the state, which was seen as partly responsible for ensuring that the relocation unfolded without violence. This talk of violence in the public sphere was therefore a way of trying to hold the government accountable; ironically, it also had the effect of generating more fear about whether violence would take place.

Playing with Information

With frustration building among the Pethikbumi leaders due to the municipal government's choice to ignore their concerns about the relocation, on 12 September 2007, the group held yet another protest against the government relocation (protests had been held every few months since Pethikbumi formed in January of that year). T-shirts that read *Laskar Mangkubumi Tolak Relokasi* (Mangkubumi soldiers refuse the relocation) had been printed by the dozens and distributed to members before the protest.[11] Although not all members wore the T-shirt, the slogan connected this dispute to larger conflicts. The term *laskar* (paramilitary group) suggested that Pethikbumi was forming just such a group. In Indonesia, many of the more extreme Islamic paramilitary groups have the word *laskar* in their organizational titles, such as Laskar Jihad (Holy War Fighters), Laskar Pembela Islam (Force for Defending Islam), and Laskar Mujahidin Indonesia (Indonesian Holy Warriors Force). Besides these Muslim organizations, various other militant youth organizations use the term *laskar,* and these groups have appeared in support of political parties, mass organizations, and the ruling government (Hasan 2002, 145–6).

In private, many of the leaders of Pethikbumi were not ready for this kind of paramilitary clash. Later, at a September 17 Pethikbumi meeting at which some members expressed their displeasure with the use of the *Laskar Mangkubumi* name, Mas Arief would explain the rationale behind the T-shirts:

> So why the name *Laskar Mangkubumi*? Because first we want to exert pressure [and show] that we are committed and ready to fight the relocation. Even if the reality on the ground is different later, in the media [the possibility of violence] has been raised already. That was our intention: [to send a message to the media], not war. If I'm honest, if there is a fight, I would run first. But if I am challenged I will be the first to be brave too. We hope that making these shirts will not be divisive or reduce our momentum.[12]

Mas Arief's explanation suggested that *Laskar Mangkubumi* had a double meaning. On the one hand, the Pethikbumi leaders wanted to show others in the public sphere that they were not afraid of bloodshed. On the other, the Pethikbumi leaders were far from ready, mentally or physically, for any kind of violent encounter with the state. Nonetheless, the laskar groups and martyrs provided a "Power-full experience" upon which Pethikbumi could symbolically draw (see B. Anderson 1990). In this case, language was not meant to represent reality – it was meant to generate the idea that violence was possible and that the Pethikbumi were willing to fight. If Pethikbumi was at other times worried about language representing the "truth," here they consciously took advantage of this confusion, playing into existing fears about the growing number of militant groups across Indonesia.

At the September 12 protest, a group of several hundred street vendors and activists (mostly university students),[13] some of whom were wearing the T-shirts, started out at the DPRD parliament building and marched to the gates of the municipal government complex. The protesters yelled slogans and demanded to meet immediately with the mayor. After waiting outside the gates for several hours, the leaders of Pethikbumi were invited to speak with government officials inside the complex. I accompanied them as they moved through the corridors to a small meeting room, where we were ushered into a space with a table that was far too small for everyone. Key Pethikbumi leaders sat at the table while the others (including myself) stood within hearing distance along with the few journalists who had been allowed in. The street vendors wanted to meet with the mayor directly, not the lower-level officials, but as usual they were told he was busy.

The meeting began like most others, with a government official explaining the rationale for the relocation. This was not a new project, the official argued; the government had been planning it for years. The official continued to defend the recent draft of the regulation that would make street vending on Mangkubumi Street illegal (see Shadow Play with Sosialisasi, Chapter 3). He stated that it should not surprise the vendors because it had emerged from earlier regulations, and he suggested that Pethikbumi and the government try to work together to resolve their problems. The government hoped that the relocation would be done peacefully and smoothly, he said – again reinforcing the necessity of an outward appearance of order. A few of the assembled leaders, however, expressed their exhaustion with this typical government story, which in their view ignored just how undemocratic the relocation process had been. The conversation quickly switched to the subject of what would happen when the final deadline for selling on the street passed. One member of Pethikbumi at the table said,

> If [the relocation] is done repressively (*cara represif*) we will just battle. Because it is what the government wants. We are already certain that the sellers on Mangkubumi do not want to move. If we are forced to move that means blood will be spilled. Is that what you want? Chaos or riots to develop? (*Keributan dan kerusuhan yang akan berkembang?*). And if that happens, it can be like Poso. We do not want chaos, but the regulation is given as the reason we must move on October 31. These men here [the government officials], however, cannot answer the question whether [the relocation] will be repressive or not (*represif atau tidak*). If you cannot answer, it is useless to have this meeting. We cannot give a clear answer to the small people (*masyarakat kecil*) [i.e., the Pethikbumi traders].[14]

In a meeting with the DPRD two days earlier, on September 10, a similar threat had been used by the Pethikbumi leadership. One leader had stated in this closed meeting, "So we hope that Yogyakarta does not become Poso or Kalimantan.[15] If the conflict comes to the point of happening, this will be the responsibility and the biggest mistake of the government because of the many obstacles [we discussed] earlier."[16]

By drawing a comparison to Poso, this leader was referencing a type of violence that had been present in Indonesia since the Reformasi period. Since 1998, the Poso region has been associated with a religious conflict between Muslims and Protestants that has seen several thousand people killed. Lorraine V. Aragon (2001), however, has argued that the conflict has less to do with religious belief per se than the "political economy of being Protestant (or Catholic) and Muslim" (47). In 2000, three thousand police and army troops were sent to control the violence between the two groups (Sidel 2006, 166). The following year, Laskar Jihad entered Poso to provide armed support to the Muslim faction (see Drawing on Deeper Sources of Fears, this chapter). It was through this talk of Poso and the *Laskar Mangkubumi* T-shirts that Pethikbumi was able to play with the uncertainty of information and situate themselves as possible threats to the ordered city.

The day after the September 12 protest, a *Kedaulatan Rakyat* article reported that the meeting with the government had resulted in a deadlock. Moreover, despite journalists being present at the September 12 meeting, and other meetings at which Pethikbumi made threats of violence, Pethikbumi's threats were not reported in any newspapers. Instead, the *Kedaulatan Rakyat* article quoted Mas Arief as saying, "We do not want to be relocated [for] a number of different reasons. But we want to be orderly. The government should not use violence to force us."[17] By calling for the mayor to not authorize the use of force, Pethikbumi brought attention to the fact that the mayor might do precisely this while also trying to hold him accountable, and yet the threats that Pethikbumi had directed towards the municipal government did not enter the newspapers.[18] Instead, these threats hovered over the discussions of violence in the newspapers as an unspoken possibility.

As discussions of state violence increased, they often slipped from unlikely rumours into the realm of reality. The Pethikbumi leadership became concerned that their members would leave their side and join the government's relocation because of the threat of repression.[19] To prevent this, the group's leaders presented their membership with statements from the government promising that it would not use violence. The leaders of Pethikbumi distributed the following statement along the street:

> You need to know, friends, that the relocation plan is not CERTAIN (*PASTI*) and not CLEAR (*belum JELAS*)! When we as the general leaders of Pethikbumi met with the municipal government there had not yet been an agreement made with those of us who are refusing the relocation. [But] the municipal government said the other day that the relocation is only for those who want to move and that those who do not want to move will be allowed to stay. Also, during the process of relocation the government promised that there will be no VIOLENCE (*KEKERASAN*), so we will not need to fight with this institution. Because of this, all the members of Pethikbumi and all the economic agents (*pelaku ekonomi*) on Mangkubumi Street do not need to panic (*perlu panik*) and be influenced by issues and stories that are not yet clear (*terpengaruh dengan isu-isu atau berita-berita yang belum tentu kejelasannya*).[20]

The leaders of Pethikbumi, ironically, were now faced with the task of countering the rumours that they had been partially responsible for starting.

By starting and participating in rumours of state violence, Pethik-bumi had tried to put the government in the position of having to deny that it would use violence. In reality, however, the government often responded to these concerns about the potential of state violence in an indirect fashion. For example, in the local newspaper *Bernas Jogja*, Pak Syahruji, a member of the government's relocation team, was asked whether the government would situate Satpol PP in the old selling locations once the deadline arrived. The article quotes Pak Syahruji as saying that the municipal government's approach will be "very technical" (*sangat teknis*), and that "the placement of Satpol PP is only one method (*satu cara*). What is clear is that we will follow the regulations that determine the rules (*aturan mainnya*). That's it! We will take action against the street vendors who still insist on selling in the old location."[21] By using the rather vague phrase *taking action*, the government perpetuated the confusion about what kind of action they might actually take against the street vendors.

Despite the government's ambiguity on this point, the Pethikbumi leaders nonetheless used such statements to report back to their membership that they need not be afraid of state violence. The traders hoped that if the municipal government was pressured into making a statement that it would refrain from repression, they could not only allay their members' fears of state violence but also pressure the government to keep its word. Despite the fact that the newspapers were a site of shadow play, what was distinctive about these strategies was the degree to which the published word was given authority as the point on which the government could be held accountable.

Drawing on Deeper Sources of Fears

Claims that an ethnic or religious conflict could emerge in Yogyakarta were based on statements that could not be trusted, yet fragments of verifiable information made these claims seem possible. Although one might assume, as I did initially, that the connections between Poso and Yogyakarta were few and far between, I was later informed by Mas Eko from Pethikbumi that there was some reality to these claims.[22] Laskar Jihad was formed in 1999 after a massacre of four hundred Muslims in a mosque in northern Maluku occurred that year (Spyer 2002, 25). Laskar Jihad set up training camps on the island of Java and based its headquarters in Yogyakarta. The organization sent thousands of fighters to Ambon, the capital of the Maluku province, in mid-2000 and again in mid-2001, and they also established a presence in Poso (International Crisis Group 2005).[23] Patricia Spyer (2002) describes how the imagination of the Ambonese was influenced by violence elsewhere in Indonesia, and how other places were in turn aware of the violence in Ambon, particularly religious violence. She states, "Ambon is not an island unto itself, which means that Christians and Muslims living there are cognizant of violence elsewhere, especially when it is religiously inflected" (26). Stuart Kirsch (2002) also argues that the "margins of Indonesia are defined largely in terms of their capacity to destabilize the whole, establishing expectations that allow state-sponsored violence to be represented as orderly and necessary" (57). Yogyakartans' imaginations were likewise shaped by these violent episodes, and this generated concerns that Yogyakarta, too, could become a violent place.

When one considers that some members of Pethikbumi were also part of Laskar Jihad, the connections between places like Ambon, Poso, and Yogyakarta are rendered even more concrete. A previous Pethikbumi group leader was among those who went to Ambon with Laskar Jihad in 2001. Pak Syafii was born in Semarang, Central Java, in 1968, and had worked since middle school as a fisherman and woodcarver because his parents were unable to support his schooling. When he finally graduated from high school, he went to Central Sulawesi and worked in a furniture factory. He moved to Yogyakarta in 1993 after studying briefly at several universities. He worked for a time making souvenirs, but then decided to use his carving skills to make Arabic calligraphy, which he initially sold from house to house, and then in shops. Pak Syafii's economic success allowed him to open a Muslim dress shop in front of Yogyakarta's Universitas Islam Indonesia.

Pak Syafii's business eventually faltered as a result of the 1997 Asian financial crisis. He then began selling refillable perfumes and Muslim clothing at the Beringharjo Marketplace (Pasar Beringharjo), even though he did not have an official location at this site. After negotiating with the government, he was allowed to sell for five hours a day in the centre of the market. However, in 2001 he sold his location and left for Ambon. In an interview with me, he explained his rationale: "I am a Muslim, and at that time there was the slaughtering of Muslims in Ambon. The country did not care, even though it was clear that the culprit was the Republic of South Maluku. Almost two thousand Muslims were massacred there."[24] For a year, Pak Syafii volunteered with Laskar Jihad.[25]

In 2002, Pak Syafii returned to Yogyakarta because he considered the situation in Ambon to be under control after the government sent elite troops to prevent further killings. Upon his return, he commenced trading second-hand goods on the street, in the mornings and afternoons on Asem Gede and then in the evenings on Mangkubumi Street.

But although Pak Syafii was no longer active with Laskar Jihad, he still knew people within the organization; the municipal government of Yogyakarta thus had to seriously consider whether street vendors could mobilize religious organizations such as Laskar Jihad to fight the relocation. In this way, the violence in places like Ambon took on a malleable quality, such that it came to signify possible violence during the relocation in Yogyakarta.

Many Yogyakartans also feared that the relocation conflict could become an "ethnic" one. Again, this fear was based on recent conflicts, especially those waged in the region of Kalimantan since 1996. At the time of the relocation project, sensationalist media reports had covered the ethnic cleansing in this region between the indigenous Christian Dayaks and migrant Muslim Madurese (Cahyono 2008).[26] For some street vendors, the horizontal nature of the conflict over the relocation reflected existing ethnic divisions. During the relocation, government officials, ordinary citizens, shop owners, and many of the pro-relocation traders made the distinction between those actors who were Javanese and those who were newcomers/outsiders. The pro-relocation group was thought to be comprised mostly of Javanese members, whereas it was assumed that the anti-relocation group was largely non-Javanese. There was some truth to this distinction: the majority of the street traders who wanted to relocate were originally from the Special Region of Yogyakarta, while their opponents tended to be either from parts of Java or from different regions of Indonesia altogether. This ethnic difference was noted early on, and it was used repeatedly to explain why there were two opposing groups.[27] The government, members of the public, and shop owners with whom I spoke characterized the Javanese group as grateful to the government for the relocation and as trusting of the government's intentions. This group did not want to be loud or showy, but instead, as "real" Javanese, were respectful to higher authority. In contrast, the members of Pethikbumi, and in particular their leaders, were characterized as "not Javanese." They were loud, held demonstrations, yelled into megaphones, and generated stories that were reported in the newspapers; there was, in other words, little subtlety to their activism. In one case, a friend from the neighbourhood where I lived counselled that I should be careful associating too closely with Pethikbumi because these traders were outsiders.

Within Yogyakarta, there are enclaves composed of different ethnic groups. These separate ethnic identities are a product of both colonial and New Order ideas of what is known in Javanese as *Bhinneka Tunggal Ika* (a national motto that translates into English as "Unity in Diversity"). Each ethnic group is portrayed as having its own dress, language, food – in essence, its own culture. Some ethnic groups tend to live in the same areas of the city and are mobilized as separate entities through ethnic organizations. As noted earlier (see Networks and Ties, Chapter 1), Mbah Ahmad, the leader of the Madurese organization KMY, also disapproved of the relocation. KMY was formed in the 1970s and, with twenty thousand members in Central Java, its political influence is significant.[28] In post–New Order Indonesia, mass organizations like KMY provide "networks of solidarity, identity and opportunity structures to fulfil material needs in the context of socioeconomic environments where there is often a distinct paucity of options" (Wilson 2015, 172). Himself a food seller in another area of the city, Mbah Ahmad had achieved prominence by virtue of his charisma and his willingness to physically fight against the government to protect his livelihood. He had reportedly stood up to the municipal government at various points, and he had won because he was willing to die rather than back down. In September 2007, Mbah Ahmad continued this trend and declared that there would be a "commotion" or "tumult" in the city if the government proceeded with the relocation.[29]

Mbah Ahmad was seventy-two years old. He moved to Yogyakarta in 1950 after living briefly in major cities like Semarang, Jakarta, and Surabaya. He sold *sate* (a dish of grilled meat) beside a railway station until the area was cleared for a parking lot in the early 1990s. After he confronted the government about the loss of his selling location – one of the occasions on which he said that he was willing to die rather than back down – the government moved him to a strategic site near another major tourist attraction. Telling the story of this encounter with the government, Mbah Ahmad told me, "I said that if that tent is taken down, either me or [the police officer] would die. If I die I will only leave my food stall. I'm brave."[30] In these early years, Mbah Ahmad developed good relations with the police because he gave them food for free. He also impressed other Madurese because he was the only one who dared to oppose the thugs who often asked for money.[31]

Located under a verandah, Mbah Ahmad's selling location enjoyed a strategic placement that protected him from the sun and the rain. Besides being the leader of KMY, he was also known to be a powerful mystic. People went to him if they were sick or to seek advice about business, politics, and love. He was also known for his ability to negotiate effectively with the police. Pak Budi, a KMY member, told me that he went to Mbah Ahmad's house any time he had a problem with either the police (concerning a criminal matter) or Satpol PP (over a non-criminal issue).[32] Shortly after his visit to Mbah Ahmad, the officer in question would visit Pak Budi and resolve the issue peacefully.[33]

Mbah Ahmad, because of his vast network, was able to raise the stakes of the relocation and the resulting crisis even higher. He was powerful because he was not afraid of violence, he claimed supernatural abilities (as a healer, he could engage in different forms of magic [*ilmu-ilmu*]),[34] and he was able to attract the support of multiple influential figures (including the mayor, Madurese community leaders, and the police). Mbah Ahmad suggested that his livelihood had depended upon his willingness to stand up to the government and to counter its threats of violence with his own. He saw himself as not only representing his Madurese "children"[35] who sold on the street, but all the traders: he considered them "little people," like himself, who were forced to go up against the government as a result of their marginalization.[36] His threats of a possible "tumult" if the relocation proceeded also helped to situate the project as a cause of possible violence.[37] As a Madurese leader, he represented a threat from outside, someone who might challenge the reified Javanese "culture" of peace.

Suharto's New Order promoted the fear of communism, the fear of Islam, and the fear of crime, but in the democratic era, these forces are subjected to less state control. Under Suharto, fears of communism, Islam, or crime weakened opposition while strengthening the armed forces and the ruling party (Roosa 2006; Sidel 2006), but in the present there is more anxiety that state intervention and violence might themselves be countered with an uncontrollable outbreak of violence due to the ethnic and religious tensions visible throughout the country (Bertrand 2004; Sidel 2006). These fears of violence in the city were made to feel more plausible for the Pethikbumi leaders, and probably for some government officials, with the knowledge that Pak Syafii had volunteered with Laskar Jihad, and that Mbah Ahmad, a leader of a large ethnic organization, had used threats of violence in the past to protect his right to the street. The Pethikbumi traders remained most fearful, however, of state violence, and they began to discuss what they would do in the face of state repression.

Laughter and Power

For Pak Toni of the NGO Forum, the government's potential use of violence was nothing new: he had faced similar threats in his previous advocacy work. Pak Toni had been actively supporting Pethikbumi in the three months leading up to the relocation. During this time he attended their meetings and took an active role in shaping the discussions and providing advice from his years of experience with anti-government organizing. At a Pethikbumi meeting near the end of October,[38] Pak Toni explained that if there was a physical fight, the

Pethikbumi members would probably be in jail for only one night. He said, "I want to be prepared for this as well. Don't let it happen that if you refuse [the relocation and are arrested], we are too long at [the] Poltabes [provincial police station]. It is cold there, lots of mosquitoes. I can only give you an image for those who haven't [experienced it yet]."[39] A member of PPIP chipped in: "I've already experienced it. It is a boarding house, rent-free." People laughed.

Despite the seriousness of talk in the public sphere, these small meetings with the street vendors sometimes included moments of levity. In the same meeting quoted above, another joking and sarcastic conversation took place:

> PAK TONI: I'm also looking for that promise as well – that if later there is fighting, then you will only be in Poltabes for one night. I hope that Pak Udin [a parliamentarian and the head of a committee with some influence over the relocation] will also promise only one night and then we are out.
>
> MAS ARIEF: If we do *not* want to get in a fight, how can we do that?
>
> PAK TONI: We can't do that. The regulation [that will officially make street vending on Mangkubumi Street illegal] will be effective on October 31. If we are selling there, our goods will be taken. If later we refuse [to stop selling on Mangkubumi Street], they [Poltabes] will take some of us [into custody]. That's certain.
>
> PETHIKBUMI MEMBER: We could start selling at the police station. At the police station [merchandise] sells quickly doesn't it?
>
> EVERYONE: [*Laughter.*][40]

Suddenly, what had been a very serious topic had taken on a different tone. This imagining of a possible encounter with the state was less severe than ones presented earlier. Like the pamphlet circulated to the Pethikbumi members explaining that there would be no violence, these jokes were made from a position of reflexivity. When the group's members joked about the violence, they also became conscious of this possible violent event as a social drama (V. Turner 1974) – an event they were performing in front of an audience, citizens of the city who would hear about it in the local and national newspapers, depending on how it unfolded. They could write and play out different scripts of how various scenarios might unfold.

As the relocation deadline approached, these scripts came to be "workshopped" at Pethikbumi meetings. The members outlined different scenarios in order to anticipate them. These exercises often shifted back and forth between the serious and the comical. At an October 31 meeting, Pak Toni started out by trying to get the group to plan for what might happen in the event of government violence. He emphasized that the group had to accept all consequences. Then Pak Akbar jumped in:

PAK AKBAR: If [state violence] really happens later [after the relocation deadline], maybe we can have an agreement with our members that if one of us is taken [by the police] then we will all act (*bergerak*). Automatically (*otomatis*) if [the police or Satpol PP] clear us [from Mangkubumi Street] it will not be done during the evening because in the evening there are lots of people – it's not likely to happen. If the municipal government announces that on this date there will be [an operation to clear vendors from Mangkubumi Street], OK, that night we make sure there are lots of people first and that they are spread out. But if we are cleared automatically before five o'clock, maybe [the police] are already ready [to clear vendors from the street]. If only –

PAK PRAMANA: We hold them up.

PAK AKBAR: We hold them up first and then use *tarung* [martial arts].

PAK TONI: Don't use tarung.

PAK AKBAR: I mean, not tarung … We must continue, but we will not start [any violence] first. Are we wrong, if we do not want to move, but they automatically use violence? When they punch us, don't we have the right to respond?

PAK TONI: Later it [the physical violence] will continue and in the end, whoa (*anu*) –

PAK AKBAR: So [the conflict will become] war (*perang*), like that.

PAK TONI: If they hit us and we do nothing, that is no problem.

PETHIKBUMI MEMBER: That will be painful, *lho*![41]

EVERYONE: [*Laughter.*]

PAK TONI: *Lho*, we are talking about strategies here. If we are punched, do not respond. Later we can report them.

PETHIKBUMI MEMBER: Usually the report [to the police] is not taken up (*ditanggapi*), *lho*. [The reports are not taken up] because [the police] are "only doing their jobs."

PAK TONI: Other citizens will report them. That [physical violence] is a criminal act.

PAK AKBAR: So we should prepare a handycam.

PAK PRAMANA: That would be good.

PETHIKBUMI MEMBER: We get ready in the mid-morning to be punched in the afternoon. If you put your body out there, make sure you get your body parts insured (*badan diasuransikan*).

EVERYONE: [*Laughter.*][42]

This laughter suggests a certain cynical distance from the situation: violence was still possible, but it was also laughable. Donna M.

Goldstein (2013), describing the *favelas* of Rio de Janeiro, argues that the laughter of their residents is a "window into the sense of injustice oppressed peoples feel about their conditions" (12). Marcyliena Morgan (2004) likewise argues that "laughter is a special category in indirect reference and serves as an indexical function in interactions by highlighting the speakers' critical attitude toward a situation or topic" (61). She argues that "the Black women's laugh" in Chicago can be misinterpreted because it "often occurs within narratives and discussions of bigotry, patriarchy, paternalism, social class privilege, sexism, and other situations that may also be responded to with outrage and indignation" (61–2). In a similar way, the street vendors were able to laugh because they were commenting on the absurdity of being jailed for wanting to refuse the government relocation. Their laughter was a comment on this power imbalance and the fact that there was little possibility that they would receive fair treatment from the police.

The conversation quoted above went on for several hours, with the Pethikbumi leaders outlining every possible scenario. Some expressed fear that someone from outside their group, a provokator, would instigate a conflict by punching people. In response, they decided that the group should receive punches first so they could be the victims. The leaders would be responsible for trying to keep their members in line with this plan. Pak Toni argued that they should make sure that their members did not fight at all, even if they were punched first. He said, "If the idea is not to fight tomorrow and you fight, the mistake is [that of] Pak Akbar and friends."[43]

The Pethikbumi leaders had to control their members and ensure that they acted together and followed the agreed-upon script. They wanted to be portrayed in the media as victims, rather than instigators, of any possible violence.[44] In private, internal meetings, the talk of state violence sometimes took the form of jokes and laughter, and this highlighted the deep inequalities between citizens, on the one hand, and the Satpol PP officers and the police, on the other. This talk and laughter about violence emphasized the continuing and entrenched power of the state to act as it wanted – with little accountability – in the post-Suharto era. In these discussions, the traders and their supporters were more clearly situated as the moral victims (*korban*) in contrast to the perpetrator (*pelaku*), in this case the state.

Signing Up to Enter Kuncen Marketplace

On November 5, the municipal government started the process of inviting the traders from Asem Gede, the Southern Square, and Mangkubumi Street to register for the relocation to Kuncen Marketplace.[45] By the next day, 578 out of the more than 600 traders who had registered had been approved for the relocation after passing the municipal government's verification process.[46] Traders who were not in the government's database did not pass the municipal government's verification process; these individuals were moved to locations in other marketplaces across the city.

As noted, some Pethikbumi traders were becoming increasingly fearful that resistance to the relocation would have a negative impact on their long-term livelihoods, and these members started to sign up for the relocation. Adding pressure to the situation, the municipal government announced in the newspaper that the registration process would close by November 7 at 3:00 p.m. The municipal government also announced that it had no plans to reopen the registration process, despite Pethikbumi's request that the registration deadline be postponed. The *Kedaulatan Rakyat* newspaper quoted Pak Ari as saying, "What is clear is that we will not open a subsequent registry (*pendaftaran susulan*). If there are people who have not registered, that is a risk [they are taking]."[47]

On November 9, the municipal government reported that 609 of the 780 traders who had now registered had passed the verification process and had been invited to participate in a lottery to distribute the kiosks, which would take place shortly. Taking a softer approach to Pethikbumi, Pak Galang estimated that Kuncen Marketplace could accommodate up to 700 traders, and he stated that "the traders who had not been drafted yet did not need to be worried that they will not be accommodated."[48] Forum Penyelamat Pedagang Pethikbumi (Forum to Save the Pethikbumi Sellers, or FP3), a group established earlier that month by a former Pethikbumi leader, stepped in to help Pethikbumi members who were already in the database but had not yet registered – even though they wanted to relocate – because they were scared of the Pethikbumi leaders. FP3 expressed the hope that the government would be able to accommodate these traders at the new location.[49] Although it was not explained in the article why these particular members were so scared of the group's leaders that they had not enlisted for the move to Kuncen Marketplace, FP3 nonetheless suggested that the Pethikbumi leaders and their supporters were forcing some of their members to resist the relocation against their will. (In fact, this was partially true since the Pethikbumi leaders had taken away the group's membership cards to try to prevent them from registering for kiosks at the new location.[50])

Also on November 9, a few more members from Pethikbumi decided to sign up for the relocation. Ibu Risti had sold blue jeans on Mangkubumi Street for the past three years. She signed up once the government extended the deadline for registering, after Pak Akbar gave her permission and said that he would not obstruct her wishes. Ibu Risti knew that Kuncen Marketplace would not be as profitable as Mang-kubumi because of the different spatial organization. Mangkubumi Street was long, so it was difficult for customers to compare prices; in Kuncen Marketplace, where comparisons between various vendors could be easily made, the competition would be much greater. Still, she claimed that she was considering the survival of her family and thus decided to register on the last official day for registration.[51] Even though a handful of other Pethikbumi members joined the relocation that same evening because of the growing uncertainty around where they might sell after the deadline passed, the Pethikbumi leaders remained firm in their rejection of the relocation.

In an article published on November 10, Pak Galang announced that there was space for around eighty kiosks above the parking lot in Kun-cen Marketplace for traders who had not yet been drafted to the market-place. The article reported that another eighteen traders had registered, of whom fifteen had passed the municipal government's verification process. Pak Galang was quoted as saying that "the decision to extend the time to register is proof that the municipal government continues to be accommodating towards the traders who wish to relocate."[52]

In the same article, Pak Herry Zudianto explained that his vision for the marketplace was "to empower the sellers in the informal sector to become formal [in the long term], so that the traders can become more prosperous, not the reverse." Pak Herry said, "We are realizing a policy that will not likely make everyone happy; this is the risk of leadership. But what is clear is that the government's intentions (*niat*) are good: to improve the welfare of the traders."[53] On 10 November 2007, in an article in *Kompas* entitled "Herry minta maaf soal relokasi" (Herry apologizes for the relocation problem), Pak Herry stated, "I apologize if until the last second there are still parties who have not understood my plan (*belum memahami rencana saya*), but I will continue to step forward." One of the reactions that Pak Herry was referring to here came from the NGO Forum, which had issued an open statement to the mayor about Pethikbumi's refusal to relocate. In this document, the NGO Forum requested that the municipal government follow the law by respecting the lawsuit that the Pethikbumi leadership had filed against the municipal government with regard to the regulation that would make street vending on Mangkubumi Street illegal. Although the NGO Forum expressed its concern in the November 10 *Kompas* article that the municipal government might act repressively and forc-ibly evict the traders who continued to sell on Mangkubumi Street, Pak Herry said that whatever the municipal government did, it would follow the relocation plan and the municipal government's vision for establishing Kuncen Marketplace.

The Deadline

On the evening of the Saturday, November 10 deadline, the NGO Forum created an advocacy post on Mangkubumi Street from which the NGOs and the Pethikbumi leaders could watch and provide support. A white banner several metres in length was strung between two green poles on the east side of the street. It read, *Posko Advokasi PKL Pethikbumi* (Pethikbumi Street Vendor Advocacy Post) in bold red and black letters. The lawyers and Pethikbumi leaders gathered a few metres behind the banner, a position that allowed for a direct view of the selling locations on the west side of the street. The advocacy post was also prepared in anticipation of an outbreak of violence. Explaining the rationale for the post to *Kedaulatan Rakyat*, Ibu Marini said, "BPHK has already prepared twelve lawyers to advocate [for the street vendors vis-à-vis the police] in anticipation of the violence that Pethikbumi will face."[54] The talk of violence had led the legal aid supporters to develop techniques and strategies for dealing with a potential clash.

That evening at 6:00 p.m., I received a phone call from Pethikbumi leader Pak Mujib; I was still at home getting ready to go out after a late-afternoon shower. He reported that several truckloads of police and Satpol PP officers, which had earlier been circling the area, had parked on Mangkubumi Street. The vendors still had until midnight to get off the street, but the warning signs of possible government action were already present.[55] Later, an article in *Bernas Jogja* stated, "With the street traders protesting the relocation, on Saturday night members of Satpol PP, backed by officers from Poltabes Yogyakarta, came to the street. This of course created an atmosphere that became intimidating and filled with pressure."[56] As the trucks circled the area and then parked, they served to mark the territory – to suggest that when the time came, it would be under the state's control again. The visible police presence also called to mind previous instances of (violent) state intervention, and thus served as an indirect threat, the decoding of which required previous experience or knowledge on the part of the observer. The state's response to the traders' talk of violence manifested itself not just in the realm of discourse, then; it was also felt as a presence on the street. This fear of violence against the relocation effort led the state to erect psychological as well as physical barriers to the street.

That night, as regular trading continued – many of the customers had come to experience the night marketplace on Mangkubumi Street for what might be the last time – members of several political parties stopped by to observe the situation. Journalists came to get the story. The NGO Forum and BPHK guarded the post until 11:00 p.m., when they decided to have an internal meeting with other NGOs to discuss how they could best support Pethikbumi in the upcoming hours and days.[57] Shortly after the NGO Forum and BPHK left, Pethikbumi decided to hold another meeting at the advocacy post – this time about another matter that had come to be of concern: that traders who claimed to be supporting Pethikbumi had in fact signed up for the marketplace as the government continued to accept registrations. Pethikbumi had held a meeting on November 7 at the DPRD in which the membership had voted to continue refusing the relocation. Now, meeting on the night of the relocation deadline, Pak Akbar decided that Pethikbumi should hold another vote over whether to refuse or support the relocation. He asked the Pethikbumi members again: Did people want to refuse the relocation or move? Three people wanted to move while all the others (approximately fifty members) agreed to continue to refuse. Despite this clear vote, Pak Akbar still focused the discussion on whether they should accept the government project. Surprisingly, as the discussion continued, Pak Akbar himself seemed to be wavering in his stance against the relocation. The discussion trailed off around 10:30 p.m., with no clear resolution. Many of the vendors, frustrated with the situation, went home. The Pethikbumi leaders remained and decided to continue this discussion internally.[58]

By 11:00 p.m., Mas Totok of PPIP, who had been observing the situation on the street, felt that Pethikbumi's position was weak and that its members – around 350 at the group's peak – were now few. He had also heard from his friends working for police intelligence that the government was going to use preman if the vendors tried to remain on the street.[59] Mas Totok had been in contact with members of Poltabes throughout the evening via text message, urging them to use restraint and to protect Pethikbumi against any preman; he felt that the Pethikbumi members would surely lose if they were up against preman, and he did not want them to experience any violence.[60] The Pethikbumi leadership also encouraged their members to go home. At this point no decisions were going to be made as a large group, and the leadership did not want any problems to arise on the street.[61]

At midnight, I sat among the few remaining Pethikbumi leaders on benches facing the west side of the street, across from where they normally sold. Several yellow dump trucks, each carrying dozens of large potted plants, pulled up, followed by streams of police and Satpol PP officers in other vehicles. Men climbed down from the backs of the trucks. They worked quickly to unload the pots (at several hundred pounds each,

Figure 4. Still image from 10 November 2007 video footage of potted plants being unloaded on Mangkubumi Street, as filmed by a journalist.

they required the effort of three to four people per pot), and then placed them along the sidewalk at intervals of several metres (see figure 4). These were similar to many of the large potted plants strategically placed around Yogyakarta by the municipal government. The leaders of Pethik-bumi watched in silence from across the street. A few of them had tears in their eyes.[62] The pots were so large and the street required so many that at 2:30 a.m. the government officials were still unloading them.

Although plants in Indonesia often symbolize modernity and cleanliness, their meanings vary depending on the context in which they are found. The placement of potted plants on city streets, for example, is closely associated with the Adipura Award. First launched in 1984, the award is given to the "cleanest and greenest" cities across the archipelago.[63] A highly prestigious civic honour, municipal governments take the Adipura seriously; it is awarded by the president and serves as an important marker of a city's "modern" status.[64] A *Jakarta Post* article from February 2011 describes it as "a political commodity to win the hearts and minds of voters and support from the central government."[65] During the Suharto era, obtaining the award was often associated with a willingness to evict poor residents or street vendors in urban areas.[66] Since the presence of street vendors is seen as a barrier to such an honour, placing potted plants on sidewalks where traders sell serves two functions: it makes the space appear "clean" and "green," and it prevents the traders from selling because it occupies the space they would otherwise use. Thus, for street vendors, the presence of large potted plants can be a sign that the government does not want them to sell on the street – they are both a symbol and a physical barrier.

Born in 1977, Pak Teguh, a media consultant, has lived in Yogyakarta since 2000. He explained to me that many of the potted plants across the city "were probably placed on the street in order to make the street look more beautiful (*keindahan*), but also to dispel (*menghalau*) the street vendors. Because if there is space [for the vendors] to sell, it will be used immediately."[67] It is no secret that municipal governments place potted plants along sidewalks in order to prevent trading on the pavement. "We build those flowerpots so street vendors cannot abuse the sidewalk," Pak Heru Bambang, head of the South Jakarta City Parks and Cemetery Agency, told the *Jakarta Post*. Moreover, Pak Heru Bambang explained that having street vendors along the sidewalk could compromise South Jakarta's ability to win the Adipura Award.[68] In *Kompas*, one article even describes how street vendors were being evicted so that flowerpots (*pot bunga*) could be placed on the sidewalk.[69] Thus, potted plants can be *both* a technology to stop traders from selling and a reason to evict them.

While the large potted plants were being placed along the sidewalks, hundreds of police and Satpol PP officers, along with other non-uniformed individuals (likely undercover police), walked up and down Mangkubumi Street. Trucks filled with police and Satpol PP officers also moved slowly up and down the street. This night operation was carried out with few witnesses besides the Pethikbumi members and a journalist who happened to live in the surrounding neighbourhood.[70] He ran alongside the trucks taking video footage as one plant after another was unloaded and placed in locations where just hours earlier the vendors had sold their wares.[71] The Satpol PP members established seven posts along the street. While all this was happening, the journalist interviewed Pak Pramana (see figure 5):

JOURNALIST: If they [the Pethikbumi traders] were already informed [about the relocation] years before, maybe there wouldn't be sellers [on Mangkubumi Street]?

PAK PRAMANA: That's clear. We wouldn't be selling. There is nobody here that is illiterate! Yeah, what we defend is right, we defend our human right to search for a living.

JOURNALIST: Maybe our friends [the Pethikbumi traders] here won't be able to sell because there are already potted plants. How about our friends [the Pethikbumi traders] who still want to sell here?

PAK PRAMANA: Yeah, actually a lot of people still sell here but with regard to violence, according to Pak Sarjono [a government official] in the newspapers, there will be no forced removal or violence. I read this in the newspaper. But the government looks at the sellers of Mangkubumi like

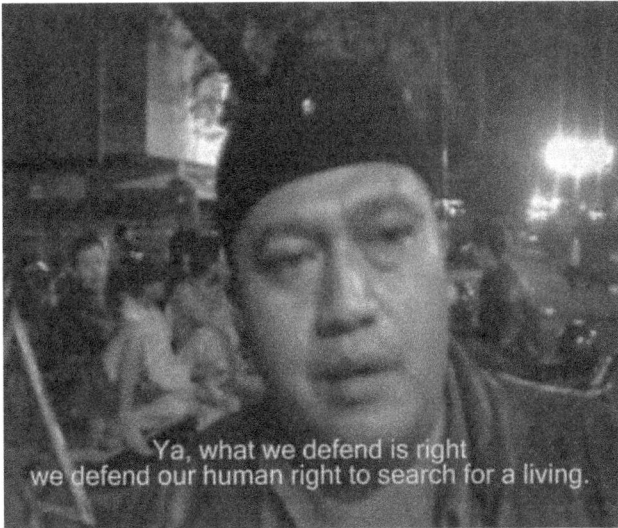

Figure 5. Still image from a 10 November 2007 interview with Pak Pramana, as filmed by a journalist.

terrorists or big-time criminals. They have to do this and that, use police and [Korps] Brigade Mobil, and maybe even the sub-district military. But they are only facing sellers [*laughs*]. Is there no other method to reduce street traders?[72]

For individuals like Pak Pramana, the "truth" about the government's actions towards the traders was determined by what was said in the newspapers. The traders were part of the emergence of an imagined community (B. Anderson 1991) whose sense of self was produced in relation to the idea of a reading public capable of judging the moral worth of their claims against those of the government. Although this form of stranger sociability had existed in Indonesia in the past,[73] it took a new form as people forged novel imaginative connections around participants' ideas of democracy and transparency. Pak Pramana did not situate the anti-relocation movement in opposition to the "order" and "culture" of Yogyakarta city, but rather in terms of human rights.

It was notable that the police, Satpol PP, and undercover officers physically occupied the street. Their presence was for all to see over the next several weeks, and it served as what Jean Bodin (1992) calls "the marks of sovereignty." The police and Satpol PP officers who appeared on the street were visible; some were uniformed while others were undercover, but all, as previously noted, were still visibly identifiable as police or Satpol PP. They stood out and represented what had been discussed for those many weeks prior to the relocation: the potential for the state to unleash an overpowering physical force. The police also represented a return to order, signalling to those who passed by that the state would ensure the security of "the people" and that anyone who opposed the government (and Java's ordered society) would be curbed.

The following day, a banner was hung on Mangkubumi Street announcing that street vendors were not allowed to sell there. An online blogger wrote approvingly of this latest eviction: "Usually the clearance of street traders is coloured by chaos between the vendors who refuse and the Satpol PP officers, but this has not happened in Yogyakarta."[74] Again, Yogyakarta was contrasted positively with other cities in Indonesia because it was able to keep the peace. In a 12 November 2007 article, local newspaper *Radar Jogja* described the activities on Mangkubumi Street:

Last night the atmosphere on Mangkubumi Street seemed quiet. There was not one street trader who laid out his merchandise. The west side of the sidewalk that stretches from the Tugu intersection [where the Tugu monument is located] to the front of the PLN [Perusahaan Listrik Negara, or State Electricity Company] seemed desolate. The sidewalk for walking is usually lit with kerosene lamps (*petromaks*) and neon lights, [but these] were not seen. What was seen was tens of police officers who guarded the length of the sidewalk. The police, both in full uniforms and undercover, were spread over many places. Besides that, you could see the Satpol Pamong Praja officers. Like the police, they were spread in a number of spots along the length of Mangkubumi Street. There were also some [Satpol PP] on alert on the south side of the Tugu intersection. The sidewalk that is usually used for selling was now used by a number of police cars and Satpol PP operational vehicles. This scene has been going on since the municipal government announced that the west side of Mangkubumi Street is forbidden [for traders] to sell klithikan on Saturday (10/11) at 24.00.[75]

The space that was once occupied by the street vendors was suddenly taken over by the police and other government personnel for a two-week period. In addition to the potted plants, the sidewalk, which was normally used for selling in the evenings, was now used by the police and other government personnel to park their vehicles. Shop owners who once struggled to get in and out of their shops and homes also parked their vehicles on the sidewalk, thus reclaiming the sidewalk as their own. Although the odd pedestrian still navigated the street, most avoided it while it was occupied.

The police presence reflected the sovereignty or rule of the state. The mayor argued that the police were there in order to "support the security" (*mendukung pengamanan*) of Mangkubumi Street, and that "the municipal government was really serious about prohibiting the second-hand traders from selling on the street."[76] In this way, the widespread fear of potential violence from the anti-relocation traders and their supporters was used as a pretext for state intervention so as to ensure that "order" was maintained. The government's strategy for removing this "threat" was to demonstrate that the state could and would mobilize an overpowering show of force if the traders decided to either continue selling or respond with violence. With this threat seemingly neutralized, Yogyakarta could now return to its privileged status as a site of order.

Conclusion

In many parts of the world, clashing with local government over the right to sell on the street is a common feature of the street vendor experience (e.g., G. Clark 1988a; Cross 1998). Sandra C. Mendiola Garcia (2017), for instance, describes how in Puebla, Mexico, "federal authorities spied on the [street vendor] organization, while local and state governments employed legal and illegal mechanisms to incarcerate their leaders, torturing some of them in order to neutralize the power of the union" (10). During street vendor evictions in Dhaka, traders often face physical violence and the destruction of their vending equipment, and they try to develop their own strategies to avoid such violence and deal with their losses (Etzold 2015, 183). Indonesia is likewise known for the degree of physical violence aimed at illegal traders (e.g., Collins 2007, 114; Guinness 2016, 207), and thus the talk of violence associated with the relocation to Kuncen Marketplace had particular meaning and weight for the traders involved.

Pemberton (1994) describes how, at election time in the New Order period, the streets of the city were the place where you could see "real campaign movements" (5). He writes, "During what the government refers to as the 'campaign season,' huge crowds of Indonesians repeatedly form in the streets … poised as if waiting for some incident to rush toward, en masse or, as Javanese would have it, *gumrubyug,* the undeniable sound of a crowd on the move" (6). Part of this feeling that something might happen was grounded in rumours that, while not described in "explicitly political terms," nonetheless implied "that the election process itself would somehow crash before election day, a sense that carried with it all the fascination of an enormous political traffic accident" (6). During the New Order, however, elections were never disrupted.

Since the fall of Suharto, the notion of order has maintained its privileged status in Yogyakarta city. In the case of the relocation project, the traders, the public, members of parliament, and government officials all discussed the possibility of violence in the context of a desire to uphold the "culture" of order and peace. When Pethikbumi and its supporters used the newspapers as vehicles to discuss their efforts to prevent state violence, they were able to convert the controversy over this relatively small relocation into a citywide concern. The newspapers were also sites where these street traders could address their fears, where they could try to dispel the uncertainty over whether the government would use violence and reassure their members, who had become fearful of the possibility of government repression. Yet even though the Pethikbumi traders used the newspapers to call on the government to eschew violence, in private meetings they also "played" with information by connecting their anti-relocation movement to violence in other parts of the archipelago.[77] These connections were tenuous but nevertheless powerful because they threatened what is seen as the "core" of Javanese culture – namely, peace and order – and they spoke to deeper anxieties about stability and peace in post–Suharto Indonesia. The talk of violence helped to shape how these fears over an outbreak of violence in Yogyakarta city were imagined, but it also perpetuated these fears because the organizing effects of this discourse worked on more than one level at once (see Caldeira 2000). In particular, the words and actions of Pak Syafii and Mbah Ahmad (see Drawing on Deeper Sources of Fears, this chapter) were likely a cause of concern for the municipal officials, who feared an outbreak of violence on the part of the traders.[78]

The question of how the talk of violence should circulate in the city was also subject to different information ideologies. With the opening of the press after the fall of Suharto, both the street traders and the government were able to move the discourse of violence into the public realm by revealing that violence might happen while also concealing exactly how it might manifest or who might be involved. It was in the newspapers that the leaders of Pethikbumi also sought to verify a rumour that the government would not use repression. The traders hoped that if they could get a clear statement from the municipal government, then they could hold officials accountable to their word and show their fellow traders that there was nothing to fear. In this sense, the newspaper was a place for the pursuit of accountability. In government meetings, the Pethikbumi leaders also played with the idea that they could engage in violence in the hope of making the government fear the vendors' ability to unleash a conflict in Yogyakarta city. Meanwhile, during internal meetings in which the Pethikbumi discussed how they would deal with state violence, laughter became a way to comment on and criticize the vast power differential between the vendors and the government and police.

While the talk of violence was sometimes used for the purposes of seeking transparency, Pethikbumi also "played" with information in less transparent ways. The group's collective action depended on its ability to use information and to circulate it in different ways, and these methods were not always in line with the goals of transparency. The Pethikbumi leaders and their supporters, as we have seen, were presented as either victims or potential perpetrators, but when they were seen as potential perpetrators of violence, the Pethikbumi movement became associated with a more threatening form of masculinity. The talk of violence also captured the wide range of information practices used by these disenfranchised traders, who saw the state as the true source of injustice even though they had to position themselves in contrasting roles to make this claim.

All this talk of violence ended in a way that most people had anticipated: with the return of order. The widespread public fear over violence was a pretext for state intervention; although not violent, this intervention showed the government's ability to intervene forcefully if necessary. The character of this state response was derived from Yogyakarta's reputation as a peaceful city, but it was also a result of globalized discourses of democracy and transparency, which encouraged the government to resolve this conflict without the use of violence.

Significantly, the resulting "order" on the street bore the hallmarks of a traditional Indonesian shadow play, or wayang kulit, which always starts and ends with images of harmony.[79] The scenes of disorder that preceded the government occupation of Mangkubumi Street, filled as they were with expectations of the moment-yet-to-come, were necessary for the return to order to occur and be felt. In the next chapter, I explore how the return to order was met by the traders. Who appeared as the winner or losers in the newspapers? Was anyone punished? Were the unruly characters made into good citizens? In wayang kulit, after all, no one wins and no one is punished, but the unruly characters always return home.

Chapter Seven

Conspiratorial Knowledge, Allah, and State Power

It is very hard for Javanese, and increasingly for all metropolitan Indonesians, to believe in any form of political spontaneity – in the accidental, or the fortuitous. Something is always going on "behind the screen," where unseen dhalang [puppeteers] are at work. The public "appearance" of the great is always regarded, less with cynicism, than with the faith that to some extent at least it is a mask.

– Benedict Anderson (1990, 150)

As the November 10 relocation deadline approached, a feeling surfaced that something radical could happen. The Pethikbumi traders had hoped that perhaps their voices would be heard and that they would be allowed to stay on the street. After the government's occupation of the street, however, this feeling gave way to a very different one: a sense of helplessness, of being up against an impossible force. In the following days, the Pethikbumi leaders struggled to remain hopeful because there seemed to be no way around the government's forceful presence, and because no alternative solution to relocation had presented itself. Without a place to sell, the Pethikbumi traders refusing the relocation no longer had a source of income. Although some had a few months' savings, most needed to be selling within a few days or weeks if they were to avoid bankruptcy. On the night of November 11, the Pethikbumi group met on Mangkubumi Street, across from where the Satpol PP stood guard, and to begin discussing their options. However, they were soon disrupted by an incident involving the Pethikbumi leaders, their NGO supporters, and pro-location lawyers at the Northern Square, an open field near the Sultan's palace where vendors sell food. This incident resulted in a breakdown of trust between Pethikbumi and its NGO supporters and the subsequent circulation of conspiracy theories around who was truly working in whose interests.[1]

The practices and ideas of shadow play are not new in Indonesia (e.g., B. Anderson 1990), and the idea that someone is working behind the scenes is an important information ideology across the archipelago. In his thirty-one years in power, Suharto relied on "dimly-lit operations of organized terror" (Strassler 2004, 69). Suspicion and fear were commonplace as citizens assumed that much of what appeared in the media was in fact concealing another reality (B. Anderson 1990, 123–51). Indeed, distrust and terror became so ingrained that they have persisted into the democratic era. Conspiracy theorizing is a form of "sensible" political communication in contemporary Indonesia, according to Bubandt (2008), an "understandable reaction to three decades of New Order state terrorism and rampant *reformasi* thug rule" (810). Paranoia has been both a "form of political critique" and a "standard political practice" (810). In the Reformasi period, political action continues to take place within "discourses of political paranoia" (810).

These discourses of political paranoia often express concerns about the breakdown of social order (Kroeger 2003, 243). Karen A. Kroeger (2003), for example, examines a series of rumours about the "AIDS club" in Surabaya: according to these rumours, a stranger would prick you with a needle and you would subsequently find a note in your pocket saying, "Welcome to the AIDS club." She describes how these rumoured encounters were often set in middle-class spaces such as shopping malls, movie theatres, games rooms, and discotheques – spaces that "embody the ambivalence" that Indonesians felt about changes in the urban landscape, such as the growing gap between the wealthy and the poor and the breakdown of moral values (249). Leslie Butt (2005) also argues that conspiracy theories concerning AIDS in Papua represented a response to the national government's unpredictable, mysterious, and inconsistent methods of regulating sex workers and dealing with AIDS. Papuans, in other words, created conspiracy theories because there were "inconsistencies" and "disjunctures" in the way AIDS was governed (414). Since Reformasi, various political, economic, and social transformations have made Yogyakartans uncertain about who has power and how that power operates in the city. People continue to be suspicious because, while they suspect certain unseen individuals are engaged in shadow play from "behind the screen," they are even less certain who these off-stage actors might be. In turn, this uncertainty has led to the spread of conspiracy theories claiming to explain how state power works, and also who is working for or against the state.

In addition to citizens questioning the actions and intentions of the state, many citizens, civil servants, and corporations are suspicious of NGOs in post-Suharto Indonesia. Marina A. Welker (2009) describes how managers of Newmont, a transnational mining company operating in Indonesia, were able to create a positive corporate identity in the eyes of the local population, while a group of concerned NGOs in the same area were deemed as "greedy, corrupt and insincere" (154). Newmont strategically planned to spread allegations against these NGOs and their allies. As Welker writes, "this strategy shows some of the coercive and, ironically, concealed ways in which corporations can use moral discourses of transparency and accountability against activists, joining a groundswell of disappointment and disaffection with NGOs" (159). Newmont, in fact, did not have to do much to make the locals suspicious of the NGOs because the NGOs were already the object of local suspicion. People assumed that they were really after money or were seeking to otherwise further their own members' personal interests (165). Likewise, in Yogyakarta, many locals do not just assume that NGOs are inherently good, honest, or transparent, with the result that the actions of NGOs are easily subject to an information practice like conspiracy theorizing.

On the evening of November 11, an unexpected gathering of different people in the Northern Square led the Pethikbumi traders to focus their own conspiracy theories on a category of non-state actors that had been deemed suspect since the New Order period. The traders made accusations against people they considered oknum because they sensed the state's off-stage play had infiltrated their group. The traders felt a sense of relief at this turn of events as it allowed them to shift the blame for their failure to oppose the relocation onto some external force. At the same time, because the traders also felt a sense of shame that their group might not be as pure or democratic as they had claimed, naming the oknum remained a private business. But while this conspiratorial knowledge circulated among the traders, the government made a version of this knowledge public through an indirect accusation that was reported in the newspapers: rather than labelling the traders' narrative as a "conspiracy," the government verified and supported a version of it by indirectly accusing the actors pinpointed in this alleged conspiracy. Daniel Hellinger (2003) argues that "conspiracy theories sometimes serve popular resistance and empowerment because they cast suspicion on the transparency and legitimacy of actions undertaken by the police, military, and intelligence agencies, whose missions include actually undertaking conspiracies" (205). While other anthropologists have likewise emphasized the importance of conspiratorial knowledge as a mode of challenging the state and its hegemonic discourses (Boyer 2006; Hellinger 2003), in this chapter I show how conspiratorial knowledge, as a central form of information politics, ended up verifying the state's narrative by framing members of civil society as the conspirators.

Harry West and Todd Sanders (2003) argue that conspiracy theories and theories of the occult have similarities. They say, "not only do occult cosmologies suggest that power sometimes hides itself from view, but they also suggest that it conspires to fulfil its objectives (each an essential trait of conspiracy theories)" (6). These occult cosmologies often contain conspiratorial knowledge within them (6–7). Alongside the conspiracies about oknum actors, theories about the role of Allah in the relocation also surfaced among the Pethikbumi traders, who drew attention to Allah's secret, mysterious, and unseen power and its role in shaping urban politics. While the conspiratorial knowledge about oknum raised concerns about the negative unseen forces behind urban politics, the conspiratorial knowledge about Allah suggested that positive forces were also operating. For the state, narratives about Allah served to identify government interests and actions as ethical in the public sphere, which in turn helped to reinforce state power. In contrast, the traders positioned Allah as an actor who would bring about justice in the private sphere. Since these narratives helped to sustain the traders' faith in justice and democracy – despite the latter's failure (see Bubandt 2014) – we could interpret the traders' turn to Allah as an attempt to compensate for the limits of democracy and transparency in post-Suharto Indonesia.

Conspiracy at the Northern Square

At six o'clock on the night of November 11, I arrived where Pethikbumi and its supporters had gathered on the east side of Mangkubumi Street in front of the *Kedaulatan Rakyat* office. This location was highly visible, just across from where Satpol PP and the police stood guard over the street. Pethikbumi and its supporters had decided to discuss their next steps, since they felt it was not a plausible option for them to continue selling on the street and face further issues with the police and Satpol PP officers.

Early in the meeting, Mas Arief received an urgent text message from Ibu Marini asking him to come to the Northern Square. Mas Arief was in the middle of leading the meeting, however, and could not leave the group. Mas Eko, another Pethikbumi leader, was sent instead. Mas Eko asked to borrow my camera in case evidence needed to be collected. After I gave it to him, he jumped on his motorbike and sped the couple of miles to the Northern Square.

Figure 6. A meeting with Pethikbumi leaders and their supporters on Mangkubumi Street, 11 November 2007. Photo by author.

Around a hundred people were by now gathered on Mangkubumi Street for the meeting, only half of whom were street traders; the others were young supporters from various organizations such as PPIP (see figure 6). We congregated around the front entrance of the *Kedaulatan Rakyat* office under a white, badly chipped overhang. Because of the many students on the street, the members of Pethikbumi could not be certain who was actually attending the meeting; most of the leaders had learned to assume that intelligence agents or government insiders were present and recording the event (see Being Shadowed, Chapter 4).

Pak Akbar did not enliven the crowd or build up their hopes for the fight against the relocation. Instead, he blamed the movement's failure on some Pethikbumi members' lack of loyalty. He said, "Many of our friends have not been true to us and they have already been drafted to the marketplace."[2] Indeed, since some vendors had signed up for the relocation, Pethikbumi's negotiating power with the government had been weakened. The government had been using the newspapers to encourage anti-relocation street vendors to move to the market-place before it was too late and all remaining places were taken.[3] In an attempt to coax the traders into joining the relocation, the government had been offering them transitional support (*bantuan masa transisi*) and adaptation assistance (*bantuan masa adaptasi*) at Kuncen Marketplace.[4] Many had taken up this call because they were scared that they might be left without a selling location.[5] The topic of group loyalty, then, came to take up much of the meeting, as those present weighed in on these concerns. But after almost an hour of back-and-forth discussion, the meeting concluded without any resolution.

While the Pethikbumi members lingered in the area after the meeting, Pak Akbar and another leader began to collect some basic information on the traders who were present; given the preceding discussion of group loyalty, it made sense for the Pethikbumi to count and document those remaining members who, in attending the meeting, had signalled that they had not signed up for the relocation and remained committed to the anti-relocation movement. After these details had been written down and the Pethikbumi members had begun to disperse from the area, Pak Akbar and I fell into conversation. He asked me, "If the remaining Pethikbumi traders relocated to Kuncen Market-place after all, had the government won?" I did not feel comfortable answering this question honestly because I was paranoid that intelligence agents were observing me; instead, I responded somewhat elliptically by saying that it depended on how you define "winning." Pak Akbar's question highlighted for me just how difficult it would be for the Pethikbumi leaders to move to the marketplace with their members after fighting for so long against the relocation.[6]

About an hour after my conversation with Pak Akbar, Mas Eko reappeared on Mangkubumi Street. He was with Pak Pramana. The two traders began to approach individual Pethikbumi and PPIP leaders, speaking to them in hushed tones. As Mas Eko and Pak Pramana spoke with each leader in turn, they all started to gather together on the street for an impromptu discussion. Mas Eko and Pak Pramana had both said that they no longer wanted to be associated with BPHK – and by extension, BPHK's close partner the NGO Forum – because Ibu Marini and her husband, Pak Suyitno (who was also in BPHK), were accusing Pak Pramana of being involved in a secret meeting with the government at the Northern Square. "BPHK was involved in some sort of conspiracy with the government," Mas Eko said. "Why else would they try to turn Pethikbumi members against each other?" Mas Eko went on to explain that upon arriving at the Northern Square, he had seen Pak Pramana engage in a discussion with Pak Didik and several police officers. The lawyers from BPHK were having their own conversation at a food stall a few metres away and were not involved in the deliberations. They had called the Pethikbumi leaders, however, to come and see for them-selves Pak Pramana in this conversation with the opposition. Mas Eko had not been able to see what was happening in detail because Pak Pramana and Pak Didik were meeting under a tent,[7] and yet he was suspicious: Why had BPHK been at the Northern Square at the exact same moment as Pak Pramana and Pak Didik's meeting? Upon hearing Mas Eko's news, the Pethikbumi leaders determined that they could no longer believe that BPHK was looking out for their interests, and they decided to hold a more formal meeting right there and then, along with leaders from PPIP, to discuss the next steps.[8]

During this meeting, Mas Eko and Pak Pramana recounted an inci-dent with BPHK from a few days earlier. They had been sitting at Pak Pramana's cell phone counter at Jogjatronik, an electronics mall, when they saw Ibu Marini and Pak Suyitno come into the mall and quickly make their way upstairs without stopping to talk or even acknowledge them. Mas Eko and Pak Pramana thought the couple was avoiding them. "Why had they not even stopped to say hello, or just wave at least, before they left?" Mas Eko asked. This seemingly unusual and inexplicable behaviour had raised their suspicions that BPHK might be up to something.[9]

At this point, the leaders of Pethikbumi decided to organize a meet-ing with government officials for later that night to discuss the possibil-ity of relocating their remaining members to Kuncen Marketplace. They also wanted to view the data on those who had already been drafted to the new location (many of whom might be among their own mem-bership).[10] Furthermore, they wanted to know how many stalls were still free in the marketplace. Pak Akbar called Pak Ari from the govern-ment's relocation team and requested an emergency meeting.

An hour later, we rode our motorbikes to a restaurant in the northern part of the city near the major national monument Monumen Yogya Kembali (Monument to the Recapture of Yogyakarta).[11] About ten of us – the Pethikbumi leaders, Pak Ari and Pak Mulyono, and myself – sat on a bamboo floor around a long table and ordered soft drinks and tea. The Pethikbumi asked to see the data on the vendors who had been drafted to the marketplace, and Pak Ari said that forty places remained – not enough for the more than seventy vendors still refusing the relo-cation. Pak Akbar demanded to see the data himself, declaring that it was his understanding that many people with no relation to Mang-kubumi Street or to street vending in general were receiving places in the marketplace. He therefore presented Pethikbumi's position as a moral argument: the group did not want to be part of a process that was tainted by private deals.

In the end, no real resolution was achieved that night, nor were the Pethikbumi leaders shown any data. But an offer had been put on the table: if Pethikbumi wanted to relocate to the marketplace, they needed to provide either Pak Ari or Pak Galang with a list of the vendors they wanted included[12] before 3:00 a.m. – or in about four hours' time.[13] Pak Ari reaffirmed many times in the meeting that he would trust (*percaya*) the Pethikbumi leaders, such as Pak Akbar and Mas Arief, to compile data on any remaining Pethikbumi members who could be included in the marketplace. Eventually, the meeting broke up. The Pethikbumi leaders opted to ride their motorcycles to a different food stall near Mangkubumi Street to discuss their options, but I decided that I was too tired and had to go home and rest, otherwise I risked getting sick after days of minimal sleep.[14]

After 1:30 a.m., I received a two-sentence text message from Pak Ferry, an undercover police officer who I knew had been monitoring the relocation and working closely with Pak Galang and Pak Didik to ensure its success. The first sentence of his message stated that the Pethikbumi leaders had submitted to the municipal government a list of seventy-one vendors who were to relocate to Kuncen Marketplace, to which the Pethikbumi leaders had then added four names, for a total of seventy-five vendors.[15] The message concluded: "The deadline is 3:00 a.m. and it [the complete and final list of vendors who would be relocating] must be submitted to Disperindagkop [the government department responsible for enlisting the vendors]."[16]

I was already at home and writing up my field notes when I received this message. I took a moment to absorb the news – relayed not by Pethikbumi but by Pak Ferry – that the Pethikbumi had accepted the government's offer to relocate to Kuncen Marketplace. I felt disappointed that the Pethikbumi's efforts to oppose the relocation had not succeeded.

At 3:00 a.m., I received a text message from Pak Toni from the NGO Forum, which was also sent to an unknown number of other people: "Please pay attention, later tonight we will not run the advocacy post on Mangkubumi because the leaders of Pethikbumi have already resigned last night at 2 a.m., please friends come and gather at 10 in the morning at BPHK to the right side of the Special Region of Yogyakarta Ombudsman Institution, to hold a press conference." I had not heard anything from Pethikbumi about this development; the group's membership had remained silent – to me, at least. Reflecting on the events of the past seven-odd hours, I recalled how, early the night before, Pak Akbar and another Pethikbumi leader had collected data on the group's remaining members – those traders who had been present at the Pethikbumi meeting outside the front entrance of the *Kedaulatan Rakyat* office. The data had likely been gathered in the event that Pethikbumi needed to submit a list of vendors to be registered for the marketplace.

At around nine or ten in the morning, shortly after I had had breakfast, I received a text message from Ibu Marini asking what was going on with Pethikbumi. She said she was getting endless phone calls from the press and members of parliament and she did not know how to respond. "Get them to call me," she pleaded. I told her that I could not promise they would, but I agreed to relay the message.

At the press conference, Pak Toni announced the NGO Forum's decision to withdraw its support from Pethikbumi, arguing that the group's leaders were "not consistent" (*tak konsisten*). As reported in *Kompas* the next day, Pak Toni stated, "We think it was a problem that on Thursday night, 9 November 2007, some of the leaders of Pethikbumi met directly with the mayor,[17] weakening the Pethikbumi movement's energy to fight because the unity of [Pethikbumi's] struggle [against the government] was undermined (*karena terpecahnya konsentrasi perjuangan*)."[18] As the press conference continued, Pak Toni said that he did not know why Pethikbumi's leaders had met with the mayor. He added that the meeting contradicted the vote at the DPRD by all Pethikbumi members on November 7 (see The Deadline, Chapter 6), according to which Pethikbumi had agreed to continue refusing the relocation.

The NGO Forum thus asserted that the leaders of Pethikbumi were no longer advocating for their members' interests in an ethical way. However, although the NGO Forum had withdrawn its support for Pethikbumi, Pak Toni declared that it was still willing to support individual traders who were continuing to refuse the relocation.[19] He also stated that BPHK had not yet made a decision about their position; they were waiting to hear back from Pethikbumi about the legal case against the government, which had already been submitted to the courts.[20]

When I met with Mas Eko later that day, I relayed the message from Ibu Marini. He said that neither Pak Pramana nor the rest of Pethikbumi's leaders were interested in talking with BPHK – they could no longer be certain that BPHK was looking out for their interests.[21] By this time, the Pethikbumi leaders' interpretation of the event had become more fixed: BPHK could not be trusted, and as a result they also could not trust BPHK's close partner, the NGO Forum.

That evening, I also received bad news. When I showed up on the street, Mas Basri, another Pethikbumi leader, called me over, and we sat together on a bench with several other Pethikbumi members. There I was told that I was no longer invited to participate in Pethikbumi's meetings or other activities while they relocated to the marketplace because they needed to work entirely on their own (in his words, Pethikbumi need to be *murni* – pure). I was among the outsiders, including BPHK and the NGO Forum, who were now banned from Pethikbumi because, as Mas Eko told me shortly afterwards, this was one of the requirements that the government had placed on the group before the traders would be allowed to join the relocation.[22] The government placed this ban on the NGOs, student activists, and other outsiders such as myself because they believed that the street vendors' activism against the relocation was driven by outsiders rather than by the vendors themselves. Although I would no longer be allowed to join in their efforts, Mas Eko promised to keep me informed over the next few hours and days through phone calls, text messages, and by meeting with me in person.[23] This banning of so-called outsiders seemed to me to violate Pethikbumi's basic rights to representation and to involve whomever they pleased, but the traders were becoming desperate to receive locations in the marketplace.[24]

Since I was banned from joining the Pethikbumi meetings until the group had entered the new marketplace, I had more time to reflect on what had taken place at the Northern Square on the night of November 11 and the significant consequences for Pethikbumi as an organization. I decided it was important to ask the different people involved for their perspectives on what had unfolded that night.

On November 13, I received a phone call from Mas Eko. He and I often met to discuss and reflect on the events taking place around the relocation project, and we decided to meet at a local coffee shop later that evening to do more of the same. Mas Eko and his fellow traders were often interested in meeting with me because I was outside of their immediate group, and I also signified to them the possibility that the story of their fight against the government might receive wider recognition.

At the coffee shop, I took my meeting with Mas Eko as an opportunity to ask him about what he had witnessed at the Northern Square. He recounted the story again. Since at the time Mas Eko had not been able to see everything in detail, the story he told me at this point was likely based on his conversation with Pak Pramana after the meeting with Pak Didik at the Northern Square had ended. Mas Eko told me about how Pak Pramana was picked up by the police and taken to the square to meet with Pak Didik. Ibu Marini and Pak Suyitno were there already. Mas Eko told me that Pak Didik had been trying to pressure Pak Pramana into influencing the remaining Pethikbumi traders to accept the relocation, and that Pak Pramana was asked to make a decision on the spot. Pak Didik was on the phone with Pak Herry Zudianto, and they were trying to negotiate a deal. Nothing came of this meeting, however, because Pak Pramana was not interested in negotiating on his own without the rest of the Pethikbumi leaders, nor did he want to accept the bribes he was being offered. Pak Pramana was surprised that Ibu Marini was also at the Northern Square.[25] The next day, at the press conference, the NGO Forum had delivered their statement separating themselves from Pethikbumi.

In addition to obtaining Mas Eko's version of the story, I was also interested in whether the secret meeting at the Northern Square was discussed in the newspapers. I was surprised to learn that it was not; after all, Pethikbumi could have gone public with a story about how the municipal government had been trying to "force" the group's leaders to negotiate individually, since Pak Pramana was essentially taken to the Northern Square without any real knowledge as to why. Instead, the story told in the newspapers was that Pethikbumi's leadership had negotiated on its own without the support of its members.[26] Indeed, the NGO Forum had previously not had a problem with the Pethikbumi leaders meeting with the mayor on November 9. It was only after the November 11 incident at the Northern Square, and after Pethikbumi had accepted the relocation, that this negotiation became a reason for the NGO Forum to withdraw its support.[27] No one was willing to discuss the events of November 11 directly in the newspapers or in public; instead, it was treated as a private matter to be discussed only among the few actors involved, and only when they were specifically asked.

A month after the relocation, I sat down for an interview with Pak Akbar, and I took the opportunity to ask him about the secret meeting at the Northern Square. Pak Akbar said that there had been two occasions when Pak Ferry asked the Pethikbumi leaders to meet, and that both times, Ibu Marini had also appeared. The first was in Jogjatronik when Ibu Marini came into the mall with Pak Suyitno. The second was when Pak Pramana was brought to the Northern Square. Pak Akbar said, "How could they come to both places? First at Jogjatronik she was there, and there was a plan here [at the Northern Square], and she is also here. It was like it was engineered, but also – I don't know exactly how – but there was suspicion from Ibu Marini."[28] Pak Akbar explained that Pak Pramana was upset because on the night of November 11, Ibu Marini had sent a text message to Mas Arief asking him to check on Pak Pramana. Ibu Marini appeared to be accusing Pak Pramana of negotiating with Pak Didik and another government official on his own.[29] Pak Pramana was upset that Ibu Marini did not ask him directly what he was doing and instead sent another member of Pethikbumi to spy on him.[30] And yet Pak Pramana never confronted Ibu Marini directly about this incident, despite her attempts to connect with him and the other Pethikbumi members.

In a conversation I had with Pak Pramana, he described the incident at the Northern Square as just another time when he was offered a bribe during the relocation.[31] He said that when he was taken to the Northern Square he was asked what he wanted. But as Pak Pramana told me, "I did not ask for anything [*laughing*]. I'm a fool. The mayor phoned me and said, 'What do you want?' I told him I don't want anything. They wanted to give us money, wanted to give it to me, but I did not want it. In reality, I'm stupid."[32] This mirrored the performances of conspicuous visibility I described earlier (see Conspicuous Visibility: Managing Impressions, Chapter 4), where the leaders of Pethikbumi portrayed themselves as loyal heroes by telling stories of the bribes they were offered but refused to take.

Pak Pramana was convinced that Ibu Marini had to have received money or some other bribe from the government. He considered that maybe Ibu Marini intended to back Pethikbumi merely to gain popularity, but he was left pondering why their own lawyers would turn people against him: "Why did Ibu Marini slander me and distribute it [the misinformation about him meeting with Pak Didik] to the members of Pethikbumi? I was in reality embarrassed at the time, even though I did not play a role at all."[33] Pak Pramana thus accounted for his own actions while shifting the accusation back onto Ibu Marini. The actions of Pethikbumi's lawyers were interpreted in relation to the already circulating idea that BPHK had unnamed interests (see Conspicuous Visibility: Managing Impressions, Chapter 4), which suggested that their efforts to work for democracy and transparency without payment or some political trade-off were not wholly sincere.

Ibu Marini also provided me with her perspective on the events of the night of November 11:

[Pak Suyitno and I] were going for our normal dinner at the Northern Square. When we arrived we were surprised to see one of the leaders from Pethikbumi there with several police and the NGO that was supporting the pro-relocation group [ILMA]. Pak Pramana was talking with Pak Didik and they were in some sort of negotiation. We had no idea what was going on, and if we had known that there was some meeting we surely wouldn't have brought our baby with us.[34] We were shocked at what was happening so we phoned another leader of Pethikbumi to come witness the event. Then we left the scene.[35]

Finally, I asked Mas Totok from PPIP about what had unfolded that evening. He gave the following response:

> It seems like there is an indication of a scenario (*indaski skenario*). Once the deadline has almost been reached, suddenly it looks as if Pak Pramana is being pitted against the [Pethikbumi] leaders. At the time of the meeting in front of the *Kedaulatan Rakyat* office on Sunday, Ibu Marini called Mas Arief and told him to come and see what was happening in the Northern Square. And it was as if to trap Pak Pramana. At that moment, Pak Pramana was meeting with ILMA [the organization run by Pak Didik]. And ILMA was working against us. It seems that we were directed to see that Pak Pramana was negotiating by himself (*bernego sendirian*). I was also disappointed with Ibu Marini, and suspected that she, too, was becoming close to ILMA.[36]

Mas Totok refers here to the idea that there might be a scenario. By this, he means that this event was the result of some form of shadow play or the actions of someone behind the scenes. For him, it was Ibu Marini who appeared to be getting close to ILMA since she had talked to them on the phone a couple of times. In the stories that emerged after the incident in the Northern Square – and especially from Mas Eko, Pak Akbar, Pak Pramana, and Mas Totok – Ibu Marini, who had made the initial accusation towards Pak Pramana, came to be considered the oknum. But this seemed to be as far as the accusation went. Besides myself, no one sought out further evidence about what really happened that night. There was instead a feeling that this incident should be forgotten – that people did not want to dig deeper into what had happened for fear of what they might find out. When I asked people about the events of November 11 specifically, they responded, but this was not something widely talked about. My desire to know what "really" took place that evening was not shared – indeed, I felt that my pursuit of information was starting to make people uncomfortable. There was no desire to report this incident to the newspapers, either. Mas Eko had used my camera to take photos that day at the Northern Square, but he had erased these photos and had never handed them over to anyone, including me. Pethikbumi members had experienced incidents with preman and oknum in the months prior to this event at the Northern Square. However, most of these incidents had involved people from outside of the anti-relocation movement, and this allowed the traders to maintain a distinction between the anti-relocation movement and those creating the conflict – the state, according to members of Pethikbumi. The events of November 11, however, caused shame among the group's membership because they indicated that those working behind the scenes might have come from within their own ranks.

Ibu Marini asked me again to request that the members of Pethik-bumi come to her office, but they continued to refuse. She thought that the incident might have been conjured up for the express purpose of instigating a conflict between Pethikbumi and BPHK, which it certainly did. But this was not a new occurrence for BPHK; I was told of similar incidents that had accompanied BPHK's efforts to help other groups such as factory workers. Had BPHK been tipped off? Was Pak Pramana a participant in the plan as well? He was known to have police and pre-man friends. Pak Didik and Pak Pramana did know many of the same people. Whatever actually happened, Pethikbumi, the NGO Forum, and BPHK ended their working relationship as a result. While others wanted to leave this incident alone and move on, I was left hoping that I would learn what had "really happened."

With this breakdown in trust, Pethikbumi turned to the government for help. They now had little bargaining power left. Pethikbumi met with the municipal government on November 13 and constructed an agreement, handwritten on a scrap of paper, requiring its leaders' signatures before the membership would be accepted into Kuncen Market-place. Sixty-two vendors were then allowed to sign up to sell at Kun-cen Marketplace, but not without a cost. The terms of the agreement included a commitment that Pethikbumi would withdraw its lawsuit against the government over the regulation that had been drafted with-out consultation (Pemerintah Kota Yogyakarta 2007).[37] Pethikbumi also had to promise to not work with outsiders, such as new lawyers or researchers such as myself. The scribbled agreement read:

We sign as the leaders of Pethikbumi on behalf of all our members, following the development of the situation, and hereby submit the following statement:

1. We agree to join the relocation of the *pedagang klithikan* [second-hand goods traders] from Mangkubumi Street to Kuncen Marketplace and will not sell again on Mangkubumi Street.
2. We agree with the City Government of Yogyakarta about the number of members of Pethikbumi that will occupy Kuncen Marketplace in the enclosed statement and will follow the procedures and mechanisms that are decided by the government in the process of drafting the traders to Kuncen Marketplace.
3. We agree to withdraw the lawsuit in the Court that is related to Regulation No. 45, 2007.
4. We will not include external people within the following process of the relocation of the pedagang klithikan from Mangkubumi Street to Kuncen Marketplace.[38]

The exclusion of "outsiders" reaffirmed the idea that only the government could help the traders, and in so doing, it once again safely secured the government as the traders' main patron. Three days later, *Kedaulatan Rakyat* reported that sixty-two of the seventy-five traders submitted by Pethikbumi had passed the verification process. In the article, the municipal government claimed that they would treat the Pethikbumi traders the same as the other traders, but that the Pethikbumi traders would be located in a less strategic area because of their delayed entry.[39]

Rumours continued to circulate in the days after the signing of this agreement. The specifics of the incident in the Northern Square were not discussed; the focus instead shifted to the question of who had generated the tensions between the anti-relocation traders and their supporters. For instance, one individual expressed a belief that "BPHK received money from the mayor in order to stop its case in the court system. This is why they are dropping the case now." Another rumour circulated about PPIP, which also supported Pethikbumi, to the effect that "the big boss behind PPIP is actually close with the mayor. This big boss was the one running the machine: he created the conflict, and then resolved it." Others said that the mayor had planned and constructed this whole conflict, only to heroically resolve it.[40] The members of Pethikbumi and their supporters each seemed to have their own idea of what really happened, but no one wanted to explore their suspicions further; these theories simply remained in the realm of rumours. And yet talking about these unresolved rumours was not without effect. Through the act of talking, the teller could establish him- or herself as both knowing and innocent, and also establish bonds with the listener (me and others).

The Pethikbumi leaders and their supporters did not bring this off-stage shadow play involving an oknum to the attention of the newspapers. A possible motive for this decision (besides wanting to avoid causing embarrassment or shock) was pointed out to me by an outside informant to whom I explained the story: Pethikbumi's leaders were afraid of finding out that no conspiracy actually existed, that it was all just a coincidence. Maybe it was easier for them to admit defeat at the hands of an unseen power than to confess that they were not able to deliver what they had promised to their members and the public.[41]

Additionally, the idea of shadow play had always been present in the minds of Pethikbumi members, not just after the November 11 incident. Consciously or not, they expected something to happen – puppet masters were always present during government projects – and maybe November 11 was the climax in their great drama, a point at which

Pethikbumi could shift course. The group's members were already slightly suspicious of BPHK and the NGO Forum. As noted earlier (see Conspicuous Visibility: Managing Impressions, Chapter 4), Pak Toni and Ibu Marini claimed that their desire to help the street vendors was based solely on their concern for human rights and democracy in the city, and not because of money. Yet when these NGO and legal supporters declared that they had "no interests" aside from the promotion of "democracy" and "transparency," their actions and the information they circulated were deemed particularly suspicious. This social distrust had already existed, and therefore it was not surprising that suspicions turned towards BPHK – the main focus of Pethikbumi's suspicions – and the NGO Forum.

The incident at the Northern Square was all that was needed to break the fragile relationship between Pethikbumi and its supporters. While the group's members could just as easily have blamed the police and Satpol PP for their failure, they did not. Instead, the November 11 incident – this chance meeting that may or may not have involved political play – became the reason for the group's failure. Thus, one potential interpretation of the situation was that Pethikbumi's leaders were too afraid to openly challenge the police and Satpol PP, because this might entail admitting that Pethikbumi was incapable as a group; in this telling, the events that transpired on November 11 and the subsequent claims of conspiracy served as an escape from this failure. The existence of an oknum deflected questions about Pethikbumi's inadequacies and contradictions while placing blame on an unknown agent, allowing the group to accept the government's relocation, but only because they were "victims" of a conspiracy. Ultimately, they could remain heroes of democracy who had refused government bribes.

Among the Pethikbumi street vendors, there was both a certain fascination with the idea of the unseen power of the oknum and an admiration for the oknum's work; both of these factors likely contributed to the lack of further inquiry. In many cases, an oknum might also be tolerated out of an acknowledgment of the material benefits accruing from their actions. Almost anyone might become an oknum as long as the opportunity and resources were available. As one informant explained to me, "It is like saying, 'Oh yeah, I'd do that too,' and therefore the tendency is to let things pass because 'It could have been me,' or 'It could be me in the future.'"[42] Many of the street vendors imagined themselves as secretly taking government bribes or playing the situation in such a way that they would receive one or more kiosks in the marketplace. For instance, Mas Tokok said in reference to becoming an oknum, "This could happen because Pak Galang himself once offered me two kiosks at the marketplace. But I did not want them because I did not want to play at that level. I am more about providing assistance. [I'm not getting involved] because of political interests or conspiracy."[43] Here Mas Tokok could see himself taking bribes and being the oknum – he did not want to do it, but it was still imaginable. This was different from cases of murder or rape, where most people could not easily place themselves in the shoes of the perpetrator.[44] In November 2006, some Pethikbumi leaders accused of illegally buying and selling locations on the street for profit had been removed from the group and reported to the police, but nothing had been done in the case of these potential oknum. Most of the street vendors understood why these traders had done what they were alleged to have done – these potential oknum stood to benefit economically – even if they personally disagreed with this kind of behaviour, which they deemed dishonest and corrupt.

The oknum was a powerful idea in the traders' political imaginations because it allowed an actor to be named under the conditions of growing inequality and unfairness in the relocation project. As a result, the oknum reoriented the search for truth and transparency. At the same time, they also prevented further truth-seeking because the figure of the oknum offered an explanation, a sense of relief, or a chance to evade one's own responsibility and role in the events – and the role of the government – in generating the suspicion between the traders and their supporters. Through efforts to reveal, name, or make known the oknum through rumour and gossip, the Pethikbumi leaders were able to blame the failure of democracy and their movement on the figure of the oknum, and to suggest that corruption and unfair play came from elsewhere. The easiest targets were the NGO supporters and lawyers who had been helping Pethikbumi, because suspicions about their "unnamed interests" already existed and they did not need to be incorporated into Kuncen Marketplace.

Indirect Accusations and NGO Oknum

The success of this relocation is a very proud achievement, because the municipal government managed to implement this relocation by emphasizing the humanitarian aspects with successful dialogues so as not to cause turmoil.
– Pak Suryadharma Ali, minister of cooperatives and small and medium enterprises[45]

In the days before Pethikbumi moved into the new marketplace, Mayor Herry Zudianto said that the Pethikbumi vendors did not want to move because they did not understand (*belum memahami*) the government's vision for Kuncen Marketplace, but that they should not be viewed as enemies.[46] When the group finally signed up for the relocation, the government's project was taken as a success: the conflict had been resolved because the traders now "understood."[47] The relocation was deemed a success because the government had been able to hold "successful dialogues" with the traders, according to the statement by Pak Suryadharma Ali, a federal minister.[48]

As reported in a press release on the municipal government's website, at a November 12 celebration to give thanks to God (*Tasyakuran*) at the marketplace, Mayor Herry Zudianto spoke briefly to journalists, promising to take care of the street vendors and reasserting himself as their rightful leader and someone they could trust.[49] This was timely, considering they could no longer trust their NGO friends, their lawyers, or even their fellow members. The mayor gave his best wishes to the street vendors (referring to them as the *rakyat*) and expressed his hope that the new marketplace would bring good luck – *berkah* and *rezeki* – to the sellers. He reminded them that the relocation was for their own good: to upgrade their status from informal to formal sellers and to protect them from being exposed to the harsh environment of the street, where they would have to face the sun, rain, and wind with little to no protection.[50]

In the press release, the mayor was also described as expressing his sympathy for the street vendors who had until recently refused the relocation:

> The mayor feels sympathy. In reality there are some street traders who are on a good path, they wish and want to believe their leader; they respect the leader because all leaders will bring good, but [they got sidetracked] because they are influenced from here and there (*dipengaruhi sana-sini*) with exaggerated promises (*janji yang muluk*). But the mayor believes that Allah will hear the prayers that are sent by all of you.[51]

In addition, *Kedaulatan Rakyat* quoted Pak Herry Zudianto as saying, "This [relocation] was influenced (*dipengaruhi*) by other sides that were not accountable (*tidak bertanggung jawab*) because there were lots of interests (*kepentingan*). The traders became only a tool (*tunggangan*)."[52] In *Merapi*, the mayor was quoted as follows: "I also understand (*memahami*) sometimes that traders get confused (*terombang-ambing*) because there are certain groups that have interests that are not necessarily the same as [the traders'] interests."[53]

In these statements, the street vendors were portrayed as victims of their nefarious patrons. The mayor, other government officials, and parliamentarians expressed their concern that these supposedly

self-interested outsiders were manipulating the "naive" and "uneducated" street vendors. The vendors, as non-agents, could be forgiven
and incorporated back into their rightful place as clients of the state. The
NGOs were the ones to be suspected and closely watched. The mayor
was thus able to argue that his government was looking out for the small
people against the interests of other (unnamed) actors. In questioning
the motivations of the NGOs and implying that they were motivated by
unnamed (as opposed to selfless) interests, the mayor used the language
of the New Order to play on lingering fear and suspicion towards NGOs.
As noted at the beginning of this chapter, this discrediting of NGOs is a
strategy used by some companies in Indonesia. Such was the case with
the mining company Newmont, which hired consultants to develop an
action plan that used discourses about transparency and accountability
against activists, helping to reaffirm citizens' concerns about the role of
NGOs in the country (M. Welker 2014, 174).

While Pak Herry Zudianto rejected the New Order model that placed
the state above society, he simultaneously drew on discourses from that
era to question the legitimacy of non-state groups. Although rumours
circulated among the actors, and they suspected each other of having
unnamed interests in the months before the relocation (see Conspicuous
Visibility: Managing Impressions, Chapter 4), the government became the
most prominent source of this conspiracy theory when it circulated it in
the contexts described above: during a brief discussion with journalists at
the November 12 *Tasyakuran* celebration, in a government press release,[54]
and in a number of newspapers. The government's interest in circulating
this rumour was to ensure that citizens and government officials, both in
Yogyakarta and across the archipelago, perceived the relocation as a success, and that the government's main opposition, Pethikbumi's lawyers
and NGO supporters, were discredited. When it came to pursuing these
aims, there was no clear boundary between unofficial discourses, such as
rumours, and their more official variants (see Bubandt 2008, 793).

By relieving the street vendors of blame, the government's message
implied that the vendors had not become agents of democracy through
their organizing, their protests, and their refusal to relocate – they were,
rather, merely victims who did not know better. It is important to note
here why it was possible for the government to separate the NGOs,
lawyers, and social organizations from the street vendors: this was a
result of their class difference. Although this was not stated directly, the
underlying difference was that the street vendors were considered by
the government to be uneducated, naive, and from a lower social class
than either the municipal civil servants or the vendors' own lawyers
and NGO supporters. (That this was not necessarily the case was beside

the point.) This was evident when the government referred to the traders as "confused" (*terombang-ambing*) and as "a tool" (*tunggangan*) for others' interests, suggesting that the Pethikbumi traders were unable to think for themselves. In contrast, Pethikbumi's supporters were viewed by government officials as educated, and for this reason, the NGOs and lawyers were blamed for acting in their own interests (*kepentingan*), even if these supposed interests were never described.

Following the mayor's indirect accusation of Pethikbumi's supporters, a November 16 article in *Kedaulatan Rakyat* referred to an official letter from the NGO Forum to the mayor.[55] The letter asked for clarification on the mayor's previous statement that "the traders became only a tool [*tunggangan*]."[56] Pak Cahyu from the NGO Forum asked what the mayor meant by his use of the term *tunggangan,* which refers to the bending of a political movement towards one's own interests. The word *oknum* was not used, but *tunggangan* basically refers to the idea that a group or person is being used by someone for their own interests. The NGO Forum asked the mayor for clarification because there were only three groups supporting Pethikbumi: BPHK, the NGO Forum, and PPIP. The mayor was thus clearly referring to these three groups when he spoke of the role of other parties (*pihak lain*). Since *Kedaulatan Rakyat*'s readers could surely decipher this veiled accusation, the NGO Forum decided to respond directly in the newspaper, just as the government had done when they were indirectly accused of organizing thugs (see The Released Story and Its Repercussions, Chapter 5). However, the government did not respond to the NGO Forum's accusation in this or any subsequent newspaper article.[57]

The indirect nature of the government's accusation was typical of a form of exchange commonly seen in the public sphere in Indonesia (see Manzella 2000) whereby the criticizer uses indirect communication to make an accusation and to prompt a direct response from the accused. Despite its accusatory nature, this style of exchange is considered a form of politeness since the actors involved are not directly named. In the case of the relocation, the government's accusation, because it was partial or incomplete, also suggested that the state was inadvertently revealing the existence of a secret. And because it was packaged as a secret that was being incompletely or indirectly revealed, citizens were eager to be in the possession of this knowledge.

James Siegel (1993) has shown how during the New Order, a rumour was thought to be problematic when the source was believed to come from outside of the government. He writes, "This is a politics of origins where the point of forgeries is not to convince anyone of the truth of their contents but to make them believe that all rumors, accurate or not, favorable or not, have their starting point in the government" (64). In her research on the "AIDS club" rumours in Surabaya, Kroeger (2003) likewise shows that the municipal government sought to control who was deemed the source of the rumours in Surabaya in order to "maintain the upper hand" (251–2). In the newspapers, the municipal government blamed the "AIDS club" rumours on what Kroeger describes as "imaginary enemies" (252). Kroeger concludes, "This served to arouse suspicion of those who might appear to undermine the nation and reestablished the moral authority of the government as the protector of the public good" (252).

In the case I have described here, the municipal government likewise used the newspapers to circulate a rumour that a pro-democracy group had unnamed interests. Rumours had already circulated among the various actors as they accused *each other* of having unnamed interests in the lead-up to the relocation, but the municipal government eventually established itself as the official source of this conspiracy theory in the public sphere. The government's version of the conspiracy reinforced state power because it suggested that it was the *only* body looking out for the interests of its citizens. Yet, as will be discussed in the next section, alongside these conspiracies about the role of the NGOs in the anti-relocation movement, narratives concerning the role of Allah in this process also surfaced, both in the public sphere and in private conversations.

Allah's Unseen Power

In his book on the intersection of politics and spirits in Indonesian democracy, Nils Bubandt (2014) argues that, "once conjured up for political reasons, spirits and gods become political actors, changing what counts as politics and what can be politically imagined and desired" (15). Aspects of politics, such as corruption and democracy, he asserts, can be "spirit-like" because both politics and spirits operate in uncertain and mysterious ways (7).[58] The politics around the vendor relocation bear some similarity to Allah in that neither is fully in view. As Bubandt states with regard to spirits and corruption, "It is this nonpresence that is the source of their power" (103). In the aftermath of the relocation, the municipal government worked hard to claim that Allah was on its side, and that the will of Allah was the same as the will of the government. For the municipal government, the relocation was conceived of and talked about as a project with spiritual virtue, not only as a social intervention but as a religious one as well (see also Rudnyckyj 2009). According to the government's publicly circulated narrative, Allah was a powerful force behind the scenes who had made the relocation successful. These narratives suggested the convergence of religious ethics and governance.

In a speech at the grand opening of the marketplace on 13 December 2007, Pak Herry Zudianto invoked a religious term to refer to the relocation – *hijrah*, which describes the undertaking of a "religious migration in order to seek sanctuary or freedom from persecution" (Elmadmad 1991, 463).[59] He said, "So we refer to yesterday not as a relocation but as a religious migration, because [the relocated vendors] are searching for a better life … and [the relocation] will bring incomes that are more blessed by Allah."[60] This statement assumed that the relocation symbolized a move from immorality to morality, from illegality to legality, and that the state's power was rooted in Allah.

It was not much earlier that the Pethikbumi traders, too, had drawn on the idea of Allah to support their right to the street. During Ramadan, in a press release responding to the newly drafted government regulation (Pemerintah Kota Yogyakarta 2007) that officially made selling on Mangkubumi Street illegal, Pethikbumi asked,

> What's the point of development through greening (*pembangunan tamanisasi*) if it will only belittle or diminish us and increase the number of poor in Yogyakarta? … Allah stated clearly in Surah Al-Ma'un [the 107th *surah* or chapter of the Quran]: "Woe unto worshippers who are heedless of their prayer, who repelleth the orphan and urgeth not the feeding of the needy." Several relocations attempted by the government of Yogyakarta have experienced failure and they are the solid proof that for us relocation is not a solution.[61]

By quoting the Al-Ma'un, the street vendors were suggesting that there was no point in doing grand things such as praying if the point was simply to be seen and praised for doing so.[62] What mattered were the little things: being kind to orphans, feeding the needy, helping the sick, being mindful in one's prayers, and doing small kindnesses. In this context, the relocation was seen as one of the "grand things" that the government was doing just to be praised and seen, in contrast to those small acts of kindness that might actually help the street vendors. This can be considered a religiously grounded hermeneutics of action, which saw Allah and his teachings as a determinant of how urban planning should unfold.

With their Ramadan press release, the members of Pethikbumi also claimed that Allah was on their side. They ended by saying, "We as the big family of Pethikbumi remind the government of Yogyakarta to rethink the relocation … before Allah SWT[63] remembers the government of Yogyakarta's method at some later moment."[64] Allah was situated as the one who knew the truth, the unseen force who would

Figure 7. Kuncen Marketplace, 16 July 2008. Photo by Dhimas Langgeng Gumilar and Alwan Brilian.

ensure that bad deeds would be brought to justice. Indeed, some of the street vendors believed that Allah would punish those who had acted unjustly during the relocation. This narrative, however, was not publicly recognized and described in the newspapers.

During the first days and weeks in the marketplace (see figure 7), the political play of the various actors transitioned from the largely invisible kind based only on rumour to a visible repertoire of verifiable actions and alliances. Some political parties, preman, and other outsiders received places in the new marketplace. Pak Halim, who took a neutral stance towards the relocation, was concerned with these developments, and he explained that many of the individuals who received kiosks in the marketplace were from one political party that supported the relocation: "[Former vice mayor] Pak Syukri [Fadholi] was someone truly from PPP. Pak Didik was from PPP. And here [in the marketplace] there are all people from PPP. They received places."[65] The street vendors from Pethikbumi who had left the group to secretly sign up for the relocation in the final days before the Pethikbumi leaders officially resigned were visible because their locations were in the better-situated areas of the marketplace. Those who had two kiosks were also visible. People such as preman also appeared to have received kiosks. This was noted by the vendors in the marketplace but not discussed in the newspapers. There was no sense that these people should be brought to justice.

Most of the vendors I spoke with said that those who had taken advantage of the process would eventually face the law: the law of karma[66] (*hukum karma*) handed out by Allah, who knew the ultimate truth.[67] As one trader, Pak Kasiyarno, said to me, "The law of karma is the law of Allah. Allah is the only one who knows. We do not know. What is clear, however, is that what is good will receive good and what is bad will receive bad."[68] The traders believed that all the oknum and political players who benefited unjustly would have to repay their debts. Maybe they would later go bankrupt or their child would die in an accident – either way, these checks and balances would ensure that things worked out.[69] In this interpretation, Allah was adjudicating the world of the living (see Bubandt 2014, 97). Although no lawsuits were filed, a spiritual mode of prosecution was underway that would provide redress by other means (86).

In the months following the opening of the marketplace, I wondered how the conflict would continue to play out. Would people be interested in figuring out what really happened? Surprisingly, few stories from the relocation process were featured in the press. The newspapers were now reporting on the business of the marketplace and events that were designed to draw shoppers' attention to it. In the marketplace itself (see figure 8), the street vendors had no real interest in continuing to investigate the corrupt practices and incidents that had taken place in the lead-up to the relocation. Talk about the past was seen as pointless; instead the vendors focused on how they could develop an organization to involve most of their colleagues in the marketplace and ensure the success of the new venture. Information about oknum was no longer viewed as particularly important because Allah would deal with the shadow play.

The Government's Account: Celebrating Dialogue

Charles L. Briggs (2004) has argued that when people in eastern Venezuela died from cholera in 1992–3, the government and the affected communities each had their own accounts of the outbreak. Rather than focusing on the different epistemologies contained in such conspiracy theorizing, Briggs asserts that we should look at the different political economies that position the different players in this drama. While some individuals can easily access the public sphere and thereby convert their narratives into public discourses, others cannot. As the vendor relocation came to an end

Figure 8. Traders in Kuncen Marketplace, December 2008. Photo by author.

and the Pethikbumi traders settled into their new lives in the marketplace, they no longer had the willpower and support to bolster their version of events in the public sphere. The municipal government, however, was able to widely distribute its narrative of the relocation by touting its success in books and newspaper articles.[70] The government now controlled the information politics governing the relocation, while Pethikbumi and its supporters, once the government's opposition, remained silent and backed away from engaging in any counter-narrative that would challenge the state's interpretation of this event.

In 2010, Pak Herry Zudianto received the Bung Hatta Anti-Corruption Award. According to the *Jakarta Post*, the award "honor[s] public servants for their integrity and leadership in creating transparency in their respective administration."[71] Although Pak Herry Zudianto is most famous for creating a one-stop licensing centre for investors, making Yogyakarta "the country's most investor-friendly city," he also received recognition for his successful relocation of the street traders on Mangkubumi Street, Asem Gede, and the Southern Square. The *Jakarta Post* article quoted above describes these efforts as follows: "By creating a dialogue with street vendors, he was able to relocate hundreds of them to a newly built market that was later named *Pasar Klithikan*, or market for second-hand goods, a few years ago … So what is his recipe for success? 'I like listening to many people,' Pak Herry said."[72]

In keeping with the widespread use of democratic rhetoric in Indonesia's public sphere during the post-Suharto era, Pak Herry Zudianto was able to represent himself as part of a new generation of leaders tapping into and trading on the symbolic capital of "dialogue" (despite the fact that he often employed a type of sosialisasi that involved informing rather than dialoging; see Getting Close and Speaking Their Language, Chapter 3). At the same time, he was an old type of leader reminiscent of the pre–New Order era in that, similar to Sukarno, he claimed to be close to the people (J.T. Siegel 1998). Like the NGOs, Pak Herry Zudianto could talk to the people, inspire them, and convince them that he could help them. In an interview with me, he said, "for me, personally, there is only one measure for being a successful leader: how far the leader is able to influence the community to participate. For me, community participation is the main target."[73]

In a 2008 memoir, Pak Herry Zudianto proudly described the street vendor relocation as an example of dialogue (*contoh dialog*):

> There are different opinions among the community and the mass media, pro and contra, regarding the ideas and the local government policies to relocate second-hand traders. Yet those who have the greatest interests are the klithikan vendors. They should be made partners in the dialogue, participate in the solution-searching despite the different opinions and interests related to the relocation policies. As the mayor, I invited them to meet in my private house, to sit together and dialogue informally from 21:00 to 3:00 in the morning.[74] Each side was given space to express their thoughts, reasons, and hopes, and they also gave their claims against the other group. Both sides agreed to listen to each other and were willing to find common ground to solve the problem together. (Zudianto 2008, 17)

Pak Herry Zudianto, as an important figure in the city, had the political and economic means to rewrite the history of the relocation in his favour. He did not, however, significantly alter his relocation plan – in fact, he did not alter the plan in any meaningful sense – in response to the protests or suggestions from the anti-relocation forces. Although the mayor presented himself as a leader who listened to the people, he pushed ahead with the project that he had helped to develop and was determined to successfully implement, excluding perspectives that ran counter to his vision. Books and newspapers played an important role in this politics of exclusion because it was through these forms of media that Pak Herry Zudianto was able to frame the Pethikbumi traders' opposition to the relocation as a straightforward reflection of their inability to understand the project. In the end, Pak Herry Zudianto's narrative of the relocation became solidified as the official version of events because he had the political and social capital to make it so. Engaging in information politics, after all, takes not only cultural capital but economic resources as well.

Conclusion

This chapter has described conspiracy theories as a central form of information politics during this street vendor relocation. These were one of the central forms of information politics because, as far as the anti-relocation traders were concerned, there had to be someone working behind the screen. The Pethikbumi leaders' conspiracy theories showed that the traders enacted their agency within a dense network of actors on the scene when they concluded that the legal aid organizations and NGOs could not be trusted (see Copeland 2014). These conspiracy theories played an important role in bringing the conflict to a climax, but they also allowed for reconciliation and resolution. The central figure of the conspiracy theories was the oknum, an individual suspected of working in secret to support the government's project while claiming to be on the traders' side. While the oknum is often imagined as a state official, in this case the incident at the Northern Square caused the Pethikbumi vendors to direct their suspicions towards their legal aid supporters. Rather than challenging the state's hegemonic discourse, this conspiratorial knowledge in fact reaffirmed a state narrative suggesting that members of civil society, especially NGOs working for democracy and transparency, could not be trusted. While Pethikbumi distrusted their legal aid supporters because they thought they were secretly working on the side of government, the government claimed the NGOs were misleading the traders. These two narratives reaffirmed each other because they led to a similar conclusion: legal aid organizations and NGOs could not be trusted. In public forums such as newspapers, the government indirectly accused the NGOs of leading the traders astray in order to discredit them, and this became the final, authoritative version of events, despite the NGOs' attempts to challenge this allegation. This conspiratorial knowledge about the role of the NGOs in the relocation reveals one of the potential limits of collective political action in Indonesia, where conspiracy theories are a central form of information politics in the democratic era. In particular, it reaffirmed a common belief that those claiming to work selflessly for the ideals of democracy and transparency cannot be taken at face value, and it reinforced the state's power as well.

Spiritual beliefs about Allah are an important part of urban politics in Indonesia. Unlike the oknum, a negative force in urban politics, Allah was interpellated as a good force, albeit in different ways by different actors. For the government, Allah served as a hidden power helping to ensure that the relocation succeeded; the government also described the relocation as a type of religious migration. For the traders, however, Allah acted more as a judge who would bring about justice in the face of the failure of democracy and transparency. The traders' occult cosmologies reflected a deep suspicion that worldly institutions are unable to bring about transparency and democracy, but also a profound sense of hope that the unseen power of Allah would restore moral order.

In an adapted version of the Mahabharata, the ancient Indian epic, told through wayang kulit, the central dispute between two sets of cousins (the Kurawa and the Pandhawa) over the Ngastina kingdom is never morally clear-cut – both sides can make reasonable claims to the throne. However, Ward Keeler (1987) found that in informal commentaries, the Kurawa cousins were often seen as bad and the Pandhawa as good (243). If we extend this scheme to the relocation project, the government claimed to represent the Pandhawa – as models of fairness, potency, and patience – whereas the NGOs and other supporters of Pethikbumi were the Kurawa – morally questionable. The traders were "good" characters who diverged from their straight and narrow path but were brought back to goodness under the triumph of the Pandhawa. Following the example of a typical shadow play, no harsh punishments were issued in the wake of the dispute between the government and the Pethikbumi. The traders did receive kiosks, however, at the back of the marketplace.

There was a moment, as we saw earlier (see Playing with Information, Chapter 6), when the traders were feared because it was thought that they might turn to physical violence. When the relocation concluded, the municipal government helped the traders to see themselves in such terms as *legal market traders*, *moral*, and *religious*. The government situated the traders not as violent or criminal but as the rakyat, the people, who could once again be spoken for and protected by their government leaders. The success of the relocation project, then, could be interpreted as the ability to convert the illegal traders into a new social identity, one that was recognized and affirmed by the state. During the relocation, the street vendors attempted to appropriate the power once possessed by the state by using its practices of revealing and concealing (see Chapter 4: Democratizing Surveillance; Chapter 5: Press Releases and Silent Critiques; and Chapter 6: The Talk of Violence). But in the end, the state was able to re-establish itself as the main source and guardian of information working for the good of the people. What was new, however, was the sense that power itself seemed to be available for capture by ordinary citizens through the use of information politics. People, even street vendors, felt that they could now accumulate power. This feeling did not exist prior to the process of decentralization that accompanied Suharto's downfall. Now, members of the urban underclass could also be leaders, using the revealing and concealing of information to accumulate and display power. Indeed, in one sense, this new power rested on the ability of the new urban underclass to know how to produce information, and how to reveal and conceal it properly.

Chapter Eight

Agents and Brothers

After the relocation, many of the Pethikbumi traders continued to feel that the conflict had not unfolded naturally but had instead been manipulated by shadow play. Certain forces had initiated the struggle, were guiding it, and would, in the end, resolve it. There was disagreement, however, about who was behind this shadow play. As noted earlier (see Conspiracy at the Northern Square, Chapter 7), some of the traders suspected that Pak Herry Zudianto had wanted the relocation to become a struggle so he could be the one to resolve it. Others thought that the masterminds behind the screen were lower-level officials with hopes of future promotion, and that they had been just as interested in generating and managing the conflict. Pak Didik, the lawyer for the pro-relocation group, was also characterized as someone who had perhaps been working behind the scenes to help fuel the conflict between the pro- and anti-relocation traders to ensure that the traders could not defend their rights against the relocation as a unified group. Although these kinds of suspicions remained after the relocation, most traders felt that the matter was over and done with, and that any wrongdoing was now in the hands of Allah (see Allah's Unseen Power, Chapter 7).

For my part, I had also given up any hope of determining what had "actually" happened, and I accepted that my ethnography would essentially be about how people perceived and used information, rather than a factual story about the government's involvement in shaping the politics around the relocation. Yet as time passed, I also wanted to know how people continued to think about and interpret the relocation. Had their theories about what happened changed over time?

When I visited Yogyakarta again in 2014, I found that most of the Pethikbumi leaders' theories had not changed significantly: they still suspected the various actors they had identified back in 2007 and 2008. I received another version of what happened in an interview with police officer Pak Ferry, who had not shared his narrative with me back in 2008. His version positioned Pak Akbar in a different way. I then went to Pak Akbar, who gave me a slightly different story than what he had shared with me in 2008.

In this chapter, I explore the different information ideologies that informed Pak Ferry's understanding of this conflict, both at the time that it was unfolding and when he shared his actions with me seven years later. Pak Ferry's approach relied on the management of informal circuits of information and money; as he himself told me, he sought to control how and through what channels information moved. Following Pak Ferry's narrative, I describe Pak Akbar's alternate version of the events surrounding the relocation. Unlike Pak Ferry, who used and controlled the flow of information to create suspicion vis-à-vis other players, Pak Akbar used information to protect himself from preman and to demonstrate that he was under threat as the leader of the anti-relocation group. While Pak Akbar described his relationship with Pak Ferry to me in order to show how he had protected himself, Pak Ferry talked openly about his involvement: enough time had passed since the relocation that his narrative about using information to break the group apart was not as controversial. Pak Ferry also claimed that he was among a small group of people who knew what "really" happened. Both of these stories, told seven years after the fact, relied on an underlying set of ideas about how to communicate secrets, and when and in what way it was appropriate for information to circulate. They also enacted different masculinities. Pak Ferry embodied a preman masculinity as he asserted his role as the mastermind behind the conflict's successful resolution and spoke of his ability to expand his network and territory through his involvement in the relocation. In contrast, Pak Akbar presented himself as someone who had been able to protect himself, not through physical strength, but through the strength of his network – the fact that he knew "the right person."

While the government had cemented the official public narrative in the months following the relocation (see The Government's Account: Celebrating Dialogue, Chapter 7), other versions continued to circulate among those involved. The narratives of Pak Ferry and Pak Akbar are not part of an official history of the relocation. The sharing of these stories with me years later can be viewed as a practice of postponement by which certain histories are eventually shared at a time when the political dangers they had once posed have subsided. Furthermore, the ways in which past events are recounted are key to how we imagine the future (Bonilla 2011, 316; Koselleck 2004), and potential futures that are no doubt always shifting. It also suggests that our ethnographic accounts of politically sensitive issues can be "a combination of truth, fear and lies" (see McGranahan 2005, 600). Carole McGranahan (2005) argues that it is helpful to understand how certain pasts become or fail to become history as processes of silencing are confirmed or contested through everyday practice (570). In this case, the state's illegal outsourcing of work to a police officer remains mostly a government secret.

Police Participation in Off-Budget Economies in Indonesia

Around the world, policing has come under greater scrutiny since 2020, when a series of violent and deadly incidents involving the police came to light in the United States. In Indonesia, too, citizens and organizations such as the Commission for Missing Persons and Victims of Violence (Kontras) have voiced increasing concern about police abuse and violence.[1] Scholars such as William Garriott (2013) have long recognized the paradoxes involved in policing. Garriott argues that police often function not as intended, but rather in relation to the unique context in which they emerge. This is a result of the fact that social, cultural, and political landscapes can undermine an optimistic view of policing's intention (2). Garriott is interested in analyzing not only how certain institutions seek to replicate standardized forms of policing, but also the emergent qualities of policing that surface when we focus on the "police in practice" (2).

In what follows, I trace the narrative of one police officer, Pak Ferry. Specifically, I consider his role in the relocation in order to understand how the police operate, both officially and unofficially, in the urban landscape of Yogyakarta city. According to Pak Ferry's narrative, his role is to protect the interests of the municipal government against unruly groups, and to help to ensure that conflicts over urban development do not escalate into something larger and more violent. His narrative suggests that the conditions for urban development are often created and managed by police who informally outsource their skills to the state in exchange for material benefits.

In the Reformasi period, the National Police (Kepolisian Negara Republik Indonesia, or POLRI) have gained greater control over domestic security (Supriatma 2013). During the Suharto era, the armed forces (Angkatan Bersenjata Republik Indonesia, or ABRI) were comprised of four different services, including the police (Honna 2010, 263). The army oversaw internal security, with ten divisions based around the country and reaching down to the village level, where they monitored political and security issues. In this system, the police worked *under* the army and helped maintain internal security and enforce the law. While up until the mid-1980s, *berpakaian preman* referred to a policeman or solider wearing civilian clothing, the term later came to be associated with criminality and violence (Wilson 2010, 12). By the 1990s, *preman* came to represent street thugs, gangsters, and networks of rackets often coordinated by the state. By the end of the New Order, Loren Ryter argues, "journalists and social critics played on this ambiguity with delight, until the thin line between criminals and soldiers (or politicians) seemed to vanish."[2]

After the fall of Suharto, the military went back to overseeing three services: the army, navy, and air force. The police were given their autonomy and assigned the role of maintaining domestic security and order, while the military was responsible for national defence (Honna 2010, 263).[3] Jacqui Baker (2013) has argued that the police, as the main providers of security in the post-Suharto era, have developed an off-budget economy by providing "protection" to businesses with the support of preman. Baker characterizes the friendships between various business owners and police officers as *parman*, short for *partisipasi teman*, or the "participation of a friend." She describes how gifts, money, and other commodities are given to police officers, often without them directly requesting it, thereby constituting an off-budget economy (127). "Revenue-raising is an important part of an officer's responsibilities," she writes. "Attracting *parman* funds is not always merely a matter of rank or position. It's about mobility and sociality. An officer must circulate and associate (*gaul*) in important sub-state spaces, particularly nightclubs, golf courses, and particular karaoke bars" (142).

Although not all officers participate in this economy, most are expected to develop contacts and networks that will generate funds for themselves and their particular police institution. If an officer is able to bring in capital from these alternative sources, they will experience greater "mobility within the police institution" (143). Thus, a police officer like Pak Ferry can bring in an alternative source of income and develop a network of preman by working for the government outside of his official duties. With the growing number of civic NGOs, student activists, and anti-government groups, police officers like Pak Ferry can provide a "conflict-management" service that helps them to accumulate the personal assets they need to sustain a middle-class lifestyle, be promoted through the ranks of the police, maintain a network of loyal friends, and undertake other personal business ventures.

Resolving Conflicts "Beautifully"

Once I was back in Yogyakarta, Pak Ferry and I decided to go out for food. He picked me up in his black SUV and we went to his favourite *nasi goreng* (Indonesian stir-fried rice) food stall. Since we last met, Pak

Ferry had married a woman from Sumatra, and they now had two children. He explained with a laugh that although he loves his wife dearly, she is forever trying various business initiatives that always seem to fail. After spending thirty minutes catching up on life, he told me he was ready for a formal interview – something he had been hesitant to do during my fieldwork in 2007 and 2008. He explained that after returning to school and doing his own research on policing, he now understood the difficulties of carrying out research. "It was so hard, Sheri," he said, laughing. "I remembered you, and I felt bad that I did not help you more." Smiling, he added, "I'm ready now!"[4] We decided to meet up several days later in a quiet hotel restaurant in order to do the interview.

The first time I met Pak Ferry, back in October 2007, I was surprised by what came out of his mouth: English swear words. He wanted to show me what he thought were his impressive English-language skills. I was visiting Kuncen Marketplace before its official opening, and a number of the independent traders and preman were gathered at the soon-to-be-filled kiosks. I was introduced to Pak Ferry by Pak Akil, a friend of Pak Didik and a preman who conducted his business at the Northern Square. Pak Akil was helping Pak Didik with the relocation by providing security, but I did not know how Pak Ferry fitted into the picture.

After meeting with Pak Ferry a couple of times, he revealed to me that he was an undercover police officer from the Brimob (Korps Brigade Mobil, or Mobile Brigade Corps), a paramilitary police force that provides support to other police units and focuses on duties such as counterterrorism and riot control. Although he had been working on the relocation project since February 2007, when the pro- and anti-relocation groups first emerged, Pak Ferry had not been a visible player in the dispute because he had been working behind the scenes. He had never openly walked the street, attended the pro-relocation meetings, or watched the Pethikbumi protests himself.

I later learned that Pak Ferry had worked in Aceh, Poso, and Timor Leste, all areas known for conflict. At the time of the relocation, Pak Ferry had seven people working under him in the field, and he worked closely with Pak Muhadjir, a well-known preman from Yogyakarta who was also a member of the elite State Intelligence Agency (Badan Intelijen Negara Republik Indonesia, or BIN). Pak Ferry spoke proudly about his relationship with Pak Muhadjir. He explained that Pak Muhadjir had taught him how to conduct telephone wiretaps. On one or two occasions, Pak Ferry had invited me to meet up with him and Pak Muhadjir to eat lunch or play pool.

The pro-relocation leaders knew that Pak Ferry was a police officer – a fact he did little to hide. He was working on this case because, as he put it, he was very likeable and could easily obtain information from people. He had two spies selling on the street as of February 2007; he had bought their selling locations with his own money so they could report to him what was happening on the street. I presume he kept a portion of their profits, although I never enquired.

From October 2007 until I left Indonesia in August 2008, I would sometimes meet Pak Ferry for outings that involved driving around in his black Toyota SUV searching for the best place to eat nasi goreng. On one particularly special occasion, on 18 November 2007, Pak Ferry invited me to join him and some of his friends – most of them semi- or underemployed youth (known to most people as preman) from the Northern Square – on a trip to Solo to watch horse racing. Most of these youths made their money acting as security during events at the North- ern Square or working as parking agents. After watching a few races, the group decided to stop at a karaoke bar on the way home. They began singing karaoke, and not long after started drinking beer and dancing, while I mostly sat in the corner watching Pak Ferry entertain his friends and treat them to drinks and cigarettes. On the way home, as I sat next to Pak Ferry in the front seat, we started talking about the relocation again. He explained to me that he was helping to resolve the opposition to the relocation because municipal government officials had been unable to deal with the emerging problems between the pro- and anti-relocation groups. He also described how he was working closely with Pak Didik to strengthen and coordinate the pro-relocation traders because Pak Ferry often could not (by his own admission) resolve these kinds of conflicts on his own.[5]

When I left Indonesia in 2008, I was still uncertain about Pak Fer- ry's exact role in the relocation. He had previously told me that he had received kiosks at Kuncen Marketplace,[6] but it was not until May 2014, when I returned to Yogyakarta, that Pak Ferry and I finally sat down for a formal interview lasting almost four hours. Pak Ferry explained that he was ready to be formally interviewed with an audio recorder, and that he wanted to tell me what really happened during the relocation. We reviewed the informed consent form and he agreed to me publish- ing the information that he provided, knowing that this information would now be more widely shared.[7] The relocation no longer seemed as sensitive and political as it had back in 2007 and 2008. We had both changed. Pak Ferry had gone back to school and had risen in the police ranks; he now oversaw 150 officers in the region. I had graduated and was no longer a student. The government had declared Kuncen

Marketplace a success, and it was bustling with customers and traders. At the same time, like he had years before, Pak Ferry continued to
enact masculine power in ways that included displays of bravado and
demonstrations of his connections and popularity with people, often
preman, across the city.

We started the interview by going over Pak Ferry's life history,
including his educational background. Pak Ferry graduated from the
academy for the Indonesian National Police Force. He was then posted
to Bandung, but soon resumed his studies for five months to enter the
Indonesian Special Police Force, with a focus on terrorism. In 1998, Pak
Ferry moved to Yogyakarta to continue his studies. He graduated with
prestige (*indeks prestasi*) after five years in an extended program in the
Faculty of Law at the Universitas Widya Mataram. Many of his police
friends had not been keen to move to Yogyakarta because it had a reputation for not providing officers with as many (illegal) opportunities to
make money on the side. However, Pak Ferry considered himself different. He claimed he was not looking for money, but instead trusted that
God would "order things." In the end, he said, "money came to me."[8]

Pak Ferry became involved in the relocation to Kuncen Marketplace
when a number of Satpol PP officers who knew of his skills asked for his
help resolving the case. "They asked me because their orientation is not
about process, but about results. What is important is the result of the
relocation, whatever the cost," he stated confidently.[9] By this he meant
that their approach to curbing political action could involve undemocratic means (like spying or generating distrust), but he said that he was
also careful not to violate the street vendors' human rights.

When I asked Pak Ferry to elaborate on his involvement in the
relocation to Kuncen Marketplace, he explained that I needed to first
understand his involvement in an earlier vendor relocation project.
This 2004 relocation involved moving traders from two areas in the
city, Shopping Centre and Sri Wedani Street, to Giwangan Marketplace,
located on the outskirts of the city. In 2000, the municipal government
moved some of the Shopping Centre traders to Giwangan Marketplace.
Giwangan Marketplace was quiet, however, and fruit and vegetable
sellers lost large sums of money.[10] Because of these losses, in 2002, the
traders from Giwangan Marketplace returned to Shopping Centre and
Sriwedani Street, and Giwangan Marketplace was left empty. After
two years, the government announced that it planned to relocate both
the Shopping Centre and Sriwedani Street traders back to Giwangan
Marketplace because they wanted to convert Shopping Centre into an
indoor children's park called Taman Pintar. In response, the traders
held a demonstration and formed an organization called the Trader

Society of Sapta Manunggal (Paguyuban Pedagang Sapta Manunggal, or PPSM).[11]

In the 2004 Giwangan Marketplace relocation, Pak Ferry had worked with Pak Didik. Pak Didik had been involved because he was close to Pak Syukri Fadholi, the vice mayor of Yogyakarta at the time. Pak Ferry explained to me that he had befriended Pak Didik because he had recognized him as an NGO advocate who was smart and interested in more than just money. They worked together to resolve the conflict, which involved not only the sellers but also groups of preman who controlled areas of the Shopping Centre and Sriwedani Street marketplaces and who were concerned about losing their source of income.[12]

I listened carefully as Pak Ferry described each group of preman. He knew the different thugs involved because he had encountered most of them through his police work:

> All of these people [he pointed to a list we had compiled on a piece of paper], I have arrested for their criminality. This person is a killer. This person forces people to destroy clubs because he doesn't receive money. This person I arrested. He got away from me two times; I shot him [*laughs*]. Why did he run? Yeah, he rode a motorbike, I chased him – *bang-bang-bang*. He was scared of me … I was closest to Pak Muhadjir because he was a preman who was very smart, clever – a genius.[13]

From Pak Ferry's perspective, the government had been increasingly annoyed (*jengkel*) and frustrated because it could not implement the 2004 relocation project successfully: "They couldn't continue; it was so difficult, and they were terrorized by thugs. The only way forward was for them to use intelligence [Pak Ferry himself]."[14] This work was also outside of his official police work, which was focused on investigating and capturing individuals involved in criminal and terrorist activities, but it was nevertheless important for Pak Ferry because it helped him develop and maintain networks in the city while also receiving additional "off-budget" funds.

Pak Ferry explained that the 2004 relocation to Giwangan Marketplace was neither easy nor fast and required that he use both a "soft" and a "hard" approach with the preman involved. For this he had to maintain "principled" relationships (*harus punya prinsip hubungan*). Pak Ferry did not want to use too much force because he feared that the more muscle he used, the more resistance he would face. Instead, he could reward the preman for their obedience by informally giving them control of property through the government, such as kiosks in Giwangan Marketplace. However, he also posed a serious threat to them because he could arrest and jail them, presumably for unrelated activities. But the purpose of meeting with the groups of preman, he admitted to me, was ultimately to divide them (*kita pisahkan dulu mereka*). He did this by determining the interests of the different group leaders, keeping these interests separate, and offering to fulfil each in turn. Most often these interests related to money and assets, and as a result Pak Ferry could offer them kiosks in Giwangan Marketplace or some other form of control over territory in the new marketplace. Pak Ferry admitted to me that he "used a little bit of intimidation also (*intimidasi sedikit juga*). I can't only use talking. 'Yeah, you are here, move there.' There is a little force (*agak sedikit paksa*)."[15]

Pak Ferry both revealed and concealed parts of his work in order to protect the government's plausible deniability. The public and government interpreted the Giwangan relocation as a success, and for his efforts Pak Ferry received a number of kiosks as well as control of security at the new marketplace. Pak Ferry gave the kiosks to others to operate, for which he received money and/or loyalty in return. The same went for security – Pak Ferry was able to place his men (many of them preman) as official guards in the marketplace. Pak Ferry was therefore able to gain control over the marketplace by placing his men there, accumulating followers, and more broadly by expanding his territorial power.

After this initial experience, Pak Ferry was asked by Pak Galang[16] to resolve the 2007 conflict between the pro- and anti-relocation traders. Pak Ferry recognized early on that the plan for Mangkubumi Street was going to involve a conflict because the government had allowed the traders to sell there too long before making it illegal. Pak Ferry also predicted that there would be resistance to the relocation because the government collected taxes from the traders, which provided them with a sense of entitlement and legitimacy even though they did not have vendor permits. Vending spots on Mangkubumi Street were also being bought and sold, which made the traders even more invested in maintaining their locations.

Pak Ferry felt that as a police officer he must support the government's relocation project. He explained to me during our interview that he would help "as long as the government's project is good for the people and for the economy."[17] Pak Ferry also thought that it would be detrimental to Yogyakarta's image if a conflict emerged, and he further justified his involvement with his belief that, if any such conflict was not managed, it could descend into violence between the traders or between the traders and the government.[18]

Pak Ferry explained that his way of operating was different from that of the municipal police (Polisi Resor, or POLRES) or Satpol PP. From

Pak Ferry's perspective, when it came to the Giwangan Marketplace relocation, the conflict between the various preman stemmed from the fact that each preman was anxious to get enough space in the new marketplace to maintain their normal income (*kepentingan ruang untuk makan*). In his opinion, if the problem of the relocation was addressed with selfishness (*egois*), it would not be resolved. "Lots of money would be spent. Many in the media would know [about the conflict]. It is possible that the government could fail and the thugs win (*menang*). That would be funny (*lucu*)!"[19] It was acceptable for preman to be involved as long as they were working only to intimidate and/or protect the various actors involved and were not engaging in outright violence.[20]

Pak Ferry wanted to help but he also expected to be rewarded for his work. A police officer's salary is meagre, and Pak Ferry needed extra income to supplement his middle-class lifestyle and to maintain his wide network of supporters across the city. He asked the lower-level government officials involved in the relocation, "How many [kiosks in Kuncen Marketplace] do you want to give me?"[21] If they were not willing to give him anything, Pak Ferry would leave the job to other police officers. After he was promised twenty kiosks in an off-the-record verbal agreement, Pak Ferry called one of his Kuncen Marketplace contacts and asked his advice about which kiosks were best. Pak Ferry was connected not only to the government but increasingly to a number of traders relocating to Kuncen Marketplace.

Even though Pak Ferry was rarely a visible presence on the streets or in Kuncen Marketplace, he was at the centre of various information networks, receiving updates from his many informants and Pak Didik. Pak Ferry had mapped the street and the stakeholders involved. He had to gather a substantial amount of background information on the different actors, and he analyzed the conflict from multiple angles as a researcher might. He methodically and conscientiously explained this process:

> I must understand the construction of this case … Who are the stakeholders (*stakeholdernya*)? What kind of conflict will happen? What kind of conflict is this? What is the solution from the government? What does the win-win solution (*win-win solutionnya*) look like? I'm mapping again (*mapping lagi*), What is the strength of this person? What are the assets of this resistance? Does he have a shop (*toko*) or financial support?[22]

Based on this analysis, Pak Ferry concluded that there were no extremely powerful people involved in the relocation. He then started to control the preman in the area surrounding Mangkubumi Street by helping them if they were arrested by the police. He said, "If the thugs had a problem with the law, I would help. If they were arrested by the police, I would help them get free."[23] Pak Ferry did not ask for money, but rather loyalty. He started to plan who would control what areas in the new marketplace so no conflict would emerge. He said, "I prepared who will [control] the parking, who will [control] the security. It became my area. So it wouldn't become a conflict when [the relocation] happened."[24] Arguably, Pak Ferry, unlike the government, could organize the thugs because he was able to build their loyalty and respect due to his police work. Pak Ferry had power that the government officials did not: he could decide when and how the law would be applied to the thugs. Through the process of the relocation, some of the preman were transformed from their informal roles as thugs into the more formalized roles that saw them work as security guards with the knowledge and permission of the government. However, they were ultimately loyal to Pak Ferry, who had gotten them these jobs in the first place.

Another one of Pak Ferry's techniques was to have individuals who worked undercover for him approach the Pethikbumi traders and encourage them to join the relocation. By doing so, Pak Ferry was intensifying the pressures felt by the traders on the street to join either the pro- or anti-relocation group. He said, "I have agents and they worked to gather the trader's KTP identity cards,[25] and we offered them places."[26] Unlike the 2004 vendor relocation project, for which Pak Ferry had to mostly control and negotiate with the preman who controlled the market, in the move to Kuncen Marketplace, Pak Ferry also had to become close to the traders. He described this process in the following terms: "I saw that [the traders'] militancy was weak. But I indoctrinated those people: 'You must be like this. If you stay here, you have no hope. If you move there, there is hope. Do you want to stay or move? If you move there, you will receive this. Don't be political (*politis*).'"[27]

Throughout this process, Pak Ferry saw his primary role as preventing potential violent conflict. If there was a conflict, the project would be seen as a failure on the part of the police, the government, and the mayor. "In the next election [the mayor] won't be elected again. Jakarta could see it as a failure. [The mayor's] career can be 'game over.'"[28] This was the reason the conflict had to be resolved "beautifully" (*indah*), in his words, and why the goals of the police, the government, and the mayor all aligned in this case. Just as they were during the New Order, "successful" urban projects (*proyek*) are important for mayors because they play a large part in determining how a mayor's legacy is remembered and celebrated. A successful project, such as a street vendor relocation, will receive significant media attention, and it will be taken as evidence that the mayor is a good leader, especially if he or she is able to resolve any problems without resorting to violence. Pak Ferry allowed the pro- and anti-relocation groups to continue their activities separately as long as they did not engage in violence. But he hoped that the anti-relocation group would eventually lose stamina. "They will become tired, and all of the traders have their own problems; we had to take advantage of this."[29]

In both of these relocation projects – to Giwangan Marketplace and to Kuncen Marketplace – Pak Ferry worked closely with Pak Didik and Pak Galang. Moreover, in both projects, Pak Didik worked closely with the traders, Pak Galang was involved in the process of sosialisasi as a government official, and Pak Ferry worked behind the scenes to resolve (or generate) conflicts so that the projects could be completed success-fully. Pak Ferry's approach to each relocation project also appeared to be similar. After mapping the anti-relocation groups' networks and power, he combined intimidation and a system of rewards to ensure that the groups causing problems received what they wanted in exchange for agreeing to the project. He also worked to ensure that the anti-relocation groups did not coalesce into a single, unified movement, whether they were preman (in the case of Giwangang Marketplace) or traders (in the case of Kuncen Marketplace).

"He Is My Agent"

I was still uncertain about Pak Ferry's undercover status during the Kuncen Marketplace relocation project, so I had to ask him directly. His response fulfilled my information ideology of wanting to know "what really happened" as it involved Pak Ferry admitting his role in vari-ous events. Similar to the instances I described earlier, in which people revealed their surveillance to those they surveilled (see Being Shad-owed, Chapter 4), this process created a new secret between two people, but it also reaffirmed the power of Pak Ferry's "play behind the scenes."

> SHERI: When you were working on the street, how many people knew about your presence and status? Maybe Pak Didik knew, and Pak Pramana, but did Pak Akbar [the leader of Pethikbumi] know?
>
> PAK FERRY: Why do you think Akbar was there [*laughing*]? Akbar was there because he used to work in a nightclub, and I knew the boss of that club. If I said, "Akbar must leave," his boss would fire him … Akbar is my agent (*agen*).
>
> SHERI: [*In disbelief*] What is he?
>
> PAK FERRY: My agent.
>
> SHERI: What do you mean?

PAK FERRY: He is my intelligence [agent].

SHERI: What? The leader of Pethikbumi?

PAK FERRY: Yeah ... Pak Akbar, right?

SHERI: [*In disbelief*] Pak Akbar? He lived near Mangkubumi. So he was placed from the start to make the people refuse the relocation?

PAK FERRY: He had already entered (*sudah masuk*) [Mangkubumi Street to operate as a trader]. [I said,] "You follow me, and you must join Pethikbumi and follow them." He had to be inside the structure of the organization so we could know. We had to follow the regulations. If there was resistance, we could not destroy the resistance organization. [We could say that] this is the aspiration of the people.

SHERI: So you had to control the organization from within? Pak Akbar had a job to make sure they didn't become too violent?

PAK FERRY: I put Pak Akbar there. [I told him,] "You join their activities there; never meet me. Make sure they aren't suspicious (*curiga dengan kamu*) of you. If there is a conflict with the pro group, join them [Pethikbumi]. You must have the same purpose of life [as the Pethikbumi traders]. You fight as the little people (*rakyat kecil*). You lie (*bohong kamu*). Fight for your family, like the others."[30]

Pak Ferry could get Pak Akbar fired from the nightclub because Pak Ferry was providing protection to this club in exchange for a fee.[31] Through his protection services, Pak Ferry provided Pak Akbar and the other nightclub employees with backing if there were any problems at the nightclub. Thus, because Pak Ferry occupied a position of power vis-à-vis the nightclub where Pak Akbar worked, it was hard for Pak Akbar to reject requests from Pak Ferry. From this position of power, Pak Ferry encouraged Pak Akbar to become a key leader of Pethikbumi, not only to lead the group but also to control it and ensure that the resistance was managed and never became violent. Pethikbumi engaged in resistance, but it was controlled resistance since Pak Ferry was directing Pak Akbar. Pak Ferry did not want the Pethikbumi leaders to be suspicious of Pak Akbar, his "agent," but he needed to keep the group's members suspicious of each other. Pak Ferry claimed to use various tactics to help foster this suspicion. He said that when the traders were gathered together, he would get a pro-relocation vendor to call over a Pethikbumi member to talk about something unrelated to the relocation. From Pak Ferry's perspective, they did not have to talk about the relocation in order to generate suspicion among the Pethikbumi. "We did this continuously. Don't let them get really solid."[32]

Prior to the relocation deadline, Pak Ferry planned to destroy the relationship between Pethikbumi and its lawyers through a special operation. He organized a meeting between BPHK, Pak Pramana, and Pak Didik in order to generate distrust. Pak Ferry explained that he had people follow Ibu Marini from the BPHK office. When she stopped to eat at the Northern Square, he called Pak Pramana to come to the location, without letting him know that Ibu Marini was there. Pak Pramana and Pak Didik sat and spoke to each other, and Ibu Marini was behind them but Pak Pramana did not know. Pak Ferry arranged for a couple of pro-relocation traders to come to the location as well. He made sure that Ibu Marini saw Pak Didik shake hands with Pak Pramana so she would think that Pak Pramana was secretly negotiating with the pro-relocation side. In the end, as described earlier (see Conspiracy at the Northern Square, Chapter 7), Pethikbumi broke off relations with their lawyer because they suspected that BPHK had been involved in creating this scenario. Proud of his actions, Pak Ferry said, "It was broken. Finished. Game over."[33]

Pak Ferry explained that, while Pak Pramana did not know that he was being used for this scenario, he also knew that Pak Pramana was not loyal to him. "Pak Pramana in the end received a kiosk at the back of the marketplace because he did not agree with me," he explained.[34] Pak Ferry felt particularly sorry for Pak Pramana because he used to date Pak Pramana's younger sister. Pak Ferry had offered Pak Pramana a number of places in the marketplace, and during the meeting at the Northern Square he had offered him a deal through Pak Didik, but Pak Pramana decided that he could not go through with it because he believed strongly in Pethikbumi's movement against the government.[35]

Ranajit Guha (1983) has shown that rumours are essential to the mobilization of peasant rebellions because they are anonymous, ambiguous, and the separate acts of "encoding and decoding of rumour are collapsed" (259–60). However, when strategically mobilized by the state, rumours can also be used to create a "chain of reactions" (261), and to divide the very groups working to undermine the state. Conspiratorial rumours were central to the break-up between the Pethikbumi traders and their legal aid supporters. They fed into already existing paranoia about the state and its ability to infiltrate groups such as theirs. But creating this scenario was not as easy as it might have looked. To be successful in his efforts to create confusion among the street vendors, Pak Ferry had to keep his involvement secret while simultaneously setting up actions that would generate rumours among the Pethikbumi traders and their supporters. A central aspect of shadow play is therefore the ability to predict how certain actions will later be interpreted and translated into information that will circulate as rumours. It took skilled knowledge, for instance, to understand that at the Northern Square, the Pethikbumi leaders would become suspicious not of Pak Didik but of their own lawyers.

In the new marketplace, those who were loyal to Pak Ferry did well. Pak Ferry assigned the underlings of the preman Pak Akil roles as official marketplace security (*transtib*). "I proposed that," he explained. "There they would need to be loyal to me, in addition to being loyal to the head of the marketplace."[36] Pak Ferry received his twenty kiosks. He contracted them out to traders and gave them to close friends. Pak Ferry was proud that he had once again resolved an issue. He had applied the skills that he had learned in conflict and crisis management – skills, he noted, that came from the West thanks to the significant foreign assistance devoted to police training in the post–New Order era (Bjorken and Payumo 2005, 1110).[37]

Having received police training and a law degree, Pak Ferry could also speak the language of police ethics and human rights. From his perspective, it was important to uphold these principles while being consistent (*konsisten*) and consequential (*konsekuen*) in his own actions. This meant that people must believe him and that he must follow through with what he promised. "I have lots of friends, and within every conflict between thugs, I am the facilitator. They believe me because I prove it with my actions."[38] While Pak Ferry generated suspicion among the Pethikbumi group and their supporters, he made sure that his own word could be trusted.

Although he believed in the government's project, Pak Ferry admitted that he was also motivated by money, although he usually received his payments in the form of assets in the new marketplaces, such as kiosks. "At minimum, I must have something that I can leave my wife and children if I die. I must study a lot and have lots of experience in the field. [*Laughing*] This case was easy."[39] The circulation of money or material benefits in exchange for "support" of the relocation was not unusual; rather, it can be considered part of how politics are organized in Indonesia. The relocation to Kuncen Marketplace could be viewed as a *proyek* – that is, what Edward Aspinall (2013) describes as a funded activity with a termed end (28). During the Suharto era, projects were carried out across the archipelago, with illicit funds directed to individuals with the "right political connections" (30). In the post-Suharto era, every social sector is looking to be involved in a proyek, and that involvement can be turned into private gain (30). As a patron of many others, Pak Ferry had to be on the lookout for proyeks to build his network and receive money that he could then distribute to his client networks around the city.

Throughout our interview, it was clear that he wondered about the ethical trade-offs involved in such work:

PAK FERRY: I often wonder, was what I did right or wrong? I say, let God
    punish me if I am wrong. Even though, Sheri, do you know my salary?
SHERI: No. Now or before, during the relocation?
PAK FERRY: Before, it was 4 million rupiah per month [approximately
    USD$400]. I must pay for many things. I must prepare things for
    marriage, and I must prepare lots of things. I came here and did not have
    family. And my family is not rich.[40]

The narrative that Pak Ferry used to describe his role in determining the outcome of the relocation (as described in this and the previous section, "Resolving Conflicts 'Beautifully'") contained different justifications. He insisted that he was only trying to make extra money to ensure his family's well-being, that he was helping to keep Yogyakarta peaceful, that he was safeguarding the mayor's career, and that he was contributing to a government project that was meant to increase the welfare of the population.

Pak Ferry's confession to me about his involvement behind the scenes contains its own information ideologies. Pak Ferry believed, for instance, that he could not share this more complete version of the story with me until years after the relocation. The scenario that he orchestrated at the Northern Square and the involvement of Pak Akbar as his agent were secrets that only a few people in Yogyakarta knew. This information could be revealed to me because I was a foreigner who did not live in Yogyakarta, but also because years had passed since the relocation; Pak Ferry was therefore less likely to face any consequences for his actions if the broader public found out. There were also fewer available channels through which this information could circulate because the networks around the relocation had largely dispersed, and the reading public was focused on other, more urgent news items. Our conversation, no doubt, was also partly an attempt on Pak Ferry's part to build up his own reputation as someone who knows what is going on in Yogyakarta and to demonstrate that he is part of an elite network that "makes things happen." As Tanya Luhrmann (1989) argues, "Secrecy is about control. It is about the individual possession of knowledge that others do not have" (161).

The sharing of secrets can equate to an exercise of power over others from whom these secrets are withheld (Colwell 2015), but it can also serve to reaffirm a friendship between two people who have not seen each other for many years, or to create an alliance to sustain a social relationship (Manderson et al. 2015, S185). Pak Ferry's choice to share his secret could have been an attempt to produce a strong social relationship between him and me (De Jong 2007, 15), and perhaps even an attempt to address our power imbalance by bringing me into his circle of knowledge (Manderson et al. 2015, S184). What made the secret a secret was not just the content but also who revealed it. Pak Ferry was a police officer who was sharing a story about his own actions. He told me that I was among only three other people in Yogyakarta who now knew his version of events. His telling felt closer to the truth for me because of my own information ideologies, which privilege confession over rumour.

Pak Ferry's version of events also suggests that engaging in secrecy and generating confusion are attempts at conflict management. Throughout this book, I have used the concept of shadow play to refer to the set of practices that government officials and other elites use to purposely generate confusion; this includes the deployment of secrecy, falsification, and obfuscation, among other tactics. Yet as I have additionally shown, shadow play can also be used by street traders, NGOs, and citizens to challenge the information politics of other groups, and indeed to assert their own power.

As I noted earlier, Pak Ferry's approach suggests that an important aspect of shadow play is mastering the understanding of how actions will be interpreted and later circulated as information. Individuals who are able to "shadow play" are therefore skilled in the field of social observation. Pak Ferry could be viewed as engaging in what Harold Garfinkel (1991) called "breaching experiments," because he set up situations in which certain individuals appeared to break the taken-for-granted "rules" of interaction during an urban conflict. When people broke these rules, rumours circulated about them, and these individuals were therefore deemed suspicious. This shows us, then, that just as there are rules about how to speak and act, those who can convince others to break these rules in a strategic manner, and to violate the associated information ideologies, are capable of mustering a significant amount of power. When norms are breached through these practices, interactions come to a confused halt, or are terminated altogether, demonstrating how fragile these interactions actually are. If these interactions are based on shared information ideologies and a resulting trust, shadow play is about breaking down the trust that enables stable and meaningful interactions in the first place – namely, by violating these shared expectations. In the context of the vendor relocation, the information ideologies of the anti-relocation traders were already unstable, shifting, and contested. For this reason, any breach was given particular significance.

"He Is My Younger Brother"

A day after speaking with Pak Ferry, I met up with Pak Akbar at a large restaurant where he worked as the managing caretaker. I did not plan on confronting Pak Akbar with the information that I had received from Pak Ferry because I needed to protect Pak Ferry's confidentiality. Instead, I would ask him about his perception of the relocation now that seven years had passed. After an initial greeting, Pak Akbar and I walked through the largely empty restaurant to a long table, where we sat down and ordered two teas before it started pouring rain.

He began our conversation by explaining that he had run for a seat in parliament in the recent municipal elections but had not won because of "money politics" – the exchange of cash for votes.[41] He was disappointed that citizens in his own neighbourhood could be bought so easily. After losing, he decided that he would leave politics for a while and focus on his work. I asked him whether he was still in contact with other members of Pethikbumi. Pak Akbar said that he did not have much contact with the group's former leaders any more since he did not have a kiosk in the marketplace, although he did ask for their support during the election. After discussing what he had been doing since we last spoke, I started asking Pak Akbar more specifically about the relocation and about the various actors involved, such as the police and intelligence agents. After he described the role of police in general terms – their job, he explained, was to provide security and to prevent violence – I asked Pak Akbar about Pak Ferry's involvement in the relocation:

SHERI: At the time there was Pak Ferry from Brimob, right?
PAK AKBAR: Pak Ferry? [*Pause.*] Pak Ferry is my friend. He is my close friend (*teman akrab saya*). He was actually sent by Pak Galang, if I'm not mistaken. Not Pak Galang … He joined in there to help with the relocation. I did not know that he was there [working on the relocation project at the time] … If it was the Department of Marketplaces [who recruited Pak Ferry to the relocation project], it was Pak Galang then. I don't know exactly (*saya nggak tau persis siapa*). But I already knew Pak Ferry at the time. Before there were second-hand traders [on Mangkubumi Street], I already knew Pak Ferry.
SHERI: How did you know him?
PAK AKBAR: I. [*Pause.*] At that time I worked at Palem. A nightclub. [*Laughs*] Pak Ferry was often at the nightclub.
SHERI: Oh yeah?[42]

Unlike Pak Ferry, Pak Akbar did not describe himself as someone who had been planted in Pethikbumi to control it from within. But as we continued our conversation, Pak Akbar mentioned that during the relocation he would often talk with Pak Ferry at the nightclub (where Pak Akbar worked as security), and that Pak Ferry was recruiting a lot of preman at the time to support the move to Kuncen Marketplace. The preman were also pressuring Pak Akbar about the relocation because they knew that he worked as a trader on Mangkubumi Street. Pak Akbar described one of the conversations he had with a group of preman to demonstrate the pressure he felt at the time:

[One of the preman said,] "If you don't move [to Kuncen Marketplace] you are in danger (*bahaya*) because later you will meet with the person behind me." I said, "Who is behind you?" "*Wah*,[43] Brimob," he said. "Pak Ferry. Later if you are known by Pak Ferry you will be scared." He said that. I said, "If it is Pak Ferry, he respects (*hormat*) me." "Pak Ferry will certainly show respect to me," I said. [*Laughing*] I already knew Pak Ferry. [One of the preman said,] "Later if Pak Ferry appears, you will see, Pak Ferry will be angry with you (*dimarah-marah*)." I said … to him [the one preman] and the other preman – about eight of them if I'm not mistaken – I said, "Now call Pak Ferry. I want to meet with Pak Ferry. If Pak Ferry is not close with me, cut off my ears (*potong kuping*)" [*laughs*]. But within my heart I wondered if it was Pak Ferry or not. I wondered if Pak Ferry was my friend or not (*teman saya atau bukan*). If that person drove an Avansa [a type of car], that meant it is Pak Ferry. [After the preman called Pak Ferry,] Pak Ferry drove by and it was a black Avansa. I saw the police plate number on Pak Ferry's car. This is really Pak Ferry. *Wah*, I'm safe [*laughs*]. We met directly and Pak Ferry says, "Hi, brother" (*Weh, abang*). He said that I was his older brother. I was embraced (*dirangkul*) by him. "This is my older brother. If you try anything with my brother, I'll hit all of you (*saya ajar kalian semua*)," said Pak Ferry [to the preman] at the time. [The preman] did not dare to touch me (*nggak berani nyentuh saya*) at the time. They [knew] that Pak Ferry was backing me (*backingan saya*). I said that Pak Ferry was my younger brother (*adek saya*). "This person [Pak Ferry] is from Medan," I said. "We are both Sumatran. Pak Ferry is my person (*Pak Ferry ini orang saya*)," I said. "A person close to me (*orang dekat saya*)," I said.[44]

Pak Akbar described Pak Ferry as being "bought" by the government. "If I am not mistaken, he [Pak Ferry] was taking orders (*suruhan*) from Pak Galang … Pak Ferry joined in to help with the relocation," he said.[45] It is common knowledge in Indonesia that corporations, the government, and other members of the elite pay the police to do work for them outside of their official policing jobs, such as protecting their businesses or helping to implement projects. A common phrase heard in Indonesia is *polisi bisa dibayar dan disewa* (police can be rented or paid).

Pak Akbar's claim that Pak Ferry had been "bought" by the government suggested that he worked on the relocation project for money or material benefits, and not because of his ideological beliefs. Pak Akbar's narrative was not told in the form of a secret; rather, it was treated as knowledge that he would share with anyone who wanted to know.

I asked Pak Akbar how he was able to negotiate his different position with Pak Ferry, since they each wanted different things out of the relocation. He replied that Pak Ferry said they should each follow their different paths, but that it was important that they did not fight (*bentrok*). He said that Pak Ferry also wanted to receive kiosks in the marketplace at the time, and that this turned out to be true: Pak Ferry did indeed receive selling locations at the marketplace. "I never did that," Pak Akbar said, contrasting himself to Pak Ferry. "These are the consequences for myself and Pak Ferry. Pak Ferry went on his own [path] and I went on my own [path]."[46]

Pak Akbar's version of what happened is clearly very different from Pak Ferry's. Although both said that they knew each other, Pak Ferry referred to Pak Akbar as his agent (*agen*), while Pak Akbar referred to Pak Ferry as his younger brother (*adek*) and highlighted the fact that Pak Ferry calls him his older brother (*abang*). While Pak Akbar viewed their relationship in familial terms, Pak Ferry referred to Pak Akbar using a word, *agen*, that describes a professional working relationship. In Pak Ferry's version, Pak Akbar worked for him because he had little choice: Pak Akbar not only benefited from Pak Ferry's protection at the nightclub – Pak Ferry could also get Pak Akbar fired from working at this nightclub altogether. In Pak Akbar's account, however, Pak Ferry is his younger brother and, as such, someone who respects him. Pak Ferry is willing to protect Pak Akbar from the preman pressuring him about the relocation because they are close. They are also both from Sumatra. Back in 2007, neither Pak Ferry nor Pak Akbar shared the fact that they knew each other with anyone except the preman. Although Pak Akbar's story is somewhat similar to other stories he told about the bribes he refused from government officials, he never shared any stories about Pak Ferry during the relocation. In 2007, he kept his relationship with Pak Ferry a secret from the other Pethikbumi leaders and their supporters, and I never witnessed them together during my fieldwork.

While Pak Ferry's story revolves around his secret efforts to resolve the conflicts over the relocation without violence, Pak Akbar's story is focused on the threats he received from preman. In my interview with Pak Akbar, he was hesitant to say definitively how Pak Ferry started to work for the government. He mentioned that it was through Pak Galang but said, "I don't know exactly."[47] Pak Akbar's interview was less about sharing a secret with me and more about telling me how he navigated the threats that preman levied at him. Here he mirrored many of the stories he told during Pethikbumi meetings about the bribes he had refused (see Conspicuous Visibility: Managing Impressions, Chapter 4). His account was also less concerned with sharing why Pethikbumi failed as a movement than with demonstrating that he had a network that could be used to fight against the government's relocation project. Pak Akbar maintained that his anti-relocation stance was genuine. According to his version of events, Pak Ferry was a sort of patron; through Pak Ferry, he received protection rather than money. And yet in some sense, Pak Ferry used coercion to keep Pak Akbar within the fold – because without Pak Ferry's protection, Pak Akbar was at risk of being targeted for violence by preman. Pak Akbar's and Pak Ferry's accounts have this element of coercion in common, even though the coercion is less explicit in Pak Akbar's version of events.

Finally, in their interviews, Pak Ferry and Pak Akbar drew on different repertoires of masculinity circulating in Indonesia (Wilson 2012a; Lee 2016). Pak Ferry performed a preman masculinity that privileged "toughness" and highlighted his own intelligence and power in resolving the conflict between Pethikbumi and the government. Pak Akbar's version also reaffirmed Pak Ferry's preman masculinity when he talked about how the preman referred to Pak Ferry as someone who should be feared. Instead of emphasizing his own "toughness," Pak Akbar explained how he was able to protect himself by knowing the right person, who just happened to be Pak Ferry. For Pak Akbar, it was not his own physical strength that saved him, but his network.

Informal Circuits

The municipal government claimed that the relocation to Kuncen Marketplace would formalize the traders since it would convert them from illegal to legal vendors. Yet, ironically, the government's own project relied on informal, off-the-book circuits of information and money. The official reports that the government produced before the relocation recommended that it take the necessary steps to engage in sosialisasi in order to address the traders' concerns about the project (see Information as Social Unrest, Chapter 2). Of course, these reports never mentioned other tactics like outsourcing this work to an off-duty police officer and offering to pay him under the table with kiosks. Pak Akbar's version of events suggests that the government also relied on informal sources of authority – Pak Ferry and the preman who were working for him – to implement the project.

If we are to consider Pak Ferry's version of events somewhat factual, we are left with little hope that the Indonesian urban underclass can organize against government projects without being controlled from within by the state. The description of Pak Akbar as an agent suggests that urban movements can in fact trust no one, not even their own leaders. This means that the Pethikbumi leaders' suspicions of their lawyers, BPHK, were not totally misplaced, either. The BPHK lawyers, too, could have been agents of the state. Pak Akbar's version of events, by contrast, gives us a little more hope. Was he really an agent or was he just using his "close" relationship with Pak Ferry to navigate the dangers he faced as someone organizing against the state? Any attempts to determine what "really happened" only lead to other possibilities. We will never know what really unfolded, but it is clear that the unreliability of information, as brought about by what I have termed *shadow play*, is a form of power utilized by the government, elites, NGOs, activists, and street traders, as well as an effect of these projects. Being able to control the movement and circulation of information, and understanding its effects, is central to the practise of shadow play. It can be a form of governance and control, or a form of activism, depending on who is using it and for what purposes.

The discussion of Pak Ferry's and Pak Akbar's roles in the government's relocation project suggests that conspiratorial thinking and shadow play are in fact sensible responses in a climate of uncertainty – after all, in such a context even the most outlandish theories might turn out to be at least partially true. As Bubandt (2008) has argued, there are periods in Indonesian history when "rumors of conspiracies and possibly real conspiracies mingle" (812). He continues, "In these murky chapters [of Indonesian history], of which the 1965 coup and the Jakartan riots of May 1998 are also examples, rumor and reality – the authentic and the fake – coproduce each other" (812). Generating rumours is one way of engaging in shadow play. But while this method is cultivated by the relevant actors, it then takes on its own momentum. Individuals like Pak Ferry attempt to predict the outcome of this momentum in advance. They are particularly skilled in understanding how actions might be interpreted and thereby translated into information, and how this information might flow afterwards. The control and manipulation of information is an important instrument of politics and governance.

Bubandt (2008) has argued, however, that rationalist explanations that situate rumours as an instrument of politics are problematic because they set up a distinction between "elites as rational actors and those who carry out the violence as cultural and emotional dupes"

(813). Pak Ferry positions himself according to standard explanations; he is a hidden instigator shaping political action in post-Suharto Indonesia. Similar to scholars interested in instrumentalist explanations, Pak Ferry also views rumours as a mere tool to be utilized by political elites such as himself. Yet Pak Ferry recognized that his approach was also effective because of pre-existing paranoid discourses. The conditions were ripe for setting up a breach in social interaction that would spiral into rumour and distrust. As I described earlier (see Conspiracy at the Northern Square, Chapter 7), because the traders were already suspicious of BPHK, the secret meeting at the Northern Square confirmed for them that BPHK might be involved with the government in some sort of political play. Pethikbumi were not dupes, but in fact acted with the knowledge that the state had likely penetrated their group through BPHK. And yet, instead of turning on the state, they turned on their own supporters. The effects of the secret meeting at the Northern Square were clear. The Pethikbumi leaders felt it was no longer possible to mobilize against the government relocation because of their lack of support from once-trusted partners. Ultimately, they turned to the state – to the very body they had been fighting against – for help.

Although shadow play can be undemocratic and unethical, elites often see it as a useful technique. It is an effective way to operate in the democratic era because the government can claim to be dialoguing with its citizens and engaging in consultative practices (see Getting Close and Speaking Their Language, Chapter 3) while simultaneously employing thugs and off-duty police officers to ensure that its projects unfold as planned. If overt physical violence and intimidation are ostensibly illegitimate in post-Suharto Indonesia, then the use of information politics becomes a feasible alternative since it is less visible while its effects are still powerful. Although shadow play is not under the exclusive control of elites, when wielded by the state, it has the ability to create distrust and break groups apart.

Chapter Nine

Marketplace Relations

"All-available, all-cheap, and all-traditional" was the slogan given to Kuncen Marketplace when it opened on 13 December 2007 after a 4.7-billion-rupiah renovation (approximately USD$350,000).[1] In the first year, the two-storey market was advertised in press releases as "a second-hand goods paradise" offering a variety of used items, including antiques, tools, electronics, clothing, and cell phones. The government claimed that Kuncen Marketplace was different from other shopping locations because it was arranged in a "traditional way," with over six hundred vendors spreading their goods on mats on the ground, as was the custom in traditional markets. As Pak Galang later put it, "Yogyakarta has always been suitable for the development of traditional markets that sell the community's cultural products. In this way, the community could participate in the operation of the market, a phenomenon that cannot be found in a mall or hypermarket."[2]

In Yogyakarta city, traditional marketplaces (*pasar tradisional*) are in competition with a growing number of modern shops, supermarkets, and malls, which have been threatening these markets' existing customer base (Rahadi, Prabowo, and Hapsariniaty 2015). Across Indonesia, traditional markets were strong in the 1960s and '70s (Malano 2011, cited in Prabowo and Rahadi 2015, 29), but during the 1998–2005 period, there was a four-fold increase in supermarkets and hypermarkets (Peters 2013, 178). In the wake of this development, the need to protect traditional marketplaces has become an important topic of discussion in the newspapers, and an agenda item for municipal and provincial governments (Peters 2013, 178).

One way of making traditional marketplaces competitive is to distinguish them from malls by treating them as "cultural sites." Thus, by billing it as an "all-traditional" marketplace, traders and government officials alike hoped that Kuncen Marketplace would become an important tourist destination for both local and foreign tourists.[3] In the lead-up to the grand opening, the municipal government worked hard to promote Kuncen as a traditional marketplace. To this end, on December 9 it encouraged the traders to wear traditional Javanese clothing during the market's inaugural week of operation.[4]

Interestingly, similar to other traditional marketplaces in Yogyakarta, more women were also found in Kuncen Marketplace. In the days and months after the market opened, I noticed that women comprised a noticeable presence, as both traders (see figure 9) and customers. Many of the male traders had turned to their wives or daughters for help in overseeing their kiosks, while some hired female employees so they could attend to other business such as purchasing merchandise. When I asked about these women, some male traders said that they still preferred that their wives and daughters stay home; in their view, Kuncen was a slightly more masculine environment than other marketplaces in the city, such as Pasar Beringharjo, which was more closely associated with femininity because of the food, clothing, and batik sold there. In contrast, Kuncen Marketplace was associated with male clothing and accessories, along with second-hand items, a small fraction of which, customers and traders suggested, may have been stolen.[5] Thus, at least in the early days and months of operation, Kuncen Marketplace remained, for these male traders, more closely associated with masculinity.

Even before the traders had been relocated to Kuncen Marketplace, it had been evident that the move was not only a spatial relocation; government officials and some of the vendors also viewed it as an upward shift in status and class. Government officials, for instance, had emphasized the positive aspects of this transformation by claiming that the traders would go from being illegal to legal subjects, from a lower to a higher social status, and from being at risk of relocation to enjoying a secure location. Yet in the first few months in the marketplace, the distinctions between life in Kuncen and life on the street were far less clear-cut. Many of the same uncertainties and practices that had accompanied the vendors' previous locations were still present in the marketplace. Although their kiosks were ostensibly secure because they could not be evicted by the government, the traders continued to pay for informal security, just as they had on the street, so that their merchandise would remain safe at night after they went home. Moreover, although these kiosks were "official," traders still illegally bought and sold spaces in the marketplace, similar to how they had bought and sold land on the street years earlier. Although government officials had emphasized how different life in the marketplace would be from the

Figure 9. A woman trading at Kuncen Marketplace, July 2013. Photo by author.

street, it became apparent – at least in the early months – that some differences were at times less obvious in practice. In fact, some of the second-hand street vendors continued to sell on the street in addition to the marketplace. This was because it was easier to sell goods on the street, especially goods of a lower quality, and it was becoming increasingly clear that, for some of these second-hand vendors, the income in Kuncen Marketplace was too little for them to survive. By April 2008, KOMPAK (Komunitas Pasar Klithikan Pakuncen, or Second-Hand Kuncen Marketplace Community), the marketplace's trader cooperative, had reported that 60 per cent of the second-hand traders had experienced bankruptcy since the relocation.[6]

When I left Yogyakarta in August 2008, I wondered how these traders would fare in comparison to those selling new goods. While those selling new goods seemed to be expanding their businesses and attracting customers, many of the second-hand traders had been expressing their concerns over how their competitors with more capital were expanding in the marketplace to occupy more and more space. Many of them had seen this before in other marketplaces: those who did not have money to invest in more and better-quality merchandise ended up back on the street, while those with more capital came to dominate the marketplace.

Changes at Kuncen Marketplace

When I returned to Yogyakarta in 2013 and 2014, I wanted to see what had happened in the years since the relocation. I was keen to learn how the traders had fared in the marketplace, what the pro- and anti-relocation leaders were up to now and how their individual circumstances might have changed, and whether the marketplace itself had undergone any transformations.

On 18 July 2013, as I walked through the newly painted marketplace (see figure 10), I saw few traders whom I knew or recognized. I wandered the bustling market for fifteen minutes, observing the customers moving through the narrow lanes looking at merchandise, the suppliers bringing in new goods, and traders chatting among themselves and their customers. I also took in all of the physical changes that had taken place since the marketplace had opened. Counter to the original "traditional" design, most traders now had their merchandise stacked a couple of metres high (which violated the government's kiosk height requirements), and they had built metal-grate walls around their kiosks, converting them into enclosed spaces that could be securely locked at night. A number of traders still occupied single kiosks, but the issue that numerous second-hand traders had pointed out back in 2008 was

Figure 10. Kuncen Marketplace, July 2013. Photo by author.

now more evident than ever: those with more capital had bought their neighbours' spaces and constructed larger spaces from which they sold hundreds of pants, shoes, or bags. As I walked to the back of the marketplace, I noticed that the space given to the former anti-relocation traders, once jokingly described as a "graveyard" because few of the Pethikbumi traders had occupied this space,[7] had changed too. Those locations had been expanded into modern shop-sized stalls with new clothing and accessories, white tile flooring, and neon lights. It was now called Zone X, and with its larger kiosks and higher-quality finishings, it was the most exclusive zone in Kuncen Marketplace.

Two levels below this new zone, I made my way to the marketplace cooperative's office, where I knocked lightly on the door and said *permisi* (excuse me) as I peered in. I was happy to see Mas Arief, Pethikbumi's original secretary, dressed in his uniform as the leader of the KOMPAK cooperative. "Few of the original traders are here any more," he confirmed after we had warmly shaken hands.[8]

When the street traders had relocated to Kuncen Marketplace, the previous street vendor organizations – Pethikbumi, Independent, Asem Gede, and Southern Square – had folded. The pro-relocation traders had, however, worked with the municipal government to create a cooperative called Ngesti Rahyu that would be ready for the opening of Kuncen Marketplace. At the time, the pro-relocation leaders had seemed well positioned to assume a leadership role in the new marketplace with the support of the government. However, after several months, the cooperative had also folded. Money had gone missing, apparently embezzled by one of its leaders, and traders in the marketplace no longer trusted the cooperative's management.[9] After Ngesti Rahyu had disbanded, control of the marketplace shifted into the hands of some of the former Pethikbumi traders. In 2008, a group of traders comprised mostly of former Pethikbumi members came together to create KOMPAK. Originally a social organization for the traders at Kuncen Marketplace, KOMPAK became a cooperative a few years later.[10]

Mas Arief is one of the former Pethikbumi leaders who has seen great success. As the leader of KOMPAK, he heads a team of three different leaders (*pengurus*), four other employees (two or three of whom are women), and hundreds of members. In the early days of the relocation, Mas Arief had rented a kiosk in Kuncen Marketplace in a more strategic location than the place he was originally given at the very back of the building. Mas Arief continues to sell shoes, and his business continues to grow and expand. He has opened another one in a marketplace on the north side of Yogyakarta, where he rents four kiosks. In 2011, he helped to develop Zone X as an exclusive area in Kuncen Marketplace, and he owns one of the eleven Zone X kiosks, where he sells clothing.

Despite Mas Arief's prosperity, many of the original traders, especially those selling second-hand goods, were no longer present in Kuncen Marketplace. The changes to the place were no secret; most of the traders who had been involved in the relocation years earlier talked eagerly about this fact during my visits to Kuncen Marketplace over the next few weeks. Pak Asep, a second-hand trader whom I had known prior to the relocation, estimated that almost 80 per cent of the traders in Kuncen Marketplace now sold new products, a change that ran against the government's original plan to have the market focused on used goods.[11] Many of the second-hand traders had sold or rented out their kiosks to traders selling new merchandise because they had found it difficult to compete in the new marketplace and needed the money. Many of the second-hand traders I spoke with during my return visits in 2013 and 2014 expressed concern that their livelihoods were at risk because they could not compete with the increasing number of traders selling new merchandise. My discussions with traders, both new and established, revealed that the relocation had had different impacts on different traders, despite the government's stated goal of empowering them and increasing all of their livelihoods.

For example, after the relocation, some of the former Pethikbumi leaders decided not to occupy the kiosks they had been granted in Kuncen Marketplace. According to himself and other sources, post-relocation, Pak Akbar never received a location in the marketplace, nor did he sell as a trader in Kuncen through other means (such as renting a kiosk from another owner). Since the relocation, Pak Akbar rarely goes to Kuncen Marketplace or meets with the other former Pethikbumi leaders. However, despite his lack of involvement in the marketplace, Pak Akbar believes that the traders there still respect him because he "did not play behind the scenes, receive money or bribes. I never did that."[12] Instead of working as a trader, Pak Akbar remains the head of security at a nightclub, and he has also begun working at a large restaurant at a resort (see "He Is My Younger Brother," Chapter 8).[13]

Although Pak Pramana received a place in Kuncen Marketplace following the relocation, he soon sold it. He never sold any merchandise there, even though he visited a number of times. He said, "I didn't want to sell there from the start because I'm embarrassed; I have my dignity."[14] Since the relocation, Pak Pramana has worked as a debt collector for various institutions such as banks and cooperatives, as well as for individuals. As a debt collector, he receives 20 per cent of the debt he collects. He makes enough money, but the job is not widely respected. Many of the original Pethikbumi leaders admitted to feeling sorry that Pak Pramana has had no other options except to become a debt collector, a job viewed by many as the work of preman.[15]

Pak Mujib respects the other leaders, like Pak Akbar and Pak Pramana, who originally decided to refuse the location and who to this day have never occupied a kiosk in Kuncen Marketplace. Pak Mujib also decided not to move to Kuncen Marketplace, and instead remains on Mangkubumi Street as a food trader (this activity was still allowed on the east side of the street). Pak Mujib originally thought that he did not receive a kiosk in Kuncen Marketplace because he was in hospital with a leg injury at the time the kiosks were allocated. However, he later discovered that he had been given a kiosk (despite not signing up for the lottery). Mas Basri (who had been the third general chair of Pethikbumi) and Mas Arief subsequently approached Pak Mujib to say that they had a buyer for his location. From Pak Mujib's perspective, however, they acted like brokers by selling his kiosk for more money than he received, something he felt that friends would not do.[16] He remains slightly suspicious of the Pethikbumi leaders who have decided to stay and sell in Kuncen Marketplace.

Mas Eko had received a kiosk at the very back of Kuncen Marketplace, with the other Pethikbumi leaders. In January 2008, he became the public relations representative of this back area of the marketplace.

However, he sold his kiosk shortly after because he needed the money, and the area was attracting too few customers (in those early days of the relocation, there was only a handful of traders selling in an area meant for approximately seventy kiosks). After selling his kiosk, he rented one at the front of Kuncen Marketplace, near other cell phone traders, but due to his continued financial struggles, he left Kuncen Marketplace in 2012. In 2013, he started to sell in Sentir Marketplace, an outdoor parking lot used as an informal market in the evenings.[17] When I met with Mas Eko in 2014, he was living with a friend in a rural area just outside of Yogyakarta city because he did not have the capital to continue selling at Sentir Marketplace.[18] He hoped to work for his friend and save enough money to resume his activities as a street vendor in the city.

According to Mas Eko, Pak Sarwan had gone bankrupt in the early years of the relocation to Kuncen Marketplace. While on Mangkubumi Street, he borrowed money from friends and family in an attempt to expand his cell phone accessories business, but because he was among the group that refused to relocate, in 2008 he was given a place at the back of the marketplace, where few customers visited. With little income in that first year in the marketplace, he was unable to pay back his loans to his friends. Embarrassed, stressed, and broke, he went to Saudi Arabia to work as a driver but was killed two years later in a car accident. Since none of the ex-Pethikbumi leaders saw an official obituary in the newspaper, some wondered whether Pak Sarwan had actually died or whether he had faked his death in order to escape his debts.[19]

Many of the second-hand traders who had supported the relocation ended up going bankrupt in their first couple of years in the marketplace. As noted earlier in this chapter, in the first months, many of the same uncertainties and practices that had existed on the street prevailed in the new marketplace. Yet as time passed, the selling conditions in Kuncen Marketplace in fact proved to be even more challenging for many of these second-hand traders. Pak Halim and Pak Edy, two second-hand traders who sold across from each other near the front of Kuncen Marketplace, explained that used items worth little money were harder to sell in the marketplace because the competition was stiffer than on the sidewalk. People selling used items from locations across the city were brought into one place, making it easier for customers to find the cheapest price. In the past, traders had often dispersed themselves across different locations, both to avoid higher levels of competition and to charge higher prices. Their profit therefore depended on the distance between the different outdoor markets.[20] Pak Dede, a former leader of the Southern Square group and a second-hand trader, told me he felt that Kuncen Marketplace has lost its community of second-hand vendors as most have left the marketplace because they could not survive there. He has been able to hold on in the marketplace because he sells household appliances – things that people still need out of necessity. In Kuncen, as Pak Dede phrased it, it is "man eats man; man eats his own friends."[21]

Besides bankruptcy, there were numerous other reasons why people left the marketplace. One left because he had to pay unexpected medical bills. Another wanted to use the money he received from selling his kiosk to renovate his home. A few found it easier to sell second-hand goods on the street or wanted to start an alternative business. By selling their kiosks, these traders could access a significant amount of capital. Others left for social reasons. For instance, Pak Warno, one ex-Kuncen trader, went to sell in Sentir Marketplace, in part because he lost most of his customers after they found trading in a market like Kuncen to be "less artisanal" (Javanese: *ra nyeni*)[22] than the street. Moreover, the experience on the street had not only economic benefits but social ones as well, with vendors and customers hanging out and getting to know each other. At Kuncen Marketplace, this, too, had changed: in Pak Warno's opinion, every relationship was counted in terms of buying and selling. Thus, many of the other traders who left Kuncen Marketplace could also be found at Sentir Marketplace.

Lingering Tensions and Differences

Changes to the original concept of the marketplace and the resulting hardships in turn changed how many of the former pro-relocation traders viewed the government. Most now distrusted the municipal government, which they felt had betrayed them. This distrust fuelled some of the lingering tensions in the marketplace. In the opinion of these former pro-relocation traders, the municipal government had failed to honour its promise to protect the interests of the second-hand traders.

These traders also distrusted a few of the former anti-relocation traders who now occupied important positions in Kuncen Marketplace and who were close to the government. In 2014, Pak Bowo, the previous leader of the Independent group, sold computer mice, cables, cell phone chargers, books, and magazines in Kuncen Marketplace. Even though he was no longer a leader of any vendor organization, he still felt responsible for the second-hand traders he had encouraged to relocate. As a result, he planned to remain at Kuncen Marketplace until all these traders were gone. This, he feared, was a reality that would come true in the next few years as the number of traders selling new goods grew. These traders had more capital – and therefore greater access to new goods that they could sell – than the second-hand traders at the marketplace (see figure 11). Pak Bowo was disappointed that

Figure 11. (top) A trader with more capital selling new goods at Kuncen Marketplace, 18 July 2013. (bottom) A trader of second-hand goods selling in an unofficial site at Kuncen Marketplace, 18 July 2013. Photos by author.

the municipal government had not upheld the memorandum of understanding it signed with the Independent, Southern Square, and Asem Gede leaders, by which it promised to help support and protect these traders in the new marketplace.[23] He was disillusioned with the government because he felt that municipal officials had done little to protect the second-hand traders. He said of the municipal government and the people generally involved in the relocation, "Everyone has interests and everyone is a liar."[24]

Pak Wahyu, the original Pethikbumi leader and a supporter of the relocation (see Postscript: Growing Unrest and Resistance, Chapter 2), had received a kiosk prior to the move. In 2014, he still had this kiosk but was allowing his friend Pak Slamat to use it. He sent glasses and antique items to Pak Slamat to be sold in the marketplace while also selling and processing antique merchandise at his home in the neighbouring town of Bantul; he even opened a place to fix bikes at his home. Pak Wahyu felt that Kuncen Marketplace was meant to empower the little people (*rakyat kecil*), but instead preman and members of the Legislative Assembly had asked for and received kiosks. Pak Wahyu no longer cared about being involved in any vendor organization. "I'm disappointed if I see bureaucrats, and I was also disappointed [with my job as a civil servant], so I retired."[25] According to Pak Wahyu, the government was filled with corruption, and he did not want to be enslaved by it. Opening a business at his home meant that he could avoid any engagement with the local government officials at the marketplace.

Many of the street vendors who had participated in the relocation distinguished themselves from the pro-relocation leaders by claiming that they, unlike their former leaders, had acted ethically during the relocation. Despite his own status as a former leader with a pro-relocation stance, Pak Wahyu was disappointed with his fellow pro-relocation leaders. Like the others, Pak Wahyu said that he could have received more than the one kiosk he was allowed from the municipal government if he had wanted, but he had chosen not to because he wished to stay honest. Pak Wahyu said that the other former pro-relocation leaders such as Pak Bowo had each received two kiosks, and as a result he thought that none of these ex-leaders actually cared about their members, but were instead looking out for their own interests.[26]

Pak Halim, who had remained neutral once the traders had divided into pro- and anti-relocation groups, was also disappointed with how things turned out with the relocation.[27] He said that it was like "thuggery" (*premanisme*) because all different types of people, including the police, had asked for and received kiosks in Kuncen Marketplace. He explained that "Pak Didik gave lots of kiosks to preman; there was a lot.

There were some who received five kiosks. They did not stay but sold their kiosks."[28] Pak Halim contrasted himself with the pro-relocation leaders, many of whom had received multiple kiosks (some, he claimed, had received up to nine). Pak Halim was proud that he had stayed "honest" during that process and only received one kiosk, as per the rules. He had also held off on entering the lottery until others had joined, to ensure that none of his friends were left behind. Pak Halim served as the leader of his block in the marketplace,[29] and he was convinced that the traders at Kuncen believed and trusted him because he did not receive multiple kiosks. "Because I helped other people maybe Allah gave me a good kiosk," he said.[30]

Some of the former Pethikbumi traders, both leaders and active members, distinguished themselves from those members who had abandoned their anti-relocation stances and signed up for the relocation surreptitiously. Pak Nur, one of the most active members of Pethikbumi during the relocation, was disappointed that many of his colleagues had signed up for the relocation behind his back and without the knowledge of the group's leaders, instead of continuing to refuse the relocation. Pak Nur had been a larger operator on Mangkubumi Street with more capital than the average trader. Thus, he was able to proudly recount to me that he could have received a place for himself at the marketplace and seven more for all his workers if he had decided to sign up for the relocation earlier on, but instead, after resisting the relocation, he had received a kiosk at the very back of the marketplace with the rest of the Pethikbumi members. It is worth noting, however, that due to the amount of capital at Pak Nur's disposal, he was able to contract three kiosks at the front of the marketplace – that is, rent them from other traders – where there were many more customers.[31]

The fact that the tensions among the traders remained six and seven years after the relocation indicated to me how significant this process had been for them. As well as the stark economic differences between individual traders – as illustrated by Pak Nur's financial power relative to the second-hand traders – there remained significant economic differences and tensions between the former pro- and anti-relocation groups. While many of the former Pethikbumi traders selling new items expanded and grew their businesses – some purchasing new motorbikes and even cars for themselves – the pro-relocation second-hand traders faced economic hardship: they lived precariously and were almost always on the verge of bankruptcy. The tensions that had developed during the relocation continued to shape the social relationships and day-to-day interactions among the traders in Kuncen Marketplace. While many government officials and traders evaluate the success of vendor relocations according to a narrow set of economic criteria, fewer pay attention to the long-lasting impact that such projects can have on social relationships.

New Interests Aligned

The stories I collected over the course of my follow-up field research suggest that the relocation impacted the pro- and anti-relocation traders in different ways. Many of the second-hand traders and their leaders, who were the keenest to join the relocation, have been the unhappiest with its outcome. They had hoped to have financial success, to shape marketplace policies and to receive protection from competition with new traders with more capital. Instead, they were eventually sidelined in the new structures of power and left vulnerable to competitive market forces. In contrast, a number of the original anti-relocation leaders who decided to sell in the marketplace slowly took up positions of power by creating the KOMPAK cooperative. By organizing meetings with the government and among the traders, they now controlled how information flowed in the marketplace. They also took a leadership role in developing Zone X, the new exclusive area in the marketplace. Although in the early days these former Pethikbumi traders were sceptical of the relocation, they were able to adapt and, for the most part, find financial success. Once suspicious of the government, they have mostly repaired their relationships with municipal officials, and have even sought to collaborate with them in order to develop Kuncen into a successful marketplace.[32]

The fact that the anti-relocation traders ended up benefiting from the relocation is not entirely surprising. They were generally economically better off than the second-hand traders from the Independent, Asem Gede, and Southern Square groups because of their strong customer base of young clients interested in their new and trendy products. These traders, and especially their leaders, had also gained a significant amount of experience in operating successful vendor organizations in the lead-up to the relocation, and had gained considerable skills in using information politics to their advantage. They knew how to negotiate with government officials, make official requests and produce official documents, and speak in terms of the popular discourses of democracy, transparency, and participation. It was unsurprising, then, that they would take up leadership roles in the new marketplace, where the government was no longer seen as the enemy. Once they were under the government's roof and part of its bureaucracy, some of the anti-relocation traders succeeded in bringing the government officials over to their side, which was necessary for the approval of projects that would make the marketplace successful from these traders' perspective. The government officials were also invested in the economic success of the marketplace, and no longer needed to use uncertainty and distrust as tactics of control, so having a reliable vendor organization and cooperative functioning in the marketplace was valuable to them. Once the government's and the former anti-relocation leaders' interests were largely in alignment, their relationship became much more collaborative and communicative. Had Pethikbumi's anti-relocation movement been successful, their relationship with the government might have been different. Pethikbumi's oppositional politics was in some sense pacified because the group underwent its own transformation after the relocation, and because, as noted earlier in this chapter, some figures such as Pak Akbar and Pak Pramana did not relocate to the marketplace. The repressive state – the object of Pethikbumi's opposition – seemingly disappeared and was replaced with what appeared to be a different and more benevolent official presence.[33]

In contrast, the second-hand traders who were part of the pro-relocation movement unfortunately were left to their own devices after the Ngesti Rahyu cooperative they had formed in the early months of the Kuncen Marketplace relocation folded. Pak Didik did not continue to advocate for these traders' interests with the government once the relocation had occurred, and they had little desire or ability to organize themselves. No NGOs, activists, or other legal aid organizations stepped in to help them organize and demand that the government protect their positions in the marketplace. Instead, the approach of many of these traders has been to leave the marketplace and return to the street, where they might have more of a say over their futures.

Chapter Ten

Conclusion

This book has provided a description of the information politics around a street vendor relocation in Yogyakarta. In so doing, it has sought to emphasize the *variety* of information ideologies and practices used by those involved in the relocation to stake their claims in the city. The first major argument of the book is that examining the creation of conspiracies, the spreading of rumours, the writing of documents, the revealing of information in newspapers, and the use of surveillance allows us to think about these tactics as part of a larger ecology of information practices, not just as isolated actions. If the information practices of the state and the various actors involved are multiple, and at times even contradictory, then our analytics must account for this multiplicity. This demands, in turn, an understanding that governance and its challenges are not straightforward, but are instead complex configurations or assemblages.[1]

The second major argument of the book is that a focus on information politics allows us to understand and study state-society relationships. In the course of this ethnography, I have shown that the ability to correctly channel, request, manipulate, and interpret information is central not only to the government's ability to implement controversial urban projects – these tactics are also necessary if the urban underclass is to challenge government policies. In post-Suharto Indonesia, the notion of *transparency* is used to imagine the future of this democratic nation, while the ideal of *sharing* information is now embedded within highly contested beliefs about how information should be distributed, circulated, and interpreted. By studying the interrelated information practices of state and society more broadly, we can understand how these relationships are produced and reproduced, and how they shift and change, through everyday encounters.

Because we are experiencing far-ranging transformations of information practices and information ideologies on a global scale, the anthropology of information should demand our attention in a variety of ways. The anthropology of information offers an exploration of the representational logic of information practices today, and how this logic shapes social and political relationships, institutions, ideas about the past, and dreams about the future. In this book, I have used the term *information politics* to refer to the repertoire of information practices and ideologies that shape the relationships that people have to each other, institutions, and the state. I have sought to lay out some analytical tools that I found useful for navigating information politics in the context of a vendor relocation in Yogyakarta. As well as paying attention to people's information practices – the way they actually seek to produce, circulate, and interpret information – this involves paying attention to people's information ideologies – how their beliefs about information shape how they use and receive information. Many of the Pethikbumi street traders, for instance, were suspicious of the information they received from government officials through the process of sosialisasi because they believed that these officials were also working behind the scenes to generate conflict, confusion, and suspicion. This ideology was verified when they determined that the government had falsified the signature of one of the traders and falsely claimed that the traders' signatures signalled their agreement to the relocation (see Shadow Play with Sosialisasi, Chapter 3).

Information practices and information ideologies are not merely the instruments of different actors or groups; they also help to shape and transform social relationships in ways that are both unexpected and predictable. As I tracked the ecologies of information practices accessed by government officials and street vendors, I was able to attend to the social forms and relationships that emerged, and to understand how these relationships shifted over time. I described, for instance, how the Pethikbumi leaders became close to a group of lawyers who helped them interpret the information they were receiving from the government and to challenge it through tactics such as the indirect revelation of information in the newspapers (see The Press Conference: Constructing a Hidden Message, Chapter 5). Yet the strategic use of information also resulted in a breakdown of the traders' relationships with their lawyers and NGO partners as rumours about the lawyers' true interests and their potential relationships with the government circulated (see Chapter 7: Conspiratorial Knowledge, Allah, and State Power). Tracing these different information ideologies and information practices allowed me to understand why certain people and groups connected with each other during some moments, and why in other moments their relationships seemed to falter.

Anthropologists are particularly well positioned to study information politics because we are skilled at showing how these behaviours and beliefs are embedded in the cultural practices and norms of particular groups and societies. I have shown that an ethnography of information practices and information ideologies involves examining the specific beliefs, skills, and efforts that actors draw upon in order to produce, interpret, and circulate information for political purposes. Tracing these associations through information politics allowed me to capture a range of practices, not all of which were official or explicitly discussed strategies of governance or resistance. The information practices and ideologies that I have highlighted during this street vendor relocation project were fuelled by a struggle for democracy in Indonesia, a prior economic crisis, and the rise of civil society in the post-Suharto era. They were also shaped by the concept of shadow play, or the idea that unseen actors are operating behind a screen, controlling events and manipulating information. As an information ideology and practice, shadow play shaped this urban conflict and the information practices that actors used, with the result that conspiratorial thinking and suspicion were widespread among the anti-relocation traders, who themselves practised shadow play in pursuit of their own interests. In such a context, however, the boundary between elites and traders is often unclear, since one of the main techniques of shadow play involves the deliberate sowing of confusion about who is working for the elites and who is working for the underdogs.

My focus on information politics began in response to the challenge of how to understand in ethnographic terms how the street traders on Mangkubumi Street negotiated their relationship with the state and other actors in the city. Across the globe, street traders in different contexts engage in diverse counter-strategies in the face of state violence, including organized relocations and removals, such as "demonstrations, strikes, party politics, legal and ritual maneuvers, and group and individual negotiations" (G. Clark 1988b, 10). This book has outlined another strategy – information politics – to add to the list of strategies and counter-strategies used by street traders and the state. In particular, information politics offered me a way into thinking about the anti-relocation traders' relationships with the state as I witnessed first-hand the wide range of information practices that government officials used to sway the anti-relocation traders, and the variety of information practices that the anti-relocation street traders and their supporters deployed to position themselves against the state's project.

My ethnographic examination of the street vendor relocation project has shown that information politics was an important space for

negotiation between the traders and the state. Recent work on street vendors has recognized that the enforcement of laws around street vending
is flexible and subject to constant negotiation (Anjaria 2016; Little 2014;
Daniel M. Goldstein 2016). Goldstein (2016) describes how the state can
cross over into the realm of informality, a process he calls "urban dis-
regulation," where the administrators chose what laws to follow and
what laws to ignore (247). In a similar way, the state administrators
of the relocation to Kuncen Marketplace chose to follow certain information practices that were officially recognized and considered democratic, while also using others that were more undemocratic and meant
to be revealed to only a small group of people in order to get the job of
relocation done. A focus on information practices has shown some of
the ways in which the state enters into this informal zone when it uses
unofficial information practices and channels to assert its power. While
the government publicly claimed to be dialoguing with the traders,
it simultaneously produced a false document to generate fear. While
municipal officials were responsible for sharing information with traders in an official capacity, they also worked with an undercover police
agent to circulate information to the traders in an underhanded way in
order to create suspicion. State control over the situation was exerted
not only through the sharing of information and documentation, but
through withholding, forging, and falsifying information. At the same
time, the traders and their supporters also used information to pressure
municipal officials. They did this through various information practices: indirectly accusing the government in the newspapers of using
preman, engaging in their own surveillance of actors associated with
the state, and claiming that they might instigate violence even though
they had no intention to follow through with this threat. The information practices used in these processes were neither straightforward nor
singular, and studying them together has allowed me to illuminate the
extent to which governance and popular resistance each involve an
array of practices that sometimes contradict each other.

In addition, addressing attention to the basic, sometimes fundamental differences in people's information ideologies and information practices can help foster a greater understanding of what democracy means,
along with both the range of possibilities and the limits that democracy provides to citizens. Scholars have noted that concepts such as
democratization come to have varied meanings and practices, resulting
in what some have called "alternative democracies" (e.g., Paley 2002;
Nugent 2008; Witsoe 2011) or "vernacular democracies" (Tanabe 2007).
While some scholars have approached the question of democratic transition narrowly by examining the formal practices of democracy (such

as voting, protesting, and engaging with political parties), this book, by contrast, has sought a wider view. In particular, it has considered both the formal and informal practices of information politics in order to argue that the information politics at play in the street vendor relocation project worked both for and against democracy. Indeed, information politics are at the heart of the paradox of Indonesia's democracy. As Bubandt (2014) writes in relation to corruption and spirits, "Democracy in Indonesia is ... dysfunctional in the sense that its success is awkwardly ensured by apparently negative means" (132). The undemocratic nature of some of the information politics discussed in this book is part and parcel of how democracy is playing out in Indonesia.

In the post-Suharto era, information politics is shaped by gender and class relationships in important ways. While there has been a "loosening" of power at the centre since the transition to democracy (Kusno 2004, 2388), street vendors' gender subjectivities have not been supplanted or greatly altered in the post-Suharto era. While men entered street vending in Yogyakarta in greater numbers after the economic crisis of 1997, in contrast to working in an office or for a formal business, street vending was and still is generally viewed in Yogyakarta as a lower-class job for men. I have also argued in this book that Pethikbumi's all-male leadership, along with their PPIP supporters, who were mostly men, at times evoked the subjectivity of pemuda, an image that is constantly circulating in the public (and private) domain (see Lee 2016). The masculinized identity of these youth activists likely shaped the kinds of information politics that the Pethikbumi leaders and their PPIP supporters engaged in. Like the activists of the late 1990s, these traders and their PPIP supporters were paranoid; fearing that they were under surveillance, they developed their own techniques for pressuring the government and obtaining information (137). By drawing on the subject position of youth activists at certain moments, the Pethikbumi leaders were able to feel that they were contributing to something larger than their small movement while also demonstrating to their NGO and legal supporters that a broader sector of people besides students could take up the cause of democracy. It was, however, only in an "urgent" situation in which the traders' livelihoods were at stake that the anti-relocation street vendors were willing to temporarily mobilize with their NGO and legal supporters. Moreover, despite the NGOs' and lawyers' desire to help these street vendors engage in information politics against the state, the government made a distinction between the traders, on the one hand, and the NGOs and activists, on the other. While the municipal government characterized the NGOs and activists as troublemakers (see Lee 2016, 206), the traders' agency was taken away when the government depicted them as unable to understand the project, a claim that could be made because it was assumed that the traders were considered uneducated and of a lower class.

Why should we care about information politics? Information politics matters because our relationships with each other, with institutions, and with the state are shaped by information practices and ideologies. Governments, international organizations, policymakers, and citizens hope that access to information will bring about better governance and transparency. This ethnography has shown, however, that despite an appetite for openness in the post-Suharto era, the official transition to democracy has seen new kinds of information politics take root in Indonesian society, the result of which has been neither transparency nor opacity, but rather an ecology of culturally specific information practices that often do not fit neatly into circulating ideals. In situations of political conflict, information politics particularly matters because people develop complex interpretations and practices around information. The Pethikbumi traders' ability to challenge the government and to stake their claims to the street was tied up in their attempt to effectively engage in information politics vis-à-vis the state and the observing public. This engagement with information politics entailed knowing when and how to use information, and it allowed for unexpected forms of participation, negotiation, and resistance.

List of Protagonists

Please note that the employment details of some individuals have been withheld in order to protect their identities.

Anti-relocation Protagonists

Mbah Ahmad	chair, Madura Family Alliance (Ikatan Keluarga Madura)
Pak Akbar	first* general chair, Pethikbumi (November 2006–November 2007)
Mas Arief	secretary, Pethikbumi (2004–7)
Mas Basri	third general chair, Pethikbumi (November 2006–November 2007)
Mas Eko	public relations officer, Pethikbumi (January–November 2007)
Ibu Marini	director, Human Rights Protection Agency (Badan Pelindung Hak Kemanusiaan, or BPHK)
Pak Mujib	research and development officer, Pethikbumi (November 2006–November 2007)
Mas Nasir	advocate with Indonesian Youth Movement for Change (Pergerakan Pemuda Indonesia untuk Perubahan, or PPIP)
Pak Nur	active member of Pethikbumi (January–November 2007)

---

* The Pethikbumi roles of first, second, and third general chair reflect a hierarchical ranking from most senior to least senior. They do not reflect the order in which each individual assumed their respective role.

Pak Pramana	second general chair, Pethikbumi (November 2006–November 2007)
Pak Sarwan	treasurer, Pethikbumi (July 2006–November 2007).
Pak Suyitno	organizer, Human Rights Protection Agency (Badan Pelindung Hak Kemanusiaan, or BPHK)
Pak Syafii	active member of Pethikbumi
Pak Toni	chair, the NGO Forum (2006–8)
Mas Totok	advocate with Indonesian Youth Movement for Change (Pergerakan Pemuda Indonesia untuk Perubahan, or PPIP)

Pro-relocation Protagonists

Pak Bowo	chair, Independent (January–November 2007)
Pak Dede	chair, Southern Square traders
Pak Didik	director, Indonesian Law Monitoring Alliance (ILMA); NGO advocate* and organizer of the pro-relocation vendor groups
Pak Ferry	member of Brimob, the mobile brigade of the police
Pak Sarjadi	treasurer, Pethikbumi (2003–November 2006); treasurer, Independent (January–November 2007)
Pak Suryadharma Ali	minister of cooperatives and small and medium enterprises
Pak Wahyu	general chair, Pethikbumi (2003–November 2006); member, Independent (2007)**

---

*   I initially thought that Pak Didik was a lawyer because his organization claimed to provide "legal" advice to citizens in Yogyakarta city. I was later surprised when, in the course of doing a life history interview with Pak Didik, he said that he was not in fact a lawyer by training.

** Pak Wahyu was the original leader of Pethikbumi. Under his leadership, the organization supported the government's relocation project. He was then removed as a leader of Pethikbumi (see Postscript: Growing Unrest and Resistance, Chapter 2), and subsequently became a member of the pro-relocation Independent vendor group.

Government Officials

Pak Ari	head, Department of Industry, Trade, and Cooperatives (Dinas Perindustrian, Perdagangan dan Koperasi, or Disperindagkop)
Pak Achmad	municipal government official, involved in the planning and redevelopment of Kuncen Marketplace in 2006–7
Pak Galang	head, Department of Marketplaces (Dinas Pasar)
Pak Herry Zudianto	mayor, Yogyakarta city (2001–6; 2006–11)
Pak Joko	employee, Regional Goods Management (Pengelolaan Barang Daerah)
Pak Susanto	employee, Department of Marketplaces
Pak Supriyanto	head, Department of Industry, Trade, and Cooperatives (2003–6)
Pak Syukri Fadholi	vice mayor, Yogyakarta city (2001–6); member of PPP
Pak Mulyono	employee, Department of Industry, Trade, and Cooperatives

Neutral to the Relocation

Pak Halim	secretary, Pethikbumi (2004–November 2007)

Minor Actors

Pak Denny	volunteer, Community-Oriented Policing on Malioboro Street; informal security officer on Mangkubumi Street
Pak Ettes	consulting firm employee (2011–13)
Ibu Fatima	employee, Study Centre at UGM
Pak Freddy	student activist during the 1990s
Pak Haris	student activist during the 1990s
Pak Johar	civil servant
Pak Kasiyarno	member, Pethikbumi
Ibu Novri	employee, Centre for the Study of Culture at UGM
Pak Nurdin	shop owner on Mangkubumi Street
Ibu Risti	member, Pethikbumi

Pak Teguh	media consultant
Pak Yohanes	civil servant

Glossary of Indonesian Terms and Abbreviations

abang	older brother
adek	younger brother
agen	agent
Beringharjo	marketplace in Yogyakarta
bermain	play
BPHK	Human Rights Protection Agency (Badan Pelindung Hak Kemanusiaan)*
Brimob	Mobile Brigade Corps (Korps Brigade Mobil) – the mobile brigade of the police
bukti	proof; evidence
curiga	suspicious
dalang	puppeteer/narrator; the source of power behind the screen
Disperindagkop	Department of Industry, Trade, and Cooperatives; an abbreviation of Dinas Perindustrian, Perdagangan dan Koperasi
DIY	Special Region of Yogyakarta (Daerah Istimewa Yogyakarta)
DPRD	Regional People's Legislative Assembly (Dewan Perwakilan Rakyat Daerah), district and provincial legislatures
Ibu	Mother; a term for an older and respected woman
ILMA	Indonesian Law Monitoring Alliance, an NGO
intel	intelligence agent
jaringan	network

---

* BPHK is a pseudonym for this organization. There are two further organizational pseudonyms listed in this glossary: ILMA and PPIP.

kampung	a lower-class residential neighbourhood, or slum, in an urban setting
kepentingan	interests
klithikan	second-hand goods, an onomatopoeic Javanese term based on the sounds that certain merchandise can make (e.g., metals hitting each other or the ringing of bells)
KMY	Madura Family Alliance (Ikatan Keluarga Madura Yogyakarta), an ethnic organization
kota	city
kotor	dirty
KTP	government-issued Indonesian identity card; the full name, *Kartu Tanda Penduduk*, is usually translated into English as either "identity card" or "personal identity card"
Kuncen	a marketplace in Yogyakarta, whose name comes from the Javanese word *kunci*, referring to someone who guards places such as graveyards
laskar	army, troops, paramilitary group
LOD DIY	Special Region of Yogyakarta Ombudsman Institution (Lembaga Ombudsman Daerah Istimewa Yogyakarta)
LSM	*Lembaga swadaya masyarakat*; often translated as "self-reliant community institution" or "NGO"
Malioboro	main street in Yogyakarta
Mangkubumi	a main street in Yogyakarta city, just north of Malioboro Street
Mas	older brother; term of address for a young man or a man who is not significantly older than the speaker
Mbah	Grandparent; a term of respect
New Order	authoritarian regime of Raden Suharto that ruled Indonesia from 1965 to 1998
oknum	rogue; an individual who uses his or her official position for secret or underhanded goals
Pak	short for *bapak* (father); a term of respect
PAN	National Mandate Party (Partai Amanat Nasional)
pasar	marketplace
pedagang	trader, merchant
pedagang kaki lima	street vendor
pemerintah	government
pemerintah kota	municipal government
Pemkot	city government (*Pemerintah Kota*)

pemuda	youth; political activist
perwal	regulation produced by the mayor (*peraturan walikota*)
Pethikbumi	association of street vendors on Mangkubumi Street (Pedagang Klithikan Mangkubumi); second-hand street vendors on Mangkubumi Street
PKL	street vendor (*pedagang kaki lima*)
Poltabes	police service at the provincial level; also known as Polisi Kota Besar
PPIP	Indonesia Youth Movement for Change (Pergerakan Pemuda Indonesia untuk Perubahan)
PPP	United Development Party (Partai Persatuan Pembangunan), a political party
preman	thug
premanisme	thuggery
provokator	provocateur; in Indonesia, a *provokator* is considered to be outside of the law and in need of punishment
proyek	project; a funded activity with a termed end
rakyat	the people
rakyat kecil	the little people, or lower classes
Reformasi	Reform; refers to the 1998 movement that ended Suharto's period of New Order rule
saat	moment; in this book, *saat* refers to a possible moment of upheaval
Satpol PP	Civil Service Police Unit (Satuan Polisi Pamong Praja)
semu	"Appearance, what shows through or is visible outwardly of something inward; what can be read on the face; to seem to, have the appearance of."*
sosialisasi	socialization, informing a group about a plan prior to its implementation
UGM	Universitas Gadjah Mada
warung	casual food stall, shop, or café usually located on the sidewalk
wayang kulit	Indonesian form of shadow puppetry

---

* This definition comes from Stuart Robson and Singgih Wibisono, *Javanese English Dictionary* (New York: Tuttle, 2013), 666.

Notes

1. Introduction

1 Unless otherwise specified, all references to *Yogyakarta* are to the city of Yogyakarta, not the region (of which the city is the administrative capital).

2 In Bahasa Indonesia, titles are often used before people's names when they are being addressed or referred to. *Pak* is the short form of *Bapak*, or father; *Ibu*, or mother, is used for older and respected women; *Mbak* is sister; *Mas* is brother. "The titles vary according to the age and status of the person addressed relative to that of the speaker, the sex of the person addressed, and the degree of intimacy or friendliness between the person addressed and the speaker" (Wolff, Oetomo, and Fietkiewicz 1992b, 17).

3 I have used pseudonyms for most of the organizations mentioned in this book, including Indonesia Law Monitoring Alliance (ILMA), Indonesia Youth Movement for Change (Pergerakan Pemuda Indonesia untuk Perubahan [PPIP]), and Human Rights Protection Agency (Badan Pelindung Hak Kemanusiaan [BPHK]). Organizations whose names have not been changed include Pethikbumi, Independent, Asem Gede, Urban Forum, Oxfam, LINGKUP Indonesia (Yayasan Lingkar Lingkungan Hidup Indonesia, or Indonesian Environmental Circle Foundation), and the NGO Forum (Forum LSM DIY; *Lembaga swadaya masyarakat*, or *LSM*, is the Indonesian equivalent of "NGO"; Daerah Istimewa Yogyakarta, or DIY, stands for the "Special Region of Yogyakarta"). I have also used pseudonyms for the individuals with whom I communicated during my fieldwork, with the exception of my research assistants and high-ranking officials such as Yogyakarta's mayor. Moreover, I have applied pseudonyms to any quoted material that mentions those individuals and organizations whose names I have altered.

4 For definitions of Indonesian terms and abbreviations frequently used in this book, see Glossary of Indonesian Terms and Abbreviations.

5 In my presentation of Indonesian names, I have adopted the approach of S. Ann Dunham (2009): "The naming system in Indonesia varies among its many cultures, but a large number do not use family names, and therefore many Indonesians, particularly Javanese, have only one name. Even when Indonesians have two or more names, the last name is not necessarily or even usually a family name. Indonesian bibliographies often alphabetize according to the first name rather than the last. I have nonetheless alphabetized according to the last name, feeling that this would be less confusing to non-Indonesian readers" (347).

6 Loren Ryter (2001) defines *oknum* as "any member of a group who acts outside of the mandate of the group, almost exclusively criminally" (126n9). Although I draw on Ryter's definition, my own definition of oknum in this book does not include the word *criminality* because not all of the oknum involved in the vendor relocation engaged in criminality.

7 In the mid-1990s, the concept of language ideologies emerged as scholars recognized that ideologies could connect language practices to such things as identity, morality, and aesthetics (Woolard and Schieffelin 1994, 56). These scholars also recognized that language ideologies often underpinned social institutions like schools, nation states, and the law.

8 Kate Lamb, "Indonesian Government to Hold Weekly 'Fake News' Briefings," *Guardian* (London), 27 September 2018, https://www.theguardian.com/world/2018/sep/27/indonesian-government-to-hold-weekly-fake-news-briefings.

9 Mike Isaac and Kevin Roose, "Disinformation and Fake News Spreads over WhatsApp Ahead of Brazil's Presidential Election," *Independent* (London), 21 October 2018, https://www.independent.co.uk/news/world/americas/brazil-election-2018-whatsap-fake-news-presidential-disinformation-a8593741.html.

10 Phillip de Wet, "Facebook Is Launching Fake News Checking in South Africa – Here's How It Works," *Business Insider*, 4 October 2018, https://www.businessinsider.co.za/facebook-fact-checking-in-south-africa-with-africa-check-2018-10.

11 In Canada, a survey by the School of Journalism and Communication at Carleton University found that 26 per cent of Canadians believed the theory that the coronavirus was engineered in a lab in China and released to the general population as a bioweapon (Carleton Newsroom, Carleton University 2020).

12 Kate Lamb, "Fake news spikes in Indonesia Ahead of Elections," *Guardian* (London), 20 March 2019, https://www.theguardian.com/world/2019/mar/20/fake-news-spikes-in-indonesia-ahead-of-elections.

13 Khidir M. Prawirosusanto, email communication with the author, 1 September 2020.

14 Joshua Barker, email communication with the author, 4 September 2020.

15 Ibid. Janet Steele (2011) argues that many of *Tempo*'s stories also focused on victims (*korban*) and were used to display the suffering of regular people in order to criticize Suharto's regime (86).

16 See Gary Roddan, "Vale George Aditjondro," *Inside Indonesia*, 21 December
     2016, https://www.insideindonesia.org/vale-george-aditjondro?highlight
     =WyJnZW9yZ2UiLCJhZGl0am9uZHJvIiwiYWRpdGpvbmRyeby dzIiwiZG
     VjZW1iZXIiLDIwMTYsImdlb3JnZSBhZGl0am9uZHJvIiwiZGVjZW1iZX
     IgMjAxNiJd.
17 Joshua Barker, email communication with the author, 4 September 2020.
18 For example, with the emergence of COVID-19 in Indonesia, the concept of
     kerpercayaan (trust) is being used by citizens in relation to government-produced
     COVID-19 data. Some citizens are asking, "Pemerintah kok dipercaya?" (Can
     the government be trusted?) in relation to this data, suggesting that the numbers
     the government is releasing are either too low or too high. Elan Lazuardi, email
     communication with the author, 2 September 2020.
19 See, for example, Fanny Potkin and Agustinus Beo Da Costa, "Fact-
     Checkers vs. Hoax Peddlers: A Fake News Battle Ahead of Indonesia's
     Election," *Reuters*, 10 April 2019, https://www.reuters.com/article
     /idCAKCN1RM2ZE-OCATP?edition-redirect=ca; see also Nadzir,
     Seftiani, and Permana (2019).
20 "Indonesia Tsunami: Authorities Fight Hoaxes," *BBC News*, 3 October
     2018, https://www.bbc.com/news/world-asia-45734861.
21 The names given to these fake or questionable documents are *selebaran
     gelap* (dark leaflets), *surat edaran* (circular letters), and *surat kaleng* (can
     letters) (Bubandt 2008, 790).
22 For further information on the conflict in North Maluku, see Christopher
     R. Duncan (2005).
23 Anthropologists during the 1960s and '70s were concerned with how
     information was transmitted in face-to-face encounters, and a number
     of terms were in use to describe these processes, such as *rumour* (Firth
     [1967] 2011), *chat* (Bailey 1971b), *gossip* and *scandal* (Gluckman 1963a), and
     information-management (Paine 1967).
24 A complete theoretical genealogy of the proposed framework of
     "information politics" is beyond the scope of this introduction, but I
     recognize that some early works in social anthropology, sociology, and
     ethnology paid attention to information practices like rumour (e.g., W.A.
     Peterson and Gist 1951; Shibutani 1966), gossip (e.g., Cox 1970; Fine 1977;
     Gilmore 1978; Haviland 1977; Handelman 1973; Szwed 1966), and joking
     (e.g., Douglas 1968; McDougal 1964).
25 Another information practice that seeks to be an expression of
     transparency is the global proliferation of "audit culture" (Kipnis 2008;
     Power 1997; Strathern 2000a). Cris Shore and Susan Wright (1999) argue
     that audit discourses are about power, and are a means for altering the
     way people associate with those in power, each other, and themselves
     (559). They note that these audit cultures often create relationships that
     are "hierarchical and paternalistic" (558).

26 Katherine Verdery (2019) likewise describes how the surveillance regime of the Securitate, the secret state police in Romania, shaped local networks of social relations. She writes, "In order to gain knowledge, officers manipulated those [local networks of social] relations in very specific ways, both in their recruitment of informers and in using them to change the shape and character of the [surveillance] target's own social relations, so as to create networks that would have certain desired effects" (66).

27 My thanks to the anonymous reviewer who drew to my attention to this.

28 At present, municipal governments are responsible for generating by-laws on street vendors who operate in their jurisdictions.

29 T. Swasono, "Tertibkan Pendjual Beras!!" [Organize the rice sellers!!], *Kedaulatan Rakyat* (Yogyakarta), 4 April 1968.

30 When the phrase *pedagang kaki lima* became more common in the 1970s, many reports tried to situate it historically (although there was general confusion over its origin). The most accepted version of its history comes from Lili N. Schoch (1986):

> The term "kaki lima" is very old. It dates back to the period from 1811 to 1816, when ... the Dutch colonies in Asia were under English administration. At that time, Sir Thomas Stamford Raffles, the Governor General, introduced left-hand traffic in Indonesia and passed a law requiring all the roads in the towns to have a pavement: 31 cm high by 150 cm wide – or one foot by five feet – hence kaki lima. Left-hand traffic is still the rule today, and although the pavements were rarely constructed, the term "kaki lima" has passed onto the roadside hawkers. (2)

31 According to these studies, the profile of the average street vendor was an uneducated male between the ages of twenty and thirty-nine who had migrated to Jakarta from another part of the country. He came to Jakarta with the help of friends or extended family. His daily income was relatively low at approximately 5,000 rupiah or less (approximately USD$0.40) but was higher than what could be earned in his place of origin (Wirakartakusumah and Pantjoro 1992).

32 A similar tactic was used in Vietnam for market traders. See Ann Marie Leshkowich (2011, 277).

33 The cooperative was officially recognized on 5 April 1982 in Document No. 1229/BH/XI.

34 Gustaaf Reerink, "When Money Rules over Voice," *Inside Indonesia*, 18 October 2009, https://www.insideindonesia.org/when-money-rules-over -voice.

35 I have translated this quotation from Dwi Ariyani Hardiyanti's original dissertation. Unless otherwise noted, all translations are my own.

36 "Joko Widodo dan Misi Mengorangkan Wong Cilik" [Joko Widodo and the mission to lift up the little people], *Kompas* (Jakarta), 1 March 2008.

37 This is in keeping with the status of Islam as the dominant religion of
    Yogyakarta. All Indonesian citizens are required to claim their religion
    on their KTP (*Kartu Tanda Penduduk*) – that is, their government-issued
    identity cards – and in 2018, 82.92 per cent of people in Yogyakarta city
    claimed Islam, followed by 10.23 per cent identifying as Catholic, and
    6.4 per cent identifying as another Christian denomination (Badan Pusat
    Statistik Kota Yogyakarta 2018).

38 Paguyuban Pedagang Klithikan Mangkbumi "Pethikbumi" Yogyakarta
    (Group of Klithikan Mangkbumi Traders "Pethikbumi" Yogyakarta),
    "Buku anggota Pethikbumi 2005–2008" [Pethikbumi member book
    2005–2008]. This document was signed on 26 August 2006.

39 Lee (2016) describes pemuda fever as "a contagious feeling of political
    belonging and identification that everybody in post-Suharto Indonesia
    recognized and that select youth experienced" (12).

40 Three male PPIP activists played major roles in the anti-relocation
    movement.

41 Formed in 2000 in Salatiga, Central Java, PPIP was created with the goal
    of educating the people (*rakyat*) to organize themselves to protest the
    municipal government and to create democracy for the people (*demokrasi
    kerakyatan*). Since its formation, PPIP has become a national organization
    with regional- and city-level leaders. Pak Toni, interview with the author,
    19 September 2007, Yogyakarta.

42 "Buku anggota Pethikbumi 2005–2008" [Pethikbumi member book
    2005–2008].

43 Based on my own observations, this final number of eight hundred
    Pethikbumi traders seems to be slightly inflated. On Mangkubumi Street
    itself, where not only Pethikbumi but the Independent street vendor group
    traded, the total final number was probably closer to six or seven hundred
    street traders. For March 2007 figures, see "Sudah miliki konsep penataan
    sendiri: Petik Bumi siap ditinjau walikota" [Ready with their own concept
    of arrangement: Pethik Bumi is ready to be reviewed by the mayor],
    Kedaulatan Rakyat (Yogyakarta), 1 March 2007; for October 2007 figures,
    see "Pasar Kuncen siap ditempati: Minta penataan PDIP tolak relokasi
    Pethikbumi" [Kuncen marketplace is ready to be occupied: PDIP requests
    the arranging, rejects the relocation of Pethikbumi], *Kedaulatan Rakyat*
    (Yogyakarta), 23 October 2007.

44 "Sudah miliki konsep penataan sendiri: Petik Bumi siap ditinjau walikota"[Ready
    with their own concept of arrangement: Pethik Bumi is ready to be reviewed
    by the mayor], *Kedaulatan Rakyat* (Yogyakarta), 1 March 2007.

45 Ibid.

46 While there are no available statistics to attest to this, it was my
    observation that the membership numbers in both the Asem Gede and

Southern Square groups generally grew over the period of the relocation project.

47 Much of my media focus in this book pertains to newspapers. This is because my informants (the vendors, their supporters, the government officials, and other individuals involved in the government's relocation project) paid the most attention to newspapers of all forms of media. The traders used newspapers as a daily source of information about the relocation and they would check other information they received against what was written in the newspapers. In comparison, my informants appeared to make minimal use of online media. Although many of them had cell phones, they did not have access to cell phone data plans and thus were not searching the Internet for news on their phones during the time of my research.

2. The Politics of Containment

1 Li (2007) describes "rendering technical" as "a whole set of practices concerned with representing 'the domain to be governed as an intelligible field with specific limits and particular characteristics ... defining boundaries, rendering that within them visible, assembling information about that which is included and devising techniques to mobilize the forces and entities thus revealed'" (7).

2 Elections in Indonesia were known as *Pesta Demokrasi* (Festivals of Democracy). However, during the New Order period, Indonesian democracy was more about appearances than reality (Pemberton 1994, 19).

3 This line is generally understood to symbolize the movement from birth to death.

4 My source material on the City for Everyone project was an archive containing various documents and related ephemera, including meeting minutes, invitations, and letters. I received the archive in 2007 from a street vendor who was involved in discussions about Mangkubumi Street with NGOs in the early 2000s, before the idea of a government-organized street vendor relocation surfaced.

5 The NGOs' approach also involved trying to shift the stakeholders' practices and behaviours to ensure that the street appeared orderly and beautiful. This shared vision of "order" was not new; rather, it fit into the rhetoric vigorously promoted and institutionalized during the New Order (Pemberton 1994; Peters 2010).

6 My thanks to Elan Lazuardi for holding a discussion with colleagues at UGM in order to further clarify the meaning of the term *sosialisasi* for this chapter. Elan Lazuardi, email communication with the author, 21 November 2013.

7 The term *sosialisasi* is commonly used alongside other terms such as *penyuluhan* (counselling).

8 Ibu Fatima, email communication with the author's research assistant, 2 June 2016.

9 Pak Yohanes, email communication with the author's research assistant, 1–2 June 2016.

10 Pak Johar, email communication with the author's research assistant, 29 May–2 June 2016.

11 "Sosialisasi program restrukturisasi angkutan umum massal" [Socialization of the mass public transportation restructuring program], Kementerian Perhubungan Republik Indonesia, http://dephub.go.id/post /read/sosialisasi-program-retrukturisasi-angkutan-umum-massal-15112 (accessed 21 November 2013).

12 "Dukung ERP, anggota DPRD DKI inginkan adanya sosialisasi" [Supporting ERP, DPRD DKI members wish there was sosialisasi], *Kompas* (Jakarta), 20 November 2013.

13 Ibu Novri, email communication with the author's research assistant, 2 June 2016.

14 Ibu Fifi, email communication with the author's research assistant, 30 May–2 June 2016.

15 I received three government reports written on Kuncen Marketplace. To my knowledge, these are the only municipal government reports on Kuncen Marketplace in existence. Hardiyanti's (2008) thesis on the relocation to Kuncen Marketplace also cites only these same three reports.

16 The title of the resulting report was *Dokumen upaya pengelolaan lingkungan dan upaya pemantauan lingkungan: Rencana pembangunan Pasar Kuncen* (referred to here and in the report itself as *UKL-UPL*) [Environmental management and environmental monitoring documents on the plans to build Kuncen Marketplace].

17 Most of the reports and documents produced by the government and/ or their consultants described all of the traders as "second-hand." Since 2001, however, the majority of the vendors working on Mangkubumi were selling new items. The Pethikbumi leaders who opposed the relocation found the government's characterization of them all as traders of "second-hand" goods as a sign that they did not understand the realities of what was happening on the street.

18 This page number refers to chapter 2, page 3. The pagination for the three consultant-authored reports that I discuss in this chapter identifies the chapter number first, then the page number, and both are separated by a hyphen.

19 It appears that through these feasibility studies, the government officials and/or consultants approached the traders and asked them individually about their thoughts on a relocation.

20 The title of the resulting report was *Laporan akhir: Kegiatan rancang bangun aset daerah, pekerjaan penyusunan (FS) eks Pasar Kuncen* [Final report: Activities to build regional Assets, compiling Work (FS) for the former Kuncen Marketplace].

21 The title of this report *Laporan akhir: Rancang bangun eks Pasar Hewan Kuncen* [Final report: Engineering/building design and construction of the former Kuncen Livestock Market].

22 In this report, much of the information regarding the layout of Kuncen Marketplace was already provided in detail. For instance, the report describes how the marketplace could be broken down into particular zones according to the type of merchandise being sold (antiques, spare parts, food, etc.). There is also a description of the potential architecture and how water, electricity, and garbage could be organized in the new marketplace (III-4–III-9).

23 Pak Joko, interview with the author, 21 November 2007, Yogyakarta.

24 Ibid.

25 Pethikbumi, "Notulen rapat" [Minutes of the meeting], 16 January 2006. The meeting was held at Yogyakarta City Hall.

26 Pethikbumi, "Hasil notulensi rapat kordinasi pada hari Jum'at, 17 November 2006" [Minutes of the coordination meeting on Friday, 17 November 2006], 23 November 2006.

27 Pethikbumi, "Pemberitahuan" [Notification], Document 01/XI/PB/2006, 23 November 2006.

28 "Pasar Klitikan menolak direloikasi" [Klitikan Market refuses relocation plan], *Media Indonesia* (Jakarta), 2 February 2007.

29 During the 1970s, second-hand goods were known in Javanese as *klithikan*.

30 Meeting with the vice mayor, 2 February 2007, Yogyakarta.

31 Ibid.

3. Dialogue, Documents, and Distrust

1 A leader from the Asem Gede group did receive information about a possible relocation in 2004, but this information was not widely circulated (Badan Pelindung Hak Kemanusiaan 2007).

2 I borrow this term from Julie Gibbings (2020), who invokes the "politics of postponement" in the Guatemalan context to describe a political strategy used by state officials, coffee planters, and others from 1860 to the 1950s to defer Mayas' full participation as citizens by suggesting they were unmodern (5). She notes that this strategy allowed the state and coffee planters to engage in feudalistic practices such as coerced labour (6).

3 See Harms (2013a) for a discussion of "eviction time," which he defines as "the complex assortment of temporalities that arise when people are displaced from their land and homes" (346).

4 Pak Herry Zudianto, interview with the author, 10 June 2008, Yogyakarta.

5 During the New Order, mayors typically had a military background and were appointed by President Suharto.

6 Pak Herry Zudianto, interview with the author, 16 May 2014, Yogyakarta.

7 Ibid.

8 Ibid.

9 Ibid.

10 For a description of this meeting, see Santoso, Budi, with Lembaga Ombudsman Daerah Istimewa Yogyakarta (Special Region of Yogyakarta Ombudsman Institution) (2007).

11 In this book, the term *lower-level* is used in a relative sense to refer to government officials/civil servants who are below the ranking of the mayor. Some of these officials, such as department heads, in fact held relatively senior roles in the municipal government.

12 *Bahasa asam* is a term used to describe everyday language (as opposed to written and formal language) in either Javanese or Bahasa Indonesia. It is also considered the language of the market (*bahasa pasar*), which can be spoken with more flexibility, and with regional accents.

13 *Bahasa gali* refers to colloquial spoken Javanese. Different cities have their own variety of *bahasa gali*, with *bahasa gali Yogyakarta* being unique to Yogyakarta.

14 Pak Herry Zudianto, interview with the author, 16 May 2014, Yogyakarta.

15 Ibid.

16 Ibid.

17 Ibid.

18 Ibid.

19 Ibid.

20 Badan Lingkungan Hidup (Environment Agency) official, interview with the author, 6 February 2008, Yogyakarta.

21 The head of the Department of Industry, Trade, and Cooperatives changed three times over the course of the relocation. The first incumbent was transferred and replaced by Pak Supriyanto, who himself was later transferred and replaced by Pak Ari, whom the mayor considered a more effective communicator.

22 Meeting at LOD DIY office, 11 September 2007, Yogyakarta.

23 Ibid.

24 Ibid.

25 Ibid.

26 Pak Herry Zudianto, interview with the author, 10 June 2008, Yogyakarta.

27 Mas Arief, interview with the author's research assistant, 26 September 2016, Yogyakarta.

28 Mas Arief, interview with the author, 14 August 2013, Yogyakarta.

29 "Konsep Pasar Klithikan dinilai kurang jelas: Tolak relokasi, Pethikbumi datangi Dewan" [The Klithikan Market concept is deemed unclear:

Refusing the relocation, Pethikbumi goes to the legislation]," *Kedaulatan Rakyat* (Yogyakarta), 17 March 2007.

30 Mas Arief, interview with the author, 14 August 2013, Yogyakarta.

31 Mas Arief, interview with the author's research assistant, 26 September 2016, Yogyakarta.

32 The only documents that could be accessed were the ones specifically meant for the public, such as Indonesia's Five-Year Development Plan (Repelita).

33 Pak Ettes, email communication with the author, 20 May 2016.

34 Ibid.

35 Mas Arief, interview with the author, 7 April 2007, Yogyakarta.

36 Mas Nasir, interview with the author, 1 August 2013, Yogyakarta.

37 Mas Arief, interview with the author, 7 April 2007, Yogyakarta.

38 Pethikbumi, "Marhaban ya Ramadhan, bersatu sehati, tolak relokasi, cabut Perwal No. 45 tahun 2007" [Welcome to Ramadhan, united together, refuse the relocation, withdraw Draft Regulation 45, 2007], press release, 12 September 2007.

39 Although the Pethikbumi traders did not have official permits, there was no written regulation at the time that banned them from selling.

40 Sheri Gibbings, untitled field note on Pethikbumi seeking a permit, 21 June 2007, Yogyakarta.

41 "Ujuk rasa: PKL Mangkubumi tetap menolak relokasi" [Protest: Mangkubumi street vendors continue to reject the relocation], *Kompas* (Jakarta), 13 September 2007.

42 For instance, according to a 1986 national law (Pasal 55, U.U. No. 5 Tahun 1986 [Pemerintah Republik Indonesia 1986]), the traders had ninety days to report their concerns regarding a new regulation.

43 Mas Nasir, interview with the author, 1 August 2013, Yogyakarta.

44 "Sidang gugat wali kota ditunda, PKL kecewa dinilai cacat hukum" [The mayor's lawsuit is postponed, the street vendors are disappointed to be judged legally flawed], *Kedaulatan Rakyat* (Yogyakarta), 8 November 2007.

45 Ibu Marini, interview with the author, 16 July 2013, Yogyakarta.

46 Mas Nasir, interview with the author, 1 August 2013, Yogyakarta.

47 Meeting with the NGO Forum, BPHK, and PPIP, 17 September 2007, Yogyakarta. These Pethikbumi supporters were concerned that Pethikbumi was not engaging in enough sosialisasi with its membership, and that it was acting on its own will based on imagined support it might not have.

48 Pethikbumi meeting, 6 November 2007, Yogyakarta.

49 My observation that the Pethikbumi leaders and their supporters were uncertain about the mayor's involvement is based on numerous informal conversations during participant observation and interviews that I had with Pethikbumi leaders and members. For example, some individuals

theorized that the mayor had created the conflict among the pro- and anti-relocation traders in order to resolve it and appear like a hero (Mas Nasir, interview with the author, 21 November 2007, Yogyakarta).

4. Democratizing Surveillance

1 Sheri Gibbings, untitled field note on Pethikbumi, 23 October 2007, Yogyakarta.
2 When using the term *social imaginary*, Erik Mueggler (2001, 4) is referring to the work of Cornelius Castoriadis (1987, 247), who argues that society uses its imagination to define its identity in relation to the world.
3 Lee (2011) describes how many women in the Reformasi activist movement did not see "gender" as an issue because they followed "activist norms" (945). She writes, "That the activist model was a masculine one was simply taken for granted" by the movement (945).
4 This hegemonic masculinist ideal saw women as less capable of "being brave and committed" despite a number of prominent female activists who emerged from the student movement of the 1990s (Lee 2011, 944). Although women's involvement in street politics has become more common and more accepted in post-Suharto Indonesia (944), women still remain sidelined.
5 Although Lee (2016) does not describe how pemuda activists engaged in surveillance themselves, she describes how the activists often mirrored state tactics. For example, she writes that, "when intel (intelligence officers or recruited informants) were discovered by activists, they were kidnapped, tortured, beaten, and punished in brutal ways, mirroring the interrogation techniques perfected by the state" (135).
6 Name withheld, email communication with the author, 1 August 2016.
7 Pak Freddy, email communication with the author's research assistant, 1 August 2016.
8 Pak Haris, interview with the author's research assistant, 1 August 2016, Yogyakarta.
9 Ibid.
10 Ibid.
11 Vigilante groups also police the sexuality of lesbian, gay, bisexual, and transgender individuals. For an example, see Jon Sharman, "Indonesian Gay Couple Beaten on Video Before Vigilantes Hand Them Over to Religious Police," *Independent* (London), 14 April 2017, https://www.independent.co.uk/news/world/asia/gay-couple-indonesia-beaten-video-religious-police-aceh-sex-vigilantes-men-assault-attack-a7682646.html.
12 Sara J. Newman, "Patrolling Sexuality," *Inside Indonesia*, 19 April 2009, https://www.insideindonesia.org/patrolling-sexuality?highlight=WyJzYXJh aCIsInNhcmFoJ3MiLCJuZXdtYW4iLCJzYXJhaCBuZXdtYW4iXQ%3D%3D.

13 See David Jansen, "Snatching Victory," *Inside Indonesia*, 1 May 2010, https://www.insideindonesia.org/snatching-victory-2?highlight =WyJtYXkiLCJtYWkiLCInbWFpIiwxLDIwMTAsIjIwMTBzIiwia3BrIiwia3 BrJ3MiLCJtYXkgMSJd.
   Pak Bibit Samad Rianto and Pak Chandra M. Hamzah, from the Corruption Eradication Commission, were accused of receiving bribes from an executive, Anggoro Widjojo, in order to overturn a travel ban on Anggoro because he was under investigation for corruption. The charges against Bibit and Chandra were dropped when a wiretap recording was played in the Constitutional Court that revealed officials plotting these false accusations about Bibit and Chandra. See "Voice Records Reveal 'Plot to Frame' KPK Deputies," *Jakarta Post*, 27 October 2009.

14 Jamison Liang, "Homophobia on the Rise," *Inside Indonesia*, 14 June 2010, https://www.insideindonesia.org/homophobia-on-the-rise-2?highlight =WyJsaWFuZyIsMjAwOV0%3D.

15 Sheri Gibbings, untitled field note on conversation with Satpol PP officers, 7 November 2007, Yogyakarta.

16 Ibid.

17 Although I do believe that Indonesian intelligence had a file on me, I am doubtful that they tried to shape what I knew, what I did, and who I went with in the way that Verdery (2014) experienced in Cold War Romania.

18 Sheri Gibbings, untitled field note on conversation with Pak Didik, 7 November 2007, Yogyakarta.

19 Sheri Gibbings, untitled field note on conversation with Satpol PP official, 9 November 2007, Yogyakarta.

20 In Indonesia, a provokator is considered to be outside of the law and in need of punishment. For instance, when a crowd emerges to protest, vandalize, or attack, individuals at the front lines of these events are described in newspapers as provokators. See, for example, "Dua provokator diamankan polisi" [Two provokators are arrested by the police], *Kompas* (Jakarta), 2 March 2010).

21 Discussing the government blacklisting during *Petrus* (a series of government executions, now known as the Mysterious Killings, that took place between 1983 and 1985), Joshua Barker (2001) argues that the state "needed to privilege its own 'truth' about peoples' identities over competing claims about *who* people really are" (33; emphasis in the original). If one was placed on a blacklist, this was viewed as irreversible (32). Barker argues that "by making the lists immutable, state representatives establish[ed] a domain where the authority of local knowledge, familiarity, and the like [were] ultimately denied, and where the knowledge produced using state surveillance techniques [was] stated to be 'true' " (33).

22 Pethikbumi meeting, 23 October 2007, Yogyakarta.

23 Sheri Gibbings, untitled field note on conversation with Pak Didik, 22 October 2007, Yogyakarta.

24 Although this letter is undated, it describes an event that took place on 14 April 2007.

25 *Aqiqah putranya* is an Islamic ritual in which animals are slaughtered in order to give thanks to Allah for receiving a child.

26 On this mirroring between state and non-state power, see Karen McCarthy Brown (2003).

27 Mas Totok, interview with the author, 21 November 2007, Yogyakarta.

28 Mas Totok, interview with the author, 14 May 2014, Yogyakarta.

29 Ibid.

30 Ibid.

31 Ibid.

32 Ibid.

33 Ibid.

34 Ibid.

35 Ibid.

36 Sheri Gibbings, untitled field note on Pethikbumi meeting, 23 August 2007, Yogyakarta.

37 The Pethikbumi traders on Mangkubumi Street were divided into eight different groups based on their location on the street.

38 Pethikbumi meeting, 9 November 2007, Yogyakarta.

39 Pak Akbar, Pethikbumi meeting, 20 September 2007, Yogyakarta.

40 Ibid.

41 Strassler (2005) also describes how, at photography exhibitions held during the Reformasi period, many students came to see the Reformasi images as "tokens of their own personal histories, blurring the lines between journalistic and personal genres of photography" (280).

42 Ibu Marini, interview with the author, 12 December 2007, Yogyakarta.

43 Pethikbumi meeting, 6 November 2007, Yogyakarta.

44 Mas Arief, interview with the author, 7 April 2007, Yogyakarta.

45 Mas Totok, interview with the author, 21 November 2007, Yogyakarta.

5. Press Releases and Silent Critiques

 1 As noted in the opening section of Chapter 6: The Talk of Violence, this deadline was later pushed back from October 31 to November 10. See "Pemkot jamin tempat lama tak ditempati PKL baru: Mundur, pemindahan Pasar Klithikan" [City government guarantees that old place will not be occupied by new street vendors: The Klithikan Marketplace relocation deadline is pushed back], *Kedaulatan Rakyat* (Yogyakarta), 25 October 2007.

2 Preman are typically found running protection rackets at nightclubs or marketplaces, but are also known to be available for hire for the purposes of intimidation (Barker 1999; Ryter 2001).

3 Team 12 was an organization that included all of the leaders from the Independent, Asem Gede, and Southern Square trader groups.

4 Although Georges Bataille has also used the term *contagious subjectivity* (Noys 2000, 74–5), I am not drawing on that usage here.

5 This chapter does not focus on how readers received or interpreted messages from the newspapers, although I assume there would be variation in how the public orients themselves to the different newspapers (see Cody 2009, 288).

6 *Harian Indonesia* published work in Chinese characters but it was under the control of Indonesia's intelligence agency – then known as Badan Koordinasi Intelijen Negara (BAKIN) – and was used by the army to reach the Chinese-speaking community (Hill 2006, 132–3).

7 "Kritik secar diam-diam, cocok demokrasi 'semi-terbuka'" [Silent critique fits with a "semi-open democracy"], *Kedaulatan Rakyat* (Yogyakarta), 2 February 1994.

8 *Kedaulatan Rakyat* (Yogyakarta), 3 March 1994.

9 After 1999, publishing companies no longer needed a Press Publishing Company Permit (*Surat Izin Usaha Penerbitan Pers*) from the government (Jurriëns 2011, 142).

10 Receiving such envelopes is not straightforward either. A journalist may receive money in order to promote a particular company or product, but sometimes without any expectation of an exchange. That is, a journalist might receive or accept an envelope with money and this will not ultimately change how they act. See Kirrilee Hughes, "A Town like Malang," *Inside Indonesia*, 29 July 2007, http://www.insideindonesia.org /a-town-like-malang-2.

11 Sheri Gibbings, untitled field note on the Independent traders, 21 October 2007, Yogyakarta. A few leaders of Pethikbumi later suggested that the decision to use preman would set the stage for a conflict, which might then require government intervention, thereby providing the police with a justification for taking control of the street. In other words, by generating a conflict on the street involving non-state actors, it would be possible to criminalize the leaders of Pethikbumi and ensure a smooth relocation. Pethikbumi meeting, 25 October 2007, Yogyakarta.

12 Some of the Independent leaders said that they had been intimidated by Pethikbumi. For instance, one explained that a couple of Pethikbumi leaders, who he claimed were drunk, had requested the signatures of traders who were refusing the relocation (Sheri Gibbings, untitled field note on the Independent traders, ca. 21 October 2007, Yogyakarta).

This data collection by Pethikbumi leaders took place on 15 April 2007. Although I know the Pethikbumi traders did request the signatures, and had also asked to see the KTP identification cards of traders who were refusing the relocation, I do not believe those Pethikbumi leaders were drunk at the time.

13 Sheri Gibbings, untitled field note on the Independent traders, 21 October 2007, Yogyakarta.

14 For the data collection to be legitimate in Pethikbumi's eyes, the pro-relocation vendor leaders and the municipal government would have had to inform them in advance and the data would have to be collected by government officials in uniforms, not by fellow traders.

15 Sheri Gibbings, untitled field note on the data collection on Mangkubumi Street, 23 October 2007, Yogyakarta.

16 Ibid.

17 This preman knew Pak Akbar because they were from the same neighbourhood.

18 Pethikbumi meeting, 25 October 2007, Yogyakarta.

19 The term *pil koplo*, a mixture of Bahasa Indonesian and Javanese, is used to refer to a street drug, a kind of mild tranquilizer, like Xanax. Elan Lazuardi, email communication with the author, 18 May 2017.

20 *Senjata tajam* usually refers to knives but it can also be used to refer to other sharp weapons such as a sickle, dagger, or sword. Elan Lazuardi, email communication with the author, 24 May 2017.

21 As mentioned in note 3 in this chapter, Team 12 included all of the leaders from the three pro-relocation trader groups. However, to avoid potential confusion, the name *Team 12* has been used sparingly in this book, and has been retained only in quoted material.

22 Pethikbumi meeting, 25 October 2007, Yogyakarta.

23 As explained in the previous chapter, the Pethikbumi traders on Mangkubumi Street were divided into eight different groups based on their location on the street. Each group had its own leader.

24 "Indonesia Editor Jailed for Libel," *BBC News*, 16 September 2004, http://news.bbc.co.uk/2/hi/asia-pacific/3662230.stm.

25 See Ann K. Cooper, "CPJ Concerned About Criminal Defamation," *Committee to Protect Journalists*, 3 October 2003, https://cpj.org/2003/10/cpj-concerned-about-criminal-defamation.php.

26 When Ibu Marini was discussing this one witness, I believe that she was referring to the preman who backed out of the data collection at the last minute. Pethikbumi meeting, 25 October 2007, Yogyakarta.

27 As well as meaning "older sister," *Mbak* is a term of respect for a younger woman who is not significantly older than the speaker.

28 Ibid.

29 Ibid.

30 Ibid.

31 The fact that the preman were drunk arguably added to the level of intimidation experienced by the Pethikbumi traders because it opened up the possibility that the preman might be less inhibited and more unpredictable.

32 Pethikbumi meeting, 25 October 2007, Yogyakarta.

33 As discussed in note 47 in chapter 1, much of my media focus in this book pertains to newspapers because of all forms of media, my informants paid the most attention to newspapers.

34 There are some common stereotypes about preman and how they can be identified. Some include the idea that preman often have protruding stomachs (*perut buncit*) because they drink alcohol, or that they have a specific haircut, such as short hair (*rambut cepak*) or dyed hair. Other stereotypical identifiers of preman include tattoos, piercings, dark clothing (including leather jackets), and metal chain necklaces. They are also often stereotypically associated with specific motorcycles, such as the Yamaha RX King, and other motorbikes with modified tailpipes that make significant noise as they travel through the city. Khidir Marsanto Prawirosusanto, email communication with the author, 23 May 2017.

35 Pethikbumi/BPHK/NGO Forum press conference, 26 October 2007, Yogyakarta.

36 Ibid.

37 Ibid.

38 While speaking at the press conference, Pak Akbar also went on to blame the leader of the Independent group, Pak Bowo, for teaming up with the preman. He called on him to remember an agreement made between the Pethikbumi and Independent traders in which they had promised to not disrupt each other during the relocation process, and he accused Pak Bowo of breaking his promise. In this instance, by blaming Pak Bowo, Pak Akbar momentarily broke the strategy of not naming anyone directly. However, this direct accusation was not of concern to anyone involved, because in this case Pak Akbar blamed a street trader with few resources and little ability to counteract this accusation. After the press conference, the NGO Forum, BPHK, and PPIP did not remark or seek to correct Pak Akbar after he had accused Pak Bowo, because other, more important actors, such as the municipal government, went unnamed.

39 Pak Nurdin, interview with the author, 14 November 2007, Yogyakarta.

40 Yogyakarta has a total of nine newspapers controlled by five different groups. The three most popular, in order of readership, are *Kedaultan Rakyat*, *Minggu Pagi*, and *Merapi* (Solihin 2008, 42).

41 "Pethikbumi tetap bertahan di lokasi lama: Pemkot jamin perekonomian di eks Pasar Kuncen tumbuh pesat" [Pethikbumi remains in its old location: The municipal government guarantees that the economy in the former Kuncen Market will grow rapidly], *Kedaultan Rakyat* (Yogyakarta), 26 October 2007. Shortly after Pethikbumi had decided on a media strategy with BPHK, the NGO Forum, and PPIP on October 25, Pak Akbar was contacted by *Kedaulatan Rakyat* to discuss the intimidation that Pethikbumi had faced during the data collection.

42 This article also describes how the governor of DIY, Sri Sultan Hamengku Buwono X, said that with the relocation, the status of the traders would automatically change from informal to formal.

43 "Gubernur beri apresiasi: Klithikan Mangkubumi diintimidasi" [The governor gives his appreciation: Second-hand traders on Mangkubumi are intimidated], *Merapi* (Yogyakarta), 27 October 2007.

44 "LABH: Tunggu Putusan PTUN" [LABH: Waiting for the State Administrative Court decision], *Radar Jogja* (Yogyakarta), 27 October 2007.

45 Ibid.

46 The newspaper article describes how Pethikbumi mobilized supporters to sign a banner in support of their opposition to the relocation.

47 Although the government threatened to engage the law, this remained only a threat.

6. The Talk of Violence

1 During such incidents, the traders' supporters were also potentially at risk because the police and Satpol PP were not always able to distinguish physically between the traders and their supporters, and because both groups were opposing the government's program.

2 The powerful effect of a saat could be related to Indonesian history, which was viewed as cyclical and involving periods in which power was created and then diffused. As Benedict Anderson (1990) explains, "Susceptibility of messianism in times of disorder ... arises from the sense that a new concentration of Power is always preparing itself within that disorder, that one must be alert for portents of its immanent appearance and then approach the germinal center as rapidly as possible, attaching oneself to the new order as it emerges" (25).

3 *Berhati Nyaman* was meant to stand for the following words: *bersih* (clean), *sehat* (healthy), *indah* (beautiful), and *nyaman* (comfortable, secure). So, more than "heart of comfort," *Berhati Nyaman* connoted a larger range of ideas within it.

4 As is noted later in this chapter (see Playing with Information), this conflict has also been viewed as a dispute over economic and political resources.

5 My thanks to an early reviewer of the manuscript for highlighting this point.

6 The traders also dealt with the fear of state violence by talking about it among themselves and their supporters. These conversations about the potential for violence often involved moments of laughter. The laughter was a commentary on the unequal relationship between the state and the traders. For a lengthier discussion, see Laughter and Power, this chapter.

7 "Relokasi Klithikan: Pedagang lolos verifikasi" [Klithikan relocation: Traders pass verification], *Merapi* (Yogyakarta), 9 November 2007.

8 "Pemkot janji promosikan Pasar Kuncen: Pendaftaran kios dibuka awal pekan depan" [The municipal government promises to promote Kuncen Market: Registration for kiosks will be opened early next week], *Kedaulatan Rakyat* (Yogyakarta), 2 November 2007.

9 Ibid.

10 "Buka lawang' awaili penggunaan pasar Pakuncen" [Door-opening ceremony marks the start of Kuncen Marketplace], *Kompas* (Jakarta), 1 November 2007.

11 Lee (2016) describes a "carefully cultivated pemuda style," explaining that this style was "the dominant vehicle for propagating the visual iconography of radical youth politics" (87). The *Laskar Mangkubumi Tolak Relokasi* T-shirts can be viewed as also connecting the Pethikbumi movement to a pemuda activist identity and style.

12 Mas Arief, Pethikbumi meeting, 17 September 2007, Yogyakarta.

13 Pethikbumi's protests against the relocation often included student activists from groups such as PPIP.

14 Meeting between Pethikbumi and the municipal government, 12 September 2007, Yogyakarta.

15 As noted in the next section of this chapter (see Drawing on Deeper Sources of Fears), Kalimantan was the site of ethnic cleansing between the indigenous Christian Dayaks and the migrant Muslim Madurese.

16 Pethikbumi meeting with DPRD Yogyakarta, 10 September 2007, Yogyakarta.

17 "Kontra relokasi ke eks Pasar Kuncen demo lagi: Dialog Pemkot-Pethikubumi 'deadlock'" [Contra-relocation to ex-market Kuncen demo again: Government-Pethikbumi dialogue in "deadlock"], *Kedaulatan Rakyat* (Yogyakarta), 13 September 2007.

18 Since I did not interview any journalists, I can only speculate as to why the journalists did not include any of these threats from the Pethikbumi leaders in the newspapers. My guess is that they preferred to portray the traders as victims of the state rather than as potential perpetrators of violence.

19 In conversations and meetings with their own membership, the Pethikbumi leaders did not repeat the threats that they themselves had

made to the municipal government about the potential unleashing of violence from their side. The violence or repression was always described to members as coming from the state and against the traders.

20 Pethikbumi leaders, "Warta Mangkubumi: Relokasi berarti repot nasi!!!" [Mangkubumi news: Relocation means a difficult living!!!], September 2007. No specific date was given on this document. *Repot nasi* literally means "the difficulty of getting rice," but is used here to mean the difficulty that the relocation will create for the street traders' livelihoods.

21 "Klithikan Pindah Paling Lambat 10 November" [Klithikan traders will move by 10 November at the latest], *Bernas Jogja* (Yogyakarta), 27 October 2007.

22 This connection was confirmed during my interview with Pethikbumi member Pak Syafii, 23 June 2007, Yogyakarta.

23 Laskar Jihad was the paramilitary branch of Forum Komunikasi Ahlus Sunnah Wal Jama'ah (the Communication Forum of the Followers of the Sunna and the Prophet, or FKAWJ), a religious organization that promoted the implementation of Islamic law in Indonesia. FKAWJ had its headquarters with Laskar Jihad just outside Yogyakarta city (International Crisis Group 2005).

24 Pak Syafii, interview with the author, 23 June 2007, Yogyakarta.

25 During our interview, we never discussed what volunteering for Laskar Jihad looked like in practice.

26 See also Gerry van Klinken, "Ethnic Fascism in Borneo," *Inside Indonesia*, 30 July 2007, https://www.insideindonesia.org/ethnic-fascism-in-borneo ?highlight=WyJkYXlhayIsIidkYXlhayIsIidkYXlhayciLCJkYXlhayciL CJkYXlha3MnIiwiZXRobmljIiwiJ2V0aG5pYyIsImV0aG5pYyciLCInZXRo bmljJyIsIidldGhuaWMnLCIsImNsZWFuc2luZyIsImNsZWFuc2luZyciIwi ZGF5YWsgZXRobmljIiwiZXRobmljIGNsZWFuc2luZyJd.

27 Sheri Gibbings, untitled field note on Asem Gede, 14 August 2007, Yogyakarta.

28 KMY also oversees several other Madurese organizations in Central Java, such as Forum Silaturahmi Mahasiswa (FSM), Forum Silaturahmi Niaga (FSN), and Forum Silaturahmi Cendekiawan (FSC). FSM is a Madurese student organization. FSN and FSC both focus on building Madurese networks in Yogyakarta. Khidir Marsanto Prawirosusanto, email communication with the author, 9 May 2017.

29 Mbah Ahmad, interview with the author, 18 September 2007, Yogyakarta.

30 Ibid.

31 Ibid.

32 The police deal with criminal activities while Satpol PP enforces non-criminal laws around such things as cleanliness.

33 Pak Budi, interview with the author's research assistant, 22 July 2016, Yogyakarta.

34 Ibid.

35 It is common for elders or people in positions of authority to refer to their supporters as their *anak buah*, or subordinates. Mbah Ahmad referred to his supporters as his children, situating them as kin and making their well-being his responsibility.

36 Mbah Ahmad, interview with the author, 18 September 2007, Yogyakarta.

37 Mbah Ahmad's threats of violence and chaos could be carried out if he decided to mobilize supporters from his Madurese organization. For instance, he could mobilize the youth from this organization to carry out violence against state actors or to create chaos by destroying state property.

38 Pethikbumi meeting with the NGO Forum, ca. 27 October 2007, Yogyakarta.

39 Ibid.

40 Ibid.; emphasis in the original transcript.

41 As noted by Wolff, Oetomo, and Fietkiewicz (1992a), *lho* (also written as *lhó*) has usages as a "particle expressing surprise at finding out that something is different from what the speaker thought," a "particle giving a reminder," and a "particle giving a mild warning" (79).

42 Pethikbumi meeting, 31 October 2007, Yogyakarta.

43 Ibid.

44 While some members of Pethikbumi and their PPIP supporters wore the *Laskar Mangkubumi Tolak Relokasi* T-shirts in public, this was never reported in the newspapers. As described earlier, the decision to wear these T-shirts was controversial.

45 "Pendaftaran kios Pasar Klithikan dibuka Senin besok: Pemot jamin seluruh pedangag tertampung" [Registration for Klithikan Market starts next Monday: City government promises all traders will be accommodated], *Kedaulatan Rakyat* (Yogyakarta), 4 November 2007.

46 "Hari ini sidang PTUN gugatan perwal: 578 pedagang klithikan lolos verifikasi" [Today the Sate Administrative Court has its lawsuit trial against the local permit regulation: 578 klithikan traders pass verification], *Kedaulatan Rakyat* (Yogyakarta), 7 November 2007.

47 "Meski ada pedagang yang belum mendaftar: Pemkot tak buka pendaftaran susulan" [Even though there are traders who have not registered: The municipal government does not open additional registration], *Kedaulatan Rakyat* (Yogyakarta), 8 November 2007.

48 "Kapasitas pasar klithikan akan dioptimalkan: Pedagang lolos verifikasi lebihi daya tampung," [Klithikan Marketplace capacity will be optimized: Verified traders passed the market capacity], *Kedaulatan Rakyat* (Yogyakarta), 9 November 2007.

49 Ibid.

50 Sheri Gibbings, untitled field note on identity cards, 3 November 2007, Yogyakarta.

51 Sheri Gibbings, untitled field note on Kuncen Marketplace, 9 November 2007, Yogyakarta.

52 "Walikota jamin Pasar Klithikan akan berkembang: Lebih 80 persen pedagang mendafter" [The mayor guarantees that Klithikan Market will develop: More than 80 per cent of traders registered], *Kedaulatan Rakyat* (Yogyakarta), 10 November 2007.

53 Ibid.

54 "Amankan Mangkubumi, Pemkot siapkan Satpol PP" [Securing Mangkubumi Street, city government prepares Satpol PP], *Kedaulatan Rakyat* (Yogyakarta), 11 November 2007.

55 Sheri Gibbings, untitled field note on Mangkubumi Street, 10 November 2007, Yogyakarta.

56 "Aliansi LSM tarik advokasi" [LSM Alliance pulls out of advocacy], *Bernas Jogja* (Yogyakarta), 13 November 2007.

57 Sheri Gibbings, untitled field note on Mangkubumi Street, 10 November 2007, Yogyakarta.

58 Ibid.

59 Mas Totok, interview with the author, 21 November 2007, Yogyakarta.

60 Ibid.

61 Sheri Gibbings, untitled field note on Mangkubumi Street, 10 November 2007, Yogyakarta.

62 Ibid.

63 Budi Widianarko, "Adipura Scandal a Slap in the Face for Indonesia," *Jakarta Post*, 6 February 2011.

64 The Adipura Award is so important that in some cases mayors will bribe award officials in an attempt to secure one, as was the case in 2010. See Basetn Gokkon, "Three Cities Take Out Environmental Ministry Award," *Jakarta Globe*, 24 November 2015.

65 Budi Widianarko, "Adipura Scandal a Slap in the Face for Indonesia," *Jakarta Post*, 6 February 2011.

66 "Adipura Award Returns to Jakarta," *Jakarta Post*, 6 June 2012.

67 Pak Teguh, interview with the author, 10 September 2016, Yogyakarta.

68 "Pasar Minggu Flower Pots a Pedestrians Obstruction," *Jakarta Post*, 19 December 2011.

69 Ponco Anggoro, "PKL harus dibina, bukan dibinasakan" [Street vendors must be nurtured, not destroyed], *Kompas* (Jakarta), 15 April 2006.

70 Sheri Gibbings, untitled field note on Mangkubumi Street, 11 November 2007, Yogyakarta.

71 I decided that I would not take any photographs during this time because I felt that tensions were high. I observed instead and the journalist provided me with his video footage of the event the following week.

72 Unpublished transcript from video recording of interview between Pak Pramana and unnamed journalist, 10 November 2007. Although the journalist collected footage of the events that night and conducted this interview, to my knowledge no resulting story was published in a newspaper or aired on television.

73 Benedict Anderson (2006), for instance, describes the important role the colonial school system played in producing colonial nationalisms in Indonesia (122).

74 misterpopo, "Penggusuran (relokasi) PKL ala Pemkot Jogja" [Eviction (relocation) of street vendors by the Municipal Government of Yogyakarta], *Angkringan Kang Popo* (blog), 12 November 2007, http:// misterpopo.wordpress.com/2007/11/12/penggusuran-relokasi-pkl-ala -pemkot-jogja/.

75 "Relokasi tanpa gejolak: Pasar Pakuncen ramai Mangkubumi lengang" [Relocation without turmoil: Pakuncen Marketplace bustling, Mangkbumi is deserted], *Radar Jogja* (Yogyakarta), 12 November 2007.

76 Ibid. The mayor partly focused on ensuring that no traders occupied the street because some of the traders who had joined the relocation were worried that if the government did not prevent it, new traders would take over Mangkubumi Street. These relocated traders felt that it would be unfair if new traders were to occupy the street.

77 Although some members of Pethikbumi and PPIP publicly wore the *Laskar Mangkubumi Tolak Relokasi* T-shirts, this action was never taken up in the public sphere for further discussion and comment.

78 Pak Ferry, the undercover police officer, did describe how he mapped Pethikbumi's networks as part of an assessment of the group's political, social, and economic strength. Pak Ferry wanted to know to what extent and for how long Pethikbumi could mobilize in opposition to the government (see Resolving Conflicts "Beautifully," Chapter 8).

79 My thanks to Dr. Abidin Kusno for drawing my attention to this point.

7. Conspiratorial Knowledge, Allah, and State Power

1 Sheri Gibbings, untitled field note on Mangkubumi Street, 11 November 2007, Yogyakarta.

2 Ibid.

3 See, for example, "Aliansi LSM Jogja minta klarifikasi walikota: 62 pedagang Pethikbumi lolos verifikas" [The Yogyakarta NGO Forum asks the mayor for clarification: 62 Pethikbumi traders pass verification], *Kedaulatan Rakyat* (Yogyakarta), 10 November 2007. (Note that Aliansi LSM Jogja and the NGO Forum are the same organization; it operates under both names.) In this news article, Pak Ari (head of the Department

of Industry, Trade, and Cooperatives) said that many of the Pethikbumi members had already been drafted to the marketplace. He explained that the traders who signed up last would be allocated the less strategic locations in the marketplace.

4 The traders who relocated would receive transition support of 40,000 rupiah (approximately USD$3.00) per day for seven days, followed by adaptation assistance of 20,000 rupiah (approximately USD$1.50) per day for thirty days. In order to obtain this money, the traders were required to show their KTP card and KBP card (*Kartu Bukti Pedagang Pasar*, or Marketplace Vendor Card of Proof). See "Walikota jamin Pasar Klithikan akan berkembang; lebih 80 persen pedagang mendaftar" [The mayor guarantees Klithikan Market will develop; more than 80 per cent of traders register], *Kedaulatan Rakyat*, 12 November 2007.

5 Sheri Gibbings, untitled field note on Pethikbumi, 11 November 2007, Yogyakarta.

6 Ibid.

7 Ibid.

8 Ibid.

9 Ibu Marini later explained to me that when she and Pak Suyitno came to Jogjatronik, their computer had broken down and they were in a rush to get it fixed. She said that they had not even seen Pak Pramana or Mas Eko. Sheri Gibbings, untitled field note on Pethikbumi, 11 November 2007, Yogyakarta.

10 Another reason why the Pethikbumi leaders wanted to view this data was because the leaders of the various vendor groups were responsible for compiling the lists of traders who were to be included in the relocation to Kuncen Marketplace. The vendor groups then submitted these lists to the government (which merely verified the lists). The compilers of such lists therefore wielded considerable power. It had come to the Pethikbumi leaders' attention that the leaders from the Independent, Asem Gede, and Southern Square pro-relocation vendor groups were accepting money from individuals in exchange for inclusion on the lists of traders to be relocated to Kuncen Marketplace. The Pethikbumi leaders therefore considered these pro-relocation leaders to be oknum. Sheri Gibbings, untitled field note on vendor relocation data, 22 October 2007, Yogyakarta.

11 Monumen Yogya Kembali is a museum dedicated to the Indonesian National Revolution.

12 Any individual Pethikbumi members who did not want to join the relocation would be free to refuse and instead find for themselves a new place to sell.

13 Sheri Gibbings, untitled field note on Pethikbumi, 11 November 2007, Yogyakarta.

14 Ibid.

15 The list would have been submitted, as per the terms of an offer made at the meeting with Pak Ari and Pak Mulyono, to either Pak Ari or Pak Galang. In turn, these government officials would have informed Pak Ferry that the list had been submitted.

16 I could not tell to whom the text message was sent, but I assume it was sent to a number of people within Pak Ferry's network because the message did not personally address me.

17 The traders had been requesting this meeting for months. When the day arrived, a couple of the Pethikbumi leaders met with the mayor privately. One of these leaders, Pak Sarwan, later told me what happened. During the meeting, the Pethikbumi leaders had raised three topics. They had informed Pak Herry Zudianto that oknum had been attempting to illegally profit from the relocation (as discussed in note 10 in this chapter, leaders from pro-relocation vendor groups were known to be accepting money from individuals in exchange for inclusion on the lists of traders relocating to Kuncen Marketplace). The Pethikbumi leaders had also pressed Pak Herry Zudianto to promise that the Pethikbumi traders who were refusing the relocation would not face intimidation or violence (*kekerasaan*) from the state. Finally, the Pethikbumi leaders had requested that all of the remaining seventy-odd Pethikbumi traders be allowed to continue selling on Mangkubumi Street into the future. As Pak Sarwan did not report to me the mayor's response to the first two topics, presumably the response was a non-answer of sorts. As for the third topic, the mayor had remained silent. Pak Sarwan, interview with the author, 9 November 2007, Yogyakarta.

18 "Tim Advokasi Pethikbumi mengundurkan diri" [The Pethikbumi Advocacy Team resigns], *Kompas* (Jakarta), 13 November 2007.

19 Ibid.

20 "Tim Advokasi Pethikubumi mengundurkan diri: Pengurus Pethikbumi dinilai inkonsisten" [Pethikbumi Advocacy Team resigns: Pethikbumi leaders are deemed inconsistent], *Kedaulatan Rakyat* (Yogyakarta), 13 November 2007.

21 Sheri Gibbings, untitled field note on the Pethikbumi relocation, 12 November 2007, Yogyakarta.

22 Ibid.

23 Ibid.

24 At first, I was surprised that Pethikbumi leaders would inform me that I was to not attend their upcoming meetings and activities, but after I went home and the news set in, I was upset. I came to realize, however, that this request was not a personal attack on me or my research by Pethikbumi; it was a request that was in fact coming from the municipal government. Sheri Gibbings, untitled field note on the Pethikbumi relocation, 12 November 2007, Yogyakarta.

25 Mas Eko, interview with the author, 13 November 2007, Yogyakarta.
26 "Tim Advokasi Pethikubumi mengundurkan diri: Pengurus Pethikbumi dinilai inkonsisten" [Pethikbumi Advocacy Team resigns: Pethikbumi leaders are deemed inconsistent], *Kedaulatan Rakyat* (Yogyakarta), 13 November 2007; "Tim Advokasi Pethikbumi mengundurkan diri" [The Pethikbumi Advocacy Team resigns], *Kompas* (Jakarta), 13 November 2007.
27 "Aliansi LSM Tarik advokasi" [The NGO Alliance pulls advocacy], *Bernas Jogja* (Yogyakarta),13 November 2007.
28 Pak Akbar, interview with the author, 13 December 2007, Yogyakarta.
29 Ibid.
30 Ibid.
31 The government had previously offered Pak Pramana a position as a bodyguard at Parangtritis (an area outside of Yogyakarta), but he had refused the job because he did not want to be involved in security work any more. He had also previously been offered money – around 2.5 million rupiah (approximately USD$276) – but he had refused this too. Pak Pramana, interview with the author, 3 December 2007, Yogyakarta.
32 Ibid.
33 Ibid.
34 The fact that Ibu Marini and Pak Suyitno had their baby with them might explain why they did not approach Pak Pramana and Pak Didik to clarify the purpose of their meeting.
35 Ibu Marini, interview with the author, 15 November 2007, Yogyakarta.
36 Mas Totok, interview with the author, 30 November 2007, Yogyakarta.
37 Pethikbumi, *Pengurus Pethikbumi pernyataan sikap* [Pethikbumi leaders' statement of intent], 13 November 2007.
38 Ibid.
39 "Aliansi LSM Jogja minta klarifikasi walikota: 62 pedagang Pethikbumi lolos verifikasi" [NGO Aliance Jogja asks mayor for clarification: 62 Pethikbumi traders pass verification], *Kedaulatan Rakyat* (Yogyakarta), 16 November 2007.
40 Sheri Gibbings, untitled field note on rumours circulating, 16 November 2007, Yogyakarta.
41 Ibu Elok Fajaruni Nur, email communication with the author, 1 June 2010.
42 Ibu Elok Fajaruni Nur, email communication with the author, 26 May 2010.
43 Mas Tokok, interview with the author, 21 November 2007, Yogyakarta.
44 Ibu Elok Fajaruni Nur, email communication with the author, 26 May 2010.
45 "Menteri Koperasi dan UKM resmikan Pasar Klithikan" [Minster of cooperatives and small and medium enterprises inaugurates Klithikan Marketplace], *Portal Pemerintah Kota Yogyakarta: Situs resmi Pemerintah Kota Yogyakarta* [Yogyakarta City Government portal: Official website of

Yogyakarta City Government], 15 December 2007, https://warta.jogjakota
.go.id/detail/index/1358 (accessed 28 December 2020).

46 "Walikota berharap Pasar Klithikan membawa berkah" [The mayor
hopes Klithikan Marketplace will bring blessings], *Portal Pemerintah
Kota Yogyakarta: Situs resmi Pemerintah Kota Yogyakarta* [Yogyakarta City
Government portal: Official website of Yogyakarta City Government],
13 November 2007, https://warta.jogjakota.go.id/detail/index/1307
(accessed 28 December 2020).

47 Ibid.

48 "Menteri Koperasi dan UKM resmikan Pasar Klithikan," https://warta
.jogjakota.go.id/detail/index/1358 (accessed 28 December 2020).

49 Pak Herry Zudianto is quoted as saying, "The mayor asserts that a leader
with all his strength, energy, mind, time and heart thinks of the welfare
of his people (*memikirkan kesejahteraan rakyatnya*), while the good people
(*rakyat yang baik*) are the people who trust and respect their leaders
(*mempercayai dan menghormati pemimpinnya*)." "Walikota berharap Pasar
Klithikan membawa berkah," https://warta.jogjakota.go.id/detail
/index/1307 (accessed 28 December 2020).

50 Ibid.

51 Ibid.

52 "Tim Advokasi Pethikubumi mengundurkan diri: Pengurus Pethikbumi
dinilia inkonsisten" [Pethikbumi Advocacy Team resigns: Pethikbumi
leaders are deemed inconsistent], *Kedaulatan Rakyat* (Yogyakarta), 13
November 2007.

53 "Trotoar Mangkubumi untuk pejalan kaki: Pedagang optimis Pakuncen
berkembang" [Mangkubumi sidewalks for pedestrians: Traders are
optimistic that Pakuncen will develop], *Merapi* (Yogyakarta), 13 November
2007.

54 "Walikota berharap Pasar Klithikan membawa berkah," https://warta
.jogjakota.go.id/detail/index/1307 (accessed 28 December 2020).

55 "Aliansi LSM Jogja minta klarifikasi walikota: 62 pedagang Pethikbumi
lolos verifikasi" [NGO Aliance Jogja asks mayor for clarification: 62
Pethikbumi traders pass verification].

56 "Tim Advokasi Pethikubumi mengundurkan diri: Pengurus Pethikbumi
dinilia inkonsisten" [Pethikbumi Advocacy Team resigns: Pethikbumi leaders
are deemed inconsistent], *Kedaulatan Rakyat* (Yogyakarta), 13 November 2007.

57 "Aliansi LSM Jogja minta klarifikasi walikota: 62 pedagang Pethikbumi
lolos verifikasi" [NGO Aliance Jogja asks mayor for clarification: 62
Pethikbumi traders pass verification], *Kedaulatan Rakyat* (Yogyakarta), 16
November 2007.

58 Bubandt (2014) writes that "a particular conjuncture opened secular
politics up to spirits in 2009 [following the landslide re-election of then

President Susilo Bambang Yudhoyono] because politics itself had come to be imagined and discussed as something increasingly spirit-like among Indonesian politicians and in the Indonesian media. The possibility of spirits becoming involved in politics had already been foreshadowed by political crisis, the increasing omnipresence of corruption, and the uncertainty of a democratic future in Indonesia at the time. All of these uncertainties gave politics a spectral character" (23).

59 In particular, *hijrah* refers to the migration of Muhammad and his followers to the city of Medina in 622 CE in order to escape persecution (Elmadmad 1991, 469).

60 Transcript of the author's video recording of the grand opening of Pasar Kuncen, 13 December 2007, Yogyakarta.

61 Pethikbumi, "Marhaban ya Ramadhan, bersatu sehati, tolak relokasi, cabut Perwal No. 45 tahun 2007" [Welcome to Ramadhan, united together, refuse the relocation, withdraw Draft Regulation 45, 2007], press release, 12 September 2007.

62 Elok Fajaruni Nur, email communication with the author, 1 June 2010.

63 *SWT* is an abbreviation of the Arabic *subhanahu wa ta'ala* (May He Be Praised and May His Transcendence Be Affirmed) (Alwani and Khalil 1995, viii, n3).

64 Pethikbumi, "Marhaban ya Ramadhan, bersatu sehati, tolak relokasi, cabut Perwal No. 45 tahun 2007."

65 Pak Halim, interview with the author, 16 January 2008, Yogyakarta.

66 For discussions on Javanese religion/culture and its relationship with Islam, see Andrew Beatty (1999, 28–9) and Mark Woodward (2010, 4–5).

67 Pethikbumi also talked about Allah when discussing whether the Pethikbumi traders would be relocated or not. For instance, Pak Pramana said that only Allah would know if they would be relocated. He said that Allah would judge the people who did not act right towards the Pethikbumi leaders. Pethikbumi meeting with BPHK, 25 October 2007, Yogyakarta.

68 In this interview, Pak Kasiyarno talked about Allah specifically, although he also used the general term *Tuhan*, which can refer to God or Allah. Pak Kasiyarno, interview with the author, 16 January 2008, Yogyakarta.

69 Such a sentiment would never be expressed openly about *specific* people, because it was believed that what was said about someone else might happen to oneself. This belief was shaped by Javanese religion/culture.

70 See, for example, Ismawati Retno's (2012, 43–5) biography of Pak Herry Zudianto. In his own memoir, which was published shortly after the Kuncen relocation project, Pak Herry Zudianto (2008, 17) describes his communication with the street vendors as an example of a dialogue undertaken between the government and the community in order to resolve a problem.

71 Sri Wahyuni, "Herry Zudianto: For the Good of Yogyakarta," *Jakarta Post*, 28 October 2010.
72 Ibid.
73 Pak Herry Zudianto, interview with the author, 16 May 2014, Yogyakarta.
74 As discussed earlier, the mayor avoided meeting with the Pethikbumi leaders until later in the relocation project, once the traders felt they had few options other than to participate in the relocation. This was part of his strategy for getting them to accept the relocation (see Getting Close and Speaking Their Language, Chapter 3).

8. Agents and Brothers

1 Budi Sutrisno, "Police Violence Is a Big Poser for Next Chief, Says Rights Group," *Jakarta Post*, 11 January 2021.
2 Loren Ryter, "Reformasi Gangsters," *Inside Indonesia*, 24 July 2007, https://www.insideindonesia.org/reformasi-gangsters.
3 Jun Honna (2010, 263) has described how in this new environment, military officers found it difficult to be promoted, and feelings of distrust and resentment against the police emerged. The relationship was also strained as the two institutions competed over the control of business activities and protection rackets across the archipelago (see Van Klinken 2007, 30).
4 Sheri Gibbings, untitled field note on discussion with Pak Ferry, 9 May 2014, Yogyakarta.
5 Sheri Gibbings, untitled field note on outing with Pak Ferry and friends, ca. 18 November 2007, Yogyakarta.
6 Ibid.
7 Pak Ferry, interview with the author, 13 May 2014, Yogyakarta. I also emailed Pak Ferry on 15 March 2019 asking for confirmation that he still approved of me publishing information from our interview. He responded on March 18 and agreed to me moving forward with the publication.
8 Ibid.
9 Ibid.
10 Paguyuban Pedagang Sapta Manunggal, "Kami mau diature, bukan untuk digusur!" [We want to be arranged, not evicted!], press release, 24 November 2004.
11 Pagyuban Pedagang Sapta Manunggal, "Kronologis aksi dan klarifikasi tuduhan komunis" [Protest chronology and clarification of communists' allegations], press release, 24 November 2004.
12 Pak Ferry, interview with the author, 13 May 2014, Yogyakarta.
13 Ibid.
14 Ibid.

15 Ibid.
16 Ibid. From our interview, it appears as if Pak Ferry was working
    specifically with Pak Galang from the Department of Marketplaces.
    Pak Ferry said, "I only help the Department of Marketplaces and the
    Department of Marketplaces only helps me."
17 Ibid.
18 Ibid.
19 Ibid.
20 Although it was possible for the government and police to engage in
    criminal behaviour, as was the case in the Mysterious Killings of 1983–5
    (J.T. Siegel 1998), Pak Ferry did not mention this.
21 Pak Ferry, interview with the author, 13 May 2014, Yogyakarta.
22 Ibid.
23 Ibid.
24 Ibid.
25 The gathering of the trader's KTP identity cards likely involved an element
    of intimidation.
26 Pak Ferry, interview with the author, 13 May 2014, Yogyakarta.
27 Ibid.
28 Ibid. The English term *game over* was used.
29 Ibid.
30 Ibid.
31 This was typical of a kind of coercive relationship between nightclubs
    and many police and military officers in Indonesia, according to which
    nightclubs are required to pay police for protection services.
32 Pak Ferry, interview with the author, 13 May 2014, Yogyakarta.
33 Ibid.
34 Ibid.
35 Ibid.
36 Ibid.
37 For instance, in 2003, the United States spent approximately $16
    million on law enforcement and counterterrorism training for
    the Indonesian police. Some of this training took place through
    educational workshops in Indonesia, while in other cases Indonesian
    officers received funding to attend workshops in the United States
    (Blair and Phillips 2003, 67). The Australian Agency for International
    Development and the US Department of Justice's International
    Criminal Investigative Training and Assistance Program developed a
    program to offer courses on democratic policing, community policing,
    and police ethics (67).
38 Pak Ferry, interview with the author, 13 May 2014, Yogyakarta.
39 Ibid.

40 Ibid. Earlier in this same interview, Pak Ferry had mentioned that he never knew his father, who had been part of the military air force (TNI Angkatan Udara) and had died in a plane crash during a training exercise when Pak Ferry was just seven months old. Pak Ferry's schooling, including his Indonesia National Police Force education, had been paid for by his older brother.

41 For a discussion of money politics in Indonesia, see Edward Aspinall and Mada Sukmajati (2016).

42 Pak Akbar, interview with the author, 14 May 2014, Yogyakarta.

43 *Wah* is a "particle of mild emotion said upon noticing something; *my!*" (Wolff 1992, 467).

44 Pak Akbar, interview with the author, 14 May 2014, Yogyakarta.

45 Ibid.

46 Ibid.

47 Ibid.

9. Marketplace Relations

1 Slamet Susanto, "Klithikan Market, a Secondhand Goods Paradise," *Jakarta Post*, 30 May 2008.

2 Ibid.

3 "Pasar Klithikan masuk agenda promosi wisata" [Klithikan market is on the tourism promotion agenda], *Kedaulatan Rakyat* (Yogyakarta), 5 December 2007; "Bule pun ada di pasar Pakuncen …" [Caucasians are also at the Pakuncen market], *Kompas* (Jakarta), 15 December 2007.

4 Sheri Gibbings, untitled field note on Kuncen Marketplace, 9 December 2007, Yogyakarta.

5 As noted earlier (see Gender and Pemuda Masculinities, Chapter 1), stolen goods were also associated with men.

6 "Pedagang klithikan Pakuncen mengeluh: Kurang promosi, pengunjung turun drastis" [Pakuncen klithikan traders complain: Lack of promotion, visitors drop drastically], *Kedaulatan Rakyat* (Yogyakarta), 4 April 2007.

7 After the relocation, rather than occupying their designated kiosks at the back of Kuncen Marketplace, many of the former Pethikbumi members and leaders rented out more strategic locations in the marketplace. They rented these better-placed kiosks from owners who were not interested in trading at Kuncen Marketplace. Alternatively, the former Pethikbumi traders did not trade at Kuncen Marketplace but held on to the kiosks they were given because they were of little value at the time. A few of the Pethikbumi traders tried operating from their allocated kiosks in the back of the marketplace, but they struggled to survive because so few customers walked to this section of the site, which was up a set of stairs and at the very back of the marketplace.

8 Sheri Gibbings, untitled field note on Kuncen Marketplace, 18 July 2013, Yogyakarta.

9 Many of the traders suggested that the cooperative failed because it was created in a top-down fashion and it did not incorporate any of the former anti-relocation traders. Sheri Gibbings, untitled field note on Ngesti Rahyu cooperative, 8 December 2008, Yogyakarta.

10 According to Mas Arief, a number of former Pethikbumi traders had formed KOMPAK because they were interested in promoting the marketplace, despite the fact that some of the traders still resisted the idea of being there. Mas Arief, interview with the author, 11 May 2014, Yogyakarta.

11 Pak Asep, interview with the author, 6 August 2014, Yogyakarta.

12 Pak Akbar, interview with the author, 14 May 2014, Yogyakarta.

13 Ibid.

14 Pak Pramana, interview with the author, 9 May 2014, Yogyakarta.

15 Ibid.

16 Pak Mujib, interview with the author, 6 August 2013, Yogyakarta.

17 Mas Eko, interview with the author, 20 July 2013, Yogyakarta.

18 Mas Eko, interview with the author, 16 May 2014, Yogyakarta.

19 Mas Eko, interview with the author, 20 July 2013, Yogyakarta.

20 Pak Halim and Pak Edy, interview with the author, 17 May 2014, Yogyakarta.

21 Pak Dede, interview with the author, 10 May 2014, Yogyakarta.

22 Elan Lazuardi, untitled field note on Sentir Marketplace, 6 August 2013, Yogyakarta.

23 The municipal government had also promised the pro-relocation leaders that they would receive a certain amount of money for helping to organize the traders to relocate to Kuncen Marketplace. Pak Bowo and a couple of the other pro-relocation leaders mentioned that they were disappointed that they had not received the full amount that they had been promised. Sheri Gibbings, untitled field note on Pak Bowo, 22 October 2007, Yogyakarta.

24 Sheri Gibbings, untitled field note on Pak Bowo, 24 July 2013, Yogyakarta.

25 Pak Wahyu, interview with the author, 13 May 2014, Yogyakarta.

26 Ibid.

27 Pak Halim was part of Pethikbumi but adopted a neutral stance vis-à-vis the relocation when the Pethikbumi leadership voted to strongly oppose the the project. He decided to join the relocation but did not want to adopt either a pro- or anti-relocation stance. Once he took the stance of neutrality, he did not join any of the Pethikbumi meetings and was not involved in the organization. He did follow the relocation closely and served as an important actor who mediated between the pro- and anti-relocation traders, as well as between the traders and the government.

28 Pak Halim, interview with the author, 3 August 2013, Yogyakarta.
29 The traders in the marketplace were organized according to numbered blocks.
30 Pak Halim, interview with the author, 3 August 2013, Yogyakarta.
31 Pak Nur, interview with the author, 15 May 2014, Yogyakarta.
32 According to Mas Arief, although government officials were initially suspicious of KOMPAK, the traders behind the cooperative built up the trust and confidence of these officials over time. Mas Arief, interview with the author, 11 May 2014, Yogyakarta.
33 The Pethikbumi leaders who did not relocate to the new marketplace, such as Pak Akbar, Pak Pramana, and Pak Mujib, continued to have a more negative view of the municipal government.

10. Conclusion

1 As Aihwa Ong and Stephen J. Collier (2005) argue, "an assemblage is the product of multiple determinations that are not reducible to a single logic. The temporality of an assemblage is emergent. It does not always involve new forms, but forms that are shifting, in formation, or at stake" (12).

References

Adam, Ahmat. 1995. *The Vernacular Press and the Emergence of Modern Indonesian Consciousness (1855–1913).* Studies on Southeast Asia, no. 17. Ithaca, NY: Southeast Asia Program Publications, Cornell University.

Ali, Arshad Imitaz. 2016. "Citizens under Suspicion: Responsive Research with Community under Surveillance." *Anthropology & Education Quarterly* 47, no. 1: 78–95. https://doi.org/10.1111/aeq.12136.

Alwani, Taha Jabir al, and Imad al Din Khalil. 1995. *The Qur'an and Sunnah: The Time-Space Factor.* Rev. ed. London: International Institute of Islamic Thought.

Anderson, Benedict R.O'G. 1972. *Java in a Time of Revolution: Occupation and Resistance, 1944–1946.* Ithaca, NY: Cornell University Press.

– 1990. *Language and Power: Exploring Political Cultures in Indonesia.* Ithaca, NY: Cornell University Press.

– 1991. *Imagined Communities: Reflections on the Origin and Spread of Nationalism.* Rev. ed. London: Verso.

Anjaria, Jonathan Shapiro. 2016. *The Slow Boil: Street Food, Rights and Public Space in Mumbai.* South Asia in Motion. Stanford, CA: Stanford University Press.

Aragon, Lorraine V. 2001. "Communal Violence in Poso, Central Sulawesi: Where People Eat Fish and Fish Eat People." *Indonesia* 72, no. 72: 45–79. https://doi.org/10.2307/3351481.

Aretxaga, Begoña. 2003. "Maddening States." *Annual Review of Anthropology* 32 (January): 393–410.

Aspinall, Edward. 1996. "The Broadening Base of Political Opposition in Indonesia." In *Political Oppositions in Industrialising Asia,* edited by Garry Rodan, 215–40. London: Routledge.

– 2013. "A Nation in Fragments: Patronage and Neoliberalism in Contemporary Indonesia." *Critical Asian Studies* 45, no. 1: 27–54. https://doi.org/10.1080/14672715.2013.758820.

Aspinall, Edward, and Mada Sukmajati, eds. 2016. *Electoral Dynamics in Indonesia: Money Politics, Patronage and Clientelism at the Grassroots.* Singapore: NUS Press.

Aspinall, Edward, and Meredith L. Weiss. 2012. "The Limits of Civil Society: Social Movements and Political Parties in Southeast Asia." In *Routledge Handbook of Southeast Asian Politics,* edited by Richard Robison, 213–28. London: Routledge.

Atkinson, Jane Monnig, and Shelly Errington, eds. 1990. *Power and Difference: Gender in Island Southeast Asia.* Stanford, CA: Stanford University Press.

Badan Pelindung Hak Kemanusiaan. 2007. *Gugatan PTUN Perwal no. 45 tahun 2007* [Lawsuit against Mayoral Regulation no. 45, 2007], 10 October 2007. Yogyakarta: Badan Pelindung Hak Kemanusiaan.

Badan Pusat Statistik Kota Yogyakarta. 2018. *Kota Yogyakarta dalam angka 2018* [Yogyakarta Municipality in figures 2018]. Publication 34710.1805. Yogyakarta: Badan Pusat Statistik Kota Yogyakarta. https://jogjakota .bps.go.id/publication/2018/08/16/8e60dd366fc77ddeee9ea008/kota -yogyakarta-dalam-angka-2018.html.

Bailey, F.G. 1971a. *Gifts and Poison: The Politics of Reputation.* Oxford: Basil Blackwell.

– 1971b. "The Management of Reputations and the Process of Change." In *Gifts and Poison: The Politics of Reputation,* edited by F.G. Bailey, 281–301. Oxford: Basil Blackwell.

Baker, Jacqui. 2013. "The 'Parman' Economy: Post-authoritarian Shifts in Indonesia's Illicit Security Economy." *Indonesia* 96:123–50. https://doi .org/10.5728/indonesia.96.0123.

Ballestero, Andrea S. 2012. "Transparency in Triads." *PoLAR: Political and Legal Anthropology Review* 35, no. 2: 160–6. https://doi.org/10.1111/j.1555 -2934.2012.01196.x.

Barenboim, Deanna. 2016. "The Specter of Surveillance: Navigating 'Illegality' and Indigeneity among Maya Migrants in the San Francisco Bay Area." *Political and Legal Anthropology Review* 39, no. 1: 79–94. https://doi.org /10.1111/plar.12132.

Barker, Joshua. 1998. "State of Fear: Controlling the Criminal Contagion in Suharto's New Order." *Indonesia* 66:7–43. https://doi.org/10.2307/3351446.

– 1999. "Surveillance and Territoriality in Bandung." In *Figures of Criminality in Indonesia, the Philippines, and Colonial Vietnam,* edited by Vicente L. Rafael, 95–127. Studies on Southeast Asia, no. 25. Ithaca, NY: Southeast Asia Program Publications, Cornell University.

– 2001. "State of Fear: Controlling the Criminal Contagion in Suharto's New Order." In *Violence and the State in Suharto's Indonesia,* edited by Benedict R.O'G. Anderson, 20–54. Ithaca, NY: Southeast Asia Program Publications, Cornell University.

– 2005. "Engineers and Political Dreams: Indonesia in the Satellite Age." *Current Anthropology* 46, no. 5: 703–27. https://doi.org/10.1086/432652.

– 2009. "Negara Beling: Street-Level Authority in an Indonesian Slum." In *State of Authority: The State in Society in Indonesia*, edited by Joshua Barker and Geert Arend Van Klinken, 47–72. Ithaca, NY: Southeast Asia Program Publications, Cornell University.

– 2015. "Guerilla Engineers: The Internet and the Politics of Freedom in Indonesia." In *Dreamscapes of Modernity: Sociotechnical Imaginaries and the Fabrication of Power*, edited by Sheila Jasanoff and Sang-Hyun Kim, 199–218. Chicago: University of Chicago Press.

Barker, Joshua, and Gerry Van Klinken. 2009. "Reflections on the State in Indonesia." In *State of Authority: The State in Society in Indonesia*, edited by Gerry Van Klinken and Joshua Barker, 17–46. Studies on Southeast Asia, no. 50. Ithaca, NY: Southeast Asia Program Publications, Cornell University.

Barrera, Leticia. 2013. "Performing the Court: Public Hearings and the Politics of Judicial Transparency in Argentina." *PoLAR: Political and Legal Anthropology Review* 36, no. 2: 326–40. https://doi.org/10.1111/plar.12032.

Barrios, Roberto. 2011. "Post-Katrina Neighbourhood Recovery Planning in New Orleans." In *Dynamics of Disaster: Lessons on Risk, Response, and Recovery*, edited by Barbara L. Allen and Rachel Dowty, 97–115. Washington, DC: Earthscan.

Bauman, Richard, and Charles L. Briggs. 1990. "Poetics and Performance as Critical Perspectives on Language and Social Life." *Annual Review of Anthropology* 19, no. 1: 59–88. https://doi.org/10.1146/annurev.an.19.100190.000423.

Beatty, Andrew. 1999. *Varieties of Javanese Religion: An Anthropological Account.* Cambridge Studies in Social and Cultural Anthropology. Cambridge: Cambridge University Press.

Benedict, Ruth. 1934. *Patterns of Culture*. New York: Mentor.

Bertrand, Jacques. 2004. *Nationalism and Ethnic Conflict in Indonesia*. Cambridge Asia-Pacific Studies. Cambridge: Cambridge University Press.

Bjorken, Johanna, and Kenneth C. Payumo. 2005. "Indonesian National Police." In *Encyclopedia of Law Enforcement*, edited by Larry E. Sullivan, Marie Simonetti Rosen, Dorothy M. Schulz, and Maria (Maki) R. Haberfeld, 1008–11. Thousand Oaks, CA: Sage Publications.

Blair, Dennis C., and David L. Phillips. 2003. *Indonesia Commission: Peace and Progress in Papua. Report of an Independent Commission Sponsored by the Council on Foreign Relations Center for Preventive Action*. New York: Council on Foreign Relations.

Bodin, Jean. 1992. *On Sovereignty: Four Chapters from the Six Books of the Commonwealth*. Edited and translated by Julian H. Franklin. Cambridge Texts in the History of Political Thought. Cambridge: Cambridge University Press.

Bonilla, Yarimar. 2011. "The Past Is Made by Walking: Labor Activism and Historical Production in Postcolonial Guadeloupe." *Cultural Anthropology* 26, no. 3: 313–39. https://doi.org/10.1111/j.1548-1360.2011.01101.x.

Borneman, John, and Joseph Masco. 2015. "Anthropology and the Security State: Public Anthropology." *American Anthropologist* 117, no. 4: 781–5. https://doi.org/10.1111/aman.12371.

Bourdieu, Pierre. 1991. *Language and Symbolic Power*. Edited by John B. Thompson. Translated by Gino Raymond and Matthew Adamson. Cambridge, MA: Harvard University Press.

Boyer, Dominic. 2005. *Spirit and System: Media, Intellectuals, and the Dialectic in Modern German Culture*. Chicago: University of Chicago Press.

– 2006. "Conspiracy, History, and Therapy at a Berlin Stammtisch." *American Ethnologist* 33, no. 3: 327–39. https://doi.org/10.1525/ae.2006.33.3.327.

Boyer, Dominic, and Ulf Hannerz. 2006. "Introduction: Worlds of Journalism." *Ethnography* 7, no. 1: 5–17. https://doi.org/10.1177/1466138106064587.

Brenner, Suzanne April. 1998. *The Domestication of Desire: Women, Wealth, and Modernity in Java*. Princeton, NJ: Princeton University Press.

Briggs, Charles L. 2004. "Theorizing Modernity Conspiratorially: Science, Scale, and the Political Economy of Public Discourse in Explanations of a Cholera Epidemic." *American Ethnologist* 31, no. 2: 164–87. https://doi.org/10.1525/ae.2004.31.2.164.

– 2007. "Mediating Infanticide Theorizing Relations between Narrative and Violence." *Cultural Anthropology* 22, no. 3: 315–56. https://doi.org/10.1525/can.2007.22.3.315.

Briggs, Charles L., and Daniel C. Hallin. 2016. *Making Health Public: How News Coverage Is Remaking Media, Medicine, and Contemporary Life*. New York: Routledge.

Brown, Alison. 2006. "Setting the Context: Social, Economic and Political Influences on the Informal Sector in Ghana, Lesotho, Nepal and Tanzania." In *Contested Space: Street Trading, Public Space, and Livelihoods in Developing Cities*, edited by Alison Brown, 55–78. Urban Management Series. Rugby, UK: ITDG Publishing.

Brown, Karen McCarthy. 2003. "Making Wanga: Reality Constructions and the Magical Manipulation of Power." In *Transparency and Conspiracy: Ethnographies of Suspicion in the New World Order*, edited by Harry G. West and Todd Sanders, 233–57. Durham, NC: Duke University Press.

Brown, Wendy. 1995. "Finding the Man in the State." In *States of Injury: Power and Freedom in Late Modernity*, 166–96. Princeton, NJ: Princeton University Press.

Bubandt, Nils. 2008. "Rumors, Pamphlets, and the Politics of Paranoia in Indonesia." *Journal of Asian Studies* 67, no. 3: 789–817. https://doi.org/10.1017/S0021911808001162.

– 2009. "From the Enemy's Point of View: Violence, Empathy, and the Ethnography of Fakes." *Cultural Anthropology* 24, no. 3: 553–88. https://doi .org/10.1111/j.1548-1360.2009.01040.x.

– 2014. *Democracy, Corruption and the Politics of Spirits in Contemporary Indonesia.* New York: Routledge.

Butt, Leslie. 2005. " 'Lipstick Girls' and 'Fallen Women': AIDS and Conspiratorial Thinking in Papua, Indonesia." *Cultural Anthropology* 20, no. 3: 412–41. https://doi.org/10.1525/can.2005.20.3.412.

Cahyono, Heru. 2008. "The State and Society in Conflict Resolution in Indonesia (Conflict Area of West Kalimantan and Central Kalimantan)." *Journal of Indonesian Social Sciences and Humanities* 1:151–60. https://doi .org/10.14203/jissh.v1i1.10.

Caldeira, Teresa Pires do Rio. 2000. *City of Walls: Crime, Segregation, and Citizenship in São Paulo.* Berkeley: University of California Press.

Carleton Newsroom, Carleton University. 2020. "New Carleton Study Finds COVID-19 Conspiracies and Misinformation Spreading Online." News release, 20 May 2020. https://newsroom.carleton.ca/2020/new-carleton -study-finds-covid-19-conspiracies-and-misinformation-spreading-online/.

Castoriadis, Cornelius. 1987. *The Imaginary Institution of Society.* Cambridge, MA: MIT Press.

Clark, Gracia C. 1988a. "Price Control of Local Foodstuffs in Kumasi, Ghana, 1979." In *Traders versus the State: Anthropological Approaches to Unofficial Economies,* edited by Gracia Clark, 57–79. Boulder, CO: Westview Press.

– 1988b. "Introduction." In *Traders versus the State: Anthropological Approaches to Unofficial Economies,* edited by Gracia Clark, 1–16. Boulder, CO: Westview Press.

– 2013. "Twentieth-Century Government Attacks on Food Vendors in Kumasi, Ghana." In *Street Economies in the Urban Global South,* edited by Karen Tranberg Hansen, Walter E. Little, and B. Lynne Milgram, 1st ed., 29–48. School for Advanced Research Seminar Series. Santa Fe, NM: School for Advanced Research Press.

Clark, Marshall. 2006. "Pipit Rochijat's Subversive Mythologies: The Suharto Era and Beyond." *Asian Folklore Studies* 65, no. 1: 21–44. https://doi.org /10.2307/30030372.

Cody, Francis. 2009. "Daily Wires and Daily Blossoms: Cultivating Regimes of Circulation in Tamil India's Newspaper Revolution." *Journal of Linguistic Anthropology* 19, no. 2: 286–309. https://doi.org/10.1111/j.1548-1395 .2009.01035.x.

Collier, Stephen J., and Aihwa Ong. 2005. "Global Assemblages, Anthropological Problems." In *Global Assemblages: Technology, Politics, and Ethics as Anthropological Problems,* edited by Aihwa Ong and Stephen J. Collier, 3–21. Malden, MA: Blackwell.

Collins, Elizabeth Fuller. 2007. *Indonesia Betrayed: How Development Fails.* Honolulu: University of Hawai'i Press.

Colombijn, Freek. 1994. *Patches of Padang: The History of an Indonesian Town in the Twentieth Century and the Use of Urban Space.* Leiden, NL: Research School CNWS.

Colwell, Chip. 2015. "Curating Secrets." *Current Anthropology* 56, no. S12: S263–75. https://doi.org/10.1086/683429.

Copeland, Nicholas. 2014. "Mayan Imaginaries of Democracy: Interactive Sovereignties and Political Affect in Postrevolutionary Guatemala." *American Ethnologist* 41, no. 2: 305–19. https://doi.org/10.1111/amet.12077.

Cox, Bruce A. 1970. "What Is Hopi Gossip About? Information Management and Hopi Factions." *Man, New Series* 5, no. 1: 88–98. https://doi.org/10.2307/2798806.

Crapanzano, Vincent. 1985. *Waiting: The Whites of South Africa.* New York: Random House.

Cross, John C. 1998. *Informal Politics: Street Vendors and the State in Mexico City.* Stanford, CA: Stanford University Press.

Das, Veena. 2004. "The Signature of the State: The Paradox of Illegibility." In *Anthropology in the Margins of the State*, edited by Veena Das and Deborah Poole, 1st ed., 225–52. Santa Fe, NM: School of American Research Press.

Das, Veena, and Deborah Poole, eds. 2004. *Anthropology in the Margins of the State.* Santa Fe, NM: School of American Research Press.

Day, Ronald E. 2008. *The Modern Invention of Information: Discourse, History, and Power.* Rev. ed. Carbondale: Southern Illinois University Press.

Dean, Jodi. 1998. *Aliens in America: Conspiracy Cultures from Outerspace to Cyberspace.* Ithaca, NY: Cornell University Press.

–. 2002. *Publicity's Secret: How Technoculture Capitalizes on Democracy.* Ithaca, NY: Cornell University Press.

De Jong, Ferdinand. 2007. *Masquerades of Modernity: Power and Secrecy in Casamance, Senegal.* Bloomington: Indiana University Press.

Douglas, Mary. 1968. "The Social Control of Cognition: Some Factors in Joke Perception." *Man, New Series* 3, no. 3: 361–76. https://doi.org/10.2307/2798875.

Drexler, Elizabeth. 2006. "History and Liability in Aceh, Indonesia: Single Bad Guys and Convergent Narratives." *American Ethnologist* 33, no. 3: 313–26. https://doi.org/10.1525/ae.2006.33.3.313.

Duncan, Christopher R. 2005. "The Other Maluku: Chronologies of Conflict in North Maluku." *Indonesia* 80 (October): 53–80.

Dunham, S. Ann. 2009. *Surviving against the Odds: Village Industry in Indonesia.* Edited and with a preface by Alice G. Dewey and Nancy I. Cooper. Durham, NC: Duke University Press.

Elmadmad, Khadija. 1991. "An Arab Convention on Forced Migration: Desirability and Possibilities." *International Journal of Refugee Law* 3, no. 3: 461–81. https://doi.org/10.1093/ijrl/3.3.461.

Etzold, Benjamin. 2015. "Selling in Insecurity, Living with Violence: Eviction Drives against Street Food Vendors in Dhaka and the Informal Politics of Exploitation." In *Street Vending in the Neoliberal City: A Global Perspective on the Practices and Policies of a Marginalized Economy*, edited by Kristina Graaff and Noa K. Ha, 164–90. New York: Berghahn.

Fakultas Hukum, Universitas Katolik Parahyangan. 1980. "Penertiban pedagang kaki lima di Kota Madya Bandung" [Order for street traders in the Muncipality of Bandung]." In *Menggali potensi pedagang kaki lima sebagai unsur pembangunan dalam pengembangan Bandung Kota Indah* [Fostering the potentiality of sidewalk vendors as elements of the development of Beautiful City Bandung; collected volume of papers from an 18–19 April 1980 workshop in Bandung]. Bandung, West Java: Fakultas Hukum, Universitas Katolik Parahyangan [Faculty of Law, Catholic University of Parahyangan].

Feldman, Allen. 2000. "Violence and Vision: The Prosthetics and Aesthetics of Terror." In *Violence and Subjectivity*, edited by Veena Das, Arthur Kleinman, Mamphela Ramphele, and Pamela Reynolds, 46–78. Berkeley: University of California Press.

Feldman, Ilana. 2015. *Police Encounters: Security and Surveillance in Gaza under Egyptian Rule*. Stanford, CA: Stanford University Press.

Ferguson, James. 1994. *The Anti-politics Machine: "Development," Depoliticization, and Bureaucratic Power in Lesotho*. Minneapolis: University of Minnesota Press.

Fine, Gary A. 1977. "Social Components of Children's Gossip." *Journal of Communication* 27, no. 1: 181–5. https://doi.org/10.1111/j.1460-2466.1977.tb01815.x.

Firth, Raymond. 1955. "The Theory of 'Cargo' Culture: A Note on Tikopia." *Man* 55, no. 142: 130–2. https://doi.org/10.2307/2794592.

– (1967) 2011. "Rumour in a Primitive Society with A Note on the Theory of 'Cargo' Cults." In *Tikopia Ritual and Belief*, 141–61. Routledge Revivals. Boston: Beacon.

Florida, Nancy K. 1995. *Writing the Past, Inscribing the Future: History as Prophesy in Colonial Java*. Durham, NC: Duke University Press.

Foucault, Michel. 1995. *Discipline and Punish: The Birth of the Prison*. 2nd Vintage ed. New York: Vintage Books.

Garfinkel, Harold. 1991. *Studies in Ethnomethodology*. Malden, MA: Blackwell.

Garriott, William Campbell, ed. 2013. *Policing and Contemporary Governance: The Anthropology of Police in Practice*. New York: Palgrave Macmillan.

Geertz, Clifford. 1978. "The Bazaar Economy: Information and Search in Peasant Marketing." *American Economic Review* 68, no. 2: 28–32. https://doi.org/10.4324/9780429494338-8.

Gershon, Ilana. 2010. *The Breakup 2.0: Disconnecting over New Media*. Ithaca, NY: Cornell University Press.

Gibbings, Julie. 2020. *Our Time Is Now: Race and Modernity in Postcolonial Guatemala*. Cambridge: Cambridge University Press.

Gibbings, Sheri L. 2013. "Unnamed Interests and Informal Leaders: A Street Vendor Relocation in Yogyakarta City." *Indonesia* 96 (October): 151–85. https://doi.org/10.5728/indonesia.96.0151.

– 2016. "Street Vending as Ethical Citizenship in Urban Indonesia." *Anthropologica* 58, no. 1: 77–94. https://doi.org/10.3138/anth.581.A05.

Gilmore, David. 1978. "Varieties of Gossip in a Spanish Rural Community." *Ethnology* 17:89–99. https://doi.org/10.2307/3773282.

Gluckman, Max. 1963a. "Gossip and Scandal." *Current Anthropology* 4:307–16.

– 1963b. "Papers in Honor of Melville J. Herskovits: Gossip and Scandal." *Current Anthropology* 4, no. 3: 307–16.

– 1968. "Psychological, Sociological and Anthropological Explanations of Witchcraft and Gossip: A Clarification." *Man, New Series* 3, no. 1: 20–34. https://doi.org/10.2307/2799409.

Goldstein, Donna M. 2013. *Laughter out of Place: Race, Class, Violence, and Sexuality in a Rio Shantytown*. California Series in Public Anthropology 9. Berkeley: University of California Press.

– 2016. *Owners of the Sidewalk: Security and Survival in the Informal City*. Global Insecurities. Durham, NC: Duke University Press.

González, Roberto J. 2017. "Hacking the Citizenry? Personality Profiling, 'Big Data' and the Election of Donald Trump." *Anthropology Today* 33, no. 3: 9–12. https://doi.org/10.1111/1467-8322.12348.

Guha, Ranajit. 1983. *Elementary Aspects of Peasant Insurgency in Colonial India*. Oxford: Oxford University Press.

Guinness, Patrick. 2016. "Land and Housing Security for the Urban Poor." In *Land and Development in Indonesia: Searching for the People's Sovereignty*, edited by John F. McCarthy and Kathryn Robinson, 206–26. Indonesia Update Series. Singapore: ISEAS–Yusof Ishak Institute.

Gupta, Akhil. 2005. "Narratives of Corruption: Anthropological and Fictional Accounts of the Indian State." *Ethnography* 6, no. 1: 5–34. https://doi.org/10.1177/1466138105055663.

Hadiwinata, Bob S. 2003. *The Politics of NGOs in Indonesia: Developing Democracy and Managing a Movement*. RoutledgeCurzon Research on Southeast Asia 3. London: RoutledgeCurzon.

Hamid, Abu, Mc. Suprapti, and Djenen Bale. 1987. "Sosialisasi pada perkampungan miskin daerah Sulawesi Selatan [Socialization in poor neighbourhoods of South Sulawesi]." Yogyakarta: Departemen Pendidikan dan Kebudayaan, Proyek Inventarisasi dan Dokumentasi Kebudayaan Daerah [Department of Education and Culture, Regional Cultural Inventory and Documentation Project].

Handelman, Don. 1973. "Gossip in Encounters: The Transmission of Information in a Bounded Social Setting." *Man, New Series* 8, no. 2: 210–27. https://doi.org/10.2307/2800847.

Hannerz, Ulf. 2004. *Foreign News: Exploring the World of Foreign Correspondents.* Chicago: University of Chicago Press.

Hansen, Karen Tranberg, Walter E. Little, and B. Lynne Milgram. 2013. "Introduction: Street Economies in the Urban Global South." In *Street Economies in the Urban Global South*, edited by Karen Tranberg Hansen, Walter E. Little, and B. Lynne Milgram, 1st ed., 3–16. School for Advanced Research Seminar Series. Santa Fe, NM: School for Advanced Research Press.

Hansen, Thomas Blom, and Finn Stepputat. 2006. "Sovereignty Revisited." *Annual Review of Anthropology* 35, no. 1: 295–315. https://doi.org/10.1146/annurev.anthro.35.081705.123317.

Hardiyanti, Dwi Ariyani. 2008. "Kebijakan relokasi pedagang Klithikan: Studi kasus di Pasar Klithikan Pakuncen Kota Yogyakarta [Klithikan traders relocation policy: A case study of Klithikan Pakuncen Marketplace Yogyakarta City]." Program Studi Magister Administrasi Publik tesis, kepada Program Pasca Sarjana [Master of Public Administration thesis, Graduate Program], Universitas Gadjah Mada.

Harms, Erik. 2013a. "The Boss: Conspicuous Invisibility in Ho Chi Minh City." *City & Society* 25, no. 2: 195–215. https://doi.org/10.1111/ciso.12016.

– 2013b. "Eviction Time in the New Saigon: Temporalities of Displacement in the Rubble of Development." *Cultural Anthropology* 28, no. 2: 344–68. https://doi.org/10.1111/cuan.12007.

Hart, Keith. 1973. "Informal Income Opportunities and Urban Employment in Ghana." *Journal of Modern African Studies* 11, no. 1: 61–89.

Harvey, Penny, and Hannah Knox. 2015. *Roads: An Anthropology of Infrastructure and Expertise.* Ithaca, NY: Cornell University Press.

Haryanto, Ignatius. 2011. "Media Ownership and Its Implications for Journalists and Journalism in Indonesia." In *Politics and the Media in Twenty-First Century Indonesia: Decade of Democracy*, edited by Krishna Sen and David T. Hill, 104–18. Media, Culture and Social Change in Asia 21. London: Routledge.

Hasan, Noorhaidi. 2002. "Faith and Politics: The Rise of the Laskar Jihad in the Era of Transition in Indonesia." *Indonesia* 73 (April): 145–69. https://doi.org/10.2307/3351472.

Haviland, John B. 1977. "Gossip as Competition in Zinacantan." *Journal of Communication* 27, no. 1: 186–91. https://doi.org/10.1111/j.1460-2466.1977.tb01816.x.

Hellinger, Daniel. 2003. "Paranoia, Conspiracy, and Hegemony in American Politics." In *Transparency and Conspiracy: Ethnographies of Suspicion in the New*

World Order, edited by Harry G. West and Todd Sanders, 204–32. Durham, NC: Duke University Press.

Heppenstall, M.A. 1971. "Reputation, Criticism and Information in an Austrian Village." In *Gifts and Poison: The Politics of Reputation*, edited by F.G. Bailey, 139–66. Oxford: Basil Blackwell.

Herriman, Nicholas. 2010. "The Great Rumor Mill: Gossip, Mass Media, and the Ninja Fear." *Journal of Asian Studies* 69, no. 3: 723–48. https://doi.org/10.1017/S0021911810001488.

Hetherington, Kregg. 2011. *Guerrilla Auditors: The Politics of Transparency in Neoliberal Paraguay*. Durham, NC: Duke University Press.

– 2012. "Agency, Scale, and the Ethnography of Transparency." *PoLAR: Political and Legal Anthropology Review* 35, no. 2: 242–7. https://doi.org/10.1111/j.1555-2934.2012.01201.x.

Heyman, Josiah McC. 2014. "Policing and Security." In *A Companion to Urban Anthropology*, edited by Donald Macon Nonini, 271–90. Malden, MA: Wiley.

Hill, David T. 2006. *The Press in New Order Indonesia*. Jakarta: Equinox.

Holbraad, Martin, Morten Axel Pedersen, and Eduardo Viveiros de Castro. 2014. "The Politics of Ontology: Anthropological Positions." *Cultural Anthropology*, 13 January 2014. https://culanth.org/fieldsights/462-the-politics-of-ontology-anthropological-positions.

Honna, Jun. 2010. "Orchestrating Transnational Crime: Security Sector Politics as a Trojan Horse for Anti-reformists." In *The State and Illegality in Indonesia*, edited by Edward Aspinall and Gerry Van Klinken, 261–79. Leiden, NL: KITLV Press. https://doi.org/10.1163/9789004253681_014.

Hoon, Chang-Yau. 2011. *Chinese Identity in Post-Suharto Indonesia: Culture, Politics and Media*. Eastbourne, UK: Sussex Academic Press.

Hoskins, Janet. 1997. *The Play of Time: Kodi Perspectives on Calendars, History, and Exchange*. Berkeley: University of California Press.

Hull, Matthew S. 2003. "The File: Agency, Authority, and Autography in an Islamabad Bureaucracy." *Language & Communication* 23, nos. 3–4: 287–314. https://doi.org/10.1016/S0271-5309(03)00019-3.

– 2012a. "Documents and Bureaucracy." *Annual Review of Anthropology* 41 (October): 251–67. https://doi.org/10.1146/annurev.anthro.012809.104953.

– 2012b. *Government of Paper: The Materiality of Bureaucracy in Urban Pakistan*. Berkeley: University of California Press.

International Crisis Group. 2005. *Weakening Indonesia's Mujahidin Networks: Lessons from Maluku and Poso*. Asia Report No. 103, 13 October 2005. https://www.crisisgroup.org/asia/south-east-asia/indonesia/weakening-indonesias-mujahidin-networks-lessons-maluku-and-poso.

Jellinek, Lea. 1991. *The Wheel of Fortune: The History of a Poor Community in Jakarta*. Honolulu: University of Hawai'i Press.

Jurriëns, Edwin. 2011. " 'Radio Active': The Creation of Media-Literate Audiences in Post-Suharto Indonesia." In *Politics and the Media in Twenty-First Century Indonesia: Decade of Democracy*, edited by Krishna Sen and David T. Hill, 141–58. New York: Routledge.

Kantor Pengendalian Dampak Lingkungan Pemkot Yogyakarta, and C.V. Bangun Cipta Persada. 2004. *Dokumen upaya pengelolaan lingkungan dan upaya pemantauan lingkungan: Rencana pembangunan Pasar Kuncen* [Environmental management and environmental monitoring documents on the plans to build Kuncen Marketplace]. Yogyakarta: Pemerintah Kota Yogyakarta.

Keeler, Ward. 1987. *Javanese Shadow Plays, Javanese Selves*. Princeton, NJ: Princeton University Press.

Kipnis, Andrew B. 2008. "Audit Cultures: Neoliberal Governmentality, Socialist Legacy, or Technologies of Governing?" *American Ethnologist* 35, no. 2: 275–89. https://doi.org/10.1111/j.1548-1425.2008.00034.x.

Kirsch, Stuart. 2002. "Rumour and Other Narratives of Political Violence in West Papua." *Critique of Anthropology* 22, no. 1: 53–79. https://doi.org/10.1177/0308275X020220010301.

Kitley, Philip. 1994. "Fine Tuning Control: Commercial Television in Indonesia." *Continuum: The Australian Journal of Media and Culture* 8, no. 2: 103–23.

– 2000. *Television, Nation, and Culture in Indonesia*. Athens: Ohio University Center for International Studies.

Kohn, Eduardo. 2015. "Anthropology of Ontologies." *Annual Review of Anthropology* 44:311–27. https://doi.org/10.1146/annurev-anthro-102214-014127.

Koselleck, Reinhart. 2004. *Futures Past: On the Semantics of Historical Time*. Translated by Keith Tribe. New York: Columbia University Press.

Kramer, Elisabeth. 2013. "When News Becomes Entertainment: Representations of Corruption in Indonesia's Media and the Implication of Scandal." *Media Asia* 40, no. 1: 60–72. https://doi.org/10.1080/01296612.2013.11689951.

Kroeger, Karen A. 2003. "AIDS Rumors, Imaginary Enemies, and the Body Politic in Indonesia." *American Ethnologist* 30, no. 2: 243–57. https://doi.org/10.1525/ae.2003.30.2.243.

Kusno, Abidin. 2004. "Whither Nationalist Urbanism? Public Life in Governor Sutiyoso's Jakarta." *Urban Studies* 41, no. 12: 2377–94. https://doi.org/10.1080/00420980412331297582.

– 2005. "The Significance of Appearance in the Zaman Normal, 1927–1942." In *Kota Lama, Kota Baru: Sejarah Kota-Kota Di Indonesia Sebelum Dan Setelah Kemerdekaan/Old City, New City: The History of the Indonesian City Before and After Independence*, edited by Freek Colombijn, rev. ed., 493–521. Yogyakarta: Ombak.

Lazar, Sian. 2007. " 'In-Betweenness' on the Margins: Collective Organisation, Ethnicity and Political Agency among Bolivian Street Traders." In *Livelihoods at the Margins: Surviving the City*, edited by James Staples, 237–56. Walnut Creek, CA: Left Coast Press.

– 2008. *El Alto, Rebel City: Self and Citizenship in Andean Bolivia*. Latin America Otherwise. Durham, NC: Duke University Press.

Lebner, Ashley, Paolo Heywood, Sarah Franklin, and Morten Axel Pedersen. 2017. "Interpreting Strathern's 'Unconscious' Critique of Ontology." *Social Anthropology/Anthropologie Sociale* 25, no. 2: 221–33. https://doi.org /10.1111/1469-8676.12368.

Lee, Doreen. 2011. "Styling the Revolution: Masculinities, Youth, and Street Politics in Jakarta, Indonesia." *Journal of Urban History* 37, no. 6: 933–51. https://doi.org/10.1177/0096144211410526.

– 2016. *Activist Archives: Youth Culture and the Political Past in Indonesia*. Durham, NC: Duke University Press.

Leshkowich, Ann Marie. 2011. "Making Class and Gender: (Market) Socialist Enframing of Traders in Ho Chi Minh City." *American Anthropologist* 113, no. 2: 277–90. https://doi.org/10.1111/j.1548-1433.2011.01330.x.

Lewinson, Anne S. 1998. "Reading Modernity in Urban Space: Politics, Geography and the Informal Sector of Downtown Dar Es Salaam, Tanzania." *City & Society* 10, no. 1: 205–22. https://doi.org/10.1525/city .1998.10.1.205.

Li, Tania. 2007. *The Will to Improve: Governmentality, Development, and the Practice of Politics*. Durham, NC: Duke University Press.

Lim, Merlyna. 2002. "Cyber-Civic Space in Indonesia: From Panopticon to Pandemonium?" *International Development Planning Review* 24, no. 4: 383–400. https://doi.org/10.3828/idpr.24.4.3.

– 2003. "The Internet, Social Networks, and Reform in Indonesia." In *Contesting Media Power: Alternative Media in a Networked World*, edited by Nick Couldry and James Curran, 273–88. Lanham, MD: Rowman and Littlefield.

Lindell, Ilda. 2010. "Between Exit and Voice: Informality and the Spaces of Popular Agency." *African Studies Quarterly* 11, nos. 2–3: 1–11.

Little, Walter E. 2014. "Façade to Street to Façade: Negotiating Public Spatial Legality in a World Heritage City." *City & Society* 26, no. 2: 196–216. https:// doi.org/10.1111/ciso.12040.

Low, Setha M. 2001. "The Edge and the Center: Gated Communities and the Discourse of Urban Fear:" *American Anthropologist* 103, no. 1: 45–58. https:// doi.org/10.1525/aa.2001.103.1.45.

– 2006. "Unlocking the Gated Community: Moral Minimalism and Social (Dis)Order in Gated Communities in the United States and Mexico." In *Private Cities: Global and Local Perspectives*, edited by Georg Glasze,

Christopher J. Webster, and Klaus Frantz, 43–60. Routledge Studies in Human Geography 13. London: Routledge.

Luhrmann, Tanya M. 1989. "The Magic of Secrecy." *Ethos* 17, no. 2: 131–65.

MacLean, Ken. 2014. "Counter-Accounting with Invisible Data: The Struggle for Transparency in Myanmar's Energy Sector." *PoLAR: Political and Legal Anthropology Review* 37, no. 1: 10–28. https://doi.org/10.1111/plar.12048.

Malano, Herman. 2011. *Selamatkan pasar tradisional: Potret ekonomi rakyat kecil* [Save traditional marketplaces: An economic portrait of small people]. Jakarta: Gramedia Pustaka Utama.

Manderson, Lenore, Mark Davis, Chip Colwell, and Tanja Ahlin. 2015. "On Secrecy, Disclosure, the Public, and the Private in Anthropology: An Introduction to Supplement 12." *Current Anthropology* 56, no. S12: S183–90.

Mann, Steve, Jason Nolan, and Barry Wellman. 2003. "Sousveillance: Inventing and Using Wearable Computing Devices for Data Collection in Surveillance Environments." *Surveillance & Society* 1, no. 3: 331–55. https://doi.org/10.24908/ss.v1i3.3344.

Manzella, Joseph C. 2000. "Negotiating the News: Indonesian Press Culture and Power during the Political Crises of 1997–8." *Journalism* 1, no. 3: 305–28. https://doi.org/10.1177/146488490000100303.

Maryati, Kun, and Juju Suryawati. 2006. *Sosiologi untuk SMA/MA kelas X* [Sociology for first grade senior high school]. Jakarta: Esis.

"Masalah pedagang kaki lima di Kodya Bandung dan penertibannya melalui Operasi Tibum [The problem of street vendors in Bandung City and the efforts to control them through Tibum Operations]." 1980. In *Menggali potensi pedagang kaki lima sebagai unsur pembangunan dalam pengembangan Bandung Kota Indah* [Fostering the potentiality of sidewalk vendors as elements of the development of the Beautiful City Bandung]. Report of Seminar at Universitas Katolik Parahyangan, Bandung, 18–19 April 1980. Bandung, West Java: Universitas Katolik Parahyangan.

Mathur, Nayanika. 2012. "Transparent-Making Documents and the Crisis of Implementation: A Rural Employment Law and Development Bureaucracy in India." *PoLAR: Political and Legal Anthropology Review* 35, no. 2: 167–85. https://doi.org/10.1111/j.1555-2934.2012.01197.x.

– 2016. *Paper Tiger: Law, Bureaucracy and the Developmental State in Himalayan India*. Delhi: Cambridge University Press.

Mazzarella, William. 2006. "Internet X-Ray: E-Governance, Transparency, and the Politics of Immediation in India." *Public Culture* 18, no. 3: 473–505. https://doi.org/10.1215/08992363-2006-016.

McDougal, Charles. 1964. "Juang Categories and Joking Relations." *Southwestern Journal of Anthropology* 20, no. 4: 319–45. https://doi.org/10.1086/soutjanth.20.4.3629174.

McGranahan, Carole. 2005. "Truth, Fear, and Lies: Exile Politics and Arrested Histories of the Tibetan Resistance." *Cultural Anthropology* 20, no. 4: 570–600. https://doi.org/10.1525/can.2005.20.4.570.

– 2017. "An Anthropology of Lying: Trump and the Political Sociality of Moral Outrage." *American Ethnologist* 44, no. 2: 243–8. https://doi.org/10.1111/amet.12475.

Mendiola García, Sandra C. 2017. *Street Democracy: Vendors, Violence, and Public Space in Late Twentieth-Century Mexico*. The Mexican Experience. Lincoln: University of Nebraska Press.

Merry, Sally Engle. 1984. "Rethinking Gossip and Scandal." In *Toward a General Theory of Social Control, Volume 1: Fundamentals*, edited by Donald Black, 271–302. New York: Academic Press.

Mitchell, Timothy. 1988. *Colonising Egypt*. New York: Cambridge University Press.

Morgan, Marcyliena. 2004. "Signifying Laughter and the Subtleties of Loud-Talking: Memory and Meaning in African American Women's Discourse." In *Ethnolinguistic Chicago: Language and Literacy in the City's Neighborhoods*, edited by Marcia Farr, 51–76. Mahwah, NJ: Lawrence Erlbaum.

Morris, Rosalind. 2004. "Intimacy and Corruption in Thailand's Age of Transparency." In *Off Stage/on Display: Intimacy and Ethnography in the Age of Public Culture*, edited by Andrew Shryock, 225–43. Stanford, CA: Stanford University Press.

Mosse, David. 2005. *Cultivating Development: An Ethnography of Aid Policy and Practice*. Anthropology, Culture, and Society. London: Pluto Press.

Mueggler, Erik. 2001. *The Age of Wild Ghosts: Memory, Violence, and Place in Southwest China*. Berkeley: University of California Press.

Nadzir, Ibnu, Sari Seftiani, and Yogi Setya Permana. 2019. "Hoax and Misinformation in Indonesia: Insights from a Nationwide Survey." *ISEAS Perspective* 92:1–12. https://www.iseas.edu.sg/images/pdf/ISEAS _Perspective_2019_92.pdf.

Newberry, Jan. 2006. *Back Door Java: State Formation and the Domestic in Working Class Java*. Peterborough, ON: Broadview Press.

Noys, Benjamin. 2000. *Georges Bataille: A Critical Introduction*. London: Pluto Press.

Nugent, David. 2008. "Democracy Otherwise: Struggles over Popular Rule in the Northern Peruvian Andes." In *Democracy: Anthropological Approaches*, edited by Julia Paley, 21–62. Santa Fe, NM: School for Advanced Research Press.

Nuijten, Monique. 2013. "The Perversity of the 'Citizenship Game': Slum-Upgrading in the Urban Periphery of Recife, Brazil." *Critique of Anthropology* 33, no. 1: 8–25. https://doi.org/10.1177/0308275X12466683.

Nuijten, Monique, Martijn Koster, and Pieter de Vries. 2012. "Regimes of Spatial Ordering in Brazil: Neoliberalism, Leftist Populism and Modernist

Aesthetics in Slum Upgrading in Recife." *Singapore Journal of Tropical Geography* 33, no. 2: 157–70. https://doi.org/10.1111/j.1467-9493.2012.00456.x.

Paget, Roger K. 1967. "The Military in Indonesian Politics: The Burden of Power." *Pacific Affairs* 40, nos. 3–4: 294–314. https://doi.org/10.2307/2754445.

Paguyuban Kawasan Mangkubumi Yogyakarta [Yogyakarta Mangkubumi Regional Organization]. 2006. *Laporan hasil persetujuan/penolakan terhadap rencana relokasi bagi semua pelaku ekonomi di kawasan Mangkubumi* [Report on the results of the approval/refusal of the relocation plan for all economic actors in the Mangkubumi area]. Yogyakarta: Paguyuban Kawasan Mangkubumi Yogyakarta.

Paine, Robert. 1967. "What Is Gossip About? An Alternative Hypothesis." *Man, New Series* 2, no. 2: 278–85.

Paley, Julia. 2002. "Toward an Anthropology of Democracy." *Annual Review of Anthropology* 31:469–96. https://doi.org/10.1146/annurev.anthro.31.040402.085453.

Pedelty, Mark. 1995. *War Stories: The Culture of Foreign Correspondents*. New York: Routledge.

Pemberton, John. 1994. *On the Subject of "Java."* Ithaca, NY: Cornell University Press.

Pemerintah Kota Yogyakarta. 2002. *Pelaksanaan peraturan daerah Kota Yogyakarta nomor 26, tahun 2002 tentang penataan pedagang kaki lima* [Implementation of Yogyakarta City Regional Regulation Number 26, 2002, on the arrangement of street vendors]. Yogyakarta: Pemerintah Kota Yogyakarta.

– 2007. *Peraturan Walikota Yogyakarta nomor 45 tahun 2007 tentang petunjuk pelaksanaan peraturan Daerah Kota Yogyakarta nomor 26 tahun 2002 tentang penataan pedagang kakilima* [Yogyakarta Mayoral Regulation Number 45, 2007, on the implementation of Yogyakarta City Regional Regulation No 26, 2002, on the arrangement of street vendors]. Yogyakarta: Pemerintah Kota Yogyakarta.

Pemerintah Kota Yogyakarta, Badan Perencanaan Pembangunana Daerah [Municipal Government of Yogyakarta, Regional Development Planning Agency], and C.V. AKA. 2005. *Laporan akhir: Kegiatan rancang bangun aset daerah, pekerjaan penyusunan (FS) eks Pasar Kuncen* [Final report: Activities to build regional assets, compiling work (FS) for the former Kuncen Marketplace]. Yogyakarta: Pemerintah Kota Yogyakarta.

Pemerintah Kota Yogyakarta, Badan Perencanaan Pembangunana Daerah [Municipal Government of Yogyakarta, Regional Development Planning Agency], and P.T. Cipta Nindita Buana. 2005. *Laporan akhir: Rancang bangun eks Pasar Hewan Kuncen* [Final report: Engineering/building design and construction of the former Kuncen Livestock Market]. Yogyakarta: Pemerintah Kota Yogyakarta.

Pemerintah Republik Indonesia. 1986. *Undang-Undang Negara Republik Indonesia nomor 5 tahun 1986 tentang peradilan tata usaha negara* [Republic of Indonesia Law Number 5, 1986, on the State Administrative Court]. Jakarta: Pemerintah Republik Indonesia.

Peters, Robbie. 2009. "The Assault on Occupancy in Surabaya: Legible and Illegible Landscapes in a City of Passage." *Development and Change* 40, no. 5: 903–25. https://doi.org/10.1111/j.1467-7660.2009.01588.x.

– 2010. "The Wheels of Misfortune: The Street and Cycles of Displacement in Surabaya, Indonesia." *Journal of Contemporary Asia* 40, no. 4: 568–88. https://doi.org/10.1080/00472336.2010.507044.

– 2013. *Surabaya, 1945–2010: Neighbourhood, State and Economy in Indonesia's City of Struggle*. Honolulu: University of Hawai'i Press.

Peterson, Mark Allen. 2001. "Getting to the Story: Unwriteable Discourse and Interpretive Practice in American Journalism." *Anthropological Quarterly* 74, no. 4: 201–11. https://doi.org/10.1353/anq.2001.0038.

Peterson, Warren A., and Noel P. Gist. 1951. "Rumor and Public Opinion." *American Journal of Sociology* 57, no. 2: 159–67. https://doi.org/10.1086/220916.

Portes, Alejandro, and William Haller. 2005. "The Informal Economy." In *The Handbook of Economic Sociology*, edited by Neil J. Smelser and Richard Swedberg, 403–25. Princeton, NJ: Princeton University Press.

Power, Michael. 1997. *The Audit Society: Rituals of Verification*. Oxford: Oxford University Press.

Prabowo, Fajar S.A., and Raden Aswin Rahadi. 2015. "David vs. Goliath: Uncovering the Future of Traditional Markets in Indonesia." *Mediterranean Journal of Social Sciences* 6, no. 5: 28–36. https://www.mcser.org/journal/index.php/mjss/article/viewFile/7456/7138.

Purdey, Jemma. 2006. *Anti-Chinese Violence in Indonesia, 1996–1999*. Honolulu: University of Hawai'i Press.

Radcliffe-Brown, A.R. 1933. "Social Sanctions." In *Encyclopedia of the Social Sciences*, vol. 13, 531–34. New York: Macmillan.

– 1940. "On Joking Relationships." *Africa* 13, no. 3: 195–210. https://doi.org/10.2307/1156093.

– 1949. "A Further Note on Joking Relationships." *Africa* 19, no. 2: 133–40. https://doi.org/10.2307/1156517.

Rahadi, Raden Aswin, Fajar S.A. Prabowo, and Alia Widyarini Hapsariniaty. 2015. "Synthesis of Traditional Marketplace Studies in Indonesia." *International Academic Research Journal of Business and Technology* 1, no. 2: 8–15. http://www.iarjournal.com/wp-content/uploads/IBTC2015-p8-15.pdf.

Retno, Ismawati. 2012. *Pak Walikota Yang Besar Kepala* [The stubborn mayor]. Yogyakarta: Gelar Semesta Aksara.

Riles, Annelise. 2001. *The Network Inside Out*. Ann Arbor: University of Michigan Press.

Romano, Angela Rose. 2003. *Politics and the Press in Indonesia: Understanding an Evolving Political Culture*. New York: RoutledgeCurzon.

Roosa, John. 2006. *Pretext for Mass Murder: The September 30th Movement and Suharto's Coup d'état in Indonesia*. New Perspectives in Southeast Asian Studies. Madison: University of Wisconsin Press.

Rudnyckyj, Daromir. 2009. "Spiritual Economies: Islam and Neoliberalism in Contemporary Indonesia." *Cultural Anthropology* 24, no. 1: 104–41. https://doi.org/10.1111/j.1548-1360.2009.00028.x.

Ryter, Loren. 1998. "Pemuda Pancasila: The Last Loyalist Free Men of Suharto's New Order?" *Indonesia* 66 (October): 45–73. https://doi.org/10.2307/3351447.

– 2001. "Pemuda Pancasila: Last Loyalist Free Men of Suharto's Order?" In *Violence and the State in Suharto's Indonesia*, edited by Benedict R.O'G. Anderson, 124–56. Ithaca, NY: Southeast Asia Program Publications, Cornell University.

Salamun, Taryati. 1993. *Sosialisasi pada perkampungan yang miskin di Kota Yogyakarta* [Socialization of poor neighbourhoods in the City of Yogyakarta]. Yogyakarta: Departemen Pendidikan dan Kebudayaan, Direktorat Jenderal Kebudayaan, Direktorat Sejarah dan Nilai Tradisional, Proyek Penelitian, Pengkajian dan Pembinaan Nilai-Nilai Budaya.

Samuels, Annemarie. 2015. "Narratives of Uncertainty: The Affective Force of Child-Trafficking Rumors in Postdisaster Aceh, Indonesia." *American Anthropologist* 117, no. 2: 229–41. https://doi.org/10.1111/aman.12226.

Santoso, Budi, with Lembaga Ombudsman Daerah Istimewa Yogyakarta (Special Region of Yogyakarta Ombudsman Institution). 2007. *Rekomendasi Lembaga Ombudsman Daerah Propinsi DIY mengenai pengaduan tentang program rencana relokasi pedagang kakilima (Klithikan) Jl. Pangeran Mangkubumi* [Recommendations of the Yogyakarta Special Regional Ombudsman Institution regarding the complaint about the relocation plan of the Mangkubumi Street traders (Klithkan)], 24 October 2007. Yogyakarta: Lembaga Ombudsman Daerah Istimewa Yogyakarta.

Schoch, Lilli N. 1986. *Kaki Lima and Streethawkers in Indonesia*. Jakarta: Indira.

Schumann, William R. 2007. "Transparency, Governmentality, and Negation: Democratic Practice and Open Government Policy in the National Assembly for Wales." *Anthropological Quarterly* 80, no. 3: 837–62. https://doi.org/10.1353/anq.2007.0048.

Scott, James C. 1985. *Weapons of the Weak: Everyday Forms of Resistance*. New Haven, CT: Yale University Press.

Sen, Krishna. 2011. "Introduction: Re-forming Media in Indonesia's Transition to Democracy." In *Politics and the Media in Twenty-First Century Indonesia: Decade of Democracy*, edited by Krishna Sen and David T. Hill, 1–12. New York: Routledge.

Sen, Krishna, and David T. Hill. 2007. *Media, Culture and Politics in Indonesia.* 1st Equinox ed. Jakarta: Equinox.

Sharma, Aradhana. 2013. "State Transparency after the Neoliberal Turn: The Politics, Limits, and Paradoxes of India's Right to Information Law." *PoLAR: Political and Legal Anthropology Review* 36, no. 2: 308–25. https://doi.org /10.1111/plar.12031.

Shibutani, Tamotsu. 1966. *Improvised News: A Sociological Study of Rumor.* Indianapolis: Bobbs-Merrill.

Shore, Cris, and Susan Wright. 1999. "Audit Culture and Anthropology: Neo-liberalism in British Higher Education." *Journal of the Royal Anthropological Institute* 5, no. 4: 557–75. https://doi.org/10.2307/2661148.

Sidel, John Thayer. 2006. *Riots, Pogroms, Jihad: Religious Violence in Indonesia.* Ithaca, NY: Cornell University Press.

Siegel, James T. 1986. *Solo in the New Order: Language and Hierarchy in an Indonesian City.* Princeton, NJ: Princeton University Press.

– 1993. "I Was Not There, But ..." *Archipel* 46, no. 1: 59–65.

– 1998. *A New Criminal Type in Jakarta: Counter-Revolution Today.* Durham, NC: Duke University Press.

Silverstein, Michael. 1979. "Language Structure and Linguistic Ideology." In *The Elements: A Parasession on Linguistic Units and Levels, April 20–21, 1979 (Proceedings)*, edited by Paul R. Clyne, William F. Hanks, and Carol L. Hofbauer, 193–247. Chicago: Chicago Linguistic Society.

Silverstein, Michael, and Greg Urban, eds. 1996. *Natural Histories of Discourse.* Chicago: University of Chicago Press.

Silverstein, Paul A. 2000. "Regimes of (Un)Truth: Conspiracy Theory and the Transnationalization of the Algerian Civil War." *Middle East Report* 214:6–10. https://doi.org/10.2307/1520185.

Sivaramakrishnan, Kalyanakrishnan. 2000. "Crafting the Public Sphere in the Forests of West Bengal: Democracy, Development, and Political Action." *American Ethnologist* 27, no. 2: 431–61. https://doi.org/10.1525/ae.2000.27.2.431.

Solihin, Lukman. 2008. "Koran Merapi dan pembaca: Sebuah etnografi surat kabar populer di Yogyakarta" [*Merapi* newspaper and readers: An ethnography of a popular newspaper in Yogyakarta]. Undergraduate thesis, Jurusan Antropologi, Fakultas Ilmu Budaya [Department of Anthropology, Faculty of Cultural Sciences], Universitas Gadjah Mada. 2008.

Spyer, Patricia. 2002. "Fire without Smoke and Other Phantoms of Ambon's Violence: Media Effects, Agency, and the Work of Imagination." *Indonesia* 74 (October): 21–36. https://doi.org/10.2307/3351523.

– 2006. "Media and Violence in an Age of Transparency: Journalistic Writing on War-Torn Maluku." In *Religion, Media, and the Public Sphere*, edited by

Birgit Meyer and Annelies Moors, 152–65. Bloomington: Indiana University Press.

Steedly, Mary Margaret. 1993. *Hanging without a Rope: Narrative Experience in Colonial and Postcolonial Karoland*. Princeton Studies in Culture/Power/History. Princeton, NJ: Princeton University Press.

– 2013. *Rifle Reports: A Story of Indonesian Independence*. Berkeley: University of California Press.

Steele, Janet. 2011. "Indonesian Journalism Post-Suharto: Changing Ideals and Professional Practices." In *Politics and the Media in Twenty-First Century Indonesia: Decade of Democracy*, edited by Krishna Sen and David T. Hill, 85–103. Media, Culture and Social Change in Asia 21. London: Routledge.

Stolee, Galen, and Steve Caton. 2018. "Twitter, Trump, and the Base: A Shift to a New Form of Presidential Talk?" *Signs and Society* 6, no. 1: 147–65. https://doi.org/10.1086/694755.

Strassler, Karen. 2000. "Currency and Fingerprints: Authentic Reproductions and Political Communication in Indonesia's 'Reform Era.'" *Indonesia* 70 (October): 71–82. https://doi.org/10.2307/3351496.

– 2004. "Gendered Visibilities and the Dream of Transparency: The Chinese-Indonesian Rape Debate in Post-Suharto Indonesia." *Gender History* 16, no. 3: 689–725. https://doi.org/10.1111/j.0953-5233.2004.00361.x.

– 2005. "Material Witnesses: Photographs and the Making of Reformasi Memory." In *Beginning to Remember: The Past in the Indonesian Present*, edited by Mary Sabina Zurbuchen, 1st ed., 278–311. Critical Dialogues in Southeast Asian Studies. Seattle: Singapore University Press in association with University of Washington Press.

– 2009. "The Face of Money: Currency, Crisis, and Remediation in Post-Suharto Indonesia." *Cultural Anthropology* 24, no. 1: 68–103. https://doi.org/10.1111/j.1548-1360.2009.00027.x.

– 2010. *Refracted Visions: Popular Photography and National Modernity in Java*. Objects/Histories: Critical Perspectives on Art, Material Culture, and Representation. Durham, NC: Duke University Press.

Strathern, Marilyn. 1991. *Partial Connections*. ASAO Special Publications, no. 3. Savage, MD: Rowman and Littlefield.

–, ed. 2000a. *Audit Cultures: Anthropological Studies in Accountability, Ethics, and the Academy*. London: Routledge.

– 2000b. "The Tyranny of Transparency." *British Educational Research Journal* 26, no. 3: 309–21. https://doi.org/10.1080/713651562.

Strömbäck, Jesper. 2008. "Four Phases of Mediatization: An Analysis of the Mediatization of Politics." *International Journal of Press/Politics* 13, no. 3: 228–46. https://doi.org/10.1177/1940161208319097.

Sumarsono, Marnis Nawi. 1987. *Sosialisasi pada perkampungan miskin (Struktur keluarga dan sosialisasi) di Kotamadya Padang* [Socialization in poor neighborhoods (Family structure and socialization) in the Municipality of Padang]. Padang: Departemen Pendidikan dan Kebudayaan [Department of Education and Culture].

Supriatma, Antonius Made Tony. 2013. "TNI/Polri in West Papua: How Security Reforms Work in the Conflict Region." *Indonesia* 95, no. 1: 93–124. https://doi.org/10.1353/ind.2013.0002.

Szwed, John F. 1966. "Gossip, Drinking, and Social Control: Consensus and Communication in a Newfoundland Parish." *Ethnology* 5, no. 4: 434–41. https://doi.org/10.2307/3772722.

Tanabe, Akio. 2007. "Toward Vernacular Democracy: Moral Society and Post-Postcolonial Transformation in Rural Orissa, India." *American Ethnologist* 34, no. 3: 558–74. https://doi.org/10.1525/ae.2007.34.3.558.

Tapsell, Ross. 2012. "Old Tricks in a New Era: Self-Censorship in Indonesian Journalism." *Asian Studies Review* 36, no. 2: 227–45. https://doi.org/10.1080/10357823.2012.685926.

Taussig, Michael T. 1999. *Defacement: Public Secrecy and the Labor of the Negative.* Stanford, CA: Stanford University Press.

Taylor, Diana. 2003. *The Archive and the Repertoire: Performing Cultural Memory in the Americas.* Durham, NC: Duke University Press.

Tidey, Sylvia. 2013. "Corruption and Adherence to Rules in the Construction Sector: Reading the 'Bidding Books.'" *American Anthropologist* 115, no. 2: 188–202. https://doi.org/10.1111/aman.12003.

Tilly, Charles, and Sidney Tarrow. 2015. *Contentious Politics.* New York: Oxford University Press.

Turner, Sarah. 2003. "Setting the Scene Speaking Out: Chinese Indonesians After Suharto." *Asian Ethnicity* 4, no. 3: 337–52. https://doi.org/10.1080/1343900032000117187.

Turner, Victor. 1974. "Hidalgo: History as Social Drama." In *Dramas, Fields, and Metaphors: Symbolic Action in Human Society*, 98–155. Symbol, Myth, and Ritual Series. Ithaca, NY: Cornell University Press.

Van Klinken, Gerry. 2007. *Communal Violence and Democratization in Indonesia: Small Town Wars.* London: Routledge.

Van Klinken, Gerry, and Joshua Barker. 2009. "Introduction: State in Society in Indonesia." In *State of Authority: The State in Society in Indonesia*, edited by Gerry Van Klinken and Joshua Barker, 1–16. Studies on Southeast Asia, no. 50. Ithaca, NY: Southeast Asia Program Publications, Cornell University.

Verdery, Katherine. 1996. *What Was Socialism, and What Comes Next?* Princeton Studies in Culture/Power/History. Princeton, NJ: Princeton University Press.

– 2014. *Secrets and Truths: Ethnography in the Archive of Romania's Secret Police.* Budapest: Central European University Press.

– 2019. "Comparative Surveillance Regimes: A Preliminary Essay." In *Spaces of Security: Ethnographies of Securityscapes, Surveillance, and Control*, edited by

Setha M. Low and Mark Maguire, 57–77. New York: New York University Press.

Warner, Michael. 2002. *Publics and Counterpublics*. New York: Zone Books.

Webb, Martin. 2012. "Activating Citizens, Remaking Brokerage: Transparency Activism, Ethical Scenes, and the Urban Poor in Delhi." *PoLAR: Political and Legal Anthropology Review* 35, no. 2: 206–22. https://doi.org/10.1111/j.1555-2934.2012.01199.x.

Welker, Marina A. 2009. " 'CORPORATE SECURITY BEGINS IN THE COMMUNITY': Mining, the Corporate Social Responsibility Industry, and Environmental Advocacy in Indonesia." *Cultural Anthropology* 24, no. 1: 142–79. https://doi.org/10.1111/j.1548-1360.2009.00029.x.

– 2014. *Enacting the Corporation: An American Mining Firm in Post-authoritarian Indonesia*. Berkeley: University of California Press.

Weller, Toni. 2011. "Introduction." In *Information History in the Modern World: Histories of the Information Age*, edited by Toni Weller, 1–12. Basingstoke, UK: Palgrave Macmillan.

West, Harry G., and Todd Sanders, eds. 2003. *Transparency and Conspiracy: Ethnographies of Suspicion in the New World Order*. Durham, NC: Duke University Press.

Wibowo, Ignatius. 2001. "Exit, Voice, and Loyalty: Indonesian Chinese after the Fall of Soeharto." *SOJOURN: Journal of Social Issues in Southeast Asia* 16, no. 1: 125–46. https://doi.org/10.1355/SJ16-1E.

Widianingsih, Ida, and Elizabeth Morrell. 2007. "Participatory Planning in Indonesia: Seeking a New Path to Democracy." *Policy Studies* 28, no. 1: 1–15. https://doi.org/10.1080/01442870601121320.

Wilson, Ian Douglas. 2010. "The Biggest Cock: Territoriality, Invulnerability and Honour amongst Jakarta's Gangsters." *Indonesian Studies Working Papers* 30 (October): 1–19. https://doi.org/10.4324/9780203197394.

– 2012a. "The Biggest Cock: Territoriality, Invulnerability and Honour amongst Jakarta's Gangsters." In *Men and Masculinities in Southeast Asia*, edited by Michele Ford and Lenore Lyons, 121–38. Abingdon, UK: Routledge.

– 2015. *The Politics of Protection Rackets in Post-New Order Indonesia: Coercive Capital, Authority and Street Politics*. New York: Routledge.

– 2012b. "Testing the Boundaries of the State: Gangs, Militias, Vigilantes and Violent Entrepreneurs in Southeast Asia." In *Routledge Handbook of Southeast Asian Politics*, edited by Richard Robison, 288–301. New York: Routledge.

Wirakartakusumah, Muhamad Djuhari, and Titik Handayani Pantjoro. 1992. "Migrants and Self-Employment in Jakarta." *Prisma* 51: 79–85.

Witsoe, Jeffrey. 2011. "Rethinking Postcolonial Democracy: An Examination of the Politics of Lower-Caste Empowerment in North India." *American Anthropologist* 113, no. 4: 619–31. https://doi.org/10.1111/j.1548-1433.2011.01374.x.

Wolff, John U. 1992. *Indonesian Readings.* 4th repr. of 1978 ed. Ithaca, NY: Cornell University, Southeast Asia Program.

Wolff, John U., Dede Oetomo, and Daniel Fietkiewicz. 1992a. *Beginning Indonesian through Self-Instruction. Book 1.* Ithaca, NY: Cornell University, Southeast Asia Program.

– 1992b. *Beginning Indonesian through Self-Instruction. Book 2, Lessons 1–15.* Ithaca, NY: Cornell University, Southeast Asia Program.

Woodward, Mark. 2010. *Java, Indonesia and Islam.* New York: Springer.

Woolard, Kathryn, and Bambi Schieffelin. 1994. "Language Ideology." *Annual Review of Anthropology* 23:55–82.

Zudianto, Herry. 2008. *Kekuasaan sebagai wakaf politik: Manajemen Yogyakarta kota multikultur* [Power as political endowment: Managing multicultural Yogyakarta]. Yogyakarta: Penerbit Kanisius.

Index

Page numbers in italics refer to figures. Indonesian names are alphabetized by first name.

Anthropological Horizons

Editor: Michael Lambek, University of Toronto

Published to date: